Angus Baxter

In Search of Your British & Irish Roots

A COMPLETE GUIDE TO TRACING YOUR ENGLISH, WELSH, SCOTTISH, AND IRISH ANCESTORS

GENEALOGICAL
PUBLISHING CO. INC.

Revised and updated 1991.
Published in the USA by Genealogical Publishing Co., Inc.
1001 N. Calvert Street, Baltimore, Maryland 21202
Published by arrangement with Macmillan Canada.

Library of Congress Catalogue Card Number 85-80180
International Standard Book Number 0-8063-1127-4

Cover design by Maher & Murtagh

Printed in Canada

FOR NAN

Who has left a scent upon my life and left my walls
Dancing over and over with her shadow;
Whose hair is twined in all my waterfalls
And all the world is littered with remembered kisses.

from "Autumn Journal" by L. MacNeice
(*The Collected Poems of Louis MacNeice*, London, Faber & Faber)

CONTENTS

ACKNOWLEDGEMENTS

I wish I could thank by name the many people who have helped me with information for this book; however, the list is too long and for the most part my thanks must be in general terms. My appreciation to the following:

First, the County Archivists of every county in England and Wales who, with minor exceptions, went out of their way to give me detailed information about their records.

Second, the officials of many public and private organizations in Scotland, Eire, Northern Ireland, the Isle of Man, and the Channel Islands, who went to considerable trouble to help me.

Third, the officials, priests, and ministers of the different denominations who patiently answered my persistent questions about the locations of registers and other religious records.

Fourth—and these I must mention by name—Joan Ferguson, secretary of the Scottish Genealogy Society; Donald Whyte, chairman of the Society and doyen of Scots genealogists; and Jeremy Gibson, England's leading expert on wills and probate records, who shared some of his vast knowledge with me.

And of course—and as always—my wife, who read every chapter as it was dumped on her knees, and who helped me beyond measure with wise comments and sound advice.

ANGUS BAXTER

People will not look forward to
posterity, who never looked backward
to their ancestors.
EDMUND BURKE

AN INTRODUCTION

We are a nation of immigrants. We—or our ancestors—came to this land to build a new life, but we still have family or sentimental ties with the countries from which we came. The reasons why our forebears came here are as varied as a patchwork quilt—the English fleeing religious persecution or immovable social barriers; the Scots fleeing the poverty of the cities or the brutal Highland Clearances; the Irish cursed by potato famines and civil war; Manxmen and Channel Islanders facing a limited future on over-populated islands.

Now many of us are looking back to far-off days. We want to know the places our ancestors came from, we want to know their names, how they lived, what they did, and—if we are lucky—what they were like.

One day we want to stand where they once stood; to walk the fields they ploughed and the cobbled streets they trod to work; to stand silent for a moment at a gravestone on some lonely hillside; to visit the old stone farmhouse or the tiny cottage where they lived and died—or perhaps the great castle or baronial mansion which once belonged to the family centuries ago. All things are possible, all dreams can become reality as you trace your family back.

If you are just starting out, there are several things you should bear in mind:

1. There is only one way you can start—you start with *you* and work back. You do *not* find someone with the same name two hundred years ago and try to trace them forward to you—this is impossible. So, if you share a surname with someone who was famous in 1780, there is only one way to find out if he or she was an ancestor—trace *back*.*

2. Don't assume that everyone with the same name is related

*This book starts "over the water"—it is not concerned with collections of records in this country. If you have not yet started your ancestor-hunting here, you should consult a book which lists sources of genealogical information available to you.

somehow. All surnames are either geographical (Wood, Hill, Field), occupational (Smith, Glover, Baker), familial (Williamson, Johnson, Peterson), or caused by strange or memorable birth circumstances (Flood, Storm, Tempest).

Before surnames became necessary towards the end of the thirteenth century because of increasing population, a man would simply be known as John of the Wood, or John the Glover, or John of the Storm. In due course, the "of" or the "the" was dropped and surnames as we know them began. In Scotland, Wales, and Ireland a variation was the use of Mac (son of), Ap (son of), or O (son of). You can see that a similarity of name is, in fact, unlikely to mean there is a blood relationship.

One more thing while we are talking about surnames—do not be confused if you find several different ways of spelling your name as you trace your family back. The changes usually occurred because few people could spell in older days and there was no absolutely correct spelling. Therefore, at baptisms, marriages, and burials, names were often written in the church registers as they sounded. Take a nice, simple name like mine, for example. How could you spell BAXTER any other way? Well, you can spell it Bagster, Backster, Bakster, Bakaster, Bacaster, and—in 1194—Baecestre! In the latter way it is a Saxon word and means baker.

3. Do not be led astray by advertisements offering you a coat of arms and a family history, or believe this will be a short cut to a family tree. It is very unlikely you or your family have any right to a coat of arms. The right to one was granted by the ruler of a country and was usually given to titled families, or owners of large estates who had rendered some service to the ruler. Most of us are descended from farmers or farm workers and our ancestors were too busy and hard-working to be bothered with frills of this kind; nor, indeed, were they in a position to qualify for such a grant.

All you will get for your money is a coat of arms originally granted a long time ago to someone with a similiar surname to yours. The odds against that person being your ancestor are very great, and, in any case, a coat of arms only descends from eldest son to eldest son.

4. Don't believe every family story you hear about the origin of your family. I am not suggesting you are descended from a long line of congenital liars, but over the years stories become a little "decorated". The small cottage becomes a country mansion on a thousand acres; the private in the army becomes a colonel; the bricklayer becomes a builder, and so on.

The changes are not always deliberate—they are often quite accidental. Let me give you a couple of examples:

A friend of mine wrote to a District Registry Office in England for a copy of his grandfather's death certificate. He knew that he had been a sawyer—a man who worked in a lumberyard. When he got back the certificate, grandfather had become a lawyer!

A family I heard about in England had always treasured the story handed down that great-great-grandfather had been the master of a sailing vessel going backwards and forwards across the Atlantic between England and Boston, Mass. They were very proud of this old seadog in the family, especially because present family members were weekend sailors. They would always refer to their love of the sea as being hereditary—a genetic gift from their brave forebear. Alas, a couple of years ago a member of the family started working on the family tree. They found their ship's master all right, but he had been the captain of a barge sailing up and down the River Ouse in the port of Boston in Lincolnshire, England!

Now let me talk with the man or woman who is ready to start the hunt overseas. Don't go rushing off to the old country. Sit down and let the feeling wear off—you have a lot of homework to do before you board that plane!

First of all, remember you do *not* need to go to the United Kingdom or Eire to trace your family. It can be done by mail and the cost will not be astronomical. Of course, when you have completed your search, your own natural curiosity will send you back to see the places your family came from—but before that you may do much better by mail than by a personal trip.

Secondly, whether you do your ancestor-hunting here or there, learn all about the records there, and where they are. That is why this book is written, and that is why you should settle down and read the first chapter, and then the chapters devoted to the area from which your family came—England, Wales, Scotland, Northern Ireland, Eire, the Isle of Man, and the Channel Islands. When you do, you will realize that each part of these islands has a different system of recording and storing sources of information. For example, just because Scotland keeps all its pre-1855 parish registers in one central place in Edinburgh, it doesn't mean you will find all the English parish registers in London.

Finally, the two questions asked most often by ancestor-hunters, and the two most difficult to answer: How far back can I get? What will it cost me?

There are no definite answers. Availability of records varies from country to country, and from county to county. Another factor is the amount of information you have about your family when you start. A lot will depend on your own patience and determination. You may get back a hundred years, or five hundred—you will not know until you start. You will not need to spend an enormous sum of money unless you employ a professional researcher to do the job for you.

Personally, I think you should do the job yourself. It will be fun (most of the time) and you will bring to the task your love and affection for your family—assets which no one else can produce. You control your own expenditure and can stop for a while whenever you think you are spending too much money.

You will become addicted—ancestor-hunting is an addiction, like drinking or drug-taking. The difference is that it does you no harm and costs far less money!

So, the time has come to turn the page and start growing your family tree!

1
STARTING THE FAMILY TREE

What *do* you do? You take a large sheet of paper and, in pencil, near the bottom, you write down *your* name and those of your brothers and sisters, if any. These should be in order of age from left to right, starting with the eldest. I am going to use as an example an entirely imaginary John Castle, whose family came from England three generations ago. It is important that you are well organized from the beginning of your search, and so I think it is worth repeating this example from my first book, *In Search of Your Roots*.

When you have your name and those of your brothers and sisters down, add the dates and places of birth:

JOHN	WILLIAM	MARY
Born: 8 June	Born: 13 January	Born: 2 February
1920	1922	1924
(Townsville)	(Townsville)	(Townsville)

Now you join the three of you together:

JOHN	WILLIAM	MARY

Next, you write in the same information about your father and mother (i.e., date and place of birth, and also of marriage and death). Your family tree begins to grow now:

DAVID CASTLE   =   MARY ADAMS

Born: 3 September 1895	Born: 4 August 1896
(Townsville)	(Freetown)
Died: 2 January 1944	Died: 5 May 1946
(Townsville)	(Townsville)

(Married in St. Stephen's Church,
Townsville, on 5 May 1918)

JOHN	WILLIAM	MARY
Born: 8 June	Born: 13 January	Born: 2 February
1920	1922	1924
(Townsville)	(Townsville)	(Townsville)

You are now going to have to find out about your grandparents and other relatives. You also, of course, want to know where the family came from "over the water". Don't keep the project to yourself: talk to your brothers and sisters, talk to aunts and uncles, talk to old family friends, look up any old family papers or photographs lying around in desk drawers or old trunks. At this point, try and get information from two major sources within the family, family stories and older relatives.

Family Stories

As I have mentioned, these can be invaluable, but they must be treated with caution until they are proved; otherwise you may start off in the wrong direction.

Let me give you an example. Thirty years ago, in England, as a beginner in genealogy (the fancy name for ancestor-hunting), I started to trace my Baxter ancestors. I had no information to go on, except for the dates of birth and death of my father (who had died when I was aged four) and the name of my grandfather. However, I found a very distant female relative who told me the Baxters originally came from a place called Tarbert. She seemed quite definite about this and I accepted it without question.

So I went up to Tarbert, in Argyll, Scotland, and searched the church registers, and read local histories in the library, and talked to local historians. I could find no mention anywhere of anyone called Baxter—and I went back two hundred years. Then I had a bright idea—the family must have come from a neighbouring parish! So I searched the registers of six more churches and talked to local historians in six more places and still no Baxters. Finally I gave up and went home again. During the next few months I wrote letters and read history books and looked up references to places of origin of surnames.

I found there were Baxters who made marmalade in Dundee, and Baxters who made soup in Grantown, and Baxters who were farmers in Yorkshire, and famous Baxters in the past like Richard the preacher and George the print-maker. None of them connected up with me.

Finally, the thought penetrated that I wasn't being very bright, and that there must be a better way! There was—I started out again as you are doing. I found the date of my grandfather's death and also his age then, and this gave me his date of birth. From my grandfather's birth certificate I discovered the names of his parents—my great-grandparents. I was off to the races—and eventually traced my family back to 1340 in Lancashire and

Westmorland. In the course of doing this, I found that some two hundred years ago they had owned a farm in Westmorland called Talbert. So you see, the story had a very slight basis of truth, but also enough error to put me on the wrong path. So, with family stories be sure you check and re-check.

Questioning Elderly Relatives

If you do not know much about your family, try and find your oldest relative—it may be like finding a watercourse in the middle of the Sahara. If you can visit this relative, rather than write or telephone, so much the better. Take along a notebook or a tape-recorder and a prepared set of questions. I hesitate a little about the tape-recorder because elderly people are often silenced by it. Use your own discretion, depending on the person concerned.

The questions should be along the following lines:

1. Where was my grandfather born?
2. When?
3. What were the names of his parents?
4. When and where did they get married?
5. Did my grandfather have any brothers or sisters?
6. What were their names?
7. Were they older or younger than he was?
8. Did they have children?
9. Do you know where they are?
10. What was my grandfather's religion? (Remember that people may change their religion, often as a result of marriage.)
11. Do you know if he left a will when he died?
12. What else can you tell me about the family?
13. Is there a family Bible or a photograph album anywhere?
14. Do you have any old family papers I can see?

There are other questions which will occur to you, depending on the size of your family and your knowledge of it. When you have asked your questions, don't rush off immediately, because, first, you will give the impression you have no interest in her, only in her information, and, secondly, now that you have her thinking about the past, you may well discover more information as she suddenly recalls something else.

If you are corresponding with distant relatives—second or third cousins—as you probably will be, you may get strange reactions. Remember, these are quite likely people you have never even met—complete strangers. Some of them may think you have found unclaimed money and are trying to get your hot little hands on it!

Almost every family seems to have a story about missing money or unclaimed money or money tied up in some court battle in years gone by.

So, when someone who has never heard of you, but has heard all about the missing millions, receives your letter, he or she may write to you and say, "Why are you asking me these questions? Have you found money in the family? My mother always said there was money tied up in chancery because of a missing birth certificate. If you have found this, I want my share."

Funny? Yes, but it really happens. The letter I have quoted was actually received by a friend of mine in Canada.

Now let us revert to the questions I listed above, and let us assume you have an old aunt who is the widow of your father's elder brother, William. You go and see her and she gives you the following answers to your questions:

1. Where was my grandfather born?
   I never knew much about him. He never got on with my husband. I know his name was John and he had a farm near Newtown. I remember that he died in 1925.
2. When was he born?
   I don't know, but he must have been about fifty-five or fifty-six when he died.
3. What were the names of his parents?
   I don't know—my husband didn't talk about his family much.
4. Do you know where his parents got married?
   No.
5. Did my grandfather have any brothers or sisters?
   He must have had a brother, because my husband used to talk about an Uncle Bill who was a farmer somewhere. Maybe, though, it was an uncle on his mother's side. I never heard of anyone else.
6. Was this Uncle Bill younger or older than my grandfather?
   I'm not sure about that.
7. What else do you know about him?
   Oh, I remember now. Bill was a brother of your grandfather's, because in 1925, when he died, Bill turned up for the funeral.
8. Did he have any children?
   No, I don't think so.
9. If there were any, have you any idea where they'd be?
   No.

10. What was my grandfather's religion?

He was an Anglican. They all were.

11. Do you know if he left a will when he died?

No, he didn't. His wife died before him, and there was just the two boys, my husband and your father. Some lawyer in Littletown sold the farm and the money was divided between the two of them.

12. What else can you tell me about the family?

Well, they were all hard-working, I can tell you that. My husband always said they came from England but I don't know how far back.

13. Is there a family Bible anywhere?

I remember one when I was first married, but I haven't seen it for years.

14. Do you have any old family papers I can see?

No, I threw everything out a few years ago when I sold the house and moved into this apartment. There didn't seem to be anything worth keeping.

Be sure you take clear notes as you search for your ancestors. You may have a wonderful memory but you are going to collect a mass of names and places and dates and you will need to write it all down.

As the result of your meeting with your old aunt, you now have some more information about your grandfather and can add to the family tree.

```
        ┌─────────────────────────┬──────────────────────┐
       JOHN                              WILLIAM
      B: 1869                           (farmer)
      D: 1925 (?)                      alive in 1925
      (Newtown)
        ┌─────────────────────────┬──────────────────────┐
      WILLIAM                           DAVID
   B: 1894 (Townsville)          B: 3 Sept. 1895 (Townsville)
   D: 1948 (Townsville)          D: 2 Jan. 1944 (Townsville)
   = Agnes Lawson                    = Mary Adams
   (no children)                 (St. Stephen's Church,
                                  Townsville, 5 May 1918)
                  ┌──────────────┬──────────────┐
                JOHN          WILLIAM          MARY
            B: 8 June 1920  B: 13 Jan. 1922  B: 2 Feb. 1924
            (Townsville)    (Townsville)     (Townsville)
```

Civil Records

At this point, you are concentrating on your grandfather. You know that, according to your aunt, he died in 1925 in Newtown, and was aged fifty-five or fifty-six. That means he was born about 1869. You must try to confirm this information—it may not be right. You then write to or visit the local office where births are registered. At the same office are records of deaths and it is, of course, wise to get confirmation of this date as well. If, where you live, these records of civil registration, as they are called, started after either or both of these dates, then you will be dependent on church registers.

Let us assume that you are lucky and unlucky. You are lucky because you get grandfather's death certificate and you now know he died in Newtown on 18 January 1925. You are unlucky because civil registration did not start until after his alleged date of birth.

Church Records

This is the moment when you move into the area of church records, and we should now talk about these sources of information. The only records dating from before civil registration started are in the church registers—Anglican, Catholic, and to a lesser degree the Nonconformist sects. The latter were restricted for many years as to the functions at which their clergy were allowed to officiate.

The church registers, of course, refer to baptisms, marriages, and burials. Baptismal records sometimes also show the actual date of birth in brackets, but not always. By and large a child was baptised on the first Sunday after its birth—although if it was ill this did not always apply. Burials usually occurred within a few days of death, and the burial records usually show the date of death and, very often, the cause.

The further back we go in time, the more difficult the tracing of these records becomes, and the records themselves become more and more unreliable. If we are trying to trace the registers of a particular church, we may find them in the church itself, or in the church archives, or in the national archives, or in a local library, or even in private hands. It is to be hoped that the day will come when all these records are in one central place, and are all indexed.

Tombstones can be invaluable, as they often have information, such as place of birth, not mentioned in church registers. Often you will find in the records of public burial-grounds the name of the person authorizing the burial or paying for the tombstone, which

may give you the name of an unknown child or other relative.
Sometimes you will find an address and this information can be of
great value.

I remember one occasion when I was tracing ancestors for
someone and I found an address in the records of a burial-ground
in a large city. From there I went to the public library and looked
up the city directory for that year. Then I worked back, year by
year (the earliest directory was 1818), and got a clear picture of
where the particular man lived and what his occupation was. His
earliest address was near a church on King Street. I took a chance
that he might have been associated with that church and searched
the tombstones. It was a long and weary job because (a) there was
no index in the church records and (b) it was a big cemetery.
Eventually I found the actual grave, and the tombstone was quite
legible. It filled in several gaps in the family, giving me names of
brothers and sisters, for example, but—and this was much more
important—it also gave his place of birth as Sligo, in Ireland. There
was absolutely no other source for this vital item of information.

With all this knowledge about the importance of church records
in mind, you write to the Rector of the Anglican Church in
Newtown and ask him if he can find the following information for
you:

1. The date of John Castle's baptism or birth between 1 January
and 31 December 1869 (you are assuming here that he was born in
Newtown, but he may very well not have been).

2. Any information about his marriage in the period from 1892
to 1894 (you know his eldest son was born in 1895).

Remember to send a small donation to the church funds.

In this particular case, let us pretend you are in luck. You hear
back that John Castle was born in Newton on 4 April 1869, the son
of William Castle and Ann Castle (maiden name Todd). You are
also told he was married on 22 June 1892 in Newtown to Jane
Adamson, of the same parish. His age is given as twenty-three and
hers as twenty. His address at the time of his birth and marriage
was given as Lake Farm, Newtown. Now you know the Castles
occupied that farm from at least 1869 to 1892.

What do you do now? You know all you need to know about
your grandfather, so you concentrate on your great-grandfather,
William. You now know he was William Castle, married to Ann
Todd some time before 1869.

At this stage a visit to Newtown and a personal search of the
registers and the graveyard seem worth while. Of course, if you
can't get there it can be done by correspondence with the rector.

You search the registers and you find several very interesting items:

1. William Castle married Ann Todd on 10 August 1867. His age was twenty-two and so was hers. His parents are shown as David and Elizabeth Castle of Keynsham, England.

2. Their first child was David and he was born 6 June 1868.

3. The second child was your grandfather, John.

4. There were four other children—Margaret (1871), Ann (1872), Ann (1873), and William (1874).

Don't be confused by the fact you have found two children named Ann. This often happened when the first child with the name died. A hundred years ago infant mortality was very high. Whenever you find a birth, always check for the death of the child—usually within days, weeks, months, or the first three or four years.

In the church graveyard you find a number of old graves. Some may be impossible to decipher because the soft stone has been worn away by the weather over the last one hundred years. However, you are in luck again, and you find a tombstone with the following information on it:

WILLIAM CASTLE
died 16 August 1897, aged 52 years
ANN CASTLE, his wife
died 10 September 1897, aged 52 years
and their son DAVID
died 10 July 1872, aged 4 years
and their daughter ANN
died 18 September 1872, aged 4 months
and their daughter MARGARET
died 4 January 1873, aged 2 years

Now the Castle family tree is really sprouting and looks like the chart on page 9.

This is the point at which you move out into the wide, wide world and explore new territory, because your sources are now overseas. The main object of all your thoughts is your great-great-grandfather, David Castle, of Keynsham, England.

What do you know about him? A little. His wife was named Elizabeth and they were alive in 1845 when your great-grandfather William was born.

What do you *not* know? You have never heard of Keynsham, and do not know where it is in England. You also do not know the exact date in 1845 when your great-grandfather was born, or whether he had brothers and sisters. You do not know when your great-great-grandparents were married (except that it was before 1845).

Of course, there are other unanswered questions which you have had to leave for the moment. You do not know what happened to your grandfather's sister Ann (born 1873) or his brother William (born 1874)—the one who was a farmer and turned up for the funeral. However, don't worry too much about them because they are not direct ancestors of yours and can be left until you have some spare time. Don't be diverted from David Castle of Keyns-

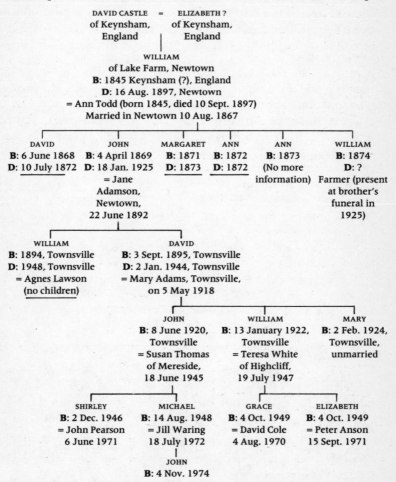

Note: Since this is a Castle family tree, only the last Castle descendant—John, born 1974—is shown. However, it is for you to decide if you will continue the tree in this way or include all the descendants of David Castle, whether they are Castles or not.

ham, England. The following chapters will show you sources of information there, and in Scotland and Ireland, the Isle of Man, and the Channel Islands.

What would have happened if you had not found your great-grandfather's place of birth in the registers in Newtown? What could you have done?

You could have searched the registers of the neighbouring parishes such as Hightown or Hillside. If you had an idea he came from England you could have written to St. Catherine's House in London, since the indexed records there started in 1837 (more about this place later on). There is also information to be obtained from wills and land records here in this country.

Family Bibles

There are two other vital sources of information about your family's place of origin which should never be neglected—family Bibles and family photograph albums.

During the last century the family Bible was very popular. It was usually the custom for one to be given as a wedding present. It was called a family Bible because there were special pages provided for listing all of the events in the new family which would stem from the wedding—births, marriages, and deaths. They were usually located in the front of the Bible, but in some editions they were inserted between the Old and the New Testament. Be sure you check in both places.

These Bibles are valuable in that the entries were made as they occurred and are therefore more likely to be accurate. However, it is always wise to check the date of an entry against the date of publication of the Bible—if the date of the entry is long before the publication date, then you know it was made from hearsay and is not necessarily accurate.

Photograph Albums

The family album can be infuriating: full of lovely pictures of stern, bearded men and shy women wearing bustles, all your ancestors, and no one has ever written the names below the pictures! Often the photographer's name and city may be your only clue to the place of origin of the family, and that is the major value of the album. Often the name and city were embossed on the front of the picture, but more often they are printed on the back.

If a photograph is pasted in, you have a problem. Try and gently remove the picture. If this fails, cut it out of the album and try steaming it off. If this does not work, you have only one alternative. Get the original photograph copied by a photographer or a friend or relative with the right camera and the right lens attachment, and then soak it off in lukewarm water. All this trouble *may* pay off with a place name on the back. I have known it to work on several occasions, and I have also known it to fail just as often. The decision is yours.

Living Relatives
If you have lost touch with one you should write to Special Section A, Records Branch (Room 1018), Dept. of Health & Social Security, Newcastle-upon-Tyne NE8 1YU. Give full name, last known address, age or date of birth, plus your sealed letter to the lost relative, with the name on the envelope. The Department will not disclose any information to you, but will forward your letter to the person concerned.

Recording Your Information

As you progress with your ancestor-hunting, you will have to decide at some time how you are going to record all the information you are collecting. There are several ways to do this, but first you must decide just what your ambitions are. Do you want simply to trace back the direct line from you to your father, then to your grandfather, your great-grandfather, and so on? Do you want to include all the brothers and sisters of your ancestors, and all their children and descendants as well? There are advantages and disadvantages to both these aims, and only you can decide what you want to do. There is no fixed law of genealogy which says you must do this or do that.

Personally, my main concern was always to trace back from son to father all the way. If in doing this I found out the names of brothers and sisters in each successive generation, I would include them in my master copy; and if I found out anything about the children of these brothers and sisters, I would include that as well.

Remember that when you are recording the brothers and sisters in each generation, and then trying to trace their children, you are setting yourself an almost impossible task. To even attempt it will cost you a great deal of time and money.

In order to build a family tree you will need several large sheets of paper, each about 2 feet x 3 feet. As you go further back into the days of large families of twelve or more children, you will find the width of the family tree increasing rapidly. In this case you can always join two pieces of paper together with glue. Of course, if you go on doing this, as you get further back you can end up with a piece of paper twenty-four feet wide and six feet high, and even rolled up this will not be manageable.

I suggest you use the large sheets I mentioned as your working copies—one fair copy and one which is available for changes and rough notes. Along with this, you can use a three-ring loose-leaf binder and a simple reference system of your own. For example, each generation, starting with yours, can be given a letter, and each person in that generation a number. This reference can be put in brackets against the person's name on your working copy of the family tree, and a page in the binder given to that person.

Imagine for a moment that you are John Castle of the fictitious Castle family. You can start the system with either yourself or your children. Personally, I always start with myself. In that case, the three of you—you, John Castle, and your brother and sister, William and Mary—would be A1, A2, and A3. Your father and mother would be B2 and B2=(signifying that your mother was married to B2). Your uncle William, of course, would be B1 because he was older than your father. This is one method.

Another system is to buy a special book for the purpose, or printed sheets which can be used in the standard binder. Both of these can be bought through a genealogical society. They can be good if they suit your aims, but sometimes they are wasteful. For example, one book I have is promoted on the basis that you can record seven generations on eight sides of the family. This is fine if you intend to trace your ancestors on eight sides, and if you only want to go back seven generations. I, for example, have traced back on *four* sides of my family, and the numbers of generations covered are seventeen on one side, ten on another, eleven on a third, and five on the last. So I would only use half the book so far as the various families are concerned, yet the book would be too small for three out of the four sides of my family because I go back more than seven generations.

Don't rush into spending money until you know what information you have and how you want to show it. If you intend eventually to frame your family tree (whether typed, printed, or hand-lettered) and display it on a wall, there is a simple way to do it which shows your descent without taking up much room. Here is an example:

THE CASTLE FAMILY

The family originated in the County of Somerset, England, in the area of Keynṣham, where it was first mentioned in a Tax Roll in 1425. Actual descent can only be proved back to 1570. It is believed that the name was originally "of the castle" and that the family was living near or in one of several castles in the district.

RICHARD CASTLE
B: 1570, Keynsham
D: 1645, Keynsham
= Eleanor Farris
in 1595

HENRY	RICHARD
B: 1598, Keynsham	WILLIAM
D: 1650, Keynsham	ELEANOR
= Mary Williams	ELIZABETH
in 1619	MARY
Tenant of Hillside	FRANCIS
Farm (100 acres)	

RICHARD	HENRY
B: 1622, Keynsham	THOMAS
D: 1700, Bath	WILLIAM
= Louise Freeman	ANN
in 1647	MARY
Tenant of Brookside	PETER
Farm (200 acres)	ELLEN
	CAROLINE
	EDWARD

HENRY	RICHARD
B: 1645, Keynsham	THOMAS
D: 1735, Keynsham	ANN
= Mary (surname	
not known)	
Farmer	

and so on, and so on. In other words, your main line of descent is shown, with all the relevant information. If you wish, the brothers and sisters of your ancestor, in each generation, are shown at the right. This is purely a matter of record, since you are not too concerned with them, except to show they existed. The family tree is manageable in size and shows your descent quite clearly.

2
SEARCHING FARTHER AFIELD

You have finished tracing your family in this country—whether your grandfather was the original immigrant, or your great-great-great-grandfather, or you yourself. You may only have traced the paternal line (that of your own surname), or you may have traced back four families (your grandparents on both sides) or eight families (your great-grandparents). It has been up to you; there are no rigid rules in genealogy.

I hope that when you did the tracing you worked on one family name at a time—it is much less confusing that way. If you are concentrating on one surname, you will find it simpler when your eyes are running down a long list of names. The same remark applies to searching overseas—unless both sides came from the same district, in which case it is obviously more sensible and economical to search for more than one name at a time.

You start tracing the generations before emigration by learning all you can about the place the family came from. You learn where all the records are kept and you find out if there are any relatives still there.

Go to a library and look up an atlas or a gazetteer of Scotland or Ireland, or whatever part of the area is of interest to you. Find out the population of the place from which your family emigrated, the exact location, and—if it is a village—the name of the nearest large town.

If your family originated in a country district, you will find a large-scale map very helpful. There are usually stores or companies in major cities in North America which stock overseas maps or can get them for you. If you experience difficulty, write to the library closest to the place you are interested in, or the nearest Family History Society, and ask them if they can tell you where you can buy a map of the area. Emphasize that you want a large-scale one.

It is very important that when you write overseas, you always send a self-addressed airmail envelope and *two* International Reply

Coupons, which you buy at your local post office. If you do not do this, you are unlikely to get a reply. There are widespread complaints in the United Kingdom and Eire that overseas inquirers often forget to enclose return postage. This applies to your correspondence with private individuals, libraries, and voluntary organizations. There is no need to do this for governments—they take enough money already without voluntary contributions!

Once you have your map, study it and try to memorize the immediate area. This may help you solve a problem. Let me give you an example:

Your great-grandfather always said he came from Upper Brookdale, Gloucestershire, England. You start searching records for that place and can find no mention of your family, and yet you *know* beyond any doubt that he came from there. Maybe you have seen an address on letters he received from the relatives he left behind when he emigrated. Look at the map and you may find that two parish boundaries met near the family farm. Legally, your family lived in Upper Brookdale parish, but the nearest church (only a five-minute walk from the farm) was in the parish of Fieldstone.

Many an ancestor-hunter has accepted defeat when all he needed to do was to search the church registers of the next parish. Remember that a hundred years or more ago a family would probably walk to church. Why walk two miles to their parish church when they could attend one at the other end of the home pasture?

It may happen that a family keeps in touch with relatives "over the water" for a long period of time, but if you are more than two generations removed from the old country, the odds are there is no contact now. When the original immigrant arrived in the new land he would probably send letters to the family he left behind (if he could write and they could read), but as time passed and older people died, the contact was usually lost.

Try and re-establish this contact by finding your relatives in the United Kingdom or Eire—it can be a valuable part of your ancestor hunt. Do this before you go if you are going in person, and not after you arrive there.

How do you set about it? There are several ways, but there is one pre-condition. If your name is a very common one and if your ancestor came from a large city, the following ideas are unlikely to work. If your name is Smith and your ancestor came from Manchester, you will probably be out of luck, but if your name is Howard and the ancestor came from Cork, or Inverness, or Swansea, then you have the odds in your favour, as Howard is an English name and unusual in those areas.

1. Write a letter to the local newspaper in the district. You should be able to find the name and address in the reference section of your local library. If not, simply write to "The Editor, the local newspaper, Inverness":

> Dear Sir,
>
> My great-grandfather, PETER HOWARD, emigrated here from Inverness in 1860. I believe he left family members behind [if you know some names, mention a couple] and I would be grateful if any descendants would write to me.

Keep your letter very short and to the point and it is almost sure to be published in a small-town paper. It will *not* be published by a newspaper in a major city, except in Dublin and Belfast. The Irish papers are very good about publishing such letters. For a large city you can try a small advertisement in the Personal column:

> HOWARD, Peter. Emigrated to North America in 1860. Any relatives in Manchester are asked to write to...

Will it bring results? Well, someone I know knew her grandfather had come from Woodbridge, Suffolk, in England. She sent a letter to the local paper, and she wrote to me some time later, saying: "I received two letters from first cousins of my father. Their father was my grandfather's brother. They say there are several members of the family in the area."

2. Try writing to people with your surname who are listed in a local directory. You can usually get a copy of the particular page by writing to the local public library, enclosing the usual self-addressed airmail envelope and two International Reply Coupons.

I should emphasize here that when you write for information, you should write a friendly, polite letter. They don't *have* to answer you, and if you send a brusque, peremptory demand you may not get an answer. You may think this is totally unnecessary advice, but you should see some of the letters I get—and no stamp or coupons enclosed, either!

3. Make absolutely sure you have got every scrap of information from your relatives. Try and sit down with an elderly aunt if you know of one. Women are the custodians of family history—they know far more than most men about the happenings in a family: the births, marriages, and deaths; the places of childhood; the family quarrels; and the achievements. And remember, it is not only her life you will hear about but what she was told as a child by

her grandparents. In this way you can often collect information covering a span of 150 years.

Even a passing remark can make a vital contribution to your family knowledge. Here is another story for you: A friend of mine had reached an impasse in her search for her English roots. No one knew the exact place of origin of her great-grandfather, except that he came from the West of England. She went the rounds of the family once again, visiting, phoning, writing, covering the same ground she had covered before. Then an elderly aunt, chatting about her grandfather, said, "I remember he told me that once, when he was a small child, he walked four miles into Gloucester with his father when he bought a horse, and then he got to ride the whole way home on it."

This was enough—four miles to Gloucester! She found there are five parishes within that area and wrote to the parson of each parish in turn, asking if he had a baptismal entry for 1835 for Thomas Burley. The third one she wrote to replied with the magic word "Yes" and all the details, and my friend was off again on a hunt which eventually took her back to 1594.

4. Make sure someone has not already done your work for you. It would be a traumatic experience to spend a great deal of time and money tracing your ancestors, only to discover that it had already been done! This has happened to many people. Family trees and family histories are to be found in many places in the old country. You will find all the details later in the book.

When I was tracing my wife's Pearson ancestors, I got back to 1705 and then found a family tree in an old local history book which took us back nearly two hundred years to 1535. Of course, we had to check that the printed information was correct, and we found it was.

Finally, let me warn you that you may meet with resistance when you talk to close relatives. They may be reluctant to help you. You will hear remarks like "Why stir things up?", "You don't know what you'll find", "Best leave well enough alone", and so on. In most cases this is because they are afraid you will discover something to the family's discredit—in their opinion. Perhaps they think that great-grandfather stole the communion plate from the church, or was hung for sheep-stealing, or, horror of horrors, was illegitimate.

Don't be discouraged by these comments; use all your well-known tact and charm to overcome the objections. You can point out with truth that you are unlikely to find out anything about the *character* of your ancestors. You will never know if they are saints or sinners but will simply find out when and where they were born, whom they married, when they died and why, and how much money they left (if they made a will).

As for illegitimacy, this really should not worry anyone in this day and age. I could not care less if my grandfather's parents were not married, and I hope you will feel the same way. In actual fact, the odds against finding a bastard in the family are very great. In searching through hundreds of church registers I have found very few illegitimate births. Admittedly I have noticed at times a suspicious number of children born seven months after the marriage!

Remember that the ancestors of most of us came from small villages where everyone knew everyone else's business. The social pressures of the day were strong enough to make premarital sex unlikely. If a girl did become pregnant, those pressures were also strong enough to ensure that a marriage took place.

The attitude to illegitimacy in those days was two-sided: on the one hand an illegitimate child was always baptised, and at the same time the entry in the church register made the illegitimacy crystal clear. I have some entries which were more than specific: "Baptised this day John, bastard son of Mary Smith, spinster"; "Baptised this day John, bastard son of Mary Smith, spinster. Confessed father, William Brown"; "Baptised this day John, son of Mary Smith, spinster, conceived in carnal lust".

These were the days of long ago. Now we are more tolerant and understanding. In any case, you are unlikely to find anything like this, and should explain so gently to any relative who will not co-operate with you.

So much for all the preliminaries. Now you can settle down with all the details in the rest of the book and, step by step, you will grow your family tree. Nobody knows what you will find waiting for you in the years long past, but as you progress, those men and women who formed you will come to life, and your roots will go deep into the earth of your family's history.

Important Notes about Genealogical Records in Great Britain and Ireland:

Regnal Years

Dates in older records are often given in what is called the *regnal year*. For example, you may find a reference in a will to an ancestor having died "on the 15th day of July in the 10th year of the reign of our Gracious Queen, Anne''. This does not tell you very much, unless you know the exact date of the commencement of each reign, and so here they are, set out below (for example, the reign of Queen Anne began on 8 March 1702. So, from 8 March 1702 to 7 March 1703 was the regnal year 1 Anne):

William I	25	Dec.	1066	Mary	6	July	1553
William II	26	Sept.	1087	Philip & Mary	25	July	1554
Henry I	5	Aug.	1100	Elizabeth I	17	Nov.	1558
Stephen	26	Dec.	1135	James I†	24	Mar.	1603
Henry II	19	Dec.	1154	Charles I	27	Mar.	1625
Richard I	3	Sept.	1189	Commonwealth‡			
John*	27	May	1199	Charles II	30	Jan.	1649
Henry III	28	Oct.	1216	James II	6	Feb.	1685
Edward I	20	Nov.	1272	(Interregnum	12	Dec.	1688
Edward II	8	July	1307	to	12	Feb.	1689)
Edward III	25	Jan.	1327	William III			
Richard II	22	June	1377	and Mary	13	Feb.	1689
Henry IV	30	Sept.	1399	William III	28	Dec.	1694
Henry V	21	Mar.	1413	Anne	8	Mar.	1702
Henry VI	1	Sept.	1422	George I	1	Aug.	1714
Edward IV	4	Mar.	1461	George II	11	June	1727
Edward V	9	Apr.	1483	George III	25	Oct.	1760
Richard III	26	June	1483	George IV	29	Jan.	1820
Henry VII	22	Aug	1485	William IV	26	June	1830
Henry VIII	22	Apr.	1509	Victoria	20	June	1837
Edward VI	28	Jan.	1547	(The Regnal Year discontinued)			

*In the case of John, regnal years are calculated from Ascension Day each year.

†Also known as James VI of Scotland.

‡No regnal year was used during the Commonwealth, 30 Jan. 1649 to 9 May 1660. At the Restoration on that date, the years of the reign of Charles II were back-dated to the death of Charles I, on the principle that he had been king *de jure* since then.

The Calendar

In trying to pinpoint an exact date of birth, marriage, or death in searching British records, there are two traps for the unwary:

1. There was a major change in the calendar in 1752.

2. In addition, in that year, the New Year was changed from March 25 to January 1.

How all this came about is a little complicated, but, unless you understand what happened, you will make some mistakes in the dates you attribute to your ancestors.

Before 1582 the Julian Calendar was used throughout the Christian world. It had been originated by Julius Caesar, hence the name. The calendar divided the year into 365 days, plus an extra day every fourth year. This system was in operation until 1582, but astronomers discovered that it exceeded the solar year by eleven minutes, or three days every four hundred years. Between the date when the Julian Calendar was instituted in 325 and the year 1582, the difference amounted to 10 days. Since this affected the calculations for Easter, Pope Gregory XIII decreed that ten days be dropped from the calendar in order to bring Easter to the correct date. To prevent a recurrence of the variation, he also ordered that in every four hundred years, Leap Year's extra day should be omitted in a centennial year when the first two digits cannot be divided by four without a remainder.

Are you still with me? Well, it means it was omitted in 1700, 1800, and 1900, but will not be omitted in 2000. The Pope also changed the beginning of the New Year from March 25 to January 1, and this new system became known as the Gregorian Calendar. All Roman Catholic countries adopted the new system in 1582. Protestant nations did so later.

However, England was having a fight with the Pope at that time, and was suspicious of new ideas anyway, so she ignored the whole idea. She continued to ignore it for another hundred and seventy years. Never let it be said the English rush into newfangled systems! So, up until 1752 in Great Britain and her colonies, the New Year still started on March 25, while in the rest of the Christian world it started on January 1. To further complicate matters, many educated people thought the change should have been made immediately, and so you will occasionally find entries in church registers and other records dated, for example, 8 January 1686/7, thus showing that although it was officially 1686, they thought it should really be 1687.

Finally, in 1752, the British government changed from the Julian Calendar to the Gregorian Calendar and ordered that eleven days be dropped between September 2 and 14 in that year. This prompted riots in various parts of the country, with mobs of people waving banners and crying, "Give us back our eleven days!"

As a result, you will find entries like 11 June O.S. (Old Style), 22 June N.S. (New Style). In addition, the change of the New Year to

January 1 meant that people born on 27 March 1692 (O.S.) had to change the date of their birth to 7 April 1691(N.S.).

Once all this is clear to you, you will not be confused to find that an ancestress of yours had one child born in one year and a second born a few months later. It was the calendar which changed and not the nine-month gestation period!

Old Handwriting

As you examine old documents you will find that handwriting will vary over the years from the Norman Conquest onwards. We are likely to be dealing at first with what is called Secretary Hand and was in use in the sixteenth and seventeenth centuries.

Bear in mind that if a letter looks like an O it is probably an E; if it looks like an R it is likely to be a C or a T; if it looks like a V or a W it may be an R; and if it seems to be a Y it will probably be a G. With this rough rule of thumb and a good magnifying glass you will probably do very well.

An example of how you can be led astray: when I was checking the 1642 Protestation Returns for Bampton, in Westmorland, I thought I had found an ancestor with the very remarkable first name of HONORIO. Later I realized that this was an example of an O being an E, and the name was really HENERIE (or Henry).

You might also remember that there used to be a letter like a Y which was pronounced "th"—so you may come across YE meaning THE and YT meaning THAT.

d.s.p.	Decessit sine prole (Died without issue)	
d.s.p.l.	Decessit sine legitima (Died without legitimate issue)	
d.s.p.m.	Decessit mascula (Died without male issue)	
d.s.p.s.	Decessit sine superslita (Died without surviving issue)	

Other common words are:

Aetas	age	maritus	husband
Agricola	farmer	marita	wife
Avator	farmer	Mortuus	dead
Arcularius	carpenter	Piscator	fisherman
Avus	grandfather	Relicta	widow
Avia	grandmother	Spurius	bastard
Caelebs	unmarried	Testes	witness
Defunctus	dead	vidius	widower

3
ADOPTIONS

If you are adopted and want to trace your natural parents, there are several organizations which exist to help you try to do this. It is not the purpose of this section of the book to argue the pros and cons of full access to adoption records. Since adoption may be part of genealogy, I am setting out below the law, as it now exists, in Britain and Ireland.

However, there are several comments to be made before we get down to the details of tracing your natural parents. If you want to go ahead with this search—and as a genealogist I can well understand your need to know your background—I do suggest you sit down and think long and hard before you make any move.

You must think of the effect it may have on your relationship with your adoptive parents, on your natural mother, and on her husband and family, if she is married; above all, think of the effect it may have on you. Do not be moved by idle curiosity without considering the results of your actions for all the people concerned.

The odds are that your mother was in her teens when you were born, and was unmarried. You may have been put out for adoption because she was alone in the world, penniless, and terrified. It may have been because she was put under very great pressure and persuasion by her parents. The years have passed; she has married, and has raised a family. Perhaps she told her husband about you, perhaps she did not. It is most unlikely she told her children.

If you eventually trace her and make contact in person or by letter, it may be a shattering experience for both of you. She may not want to have anything at all to do with you and the door may be slammed in your face. Your arrival on the scene may destroy her marriage and her relationships with her children. You may discover she is an utterly reprehensible person with whom you could not possibly have anything in common. Your search may destroy your adoptive parents, whom you love and who have cared for you all your life. They may think that all this time you have had a secret wish to search, and that you have no affection for them at all.

Under certain circumstances your search may have even more tragic consequences. Is this what you want?

In any case, the procedure I am setting out below is not as simple as it sounds. The information about your natural mother may not be available—it depends on how your adoption was arranged and whether there were any records. Even if there were, they may have been destroyed years ago. Your adoption could have been arranged through an adoption society, or a local council, or by a doctor, a lawyer, or a friend. Perhaps your mother arranged everything privately, or it was done by your grandparents.

If your adoption was arranged by a voluntary organization or a local municipal authority, the records may be available, but very often they were kept only for a few years and then were destroyed. For adoption agencies the legal time limit for retention of records was twenty-five years. Even if the records are available, you may find that the information given is so brief that you have made no progress. The longer ago the adoption took place, the less likely it is that you will get anywhere.

England and Wales

A new Children's Act became law in 1975. This made important changes in the regulations relating to access to birth records. It provided that adopted adults (at least eighteen years old) could apply to the Registrar General for access to the original record of their birth.

In the past it was thought best for all concerned that an adopted child's break with the past should be total. Parents who placed a child for adoption were told that the child would never have access to his or her birth records. However, the government now believes that, although adoption makes a child a full member of a new family, information about his or her origins may still be important.

If you were adopted before 12 November 1975, you will have to see an experienced social worker before you can obtain information from your original birth records. However, as there are no provisions under the Act for people to receive counselling outside these two countries, it will be necessary for you to go to England or Wales to discuss the question with a counsellor before your application for information can be considered.

The Act provides that you can be given the necessary information to obtain a certificate of your birth. This document will show your name before adoption, together with your mother's name and address at the time your birth was registered.

The object of counselling is:

1. To give adopted people basic information about their adoption;

2. To help adopted people to understand some of the possible effects of their inquiries on other people;

3. To tell adopted people about some of the complicated regulations concerning adoption.

The law requires such counselling because, in the past, natural mothers and adoptive mothers were told that the children being adopted would never be able to find out their original names or the names of their parents. These arrangements were made in good faith at the time, and it is very important that adopted people should understand this.

In England and Wales your first move is to write to the General Register Office (CA Section), Titchfield, Fareham, Hampshire PO15 5RU, and ask for an application form. At the same time, tell them when you plan to be in the country. You will then receive the form to complete and return.

By the time the counselling interview has been arranged, the Registrar General will have sent the counsellor most of the information from your adoption order. This includes your original name; the name of your natural mother; possibly, but not certainly, the name of your natural father; and the name of the court where the order was made. The counsellor will give you this information at your request, and you will then be able to obtain a copy of your birth certificate, if you decide you want one.

If the adopted person is not you yourself but a parent or grandparent, then try to obtain more information by all means, but do not count on finding out anything. Give all the details in a letter to the Registrar General, enclose proof of relationship, and see how you get on. There may be an adoption society or a local council whose adoption records still exist. It is unlikely, but worth the try.

Scotland

The Adoption of Children Act (Scotland) became law in 1930. Before this date, legal adoption was not possible in Scotland. There was one important difference between the Act of 1930 for Scotland and that of 1926 for England and Wales. In Scotland it was made possible for the Registrar General to issue an extract from the original birth entry, or provide other information, for the adopted person, as long as he or she was over seventeen years of age.

The staff of the Adoption Unit of the General Register Office in Edinburgh are responsible for recording every adoption order granted by the courts in Scotland and, in some cases, adoption orders granted abroad for children born in Scotland. The majority of Scots adoptions are granted by the Sheriff Courts.

Entries in the Adopted Child Register are indexed and the indexes may be searched by the public. However, the link between the entry in the register and the original birth entry can only be made by the very few staff members who have access to the special index.

Facilities exist for counselling in Scotland, as they do in England and Wales, but here counselling is not compulsory. For further information you can write to the General Register Office (Adoption Unit), Edinburgh, or to the Social Work Services Group, 43 Jeffrey Street, Edinburgh EH1 1DN.

It must be emphasized that the "right" under the law for adopted persons is that of access to birth records and *not* that of tracing natural parents. Records in Scotland, like those in England and Wales, do not go far back, have often been destroyed already, and in many cases never existed.

The Isle of Man

The considerable relaxation of the rules governing the confidentiality of adoption records in England and Wales has not automatically followed in the Isle of Man.

Basically, if the Chief Registrar is satisfied that the inquiry is from an official source or from a lawyer, the information will be released. If the inquiry is from a private person, the information will be divulged only if a satisfactory reason is given to the Chief Registrar, and he is satisfied that curiosity is not the only motive. The authorities point out that in such a small community, caution must be used in giving out information.

Legal adoption through the courts did not commence in the Isle of Man until 1928.

Northern Ireland

Legal adoption in Northern Ireland came into effect on 1 July 1930. All adoptions are entered in an Adopted Children Register maintained in the General Register Office, 49-55 Chichester Street, Belfast BT1 4HL. A copy of the entry may be obtained for a small fee, and will provide evidence of adoption and date of birth. Under the provisions of the Adoption Act, the office is unable to divulge any information linking an entry in the Adopted Children Register with the original entry of the birth in a Birth Register. Of course, if the name and surname before adoption are known, search may be made for a record in the Birth Register.

Eire

When a child is adopted, an entry is made in the Adopted Children's Register. The Chief Registrar is obliged to maintain an index to make a connection between each entry and the corresponding entry in the register of births. The index is not open for public inspection. The Adoption Act states that no information may be given except by order of a court or the Adoption Board, and this can be done only if it is in the best interest of the child. Adopted children are never informed of the names of their natural parents. It is possible, however, for a person to contact the adoption society making the original placement, and the society may, if both natural parents are agreeable, put the child in touch with them.

4

THE MORMON RECORDS

The Genealogical Society of the Church of Jesus Christ of Latter Day Saints (popularly known as the Mormons) possesses the greatest single source of genealogical information in the world, and no one starting off on an ancestor-hunt should do so without checking the records available from this society. It is not necessary to be a member of the Church, or even to approve of its teachings, to be able to use its records. There are no strings attached to their use and no one will try to convert you if you contact the Mormons for information.

The Mormons' interest in genealogy stems from their theological belief that family relationships and family associations are intended to be eternal, and not limited to a short period of mortality. Church members "sealed together" are not married only "until death do you part". It is believed the husband and wife and their children remain together throughout eternity as a family unit, with their ancestors and posterity. Members of the Church collect genealogical data about their ancestors in order to perform "sealing" ceremonies in temples erected for the purpose. Before the sealings of families from generation to generation can be performed, the families must be properly identified. This is done by using the records of the Genealogical Society, which is located at 35 NW Temple Street, Salt Lake City, Utah 84150.

The Society is engaged in the most active and comprehensive genealogical program ever known. Microfilming is the heart of the operation, and trained specialists are microfilming records every day in thirty-eight countries around the world. Documents such as parish registers, land grants, deeds, probate records, marriage bonds, and cemetery records are being microfilmed. More than 1,100,000 rolls of microfilm are in the library, and 30,000 new rolls are added each year. There are over 200,000 printed volumes on the shelves, and over 300 new books are being added monthly. There are records of over ten million families in the archives, and sixty million names in the International Genealogical Index (the new name for the computer file index, or CFI as it was known to genealogists and archivists). A microfilm copy of the card catalogue, showing the holdings of the library, is available at all Church branch libraries. There are over fifty thousand microfilms containing genealogical information from the United Kingdom and Eire. Microfilms can be ordered through any Mormon branch library and viewed at that library. You must, of course, be specific in your order—a microfilm of pre-1858 Somerset Wills; a microfilm of Baptisms, Marriages, and Burials for the Catholic Church at Litter, Co. Wexford, Eire; and so on.

For many counties of England and Wales the Church has compiled an index of names contained in the parish registers which they have microfilmed. By contacting the Genealogical Society or your nearest Mormon Library, you can obtain—for a small fee—a print-out of the entries of a specific surname in a particular county. Bear in mind that not all parishes will be included, and that the alphabetical index is not always accurate. The index is a guide to a particular area of a county where the surname may be concentrated, and you can then do a double-check by writing to the County Record Office.

The percentage of registers copied ranges from 3 per cent in Somerset and Northants, to 100 per cent in Wiltshire. In Scotland the coverage is 100 per cent for the period 1553 to 1855 for the parishes of the Church of Scotland.

If you are able to visit the library in person (three thousand people do so every day), you will find four hundred microfilm viewers available, and all the printed volumes on open shelves for easy access. The parish registers are indexed and printed in alphabetical order, so that a search for a particular individual can be made very quickly.

In 1979, cataloguing of records was automated. Records are described on computer-generated microfiche catalogues. In the near future, visitors to the library will have on-line access to the information in the computer catalogue.

The Society library does not have sufficient staff to do detailed research for individuals but will answer one or two specific questions. If more detailed information is required, the library will mail you a list of accredited researchers. When asking for this list, be sure you specify the country in which you are interested, since the researchers are specialists in a particular area. You will then be able to make your own financial arrangements with the researcher you have selected.

Branch libraries are established in eight countries outside the

United States. The names of the countries and the number of branches is given below:

Australia(8), Canada(13), England(5), Germany(1), Mexico(2), New Zealand(6), South Africa(1), and Wales(1).

The Genealogical Society has made sure its records will never be accidentally destroyed. In the Wasatch Range of the Rockies is Granite Mountain. Inside this mountain is the Records Vault. There is three hundred feet of solid granite above the office area, and seven hundred feet above the enormous storage rooms which contain the negative prints of the microfilms.

When using the Mormon records, remember that the extracts from parish registers are not always accurate; they are not always complete for baptisms, marriages, and burials; and they have been known to be missing a page of entries. In addition, not all church authorities are prepared to co-operate with the Mormons on theological grounds, believing that people should not be ''baptised'' into another faith, willy-nilly and perhaps against their will, long after they are dead. The Mormon records are vast, they are superb, but they are not the final word.

The LDS Church has now completed microfilming and indexing the following records in the United Kingdom:

England and Wales:
Civil Registration of BMD, 1837-1903

Scotland:
Parish Registers (Church of Scotland), 1552-1855
Civil Registration of BMD, 1855-1955
Census Returns, 1841-1891

5

JEWISH RECORDS

Many people of Jewish descent are so convinced of the absolute impossibility of tracing their ancestors that they do not even try. Certainly there are problems because of the diaspora (the dispersion of the Jews) and the later persecutions and pogroms in Eastern Europe. However, so far as Jews of English descent are concerned, the problems are not nearly so great as those faced by Jews who trace their descent from Europe.

The Jews of Europe were divided into two main groups—those living in Spain and Portugal were Sephardim (a medieval Hebrew word meaning "Spaniard"); those living in the Rhine Valley and later in Poland and Russia were called Ashkenazim (Germans). The differences between the two were minor—mainly Hebrew pronunciation and a variety in liturgical tradition and religious practice.

A few Jews from Rouen arrived in Britain with William the Conqueror. From then onwards there were communities of French-speaking Jews in many of the main towns of England. In 1290 Edward I expelled them all. By the early sixteenth century some two hundred Jews had again settled in the country. Their stay was a short one: when a Jewish leader was executed they left England once again and did not return until the middle of the century.

No synagogue records exist for this period, but there are a few taxation and business records in the Public Record Office, the British Library, and St. Paul's Cathedral.

The first Jews to settle in England after this time were Sephardic Jews from Portugal, and they arrived in increasing numbers from 1541 until 1760. The main Jewish settlements were in London and Bristol, and by 1680 there were over two thousand Sephardic Jews in London alone. In 1656 Cromwell gave the London Jews permission to establish a synagogue. A rented house in London in Creechurch Lane was adapted for the purpose, but in 1701 the congregation moved to a new building on Bevis Marks at Hineage Lane, a stone's throw away. The Sephardic congregation still worships at this synagogue, and its records are kept in the offices next to the main building. The entries are in Portuguese until 1819, but after that in English. The surnames in the registers of births, marriages, and deaths are indexed.

A group of Ashkenazi Jews emigrated to England in the late seventeenth century from Poland, Germany, France, the Netherlands, and Central Europe. During the eighteenth century the emigration from Europe eventually resulted in the Ashkenazim becoming a majority in English Jewish centres. By the middle of the eighteenth century there were over six thousand Jews in England. Many were absorbed into the general population by intermarriage.

As far as records are concerned, the early Jews in England practised their faith in secret because there was always the risk of persecution. For this reason, many of them were married, had their children baptised, and were buried in the local Anglican church. It was also quite common for a Portuguese or Spanish Jew living in England in the seventeenth century to use an alias, or several aliases, to protect his relatives still living in the Iberian peninsula. This complicates matters for the ancestor-hunter when he gets back that far. Let me give you an example. Isaac Haim Pereira was known outside the synagogue as Manoel Lopes Pereira, but in business he was also called Manuel de Velasquez and Jacques Vendepeere. These various names appear in his will dated 1709. The Spanish and Portuguese Jews usually used normal family names, but sometimes followed the Iberian system of adding the mother's name, or taking over the surname and forename of a godfather.

It was not easy for the Jews to become established in England— many occupations were closed to them because of the anti-Semitic guild system, which forbade Jews to enter the various guilds of furniture-makers, weavers, builders, etc. As a result, a great many spread out across the country as pedlars, tailors, jewellers, and dealers in old clothes. One enterprising Jew arrived in Bristol and set up a glass factory—two centuries later, Bristol glass is world-famous and very valuable.

Outside London there were at least thirteen congregations by the early part of the nineteenth century—Brighton, Bristol, Dublin, Edinburgh, Exeter, Hull, Liverpool, Manchester, Nottingham, Plymouth, Portsmouth, Sheffield, and Swansea. If your ancestor came from one of these places, it will be worth your while to write to the City Archivist and find out what records exist of the Jewish community.

There are a number of other early synagogues in the places of major settlement. Most of them were Ashkenazi. Their registers are not easy to follow, as they were, of course, written in Hebrew or in Yiddish in a Hebrew script, and also because the names recorded do not always correspond to the names used by that person outside the synagogue. Sometimes no surname is given, and in other cases the surname used in the registers was obviously a nickname. How else do you explain "Hayim ben Eleazar Greyhound"? Yes, this name and others like it actually appear in a seatholders' list issued in 1766 by the Great Synagogue in London!

Births were not always recorded in the registers, but marriages and deaths were. Sometimes the marriage record was actually a copy of the marriage contract. Fortunately for those trying to trace a Jewish birth, the records of circumcision are virtually complete. Circumcision took place eight days after birth, and the records are either in the actual registers or in the surgeon's own register, a copy of which is also in the synagogue records. Other records available include offering books, legacy lists, and membership rolls.

Those early synagogue registers which survived are listed below, together with the founding date of the synagogue and the location of the registers:

In original synagogue: Birmingham (1730), Brighton (1800), Cheltenham (1824), London (1656), Plymouth (1750), Spanish and Portuguese Synagogue, Western Synagogue, London (1760).
Jewish Museum: Canterbury (1760), Dover (1833), Exeter (1734).
United Synagogue Archives: Borough Synagogue, London (c. 1820), Great Synagogue, London (1690), Hambro Synagogue, London (1707), King's Lynn (1747), New Synagogue, London (1761).

It is advisable to check with the various Jewish archives for information about synagogues in Bath, Bedford, Bristol, Cambridge, Chatham, Falmouth, Gloucester, Hull, Ipswich, Leeds, Liverpool, Manchester, Newcastle-upon-Tyne, Norwich, Nottingham, Penzance, Portsmouth, Ramsgate, Sheerness, Sheffield, Southampton, Sunderland, and Yarmouth. Also Swansea (Wales); Belfast, Cork, and Dublin (Northern Ireland and Eire); Edinburgh and Glasgow (Scotland).

In several of these places, synagogues have been re-established but they rarely have any historical connection with the earlier congregation, nor do they often have its records.

The Jewish Circumcision Registers in the Jewish Museum are

those of London, Bedford, Chatham, Chelmsford, Newmarket, Penzance, Plymouth, and Sheerness. They all start in the late eighteenth or early nineteenth centuries.

There are a number of inactive Jewish cemeteries in London. They are supervised by the Jewish Board of Deputies.

An alphabetical list of Jewish wills, compiled by Arthur Arnold, is in the Principal Registry of the Family Division, Somerset House, Strand, London WC2R 1LP.

One final source of information is the Colyer-Fergusson collection in the Jewish Museum. This lists marriages, deaths, and other records, taken from every known source, plus a number of Jewish family trees and abstracts from wills.

The address of the Jewish Museum and the United Synagogue Archives is Woburn House, London, England.

6
ENGLAND AND WALES

The genealogical records of England and Wales are so intertwined that it is impossible to have a separate section for Wales without a great deal of duplication. This applies particularly to records of civil registration and present-day wills. However, when we come to records at the county level, you will find a separate chapter on Welsh records.

Civil Registration of Births, Marriages, and Deaths

You may have heard of "Somerset House" in London as a place where family records are kept. This is not true. What was kept there at one time were the records of births, marriages, and deaths for England and Wales, but these are now located in the General Register Office, St. Catherine's House, 10 Kingsway, London WC2B 6JP.

The compulsory civil registration of births, marriages, and deaths started on 1 July 1837 for England and Wales *only*. The records are not dependable during the first few years because it took a while for people to obey the law. They baptised their children in church, were married by a clergyman, and were buried with a funeral service—and they saw no reason why they should report these events to the government. There were all sorts of objections: it was a sneaky way of getting information for taxes; it was an anarchist plot against individual liberty; it was the forerunner of other more sinister measures!

The indexes are kept complete to within the last twelve months. They cover the whole of England and Wales in one alphabetical order for each quarterly volume. They each measure 24 inches by 18 inches and weigh about ten pounds (the earlier parchment ones weigh twice this amount). So you should start getting into good physical shape if you intend doing your searching in person. If you pay the officials there to search for you, it will cost you twice as much, but you may be better off physically!

The Birth Indexes from September 1911 onwards also contain the maiden name of the mother; the Marriage Indexes from March

1912 onwards also show the surname of the second party beside the name and surname of the first party; and the Death Indexes from March 1866 onwards show the age at death.

If the first name and the surname for which you are searching are common ones, you will be astonished to discover a number of people with the same names born in the same year in different parts of the country. It is important, then, that when you search in person, or apply for a certificate by mail, you know something more than a name and a year. If your ancestor has more than one name, be sure you know it. Also try and discover the exact date of birth or marriage or death and find out as much detail as you can about the exact place where the event took place. If you know the first names of the person's parents, this will help a great deal in the search for a birth or marriage entry.

All applications by mail should be sent to General Register Office, (Postal Applications), Room 09, Smedley Hydro, Trafalgar Road, Southport, Lancashire PR8 2HH.

If you are applying by mail for a certificate, you will not have this freedom of choice—you will *have* to give some details. You will have to supply at least the date and place of the event in addition to the first name and surname of the person. If you cannot supply all the details, the office will still undertake a search if sufficient details have been given to identify the entry. The search will cover a period of five years inclusive. However, a search will *not* be undertaken if you can only supply a name and a year, simply because there will probably be more than one person registered with the same name and they will not be able to identify the correct one for you.

Let me give you an example of this. An application was made for a copy of the birth certificate of Richard Clayton, born in 1838 in Nottinghamshire. One would think that the names were not very common, but the office refused to make a search with so little information. The applicant mentioned this to me in the course of a conversation, and at my request the officials at St. Catherine's House were kind enough to make a search in order to test the result against their policy. *Three* entries of birth for a Richard Clayton were found in Nottinghamshire in the year 1838. So you can see that even an apparently uncommon name can present a problem.

We always have to bear in mind that what appears to be an uncommon or even a rare name at the present day may have been very common in a particular small area a century ago. My mother's maiden name—Cantle—is very unusual and I have come across it only a couple of times. However, when I traced that side of my family, I found that in the early part of the nineteenth century in a village named Keynsham, in Somerset, nearly half the population had that name!

So, quite rightly, the information you are required to provide for each type of certificate is:

Birth: Full name at birth; date; place; father's full name; mother's full name; mother's maiden name.
Note: You can ask for either a *short* or a *full* certificate. The former is slightly cheaper but gives no information about the parents, so obviously you should ask for a full one.
Marriage: Names in full of both parties; date of marriage; place of marriage; name and occupation of man's father; name and occupation of woman's father.
Note: If you cannot supply information about the parents, they will still search if you supply the rest of the required information.
Death: Name; date of death; age at death; place of death; occupation.
Note: If you do not know the occupation, they will still search.

The information you will be given on each certificate is:

Birth (full certificate): Place and date of birth; sex and names of child; name and occupation of father; name and maiden name of mother; name, description, and address of the informant.
Marriage: Place and date of marriage; names, ages, occupations, addresses, and marital status of the bride and bridegroom; names and occupations of the fathers of the bride and bridegroom; names of the witnesses. (The latter information is often very useful, because the witnesses were usually relatives of either the bride or the bridegroom.)
Death: Name, age, sex, and occupation of the deceased; place, date, and cause of death; name and address of the informant.

I am not quoting you any fees because that information will be out of date almost immediately. As a very rough guide, you must expect the fees to be three times the charge in this country. Costs of genealogical research in the U.K. and Eire have increased in recent years at a greater rate than the increase in the cost of living.

If you search in person at St. Catherine's House, you can collect your certificate the next day, or arrange for it to be mailed to you. The great advantage of a personal search, apart from the saving in cost, is that you can follow up clues on the spot. For example, in searching for one relative you may find references to others, and you can then search for them at the same time.

It is also worth noting that the Genealogical Society of the Mormon Church now has the civil registration indexes (listed by year only) for England and Wales for the years 1837-1906 for births, and 1867-1903 for marriages. Searches must be made in person at any Mormon library.

There are many other records at St. Catherine's House which may be of value to you, depending on your individual requirements:

Records of Still-births since 1 July 1927
Certified copies of these records can be obtained only with the special permission of the Registrar General.

Records of Births and Deaths at Sea since 1 July 1837
This is the Marine Register Book, and the returns relate chiefly to British subjects from England and Wales.

Records of Births and Deaths in Aircraft since 1949
This is the Air Register Book and relates to births and deaths in any part of the world in aircraft registered in the United Kingdom and Northern Ireland.

Service Records
Births, marriages, and deaths occurring outside of the United Kingdom among members of the armed forces and certain other persons, or occurring aboard certain ships and aircraft, are recorded in the Service Records. The entries in the army registers date mainly from 1881, but there are some entries going back to 1796. The Royal Air Force returns commenced in 1920.
Note: If you are tracing an ancestor who served in any of the armed forces, you are referred to Chapter 8 on this subject.

Consular Returns
Births, marriages, and deaths of British subjects in foreign countries have been recorded by consular officers since July 1849.

Miscellaneous
Births, baptisms, marriages, deaths, and burials form a large series of miscellaneous records (army, colonial, and foreign), some dating back to 1627. These include births and deaths registered by, and marriage certificates forwarded by, the British High Commissioners for India and Pakistan from 1950, and by High Commissioners in other Commonwealth countries at a later date.

Records of Adoption since 1 January 1927

These records consist of entries of adoption made in the Adopted Children Register in accordance with the adoption acts. The fees for certificates are the same as those for births.

When applying for a search to be made, the applicant should give as much of the following information as possible:

1. Date of the adoption order and name of the court making the order;
2. Name of the child;
3. Full name and surname of the adoptive parents.

Applications by mail for these certificates should be sent to General Register Office (Registration Division), Titchfield, Fareham, Hampshire.

Note: You are referred to Chapter 3 for further information.

One final word before we leave the General Register Office and move elsewhere: All fees sent to the GRO for any kind of search or certificate should be paid in sterling funds by international money order, cheque, or draft, payable to the Registrar General.

Please remember that, apart from the central records at St. Catherine's House, there are District Registry Offices in each locality. The cost of a search is considerably cheaper, and you will also be relieved to learn that if you search in person you have smaller and lighter indexes to heave about. If you search by mail, you may well find that a small local registry office will be staffed by people who may be more helpful in searching on a basis of little information. In either case, you can only make use of a district office if you know the exact location of the particular event.

Census Records

Once you have obtained all possible information from the General Register Office (St. Catherine's House), you must decide whether to search church registers, census returns, or wills. There is always debate as to which source of information is the most important. Personally, I would go for the census returns first.

We now have to go to the next most important building so far as the ancestor-hunter in England and Wales is concerned. This is the Public Record Office, now in two separate locations: Chancery Lane, London WC 2A 1LR, and Ruskin Avenue, Kew, Richmond, Surrey TW9 4DU. At the first place you will find census returns, wills, and non-parochial church registers; and at the second, records of government departments. These include military and naval records of major interest to the genealogist, and are described later in the book.

So, back to the census returns. The first census of England and Wales took place in 1801. There had been several attempts before that to establish a regular census of the population, but the opposition to the idea was based on the belief that it would give valuable information to the nation's enemies, and so the various proposals were always defeated. What with losing eleven days, and changing the calendar, and now the idea of counting heads, our ancestors certainly went through some harrowing experiences!

Since 1801 the censuses have been held every ten years (except in 1941, during the Second World War). The early censuses are of little interest to the ancestor-hunter because they have only the number of people in each household, and not the names.

The 1841 Census is the first of interest. It gave the name of all persons in the household, with their approximate age (to the nearest five years below), their sex, their occupation, and whether they were born in the same county or not. Unfortunately it did not ask for the place of birth, nor did it list the relationship of each member to the head of the household.

The 1851 Census is far more valuable. It gave the exact address or location of the house; the names of all the people in the house; their marital status; and (praise be!) their exact place of birth. It also showed the head of the household (this was in the days before Women's Lib) and the relationship of each person to him (e.g., wife, son, mother, aunt, visitor, servant, etc.). The same information is given in the census returns for 1861, 1871, and 1881, which are also available for inspection in the Public Record Office. The census returns for 1891 and later years are in the custody of the Registrar General at St. Catherine's House, and will not be available for public search until one hundred years after the date of the census. This is designed to protect the privacy of the individual.

The Registrar General may release from the returns of 1891 and 1901 the age and place of birth of named persons, on condition that the person concerned gives permission in writing, or that application is made by a direct descendant, able to prove a relationship.

Census returns are produced free of charge for people visiting the PRO in person, but a fee is charged for those requested by mail.

In 1851, in addition to the Population Census there was an Ecclesiastical Census and an Educational Census. The return was voluntary. However, most places of worship made returns, and those for England and Wales are in the Public Record Office. The ecclesiastical returns showed the name and denomination of each place of worship, the estimated attendance on 30 March 1851, and the average attendance. They can be of value in tracing what churches existed in a particular district in 1851. The educational returns are also in the PRO but are not of any interest to the ancestor-hunter.

The main problem in using the census returns lies in finding the exact address of the person you are looking for. In a village this does not matter because the entire return for the area will be contained in a few pages. The cities present more of a problem, but this can usually be overcome. If you know that your ancestor, William Evans, came from Bristol, for example, but you have no address, you can probably find this in a local directory. Most major cities and towns published directories as far back as the late eighteenth or early nineteenth centuries, and they are to be found in the British Library, the Guildhall Library in London, and the Society of Genealogists, and in County Record Offices, city archives, and local libraries. However, usually only the householders were listed, so if your ancestor was a lodger, he will not be recorded.

You may find several William Evanses listed in the directory, and in that case you will have to note them all and check each one out in turn. Presumably you know the first name of William's wife or son or daughter, and this will show up in the census and enable you to make a positive identification.

The census returns can often be the key to taking your family a long way back. For example, you may find William Evans in the 1851 Census living at 24 Rhondda Road, Cardiff, with his wife and children. His place of birth is shown as Cardiff, *but* you also find he had an aunt, Mary Evans, spinster, living with him. She was eighty years old and was born in the village of Merthyr Tydfil. Do you realize the value of this one entry? It means that if Mary Evans was born in Merthyr Tydfil, it is ninety-nine per cent certain that her brother, William's father, was born there, too. Without this census return you might never have made the link between Cardiff and Merthyr Tydfil.

Church Records
After census returns, you should turn to the parish registers of the state church (the Church of England) and to the non-parochial registers which contain entries of baptisms, marriages, and burials for Nonconformists or Dissenters. These include those of Jews,

Quakers, Catholics, and the Protestant Nonconformist sects. The registers are in many different places in England and Wales. Before I give details of all these locations, we must go into the whole story of the registers—the single most important item for the ancestor-hunter, because without them no completely accurate and verifiable family tree is possible.

Parish Registers

In medieval times there were no official parish registers, although some monasteries and parish priests did keep some sort of record of baptisms, marriages, and burials of leading local families. Records of this kind do exist as far back as 1344 for a few parishes. However, this is very exceptional, and for the average ancestor-hunter the starting date for parish registers is 5 September 1538. All parsons, vicars, and curates were ordered to enter in a book every wedding, christening, and burial in the parish, with the names of the people concerned. They were also instructed to provide a ''sure coffer'' with two locks in order to protect the records from theft or destruction. The parson kept one key and the churchwardens the other.

These entries were made on paper, and often only on loose sheets. In 1598 all the entries were supposed to be copied into parchment books. When this was done, the paper books and the loose sheets could be destroyed. Unfortunately the wording of the Act said that the entries should be copied from the beginning, ''but especially since the first year of Her Majesty's reign''. In most cases this loose phrase was taken to mean that entries *before* the first year of Queen Elizabeth's reign need not be copied, and so few records exist before that date (1558). Of course, there are other gaps caused by fighting in the Civil War (1642-49) when a number of churches were destroyed or their records were stolen; by fire or storm damage; by damp or flood damage; by theft; and by loss caused by the carelessness or stupidity of a number of parsons. Only a couple of years ago the registers of a parish church in the south of England were stolen from an unlocked box in a church and were never found. Over the previous several years the parson had refused to surrender the registers to the County Record Office, refused to allow them to be microfilmed, and refused to place them in a safety-deposit box in a bank. Fortunately, many registers have now been published, microfilmed, or lodged in archives.

The National Index of Parish Registers is a monumental work sponsored by the Society of Genealogists in London, and when completed it will give the location of church registers throughout the United Kingdom. Some eight volumes have been published so far. To a degree, it has been overtaken by the recent Act directing the deposit of church registers in County Record Offices in England and Wales.

Less expensive is a series of booklets containing a location list of parish registers which is being published on a biannual basis by the Local Population Studies Group, Tawney House, Matlock, Derbyshire.

Bishop's Transcripts

The Act of 1598 also specified that once a year a copy of all entries for that year should be sent to the diocesan registry at the bishop's office, and these are now known as the *Bishop's Transcripts*. In many cases, where parish registers have been destroyed or lost, the Bishop's Transcripts have been preserved. I am always a little amazed when I meet fairly experienced amateur genealogists who have only a vague knowledge of the transcripts, and have never made use of them. In my own ancestor-hunting in two different parishes, I found mysterious gaps of about fifty years each in the registers. In each case I was able to make use of the transcripts. Without them I would never have been able to trace my family as far back as I have done.

Most of the Bishop's Transcripts are deposited in the County Record Offices most closely concerned with the areas of jurisdiction of the bishops. A notable exception is Kent, where those of the Diocese of Canterbury remain at Canterbury Cathedral. Those for the Diocese of Lichfield, which covered serveral counties, are all in the County Record Office at Lincoln. In the Diocese of London, no transcripts were kept before 1800, and in that of Winchester there are none before 1770. (This diocese also included the Channel Islands, so searchers in that area should remember this.)

From 1660 the parish registers are, generally speaking, complete. The only exceptions are those lost through natural disasters. Here again the Bishop's Transcripts are very useful—depending on the date of the disaster, and the date on which the transcripts were sent to the Bishop (they were supposed to be sent after Easter in each year).

In 1753 the Marriage Act tightened the regulations for a church marriage. Among other provisions, it set out that one of the parties must reside in the parish where the marriage was to take place, and that the marriage was not valid unless the banns had been read or a special licence issued. These assured more dependable marriage records and also reduced the chances of bigamous marriages.

I should, perhaps, explain about banns and special licences. The banns, or notices of intention to marry, were called out three times on successive Sundays in the church in which the marriage was to take place, and also in the church of the bride or groom if it was different from the one where they were getting married. When for some reason the people concerned wanted to dispense with the calling of the banns, they could do so by being married by licence. Usually, since special licences were costly, their use was automatically restricted to people of wealth and position. Application was made for a special licence for privacy or because the groom was leaving for military or government service overseas.

As the years passed, the question of special licences became a matter of "keeping up with the Joneses". It developed into a status symbol to be married by licence, and eventually merchants and farmers and clerks all followed the example of the aristocracy. This development was very helpful to the ancestor-hunter because the licence records were well kept and well preserved, usually in the diocesan office. You will also come across references to marriage bonds. These were records of sureties given by the friends of the bride and groom to the authorities, stating that there was no impediment to the marriage. Many of these records of licences and bonds have been published or indexed, and most of them are now in the County Record Offices.

In 1812 Rose's Act, as it is known, set out stringent rules for the preservation and custody of the parish registers. It also abolished the parchment registers and replaced them with the form of book still in use today.

If your ancestors belonged to the Church of England the parish registers will, if you are lucky, provide you with much information about them. Even if they were Catholics or Nonconformists, Dissenters, or Quakers you may still find them in the parish registers. In less tolerant days, people who did not belong to the Church of England were forced, at certain periods, to be baptised, married, or buried according to the rites of that church. We will talk about this when we come to the section about non-parochial registers.

One other thing will help you in your search through the registers. By and large, there was not a great deal of movement of population before the latter half of the eighteenth century; then the start of the Industrial Revolution meant a general drift from the countryside into the towns. This static population over many centuries meant that men and women were most likely to marry someone from their own village, or at least from the neighbouring one. This is why, when you search for ancestral records in a particular village and fail to find them, you should always search in the adjoining parishes.

I was particularly lucky when tracing the Baxters back. The first Baxter appeared in the valley of Swindale, Westmorland, in 1195, when John Baecastre was mentioned in a tax roll. The family was mentioned again when a John Baxter and his wife, Beatrice, were left forty sheep in 1362 in the will of Sir Thomas Legleys. From then on, descent was proved right down to the present day. The task was relatively easy because for six hundred years—from 1195 to 1795—the Baxters lived in that remote valley. The wars and civil wars and revolutions and rebellions passed them by to the east and the west. The invading armies from Scotland into England, and from England into Scotland, also left the valley alone. Farming the valley and pasturing their sheep on the high fells, the Baxters raised their children and minded their own business.

Often, however, one is not so lucky. My father's maternal family were named Caley. I traced them back to a Henry Caley who was married in 1778 to Ellen Webster in Cockerham, Lancashire. She had been born in the small coastal village but Henry Caley had not. So, as I advised you to do, I searched neighbouring registers, but I found no trace of him. Over the years since, I have searched every register for fifty miles around without success. This is one of my failures. I believe him to be the younger son of the Cayley family of Norfolk, who are descended from Simon de Caillet, one of the Conqueror's knights, but I cannot prove the connection yet. I am still trying—in ancestor-hunting one never gives up. There is always a new lead, a new source, a new possibility.

The Transfer of Records to County Record Offices

The parish registers were, until recently, always in the custody of the parson of the particular church. However, the closing of so many churches because of lack of attendance, and increasing concern about the conditions under which the registers were kept, have led to changes.

The Parochial Registers and Records Measure 1978 came into force of law on 1 January 1979. Under this measure, each bishop is required to designate an existing Record Office as the Diocesan Record Office, but his choice is restricted to the County Record Office, a City Record Office, or some other place recognized under the Public Records Act of 1958 (for instance, the Borthwick Institute of Historical Research for York, or the Bodleian Library for Oxford).

Under the Measure, every custodian of parish registers and records that are over one hundred years old has to deposit them in the designated Record Office unless specific exemption is obtained from the bishop. Where the records are retained in parish custody, they must be kept in accordance with very detailed conditions set out in the Measure. These conditions are so restrictive that very few applications for exemption are made—it is far simpler to hand over the registers to a Record Office:

1. Every register shall be kept in a rust-proofed, vented steel cupboard, the door of which is fitted with a multi-lever lock, and the cupboard shall be kept in the parish church.

2. The place in the church in which the cupboard is located shall be a place where there is least risk of damage in the event of flood or fire.

3. The temperature and relative humidity in the cupboard shall be checked at least once a week by means of a thermometer and a hygrometer, each of which shall be kept in the cupboard.

4. The difference between the maximum and the minimum temperature in the cupboard during any week shall not be allowed to exceed ten degrees Celsius.

5. The relative humidity in the cupboard shall not be allowed to fall below 50 per cent, or to rise above 65 per cent.

6. Nothing, except books or other documents, shall be kept in the cupboard.

7. The person or persons having custody of the register shall take all such steps as are reasonably practicable to ensure that the book is protected against theft, loss, or damage.

A final requirement of the Measure is that a periodic inspection of all registers in parish custody shall be arranged by the bishop. The first inspection shall take place within five years of the initial operation of the Measure, and the person making the inspection shall be appointed by the bishop, in consultation with the chief officer of the diocesan record office.

All of this means that you should check the location of the registers before rushing off to search in person at some remote church halfway up a mountain in Wales, or wherever! Write to the County Record Office or the church first and find out where the registers are.

In some ways I regret the passing of the days when it was necessary to visit the local parson and ask politely whether he would allow you to look through the registers. He was often quite a character—mostly good, but sometimes bad. If you find a particular register is still in the parish church and you are going there in person, you must be quite prepared to do your searching under difficult conditions and under the close supervision of the parson, unless he decides you look trustworthy. I hope he does *not* trust you, because there have been instances where an unscrupulous searcher has torn out and tucked in a pocket an entire page because it contained an entry referring to an ancestor.

If you are writing, be sure you send the usual self-addressed airmail envelope and the two International Reply Coupons. Before you write, go into your nearest library and see if it has a copy of *Crockford's Clerical Directory*. This will give you the parson's name, full address, and any degrees or decorations he possesses—some of them are very sensitive about the omission of these. There is a scale of fees for finding a particular entry, or searching for records which span several years. The fee for a long search is usually negotiable. So tell him what you want done and ask him what it will cost. Incidentally, if you are arranging a search spanning, say, twenty years, it will be worth while to ask for details of any entries with the particular surname. This may produce brothers, sisters, etc., of your ancestor, and thus help to add a few branches to the tree.

The likelihood is, however, that you will be dealing with a County Record Office. The office will usually search for one particular entry without charge, or for a small fee. If you want a long search made, you will be referred to a professional researcher and you must negotiate the charge with him or her. The County Record Offices were not set up for genealogical correspondence, so do not ask for too much!

Some final comments about reading the registers yourself. Be prepared for difficulty in deciphering the writing in the early ones. Sometimes it is copper-plate and easy to read, but very often great concentration is needed and a magnifying-glass is a great help. Remember that until fairly recent times a double s(ss) was written fs (ʃs). You will also find the considerable variation in the spelling of your name which I mentioned at the start of this book. Very often the entry was made by a churchwarden or a parish clerk who could not necessarily read and write too well. He would ask the surname and then write it down as it sounded. First names can also be a problem, because, in the early registers, the name was often written in Latin, and it is not easy to realize that James and Jacobus are the same, as are William and Guglielmo. A further complication is the fact that many first names are applicable to both male and female children, for example Evelyn, Leslie, and Hilary.

If you are lucky, you will find that the surname for each entry is shown first, on the left of the page, followed by the first name and the rest of the information. I am always delighted to be able to run straight down a page when this happens, rather than reading painstakingly across each line.

You may also run into another difficult problem if there were a number of members of your family living in the village or area at any one time. Many years ago I found two separate Baxter couples producing children at the same time, and each couple was named William and Elizabeth. The two Williams were first cousins. This complicated matters, but I was able to solve it eventually by reference to wills, and to the naming patterns of that particular time (1700-1875):

> The first son was named after the father's father,
> the second son after the mother's father,
> the third son after the father,
> the fourth son after the father's eldest brother,
> the first daughter after the mother's mother,
> the second daughter after the father's mother,
> the third daughter after the mother,
> the fourth daughter after the mother's eldest sister.

There were exceptions to the pattern when the naming system produced a duplication of names. In that case, the name was taken from the next on the list; i.e., if the eldest son was named John after the father's father, and the mother's father was also John, then the second son could not be named after him and was, therefore, named after the father.

Another break in the pattern could be caused by death. A century or so ago it was not unusual for at least half the children to die in infancy. Nowadays, parents who lose a child by death are not inclined to use his name for a subsequent child, but this is a comparatively recent development. I have known cases where five sons in succession were named John because each one died in turn. This is why it is essential to check the deaths in the register as well as the births.

You must remember, too, that you are searching the *registers* of baptisms, marriages, and burials, and not actual births, marriages, and deaths. Often the date of birth or death was given as well, but this depended on the individual parson's own policy. You may have to settle for the date of the event recorded in the registers, unless you can find a date of death from a tombstone in the churchyard.

Tombstones

Quite often the information on a tombstone is far more detailed than the entry in the church registers. Even if the registers are not in the church, it will be worth writing to the parson to ask if the surname appears on any tombstones or memorials in the church. Many churches have a typed and indexed list of tombstones and the wording on them, and so you are not *necessarily* asking the parson to wander miserably through the long grass in the churchyard on a wet day looking for a tombstone that will help your search. Nevertheless, write as if you are!

If *you* are visiting the church, check for the typed list first, and then start your wandering through the wet grass. You will find that many tombstones have been cemented into the outside church wall or the floor in the interior; in some cases you will find them piled up in a corner.

You may also share an experience with me. My great-grandfather, Robert Baxter, is buried in the churchyard of the Priory Church in Lancaster. A few years ago I paid a return visit to the churchyard and found that Robert's flat, plain tombstone was no longer there. I searched for the sexton and asked what had happened. He explained that many of the tombstones had been moved so that the grass could be cut more easily. I asked where they were now. "Oh," he said, "I expect it'll be down the hill there. We've built an amphitheatre for stage shows in the summertime, and we used the old tombstones for the seats."

So down the hill the two of us went and in due course I found the tombstone of Robert Baxter (1816-90). I sat on it and looked down at the stage, and then asked if I would be entitled to a free seat at all theatrical performances. The sexton took me very seriously and said, "Oh no, sir, we couldn't do that. If we did it for you we'd have to do it for everyone." Poor great-grandfather lying in an unmarked grave, while the tourists sit on his tombstone and watch a play!

Often the writing on a tombstone may not be readable at all, or it may be readable only in a certain light at a certain angle. If you run into difficulty in deciphering the words, try taking photographs from several different angles. Oddly enough, by some trick of the light or the angle, a photograph often produces legible words.

Non-Parochial Records

Let me start by saying that if your ancestors were not members of the established Church of England you will have a much more difficult task, because the records of the other denominations are incomplete and widely scattered. The search may well be successful but it will call for all your patience and determination, the two essential qualities for any ancestor-hunter!

The Public Record Office

As previously mentioned, one section of the Public Record Office is located in Chancery Lane, London, and this is where the non-parochial registers are to be found. These are the registers which were surrendered in 1840 by the various Nonconformist denominations.

Further registers and records came to light later and a new Act in 1858 ordered their surrender. In 1961 the General Register Office transferred all the non-parochial registers to the Public Record Office. They are open for inspection in the Search Room. There is no general index, and for a search to be practicable you need to know at least the approximate place in which a birth, marriage, or death occurred, and preferably the denomination. (Remember, there is an index to Quaker records at Friends' House.)

Extended searches will not be undertaken by the staff of the Public Record Office, and overseas inquirers by mail will be referred to a list of authorized searchers approved by the Public Record Office.

The non-parochial registers cover only England and Wales. They include those of the Protestant Nonconformist churches; several registers of Huguenot and other foreign Protestant churches in England; and a few Catholic registers which come mainly from the north of England. A few registers relate to non-denominational institutions, such as the City of London burial-ground at Bunhill Fields and the British Lying-in Hospital in Holborn. There are no Jewish registers.

Most of the registers cover the period 1775-1837, although a few continue up to 1857, and several go back to the middle of the seventeenth century or even, in the case of some foreign Protestant churches, to the sixteenth century.

Catholic Records

At varying periods in British history, religious tolerance has been sadly lacking and life was made very difficult for people who followed a religion other than that favoured by the state. Before the fight between Henry VIII and the Pope in 1534, the English Church was Catholic and monolithic. If there was an opposition, it was not very apparent.

With the founding of the Church of England, Catholics and their religion went underground. Services and confessions were held in secret, and as a result Catholic registers were kept hidden in various places. Consequently, a great many of the early ones have disappeared. Those that did survive have been retained by the Church and are not in the custody of the Public Record Office. The Catholic Record Society has published a number of the early registers for the years prior to 1754. In that year the Hardwicke Marriage Act came into force. It ordered that all Catholics were to be married in the Church of England or the marriage would not be legal. The Catholics were forced to obey, as otherwise there would have been later complications with inheritance. Many Catholics, however, followed their marriage in the parish church with a later and secret one by a Catholic priest.

In general terms, current Catholic registers (and in small parishes this may mean those dating back to the early nineteenth century) are kept in the original church, and there are no microfilm copies. However, in certain dioceses, notably Westminster, Lancaster, Birmingham, and Southwark, original registers from before 1850 (or, in rare cases, microfilms) have been deposited in the central Diocesan Archives.

Two first steps are always useful:

1. Find a copy of the current Catholic Directory in your local library or in the Chancery Office of the local Catholic diocese. This lists all Catholic churches in England and Wales. With this you can locate the church you want and write to the parish priest.

2. If you get no reply, you should then write to the archivist or the bishop of the diocese (the Catholic Directory will give you the address) and ask if the registers of the particular church have been deposited.

If these steps fail, write to the Catholic Family History Society, 5 Winscombe Crescent, London W5 1AZ (with two IRCs please).

Nonconformist Records

Many Nonconformists were also married in the Church of England because before 1806 their own ministers were not permitted to officiate at marriages, and only marriages in the recognized church were legal.

Congregationalists: The oldest body of Nonconformists, they came into existence immediately after the Reformation. They disagreed with the idea of the King being head of the Church and did not believe church membership should be open to everyone— only to true believers and people who made open confession of their faith. The Puritans were basically an offshoot of the Congregationalists and, of course, the Church suffered accordingly when the monarchy was restored in 1660.

The Corporation Act of 1661 prevented members of the Congregational Church from holding any kind of public office, and the Conventicle Act of 1664 declared illegal all religious meetings except those of the Church of England (also known as the Anglican Church). The Five Mile Act of 1655 forbade Nonconformist ministers from teaching in schools or living within five miles of a town. In 1673 the Test Act ordered that all people holding office under the Crown should take the sacrament according to the rites of the Church of England.

During the eighteenth century there was an increase in religious tolerance, and although the Acts remained on the statute books, very little attempt was made to enforce them. By the nineteenth century they were abolished.

Many Nonconformist records have disappeared. The National Union of Congregational Churches was established in 1832 and set up the Congregational Library, where many early records are preserved. The registers which did survive are in the Public Record Office. The information in them is more detailed than in the Church of England registers; for example, baptismal entries include the maiden name of the child's mother, a very valuable addition. The Congregational Historical Society has published a number of early records.

Methodist Records: This church was established as a result of the preaching of the Wesley brothers, John and Charles. They were both Church of England parsons who had a falling-out with the church. Originally their intention was to revitalize the Church of England, but eventually, with the urging of their supporters, a separate church was founded. Methodist ministers started baptising, marrying, and burying their followers, although many members continued to use the facilities of the established church. If your ancestors were Methodists, it is vital to bear this in mind.

Originally the Methodists did not establish churches in each district but held services at what were called district meetings. These were held in different places and at irregular intervals. In the early 1790s local churches were built and the church became organized on a central basis. By this time the Wesley brothers were both dead and, inevitably, with no strong direction from the top, there were splits in the ranks and a great variety of different sects of the church appeared: the Wesleyan Methodists, the New Connexion, the Primitive Methodists, the Bible Christians, the Protestant

Methodists, the Wesleyan Methodist Associates, and the Wesleyan Reformers. In addition, there were other minute meeting-houses established in various localities as the result of local conditions and local animosities and feuds. In 1907 the United Methodist Free Church and the New Connexion united to form the United Methodist Church. In 1932 there was a merger of the Wesleyans, the Primitive Methodists, and the United Methodists to form the Methodist Church.

In 1818 a Methodist registry was set up for the central recording of baptisms being performed in the various chapels throughout England and Wales, and this register is now among the holdings of the Public Record Office. You will also find there the records of the early Methodist burial-grounds—an invaluable source of vital information. For example, Wesley's chapel in City Road, London, had its own graveyard, and the records of it date back to 1779.

All the 856 Methodist registers of baptism and burials were handed over to the General Registry in 1840 and are now in the PRO. The marriage registers of many Methodist chapels are now in the various County Record Offices, but marriages were not recorded until 1898.

The Methodist Archives, now located in the John Rylands University Library, Deansgate, Manchester, do not have any church registers or burial records. The Methodist Church Archives and History Committee (Central Hall, Oldham Street, Manchester M1 1JQ) can supply information about ministers, and copies of obituary notices of church members if they appeared in Methodist magazines.

Baptist Records: The Baptist Historical Society, 4 Southampton Row, London WC1B 4AB, does not hold any church registers. Those not handed over to the General Registry in 1840 may be in local chapels, or more likely in County Record Offices. Those in the CROs are listed under the various counties later in the book, but no overall list of locations exists.

The Historical Society holds early handbooks, the *Baptist Magazine*, and various published memoirs. They can be useful if you are searching for information about an ancestor who was a Baptist minister, but are not of general interest to the ancestor-hunter.

There are two important facts to bear in mind if your ancestors were Baptists. First, between 1759 and 1837 *all* marriages had to take place in the parish church, and not in a Baptist chapel. Second, you are unlikely to find *birth* records in Baptist registers, since the church believes baptism is the real birth. Only believers may be baptised, and their ages range from nine to ninety!

Quaker (The Society of Friends) Records: The Quakers have kept good records from their foundation by George Fox in the seventeenth century. These were also handed over in 1840 and are in the Public Record Office. However, before doing so, the Quakers made digests of the records and indexed them. These are kept at Friends' House, Euston Road, London NW1 2BJ. There are 85 volumes, containing the records of 260,000 births, 40,000 marriages, and 310,000 burials.

From the mid-seventeenth century most monthly meetings, some particular meetings, and some quarterly meetings kept records of births, marriages, and burials. The digests contain all the information in the originals (now at the PRO) except the names of witnesses to marriages. The indexes are not strictly alphabetical, but chronological within each letter of the alphabet. In some cases there are supplementary registers for material surrendered after 1840. A separate series of digests covers the period from 1837 to the mid-twentieth century.

It must be remembered that Friends, like other denominations, often failed to make entries in the original registers. Also, a number were lost before the registers were surrendered to the PRO in 1840.

The Friends' House also holds many books about Quaker history, many manuscripts of meeting records, and a number of private and family papers. There are more Quaker records in a number of County Record Offices.

The Religious Society of Friends, which has custody of the above material, will provide, at a small charge, photocopies of any document within reason. They will not supply photocopies of very old documents or those in a frail state. The library is open to individual researchers who have a letter of introduction. Overseas inquirers requiring lengthy searches will be referred to accredited researchers.

The Protestation Returns

The Protestation Returns of 1642 are in the custody of the Record Office of the House of Lords. They were intended to list the names of all males over the age of eighteen in every parish who were willing to swear their allegiance to the established church, the Church of England. They vary greatly in format and appearance, some having original signatures or marks, and some being lists in the same hand, presumably that of the parish clerk. The names are arranged in parishes within *Hundreds* (i.e. segments of counties), and these parishes have been listed in the Appendix to the Fifth

Report of the Historical Manuscripts Commission. The names have not been indexed except in those volumes of local history which print the Protestations. Check with the particular County Record Office to find out if there is such an index for your area. The Protestation Returns can be of great genealogical value, but unfortunately there are no Returns for a great number of parishes.

(Note that the Return for Cheshire is in the British Library.)

The staff of the Record Office will check lists of one or two specific parishes without charge. For an extended search you will have to engage the services of a record agent. The Search Room at the House of Lords is open to the public from Monday to Friday, 0930-1730 hours. The production of documents stops at 1640 hours. The address is: Record Office, House of Lords, London SW1A 0PW.

Tithes

Another possible source of information about your ancestors—or at least one ancestor living in 1840—is the tithe records. Originally tithes were designed to make sure the established church received a regular income. Payment of tithes was compulsory for members of the church, and even non-members and non-believers—subject to social pressures—found it expedient to make their contribution.

A tenth part of the main produce of the land (corn, oats, barley, wood, etc.) was known as the Praedial Tithe, and a tenth part of the produce of both stock and labour, such as wool, pigs, milk, etc., was known as a Mixed Tithe. A tenth part of the profits of labour was called a Personal Tithe. You can see that the ecclesiastical net was cast pretty wide, and very few escaped.

In the early part of the last century the government decided that tithes should be changed to fixed charges on land. This was done in 1836. Three Commissioners were appointed to oversee the administration of these changes. The need to obtain accurate information on which the Commissioners could base their decisions caused the most detailed land survey and record since the Domesday Book was made in 1080. Three copies of the map and the land description for each district were made, one for the parish, one for the Bishop, and one for the Commissioners.

The Tithe Maps, of which there are about twelve thousand, are not uniform in size; they can be anything from one foot to fourteen feet in width, with corresponding variations in the length. The Tithe District was usually a parish or a township. The map was hand-drawn and showed the location and area of the land within the district. The Apportionment (21 in. x 18 in.), a document accompanying the map, gave the acreage, and the name of the owner or occupier of each area.

The records are in the Public Record Office at Kew, and will show you exactly where your ancestor was living in a particular area in 1840.

Finally, bear in mind that the records will give you only the location and the name of a particular person living in a particular place in 1840; they will not give details of parentage or names of descendants.

You can write to the Photo Ordering Section at Kew, giving all possible information to enable the right Tithe District to be identified. You will then be advised of the amount of the fee, which will depend on the information you give and the number of photocopies needed. Remember the variation in the size of the maps—a number of photocopies may be needed to give you complete coverage of a Tithe District.

A number of the County Record Offices in England and Wales also have copies of the diocesan or the parish maps, but, by and large, those at the PRO are in better condition.

Passenger Lists

The question is often asked, "Where are the lists of ships' passengers kept?" Unfortunately, these are few and far between, and those that do exist are not kept in any one central place. The PRO in England has a few records from 1890-1913 (outwards) and 1878-1914 (inwards). In Scotland, Donald Whyte has published two books listing several thousand Scots who emigrated to the U.S.A. and Canada. There are other books which have been published for other parts of the world, but all of them added together only list a tiny percentage of the names of emigrants. Various County Record Offices in England and Wales have a few lists; overseas archives have a few; and searches are still being made for a forgotten hoard in some forgotten vault.

Very few records were kept before this century of people leaving the old country or arriving in the new. If you are lucky you may discover the details of your ancestor's voyage from overseas, but do not count on finding this information.

The Free and Voluntary Present (1661-62)

This was a national appeal in England for money to pay the debts of Charles II during his exile. Lists of the contributors (on a county basis) are in the PRO. A little over half the county lists have survived and are usually listed by parish. They are of value because they give the occupation of the donors.

Public Record Office

I mentioned this office in passing when we talked about census returns. We should now speak in more detail about the records in the two locations of the PRO. The holdings are vast, and it is unlikely that you can trace your ancestors without having some dealings here. It is not the place to *start* your tracing, and I hope this has been made clear already. It is a place to add leaves to the tree, or a place to search more obscure sources if you have failed elsewhere.

The PRO originally had all its holdings in the old building in Chancery Lane, London WC2A 1LR, but it now has a second building at Ruskin Avenue, Kew, Richmond, Surrey TW9 4DU. In spite of the address, this is really a suburb of London. You take the District Line to Kew Gardens Station, and the PRO(Kew) is a ten-minute walk away. It can also be reached by British Rail.

The odds are that you will be doing your searching at Chancery Lane, because that is where most of the genealogical records are kept. Kew is primarily the place for records of government departments and is less likely to be of use to you except in certain specialized areas. However, there are plans being discussed to move most of the records from Chancery Lane to Kew over the next few years, so you should check with the PRO for the latest information about this projected move of the records.

You will find the following records at Chancery Lane, besides the Census Returns, which we have already covered (see page 38):

Wills

These are wills proved in the Prerogative Court of Canterbury for the period 1384-1858. They are mainly those of wealthy men and widows dying in the south of England or abroad. The wills are on microfilm in the Wills Room and also in many County Record Offices (see Chapter 7).

Death Duty Registers

Since 1796 many estates have been liable to duty. (The word "estate" refers to property and personal wealth, and not to a land acreage.) The indexed registers give details of the estates and are also located in the Wills Room.

Nonconformist Registers

These have been covered in the section on Church Registers (see page 40). They are available in the Long Room and are not indexed, except for the Quaker records. The Quaker index is at Friends' House, Euston Road, London NW1 2BJ. It is much better to check with the appropriate County Record Office first, because a local office may have copies of the Nonconformist registers for the county, and they may have been indexed.

Deeds

There are many thousands of deeds of various kinds in the PRO. Here again it will be wiser to go to the County Record Office first. It is not easy to find your way around the ancient records in the PRO, whereas the County Record Offices frequently have indexes to local deeds. The deeds called *Feet of Fines* are in the PRO but they are difficult and complicated to search, and many have been printed by local record societies and are in the County Record Offices. The *Close Rolls* are much simpler. They are kept in the Long Room and are indexed by grantee and grantor from the sixteenth to the nineteenth centuries.

Tax Returns

There are two sets of tax records of value to the ancestor-hunter, *The Hearth Tax (1662-74)* and the *Land Tax Redemption Office Quotas and Assessments (1798-1914)*. The former relates to a tax on every hearth, arranged by place, and giving the number of hearths for which the householder was responsible. The indexes are on the search-room shelves. Many of the returns have been printed on a county basis and are in the CROs. The Land Tax was very unpopular and in many cases was evaded by landowners, so many names fail to appear. The records list owners of property.

Fleet Marriage Registers

In the seventeenth and eighteenth centuries there were a number of "marriage shops" in London where dubious clergymen performed dubious ceremonies for brides and grooms. If you have searched all available normal sources for information about a London marriage, it may be worth your while to look through the registers of marriages that took place in and around the Fleet Prison. There are a great number of them and no indexes. They are in the Long Room.

Crown Employees and Civil Servants

Modern records are kept at Kew, but in Chancery Lane you will find, for example, lists of employees of the Royal Household (1641-1902), registers of the Chapels Royal, and civil servants' wills (1836-1915).

Chancery Records

The Chancery Courts have been in operation from the fourteenth century and deal with disputes over wills, land, marriage settlements, etc. "Chancery" is always mentioned in the family stories about missing money—"There's money tied up in Chancery because of a missing birth certificate!"

The Chancery records are badly arranged and indexed, and there is no comprehensive guide to their contents or to the necessary procedures in searching them. The staff at the PRO, knowing the problems, are not very encouraging to would-be searchers. I hesitate to suggest you search the records because it will be a long and difficult task and I do not know how patient and determined you are! There are one or two aids—*Indexes to Disputed Estates in Chancery, 1649-1714* by Peter Coldham, and the *Bernau Index* (see the Society of Genealogists on page 66). One problem is that, for example, a man named David Castle may have died, leaving problems in connection with his property, which led to a legal battle between his executor, Peter Grayson, and a creditor, Thomas Allen. This case is likely to be listed as Allen versus Grayson, with no mention of the name Castle.

The Chancery Court dealt with all of England and Wales, except for the County Palatinate of Lancaster, which had its own separate judicial system. If you do search the records and are lucky enough to find a reference to an ancestor, it may give you a lot of information. For example, a dispute over inheritance of an estate by a distant relative may have left in the court records a complete family tree over several generations, duly attested to and entered as evidence in the case.

The holdings of the Public Record Office at Kew are, as stated, primarily those of government departments. The following are of interest to the genealogist:

Apprenticeship Records

Between 1710 and 1811 stamp duty was payable on indentures of apprenticeship. The entries give the names, addresses, and trades of the masters, and, until 1752, the names of the apprentices' parents. The Society of Genealogists has a partial index to these records.

British Nationals Abroad
These are records of people serving in the colonial or foreign service. In addition, for people abroad not necessarily in an official capacity, there are registers of birth, marriage, and death at Chancery Lane.

Military Records
These are located at Kew and are described in much more detail in Chapter 8 (page 79).

Emigrants
There are many references to emigrants in records in the PRO, but unfortunately there is no single index to the names. Some of the information has been published in the United States and in Australia. It will be a long-drawn-out process to look for a particular name in the records, but the most important of these papers are listed below:

Convict Transportation Registers: These cover the period 1787-1871 in 21 volumes. Each volume is indexed by ship, and the ships' names are listed roughly in order of departure. Under each ship are listed the full name of the convict, the term of his or her transportation, and the date and place of conviction.

Convicts, New South Wales and Tasmania: There are 64 volumes which, although primarily concerned with convicts, are really a series of censuses of these colonies for the period 1788-1859.

Passenger Lists, Outward: These are lists of passengers leaving the United Kingdom by sea. Lists before 1890 no longer exist. They are arranged year by year under the names of the ports of departure and show age and occupation of each passenger, and usually the place of residence. If you know the place from which your ancestor sailed, the date, and the name of the ship, these lists may give you information about where he lived before sailing. On the other hand, if you know the place and date of sailing and the name of the ship, the chances are you know where he came from!

Registers, Various: These three volumes give details of emigrants from England and Wales to North America and other places between 1773 and 1776. There is a card index for them. There is also a list of emigrants leaving Scottish ports for America between 1774 and 1775, but it is not indexed.

Passport Registers: These contain the names and intended destinations abroad of all applicants to whom passports were issued for the period 1795-1898. There are indexes for the years 1851-62 and 1874-98.

It must be emphasized that the PRO will not undertake genealogical searches, but will refer you to an approved list of record searchers.

The British Library

Another major source of information for the ancestor-hunter of British and Irish descent is the British Library, Great Russell Street, London WC1B 3DG—originally known as the British Museum.

This vast source of knowledge is so vital to you in tracing your roots that you should know how to find your way about it, and how to find information about its holdings. To make adequate use of the Library a personal visit is essential, and this section is based on that fact.

The Bibliographical Information Service, for which there is no charge, will answer questions by mail but cannot undertake detailed research. It will provide names of professional record agents who will undertake work for a fee.

It is important to realize that admission is not granted for the purpose of consulting books or documents available in other libraries. You may find in such a case that you are referred to the Guildhall Library, Aldermanbury, London, for example.

The main sections of the British Library of value to you are:

The Department of Printed Books
The Department of Manuscripts
The Map Library
The Newspaper Library

The first three of these are located at the address above; the fourth is at a separate location, and information about it will be given later.

The opening hours of the British Library are Monday, Friday, Saturday, 0900-1700 hours, and Tuesday, Wednesday, and Thursday, 0900-2100 hours. You are required to be outside the building by closing-time.

A temporary photographic pass for fourteen days can be issued without delay on application at the Reader Admission Office. No character reference is required for admission to the Department of Printed Books, or to the Map Library, but a written reference is needed for the Department of Manuscripts. This can be a letter from a librarian, clergyman, or university professor who knows you, or, probably, an introduction from a High Commissioner's Office, your Embassy, or someone in an official position in the United Kingdom who can vouch for you.

In the *Department of Manuscripts* you can locate information likely to be of interest to you by using the amalgamated index. This is a card index of persons and places, alphabetically arranged and compiled from the indexes in the printed catalogue. This Department holds a considerable amount of genealogical material in manuscript form—particularly histories of families of some prominence, either locally or nationally.

The *Department of Printed Books* holds, as well as family histories, copies of many newspapers. The books, apart from general reference books, are not on open shelves, and it may take up to two hours to obtain the ones you have requested. If they are particularly obscure books, not in common demand, they may be stored in another building at Woolwich, and you may have to wait twenty-four hours to consult them. There is no separate catalogue of genealogical works held in the Library, but published family histories are entered in the General Catalogue of Printed Books. Copies of the General Catalogue of Printed Books are held in most national and university libraries throughout the world.

The *Map Library* is on the mezzanine floor of the King Edward Building and is open Monday-Saturday, 0930-1630 hours. It contains many early maps of all parts of the country, and present-day ordnance survey maps.

There are a number of explanatory leaflets published by the British Library, and available without charge. They include the following:

Regulations for Use of Reading Room
Regulations for Admission to Department of Manuscripts
Official Publications Library
Notes for Readers—Department of Printed Books
Map Library
Newspaper Library (see below)
A Brief Guide to Some Libraries in London
British Library Publications
Readers' Guide No. 6: English Places
Readers' Guide No. 8: Family and Personal Names

Before we talk about the *Newspaper Library*, it should be mentioned that the Department of Printed Books has the Burney Collection of early London and provincial newspapers.

The National Collection of Newspapers is housed at the Newspaper Library, Colindale (opposite the Colindale Underground Station). It contains about half a million volumes and parcels of daily and weekly newspapers and periodicals, including London newspapers and journals from 1801 onwards, English, Welsh, Scottish and Irish newspapers from 1700 on, and large collections of Commonwealth and foreign newspapers. A bomb demolished the original building in 1940 and destroyed ten thousand volumes of provincial and Irish newspapers, damaging fifteen thousand more. Apart from gaps caused by this, the U.K. collections are complete from about 1840. The Library's photographic service can supply microfilm and photocopies of items from the newspapers in the collection. In addition to the volumes of original newspapers, there are 90,000 reels of microfilm on twenty miles of shelving!

The purpose of the Newspaper Reading Room is to provide readers with facilities for research and reference which are not readily available in other libraries normally accessible to them.

The Reading Room is open every weekday, including bank holidays, from 1000 to 1700 hours throughout the year (except for Good Friday, Christmas Eve and Day, New Year's Day, May Day, and the week following the last complete week in October). Admission is conditional on the same information as that required for the Department of Manuscripts, plus a passport or other document containing a photograph and a signature. Persons under twenty-one years of age are not normally admitted.

There is another regulation which I find quite justifiable, but very amusing: *In the interests of the preservation of the collections, admission is not granted for the purpose of research into football match results and horse and greyhound racing, or for competing for prizes*.

Although the collections contain a wealth of information, the newspapers do not always have an index. For this reason, the office will not undertake genealogical research unless the inquirer provides specific information, i.e., name of newspaper, date, and name of person mentioned. Otherwise, a list of researchers will be provided and a fee can be negotiated directly. You should bear in mind that the searching of newspapers for the mention of a particular name is a very long, and therefore expensive, business.

The Library publishes a booklet listing microfilms of newspapers and journals which are for sale. Some examples:

Bristol Mirror 1811-32
Inverness Courier 1870-90
Carnarvon Herald 1831-82
Belfast Morning News 1860-65

Irish Times 1861-65

The Guildhall Library

This extraordinary repository of genealogical knowledge is located in Aldermanbury, London EC2P 2EJ. (Open 0930-1700 hours, Monday-Saturday.) The Library is most useful to those who are ancestor-hunting within the area of the City of London with its hundred-odd parishes. The records for Greater London are in the Greater London Record Office (see Chapter 9, page 166). However, much of the information in the Guildhall Library does cover a wider area of London and even other areas of the country. If you are in London and have the time, it may be worth while to spend a day there looking through the open shelves—it is quite likely that you will find something about the other parts of the country in which you are interested.

It is impossible to list all the sources of information here, so if you are interested in London and its genealogical records, I suggest you send the equivalent of three English pounds and ask for the 42-page booklet entitled *A Guide to Genealogical Sources in Guildhall Library*. I will list below what I think are the records of major importance, although the booklet will tell you much more about them.

Books

There are a great many books on the open shelves: directories from 1677 for the city (from 1860 for the suburbs); many directories from other major cities in England; Poll Books and Election Registers from the late 1600s; *Debrett's Peerage* from 1809 up to today; *Burke's "Landed Gentry"* from 1834; and *Walford's County Families* from 1864.

Parish Registers

The Library holds the original registers of 106 parishes in the City of London. As a matter of fact, only three of the parishes are *not* included, and by the time you read this they may all be there.

Marriage Licences

These start in 1597 and continue into the nineteenth century.

Bishop's Transcripts

There are only a few of these.

Burial-Grounds

There are indexed records of burial-grounds in the City from 1713.

Census Returns

Census records for the period 1841-71 are on microfilm.

Nominal Lists

These are lists of names contained in rate books; assessment records; Protestation Returns (from 1642); Marriage Assessments (from 1695); Return of Owners of Land (from 1873); and Boyd's *The Inhabitants of London* (in 238 volumes listing names from the fifteenth to the nineteenth centuries—only the index is in the Library; the actual books are kept by the Society of Genealogists).

Monumental Inscriptions

These are lists of tombstone inscriptions. The Library holds two manuscript lists of these. However, use them with caution, as they contain a number of errors.

Wills

The Library holds the original records of the Commissary Court of London, the Archdeaconry Court of London, and the Royal Peculiar of St. Katherine's by the Tower. They are indexed.

Parish Clerk's Notebooks

These are working notebooks and contain the same information that was later inscribed in copper-plate writing in the parish registers. If you find a gap in the registers or have a query about a name, perhaps because of the spelling or of deterioration of legibility through aging, then a check in the notebooks may solve the problem. Sometimes the notebooks contain much more information than the registers, such as occupation and exact address of the persons concerned.

Churchwarden's Accounts

These are often ignored as being of no genealogical value. Quite frequently this is so, but the accounts do list burial receipts as far back as the fifteenth century—*before* parish registers started! Now you can see how vital they may be to you.

Other Records

These include school attendance lists; records of the various guilds and livery companies; lists of the freemen; and many records of professions and trades, such as law, medicine, the clergy, brokers, goldsmiths, clock- and watchmakers, and army and navy lists.

Catholic Record Society

The function of the Society is to make available in print the essential sources relevant to the history of Catholicism in England and Wales since the Reformation. The Society does not undertake any research but will direct inquirers to the sources available. A catalogue of its various publications will be forwarded at a small charge. The Society's publications are available through the public library system in England and Wales, or they can be bought, if still in print, from William Dawson and Sons Ltd., Cannon House, Folkestone, Kent—as either originals, photocopies, or microfilms.

An annual conference is held at Oxford in July and non-members of the Society may attend. Details from the secretary, c/o 114 Mount Street, London W1Y 6AH.

Barnardo's Homes

During the last century many thousands of boys and girls were sent from Britain by philanthropic societies like Barnardo's Homes to work and live with farming families overseas. Over 30,000 boys and girls were settled in Canada between 1882 and 1939 (many of these moved later in life to the United States), and some were sent to other countries. Some of the children were orphans or had been abandoned; others had been placed in the care of Barnardo's Homes by parents unable to care for them properly. The luckier children were loved and adopted by the people for whom they worked, but some of them led lives which do not bear thinking about today.

Their descendants are scattered around the world and may not be aware that, under certain circumstances, they may be able to trace their ancestry.

The head office of Barnardo's Homes still exists at Tanners Lane, Barkingside, Ilford, Essex, England IG6 1QG. Inquiries should be sent to the After Care Section, and as many basic facts as possible should be given, such as full names, date of birth, and date of sailing. Generally speaking, the records contain details of parents and location (if these facts were known at the time the child came into the care of the Homes) and a photograph of the child taken before sailing.

It must be appreciated that before personal information is disclosed to the inquirer, the Homes must be satisfied that there is a direct relationship. A letter of reference from a clergyman or some other responsible person will be helpful.

The records are not complete and you should not expect certain success. A careful search will be made and this may take several hours. No charge is made but a donation will be appreciated. My suggestion, based on information given to me, is that a minimum of $20 is a fair sum. If the search gives you information about your ancestor's parentage and also a photograph, it will be money well spent.

The Society of Genealogists

This organization was formed in 1911 and its expert staff and immense collection of genealogical material can be of great help to anyone searching for ancestors in the U.K. and Eire. It has a membership of some seven thousand, many of whom live overseas. There is an entrance fee plus an annual subscription, and full information can be obtained by writing to the Honorary Treasurer. The Society is located at 14 Charterhouse Buildings, London EC1M 7BA.

Is it worth joining? You must decide this for yourself. If you are a member and are visiting London, you will have free use of all the facilities. If you are not a member, you will have to pay for the use. If you are a member, you will get the quarterly magazine (about three months late), and you will receive notice of meetings (long after they have been held). If you are a member, you can put a query in a special section of the magazine, but you must pay for it.

There is a chance that a few lines in the magazine will produce results for you. For example, you could put in the following kind of query:

SMITH, David. Believed born in Keynsham, Avon, in 1820. Wife Elizabeth. Any information to John Smith, 1105 Main Street, Townsville, Canada.

A member may have traced his Smith ancestors in that area already, or someone who lives at Keynsham may write and tell you he has noticed a tombstone there which gives the dates of birth and death of a David and Elizabeth Smith, or someone named Jones may write and tell you he had an ancestor named Elizabeth Jones who married a David Smith. There is slight chance of success, but if you have tried every other way of tracing your ancestor, a little more money is worth spending. I have written perhaps half a dozen queries during my years of membership and have never had any information as a result. You may be luckier!

The Society will also undertake research for both members and non-members for a fee. For details you should write to the Director at the address above. Don't hold your breath waiting for a reply—it may be several months before you hear anything. Of course, they are short-staffed and receive many inquiries. This, plus a certain lack of organization which is all too apparent, means you must be patient!

The library is open Tuesday, Friday, and Saturday, 1000-1800 hours; Wednesday and Thursday, 1000-2000 hours. However, it is liable to be closed for redecoration or repairs without much warning. If you are planning a trip to London, be sure you write as soon as possible and ask if the library will be open. It is to be hoped you will hear back before you leave.

All the books in the library are on open shelves and this saves a considerable amount of waiting time. However, thefts of books are a problem, and there is some talk of restricting access to the shelves for this reason. A better solution might be the installation of an electronic scanning device.

The main collections of the Society are detailed below:

Documents
The document collection, built up from the donations of members and non-members and the purchase of genealogical material, is divided into two sections. All the documents which relate to one particular family are filed in envelopes in alphabetical order of surname in some eight hundred file boxes. There are approximately eleven thousand names. In the second section are those documents which relate to several persons or families in a particular place. These are filed in envelopes under the name of the place, and arranged in alphabetical order by counties. The "documents" range from complete and detailed family trees to a few notes on a scrap of paper. In other words, they form a mass of information, parts of which may be of vital importance to you.

Here again, if you send an inquiry you must be patient. Recently I knew that I would be appearing on a TV show to talk about genealogy. The host of the program was named McLean, and his family came from Lochmaddy, North Uist, in Scotland. I saw that the name McLean appeared in the index to the Document Collection and decided that it might be worth while asking if the McLean papers there referred to a family of that name from North Uist. The name is common, of course, and I was not too hopeful, but I thought it might be fun if I could talk to the TV host about his own family. So I wrote to the Society, explaining that in six weeks I would be on a TV show, and asked if they could check the McLean papers for a family from North Uist. I emphasized that there was a deadline, stated I was a member, offered to pay whatever fee was required, and enclosed a reply-paid coupon and a self-addressed airmail envelope.

Weeks and months went by, the TV show came and went, and *five months* after I sent my letter I received a reply which informed me that on receipt of five pounds they would check on the name for me! This is why I counsel patience. How did I do on the TV show? Oh, fine, because, based on my previous experiences and those of other members, I doubted very much whether I would hear from the Society in time—and so I wrote to the parish priest at Lochmaddy, in North Uist, and to a local newspaper. I had a long letter full of information about the family from the priest, and half a dozen letters containing further information from people who read my letter in the paper. As a result, I was able to tell the TV host about his family back to 1780.

Directories and Poll Books
The Society has a fine collection of these covering many parts of the country and dating back to the early eighteenth century for poll books, and to the latter part for city and county directories.

Family Histories
The library has a good collection of printed and manuscript family histories.

The Great Card Index
This contains some three million references from the Norman Conquest to the nineteenth century. It is not an index to anything in particular—just a mass of names from registers, marriage licences, and printed pedigrees, all lumped together and sorted under surnames and subdivided under first names.

Boyd's Marriage Index
For details of this, see Chapter 9 (page 89).

Bernau's Index
This is on microfilm and covers about four and a half million slips referring to unindexed material in the Public Record Office, mainly Chancery and Exchequer Court records. It is arranged by surname and subdivided by first name.

Wills and Marriage Licences
The originals are in the Public Record Office or the County Record Offices (see Chapter 7, pages 44 and 49). However, the Society has a unique collection of indexes to the wills. These indexes are being

added to from time to time, and should certainly be checked while you are on the premises.

Welsh Pedigrees
The library includes the Williams Collection, which consists of 104 volumes of manuscript notes on Welsh pedigrees.

Scottish Collection
This collection is not a particularly good one, and in the main consists of the MacLeod Papers covering a period from 1880 to 1940. The MacLeods, father and son, were professional record-searchers, but the collection is of only limited value.

The Society is at present publishing the National Index of Parish Registers, and when the project is complete, full details of the location of all parish and Nonconformist registers and Bishop's Transcripts will be covered.

There are also a number of Society publications which are very useful. For example, you can buy a catalogue of parish registers, or a key to Boyd's Marriage Index, or *Examples of Handwriting*, or *Monumental Inscriptions of Jamaica*, or *Further Light on the Ancestry of William Penn*.

To sum up, a visit to the Society's offices may be a worthwhile trip, but do not expect a miracle. Make sure you know exactly what you are looking for before you go—otherwise you will waste a lot of time wandering from room to room, and from shelf to shelf. The staff are helpful up to a point, but one often has the feeling one's intrusion into their little empire is not particularly welcome. However, this sort of thing is not unique in England, so do not be put off.

Settlement Act, 1662
This was a measure to give a local council the right to expel paupers who had not settled in the place, and to send them back to their place of origin. At intervals various changes were made in the Act, but, basically, it remained in force until 1876. Most of the records survive in the CROs and may be of considerable value to you if your ancestors were paupers at any time. The records give details of the family members and place of birth.

Dr. Williams' Library
This is located at 14 Gordon Square, London WC1H 0AG, and contains a great deal of information about ecclesiastical history,

particularly that of the Nonconformists during the seventeenth to nineteenth centuries. No genealogical research is undertaken.

Huguenot Records

Following the revocation of the Edict of Nantes by the French government in 1685, over 50,000 Protestants (Huguenots) fled overseas to England, Ireland, North America, and South Africa. There were several Huguenot churches established in England, and the registers and other records are in the custody of the Huguenot Society of London (Hon. Secretary, 67 Victoria Road, London W8 5RH). See also page 270 for Irish records.

7

WILLS
(ENGLAND & WALES)

The discovery of an ancestor's will can be of tremendous value. It may give you an exact address, the names of relatives of the deceased and their location, the style of life of the ancestor, the names and locations of farms and other property, insights into his character, and, of course, the fun of finding out how much money he left—and wondering to yourself where it all went over the years! Although the subject is a most complicated one, do not be discouraged, because the prize will be worth the hunt.

Wills became fairly common about 1550, although some exist dating back for nearly three centuries earlier. The normal procedure in England was for a will to be proved in the archdeaconry court, or the diocesan consistory court if there was no archdeaconry in the area in which the man or woman died. These ecclesiastical courts were under the jurisdiction of the established church in England and Wales.

If I could stop right here, life (and will-finding) would be simple, but it is all the "ifs" and "buts" that add the complications.

1. If the possessions were in two separate places far enough apart to be in two different archdeaconries, the will had to be proved in the consistory court of the bishop.

2. If the two separate places were so far apart that they were in separate dioceses (that is, under two bishops), then it went to the prerogative court of the archbishop. In England and Wales there were two archbishops—Canterbury and York—and each headed up his own province. Basically, Canterbury covered that part of England south of Cheshire and Yorkshire, but excluding Nottinghamshire. It also included the whole of Wales. York covered the rest of England—in other words, the northern counties.

3. If the two separate places were so far apart they were in two provinces, the will went to the prerogative court of the senior province (Canterbury).

That was the complicated rule, but now here come the exceptions!

1. Very often the executor of a will would bypass the lower court—the archdeaconry one—and deal directly with the consistory court of the bishop. This was for several reasons: a desire for more privacy and secrecy about a family's financial affairs; or perhaps the location of the consistory court was more convenient for the executor.

This latter little ploy can really throw you off the track. A man dies in Bristol and owns no property anywhere else in England. No problem, right? Wrong. His executor lives in London and so that is where the will is to be found!

2. You must know about "peculiars". Throughout England there were "peculiar" jurisdictions. These were a parish, or a group of parishes, which were (for some reason which has been lost in the mists of time) exempt from the normal jurisdiction and placed under some other jurisdiction. If your ancestors lived in a peculiar, as did some of mine, you will have to go carefully.

An extreme example is that of the parish of Eton, in Buckinghamshire. This is a peculiar of the Provost of Eton College, and you have to go to the school to look at the will of anyone living in the parish before 1858. More normal examples—if there is anything normal about a peculiar—can be found in the county of Gloucester. The county came under three major jurisdictions: the Diocese of Gloucester, the Diocese of Bristol, and the Archdeaconry of Hereford, *but* the peculiar of Bibury, the peculiar of Bishop Cleeve, and the peculiar of Withington—all in the middle of the county—came under the Bishop of Bristol.

However, now that you know peculiars existed, forget about them—they may not bother you at all. I simply bring the matter up so that if you don't find a will, you can always say "Ah, the peculiars!" and try again somewhere else. Anyway, in most cases the peculiars are in the same record office as the surrounding jurisdictions.

As you will see, it is much simpler if you know in which parish your ancestor lived. This will give you the archdeaconry court or the diocesan court under whose jurisdiction the parish lay.

However, if you know only the county and not the parish, all is not lost. You have two possible sources of information:

1. Indexes to the wills of the county, or of the jurisdiction covering it, may have been published.

2. Any record office with probate records will have some form of index. If there is no published one, there may be a card index.

There are a number of general comments about wills which you should bear in mind:

1. Wills were often not proved at all. If the inheritance was straightforward—everything to the wife, or to the eldest son, or an equal division—the family might not bother with probate, as this saved time and money and effort. This is why you may not find a will even though you are absolutely sure that the ancestor was wealthy and owned property.

2. Usually a will was not made until the testator was dying, so you will often find the wills start off, "I, Richard Castle, being sound of mind but frail of body..." This will help you because if you know a date of death you may assume the will was made within a year before, and probated or proved within a year after. This narrows your search a little if you have a common name to deal with. On the other hand, this habit of death-bed wills also means that someone dying suddenly or by accident left no will for you to find.

3. Quite often the estate was divided up *before* death. The testator, knowing death was near, would divide up his property between his wife and children, giving, for example, one farm to the eldest son, another to the second, and various cash payments to other members of the family.

4. Until the middle of the last century, the more possessions your ancestor owned, the more likely it was that he left a will. The reverse was also true, which is why the practice of will-making was not all that common before the middle of the last century.

The systems in other parts of the United Kingdom and Eire were similar in that wills were originally under church jurisdiction, but there were minor variations. You will find full information about this in later chapters.

In 1858 probate matters in England and Wales were transferred from ecclesiastical to civil control. In that year a Principal Probate Registry was set up in London to which district registries sent copies of all wills and administrations proved locally. This is now known as the Principal Registry of the Family Division and is located at Somerset House in London (where the Civil Registration records used to be before the move to St. Catherine's House). All wills and administrations in England and Wales since 1858 can be consulted there. An annual printed index was produced, and in addition to the copy of this at Somerset House, sets of the index were sent to the district registries. Most of those over fifty years old have now been transferred to the local record offices or libraries— their location is given in *Where to Look For Wills* by J. S. W. Gibson

(Gulliver Press, Banbury, Oxford, 1980). Duplicate copies of the wills over fifty years old proved at district registeries have often been transferred to local record offices (see Chapters 9 and 10). However, for visitors to England or those writing from overseas, it is easier to deal directly with Somerset House. Ask for a will or a grant of representation, and send one pound with your application. A grant of representation tells you the names of the executors and the total value of the estate. A copy of the will alone does not give this information. If you are calling in person at Somerset House, the hours of opening are 1000-1630 hours, Monday to Friday.

Prerogative Court of Canterbury (PCC)

This court had overriding jurisdiction in England and Wales, and sole jurisdiction when a testator held possessions ("bona notabilia") in more than one diocese or peculiar in the Province of Canterbury—that is, England south of Cheshire and Yorkshire, except for Nottinghamshire, and all of Wales. It also had jurisdiction over those with estates in England or Wales who died overseas or at sea.

During the Commonwealth period (1653-60), it had sole jurisdiction over the whole of England and Wales. In actual fact this sole jurisdiction covered the period from 1642, when the civil war started, to about 1666, six years after the Restoration. This was because so many lower courts had ceased to exist, and it took time to re-establish them.

The records of the court are in the Public Record Office. There are printed indexes until 1700. After this date it is necessary to search the *Calendars* (in manuscript form until 1852, printed since then), which are arranged in one or more volumes per year. Names are listed chronologically within their initial letter.

A fully alphabetical, consolidated card index to PCC wills from 1750 to 1800 has been prepared by the Society of Genealogists. The first part of this (A-G) has been published in three volumes and others will appear in due course. Meanwhile, the Society will make searches in the remainder of the index for a small fee. The address is 14 Charterhouse Buildings, London EC1M 7BA.

Ecclesiastical Courts

The following list shows the ecclesiastical courts having some jurisdiction in each county of England and Wales. For this purpose I have followed "old" (pre-1974) boundaries. I have not listed peculiars and their separate courts because this would make the list too long. Much fuller information can best be obtained from Jeremy Gibson's *Wills and Where to Find Them*,* or from the County Record Office concerned:

England

BEDFORDSHIRE: Archdeaconry of Bedford (Diocese of Lincoln until 1837, then of Ely).

BERKSHIRE: Archdeaconry of Berkshire (Diocese of Salisbury until 1836, then of Oxford).

BUCKINGHAMSHIRE: Archdeaconry of Buckingham (Diocese of Lincoln until 1845, then of Oxford).

CAMBRIDGESHIRE (AND ISLE OF ELY): Archdeaconry of Ely (Diocese of Ely).

CHESHIRE: Diocese of Cheshire.

CORNWALL: Archdeaconry of Cornwall (Diocese of Exeter).

CUMBERLAND: Dioceses of Carlisle and Chester.

DERBYSHIRE: Diocese of Lichfield.

DEVONSHIRE: Archdeaconries of Barnstaple, Exeter, and Totnes (Diocese of Exeter).

DORSET: Archdeaconry of Dorset (Diocese of Bristol).

DURHAM: Diocese of Durham.

ESSEX: Archdeaconries of Essex, Middlesex, Colchester (Diocese of London).

GLOUCESTERSHIRE: Diocese of Gloucester and Bristol, Archdeaconry of Hereford.

HAMPSHIRE: Archdeaconry and Diocese of Winchester.

HEREFORDSHIRE: Diocese of Hereford, Archdeaconry of Brecon.

HERTFORDSHIRE: Archdeaconries of Huntingdon, Middlesex, St. Albans, (Dioceses of Lincoln and London).

HUNTINGDONSHIRE: Archdeaconry of Huntingdon (Diocese of Lincoln, until 1831, then of Ely).

KENT: Archdeaconries of Canterbury and Rochester, Dioceses of Canterbury and Rochester.

LANCASHIRE: Diocese of Chester, Archdeaconries of Chester and Richmond.

LEICESTERSHIRE: Archdeaconry of Leicester (Diocese of Lincoln).

LINCOLNSHIRE: Diocese of Lincoln, Archdeaconry of Stow.

---

*I wish to acknowledge my indebtedness to Jeremy Gibson for permission to quote from his book *Wills and Where to Find Them* (Phillimore, Chichester, 1974). It is without doubt the clearest and most concise book on the subject, and all genealogists are in his debt.

LONDON AND MIDDLESEX: Archdeaconries of London and Middlesex, Diocese of London.

NORFOLK: Archdeaconry of Norfolk and Norwich (Diocese of Norwich).

NORTHAMPTONSHIRE (AND SOKE OF PETERBOROUGH): Archdeaconry of Northampton (Diocese of Peterborough).

NORTHUMBERLAND: Diocese of Durham.

NOTTINGHAMSHIRE: Archdeaconry of Nottingham (Diocese of York).

OXFORDSHIRE: Archdeaconry of Oxford (Diocese of Oxford).

RUTLAND: Diocese of Peterborough.

SHROPSHIRE: Dioceses of Hereford, Lichfield, St. Asaph, and Worcester.

SOMERSETSHIRE: Archdeaconries of Wells and Taunton (Diocese of Bath and Wells).

STAFFORDSHIRE: Diocese of Lichfield.

SUFFOLK: Archdeaconries of Suffolk, Sudbury, Norfolk, and Norwich (Diocese of Norwich).

SURREY: Archdeaconry of Surrey (Diocese of Winchester).

SUSSEX: Archdeaconries of Chichester and Lewes (Diocese of Chichester).

WARWICKSHIRE: Dioceses of Lichfield and Worcester.

WESTMORLAND: Dioceses of Carlisle and Chester.

WILTSHIRE: Archdeaconries of Salisbury and Wiltshire, and subdeanery of Salisbury (Dioceses of Salisbury, Gloucester, and Winchester).

WORCESTERSHIRE: Dioceses of Worcester and Hereford.

YORKSHIRE: Archdeaconry of Richmond (Dioceses of York and Chester).

Wales

ANGLESEY: Diocese of Bangor.

CAERNARFON: Diocese of Bangor, but 3 parishes in St. Asaph.

DENBIGH: Dioceses of St. Asaph and Bangor, but 1 parish in Chester.

FLINT: Dioceses of St. Asaph and Chester.

MERIONETH: Dioceses of Bangor and St. Asaph.

MONTGOMERY: Dioceses of St. Asaph, St. David's, Hereford, and Bangor.

The counties of BRECKNOCK, CARDIGAN, CARMARTHEN, GLAMORGAN, MONMOUTH, PEMBROKE, and RADNOR were all in the Dioceses of St. David's and Llandaff.

Glossary

These terms are the ones you are most likely to come across in your search for and reading of wills. They apply in England and Wales. Other words used in other parts are given in the appropriate chapters:

Act Book: A day-by-day account of grants of probate of wills, letters of administration, and other business in connection with wills.

Administration, Letters of: These are often referred to as "admons" and are a grant to the person applying to administer an estate.

Archdeaconry: The court most likely to deal with probate of a will. In large dioceses there could be several of them.

Bona Notabilia: A Latin phrase meaning considerable goods, usually five pounds or more. When the deceased had "bona notabilia" in more than one place, it meant the will would be proved in a higher court.

Bond: A signed declaration by the administrator setting out his obligation to administer an estate, prove a will, or act as the guardian of a minor.

Caveat: A warning that a will is under dispute.

Consistory Court: The bishop's court with higher rank than an archdeaconry court. Often, in a diocese, it would replace the lower court entirely, and there would be no archdeaconry court. (See also under *Inhibition*.)

Curation: Guardianship of orphan minors.

Dean and Chapter: Clergy who were members of a cathedral chapter; usually those who administered a peculiar either in their own right, or on behalf of the bishop.

Diocese: The area over which a bishop has authority. Also known as a see.

Executor (or Executrix): The man (or woman) appointed by the testator to see that the provisions of the will are observed.

Grant: Approval of the report of the administrator or executor of an estate, and the conclusion of the work, i.e., probate was granted.

Inhibition: When a bishop visited an archdeaconry, which he would do every few years for a couple of months, the archdeaconry court would be closed (or *inhibited* from operation) and all probate business would be referred to the consistory court of the diocese.

Intestate: A person who died without making a will.

Inventory: A list of personal and household goods left by the deceased, with their appraised value.

Jurisdiction: The area within which a particular court could grant probate.

Noncupative will: A will made orally, normally by a testator on his deathbed, written down and sworn to by witnesses but not signed by the deceased.

Peculiar: A parish or a group of parishes which were exempt from the jurisdiction of one court and came under the jurisdiction of another, even though they were geographically within the normal jurisdictional boundaries of the first court.

Personalty: Personal property (e.g., jewellery and furniture) as opposed to real property (land).

Probate: Evidence that a will has been accepted by the court, and that the executor has been granted permission to carry out its provisions.

Proved: A will has been "proved" when probate has been granted.

Realty, Real Property, Real Estate: Property or interests in land, as opposed to personalty.

Registers and Registered Wills: Volumes of copy wills, made at the time of probate. It is these you will probably see, although often only original wills are available. At times only the registered copies survive.

See: Often used instead of diocese to describe the area of jurisdiction of the bishop, although actually it should only be used to describe the centre of the diocese where the bishop has his seat.

Surrogate: A deputy appointed by an ecclesiastical court to deal with probate matters.

Testament: A will.

Testator: A man who has made his will. A testatrix is a woman.

Will: A written statement by which a person sets out his wishes regarding disposition of his property after his death.

8

ARMY & NAVY RECORDS (ENGLAND & WALES)

Before the Civil War (1642-49) there was no regular standing army in England. Regiments were raised to meet special occasions and were usually known by the names of the colonels who raised them. There are no surviving records of such regiments, although you will find an occasional reference to individual officers in State papers and Privy Council registers.

For the period of the Civil War and of the Commonwealth which followed it, the officers of both sides are listed in *The Army List of Roundheads and Cavaliers* by Edward Peacock (1865), and for the Parliamentary troops much detailed information can be found in *The Regimental History of Cromwell's Army* by Frith and Davies (1940).

It has been said that everyone of British descent has at least one soldier among his ancestors. I have no idea if this is true, nor does anyone else. I suspect that in actual fact very few of us have military ancestors, if we exclude the period of the wars of this present century. Even when there was a standing army its numbers were small in proportion to the civilian population. The hazards of the profession also reduced the number of children fathered by the soldiers and sailors—within wedlock, at any rate.

On four sides of my family I never found a soldier or a sailor, except in this century when my father was in the Boer War and the First World War, and I was in the Second World War. On my wife's side we found an officer in the Black Watch who fought at Waterloo, and in this century her father served in the army in the First World War, as did she in the Second World War. I am inclined to think this is about average.

However, there may be many of you with military backgrounds, so let us talk about the available records.

Once the monarchy was restored in 1660 the records became more plentiful. The main War Office records contain a great deal of information about military operations and administration, finance, supplies, courts martial, etc. All records for officers and other ranks up to the start of the First World War are kept in the Public Record Office at Kew. The records since then remain in the custody of the Ministry of Defence. Fuller information can be obtained from the Army Historical Branch, Old War Office Building, London SW1A 2EU. Similar information about naval personnel of this period can be obtained from the Naval Historical Branch, The Admiralty, London.

The military authorities acquired a great deal of personal information about serving officers and men over their years of service, and it is all on record. If you have a military ancestor and you do find his records, you will gain a great deal of new knowledge about him. However, it is not an easy job and it is not one which you can do yourself. The records and the system under which they are filed are complicated, and a professional record agent must be employed.

Army Records

Officers

The service records of officers can be traced from 1660, although family details and places of birth were not often recorded until about 1800. Systematic records of officers' services were introduced in 1829. They are arranged by regiments, but some of these have been lost.

The main sources of information about officers are:

1. Returns of Officers' Services (military service only, 1808-10). These contain no personal details.

2. Services of Officers Retired on Full and Half Pay (1828). These give age on being commissioned, date of marriage, and birth of children.

3. Services of Officers on the Active List (1829-1919). These are the best source and include date and place of birth, details of marriage, and names and ages of children.

4. The date of an officer's death can usually be found in the Paymaster General's Records of Full and Half Pay.

Other Ranks

The records of other ranks are listed in most cases by regiment, so that it is almost essential to know the name of the regiment in which the soldier served in order to trace his records. If it is known where he was serving on a given date, it may be possible to discover his regiment from the Monthly Returns, which show where particular regiments were stationed during any particular year. Once the regiment is known, the main sources of information about an other rank are:

1. **Regular Soldiers' Documents:** These date back to 1756. Among other records they contain the Discharge Certificates. Up to 1883 the certificates of soldiers "discharged to pension" were kept separately from those of men discharged for other reasons, such as "discharges by purchase" or "conclusion of limited engagement". After 1883 all the discharge certificates are listed in one group. The records of soldiers who died on active service and thus never received discharge certificates, together with those of soldiers who were not pensioned, were destroyed in a fire many years ago. It is ironic that if you have a gallant ancestor who was killed in action, it will be harder to find him than one who stayed home in the regimental depot!

All discharge certificates, except for a few of the earliest ones, record the place of the soldier's birth and his age on the date of enlistment. After 1883, details of the next of kin—parents, wife, children—are usually given.

2. **Pay Lists and Muster Rolls:** These are very comprehensive and detailed. They date from 1760 and may give you the date of an ancestor's enlistment, his areas of service throughout the world, and the date of his discharge or death. They are arranged by regiment in volumes, each covering a period of one year. In many of them a list entitled "Men Becoming Non-effective" appears at the end of each quarter. Where this exists, it should show the birthplace of the man discharged or dead, his trade, and his date of enlistment. Before 1883 this sometimes provides the only method of discovering the birthplace of a man not discharged on pension. By tracing him back through the Muster Books it may be possible to find his age shown on the day of his entry as a recruit.

3. **Other sources of birth information:** Description Books were used by the military authorities as a means of tracing deserters. If your ancestor went on the run at some time you may find out that he was six feet tall and had red hair and blue eyes, a wart on his left cheek, and a tattoo of an elephant on his right arm!

Details of marriage and children may be found in the Marriage Rolls, which are at the end of the Musters and Pay Lists, but they only exist from 1868. There are some miscellaneous "Regimental Registers of Soldiers' Marriages and the Births or Baptisms of their Children" in the General Register Office, St. Catherine's House, London.

There are also Casualty Returns; Chelsea Hospital Pension Registers; Royal Hospital, Kilmainham, Dublin, Pension Registers; Regular Soldiers' Documents 1760-1900; and Royal Artillery Records of Service up to 1877.

In Scotland there was no regular army before the Act of Union in 1707. Fuller information about Scots military records can be found in Chapter 11. Details of Irish military records can be found in Chapter 12, and those for the Isle of man in Chapter 13.

Naval Records

The Admiralty Records are also in the Public Record Office at Kew. Information about naval officers is much easier to find than that about naval ratings. Strictly genealogical information about an individual (birth or baptism, marriage and death, names of parents, wife, and children) cannot always be found among the surviving records. In any case, it may require an involved search through many different types of records, since there is no general index of names. Records which supply information about a man's career (such as ships on which he served, with rank and date) do not always include genealogical information.

For men serving before 1660, no systematic records of service survive in the PRO. Mention of individuals and ships may sometimes be found among the State Papers Domestic in the Chancery Lane office of the PRO by means of indexes to printed Calendars. Records since 1660 are described below.

Records of Service

Until the present century the personnel of the navy was divided into commissioned officers, warrant officers, and ratings. The first were the executive officers of the ship, answerable only to the Admiralty. Warrant officers were responsible heads of their own departments (boatswain, carpenter, cooper, engineer, gunner, master, purser, sailmaker, surgeon) and were answerable to the Navy Board. There was no naval equivalent of the NCOs and "other ranks" of the army—all other members of the ship's company were "ratings" (petty officer, able seaman, boy, stoker, gunner's mate, steward, cook).

Commissioned Officers: Their career may usually be traced from printed lists in the PRO. There is also a typescript list in the National Maritime Museum, based on material *not* deposited in the PRO. This covers the period 1660-1815. Other sources of information are:

Lieutenants' Passing Certificates: These summarize the training and career of the candidate and often have certificates of birth or baptism attached. These are indexed for the period 1691-1902.

Records of Officers' Services: These include both commissioned and warrant officers and begin in the last quarter of the eighteenth century. They are in several different sections, each of which is indexed. There is some overlapping and it may be necessary to check more than one index for full information about an individual. Many give dates and places of birth and death, and all list the ships on which the man served, with dates.

Returns of Officers' Services: These consist of two censuses—of officers in 1817-22 and in 1846. The latter census also gives the age of the officer in that year.

Other returns provide more specialized information:
Officers appointed 1660-88;
Lieutenants unfit for service 1804-10;
Lieutenants serving in 1847, with service and age;
Candidates for Royal Naval College 1816-18 with birth;
Officers passing gunnery course 1833-42.

Bounty Papers: These are complete for 1675-1822 and give the name and address of the next of kin to whom a bounty was to be paid if the officer or rating was killed in action or died. The baptismal certificate of the next of kin is also included.

Register of Lieutenants Soliciting Employment: This was kept from 1799 on and lists the address of the applicant.

Warrant Officers: Incomplete lists are available for several departments.

Warrant Officers' and Seamen's Services: These give a brief service record of warrant officers sent into retirement with a pension after 1802. They include chaplains, cooks, masters, and surgeon's assistants.

Engineers: There are Passing Certificates from 1863, and lists of those serving from 1836 to 1849.

Surgeons: These are recorded between 1774 and 1886. There are also incomplete lists between 1742 and 1815.

Masters: There are details of Masters' Qualifications from 1660 to 1830, which include certificates of baptism. Passing Certificates from 1851 to 1863 also include baptism certificates.

Clerks: A register of those serving between 1835 and 1849 is also in the PRO.

Midshipmen: Passing Certificates are available from 1857 to 1899, and also an indexed survey of those serving in 1814, giving age and place of birth.

Chaplains: A list of these serving between 1626 and 1903 is in the PRO.

Ratings: There are various sources for this information.

Ships' Musters: For records of service before the nineteenth century it is necessary to know the name of the ship on which the man served on a particular date. The Ships' Musters, which survive from 1667, may then be consulted. In many cases the musters record the man's age and place of birth. Sometimes they also include descriptions of the rating—age, height, complexion, scars, tattoos, etc. As in the Army Description Books, this information was kept on record to enable the authorities to trace deserters from the service.

Continuous Service: From 1853, when a Continuous Service engagement was started, seamen were given CS numbers. On entry, a CS Certificate was completed showing date and place of birth, description, and name of ship. These records are in the Continuous Service Engagement Books for the period 1853-72. There is an index, together with a list of the new Official Numbers which replaced CS numbers from 1873.

Register of Seamen's Services: This is available from 1853 to 1891, arranged in numerical order, giving date of birth, period of service and first ship.

List Books: If it is known *where* a man was serving at a particular time, but not in which ship, the List Books for 1673-1893 can be checked to find out the location of all ships on a certain date.

Inquiries about ships of the Royal Navy should be sent to the National Maritime Museum, Greenwich, London SE10 9NF.

Royal Marines

The records of the Royal Marines are also in the PRO. Many of the early documents are lost, including most of the Description Books. The Attestation Forms (1780-1883) give the age, place of birth, and physical appearance of each recruit. These are arranged alphabetically. Those Description Books which survive cover the period 1750-1888 and are also in alphabetical order. The Registers of Service (1842-1905) give similar information.

Inquiries about serving officers since 1906 should be sent to Royal Marines, Ministry of Defence, Whitehall, London SW1A 2HB, and for other ranks to Records Office, Royal Marines, HMS Centurion, Grange Road, Gosport, Hampshire PO 13 9XA.

In addition to the PRO records there are several published books which give more information, and some of these are listed in the bibliography at the end of this book (in particular, John Kitzmiller's book about British regiments—see page 303).

Royal Air Force

This was formed under the name of the Royal Flying Corps in the First World War and therefore there are no records of interest to ancestor-hunters, unless they are concerned with the very recent past. In that case, they should write to the Ministry of Defence, Old War Office Building, Whitehall, and ask for the letter to be forwarded to Personnel Records, Royal Air Force.

9
ENGLISH COUNTIES

Before you start searching for records in England and Wales, it is essential that you know about the major changes made in 1974 in the county boundaries. As a result of this, several counties disappeared and others were divided or renamed. The new county of Cumbria, for example, includes the old counties of Cumberland and Westmorland, parts of Lancashire, parts of the old West Riding of Yorkshire, and the County Borough Councils of Carlisle and Barrow-in-Furness. This can be confusing when you are searching for a county and find it has disappeared.

The English counties and the areas they now include are listed below.

Note: M after the county name indicates a Metropolitan County, CBC means County Borough Council, C stands for city. The name of the county town and seat of government is shown in brackets.

AVON: Bath and Bristol CBCs, parts of Gloucestershire and Somerset (Bristol)

BEDFORDSHIRE: Luton CBC and Bedfordshire (Bedford)

BERKSHIRE: Reading CBC, most of Berkshire, parts of Buckinghamshire (Reading)

BUCKINGHAMSHIRE: Most of Buckinghamshire (Aylesbury)

CAMBRIDGESHIRE: Cambridgeshire, Isle of Ely, Huntingdon, and Peterborough (Cambridge)

CHESHIRE: Chester and Warrington CBCs, most of Cheshire, parts of Lancashire (Chester)

CLEVELAND: Hartlepool and Teesside CBCs, parts of Durham, parts of North Riding of Yorkshire (Middlesbrough)

CORNWALL: Cornwall (Truro)

CUMBRIA: Barrow-in-Furness and Carlisle CBCs, Cumberland, Westmorland, parts of Lancashire, parts of West Riding of Yorkshire (Carlisle)

DERBYSHIRE: Derby CBC, Derbyshire, parts of Cheshire (Matlock)

DEVON: Exeter, Plymouth, and Torbay CBCs, Devon (Exeter)

DORSET: Bournemouth CBC, Dorset, parts of Hampshire (Dorchester)

DURHAM: Darlington CBC, most of Durham, parts of North Riding of Yorkshire (Durham)

EAST SUSSEX: Brighton, Eastbourne, and Hastings CBCs, most of East Sussex (Lewes)

ESSEX: Southend-on-Sea CBC, Essex (Chelmsford)

GLOUCESTERSHIRE: Gloucester CBC, most of Gloucestershire (Gloucester)

GREATER MANCHESTER M: Wigan, Bolton, Bury, Rochdale, Salford, Manchester, Oldham, and Stockport CBCs, parts of Lancashire, parts of Cheshire (Manchester)

HAMPSHIRE: Portsmouth and Southampton CBCs, most of Hampshire (Winchester)

HEREFORD and WORCESTER (amalgamated in 1975): Worcester CBC, Herefordshire, most of Worcestershire (Worcester)

HERTFORDSHIRE: Hertfordshire (Hertford)

HUMBERSIDE: Grimsby and Kingston-upon-Hull CBCs, most of the East Riding of Yorkshire, parts of Lindsey (Lincolnshire), and parts of the West Riding of Yorkshire (Kingston-upon-Hull)

ISLE OF WIGHT: Isle of Wight (Newport)

KENT: Canterbury CBC, Kent (Maidstone)

LANCASHIRE: Blackburn, Blackpool, Burnley, and Preston CBCs, most of Lancashire, parts of the West Riding of Yorkshire (Preston)

LEICESTERSHIRE: Leicester CBC, Leicestershire, Rutland (Leicester)

LINCOLNSHIRE: Lincoln CBC, Holland, Kesteven, some of Lindsey (Lincoln)

MERSEYSIDE M: Bootle, Southport, Liverpool, and St. Helens CBCs, parts of Lancashire, parts of Cheshire (Liverpool)

NORFOLK: Great Yarmouth and Norwich CBCs, Norfolk, parts of East Suffolk (Norwich)

NORTHAMPTONSHIRE: Northampton CBC and Northamptonshire (Northampton)

NORTHUMBERLAND: Most of Northumberland (Newcastle)

NORTH YORKSHIRE: York CBC, most of the North Riding of Yorkshire, part of the East Riding of Yorkshire (Northallerton)

NOTTINGHAMSHIRE: Nottingham CBC, most of Nottinghamshire (Nottingham)

OXFORDSHIRE: Oxford CBC, Oxfordshire, part of Berkshire (Oxford)

SALOP: Salop (Shrewsbury). Note: Salop is also known as Shropshire.

SOMERSET: Most of Somerset (Taunton)

SOUTH YORKSHIRE M: Barnsley, Doncaster, Rotherham, Sheffield CBCs, part of the West Riding of Yorkshire (Barnsley)

STAFFORDSHIRE: Burton-upon-Trent and Stoke-on-Trent CBCs, most of Staffordshire (Stafford)

SUFFOLK: Ipswich CBC, West Suffolk, most of East Suffolk (Ipswich)

TYNE AND WEAR M: Gateshead, Newcastle-upon-Tyne, South Shields, Sunderland, Tynemouth CBCs, parts of Northumberland, parts of Durham (Newcastle-upon-Tyne)

WARWICKSHIRE: Most of Warwickshire (Warwick)

WEST MIDLANDS M: Birmingham, Coventry, Dudley, Solihull, Walsall, Warley, West Bromwich, Wolverhampton CBCs, parts of Staffordshire, parts of Warwickshire, parts of Worcestershire (Birmingham)

WEST SUSSEX: West Sussex, parts of East Sussex (Chichester)

WEST YORKSHIRE M: Bradford, Dewsbury, Halifax, Huddersfield, Leeds, Wakefield CBCs, parts of the West Riding of Yorkshire (Wakefield)

WILTSHIRE: Wiltshire (Trowbridge)

It will be seen from the above that the two smallest counties in England (Rutland and the Isle of Ely) have disappeared, as have Huntingdon, Westmorland, Cumberland, and Middlesex. Only Bedfordshire, Cornwall, Essex, Hertfordshire, Isle of Wight, Kent, Northamptonshire, Salop, and Wiltshire have no boundary changes.

County Records

We have talked about the main national sources of information— St. Catherine's House, the Public Record Office, Somerset House, the British Library, the Newspaper Library, the House of Lords, various religious organizations, the Society of Genealogists, etc. Now it is time to examine genealogical sources on a county basis in England and Wales.

It was only in 1914 that the first County Record Office was established, and it is only since the Second World War that the idea of archives for each county has really developed. Now, in some form or another each county has its record office. Other authorities are co-operating and an enormous amount of material—not all genealogical, of course—is being handed over to the County

Record Offices. The churches are also being most co-operative and it brings joy to my heart to know that priceless old documents are now being cared for as they should be. Our thanks as genealogists must go out to the County Archivists and their staffs—they are making our task easier for us.

Family History Societies

Accessibility of genealogical records in the County Record Offices has been a major factor in another postwar development—the formation of Family History Societies in the 1960s and 1970s. These are organized on either a county or a one-name basis. To all intents and purposes they are genealogical societies. In 1974 the Federation of Family History Societies was formed to co-ordinate and assist the work of individual branches and to encourge the formation of branches where none exist.

Some Societies will undertake simple research for a fee, others will not. If you need research in a particular area you should contact the FHS for that county or area. Although there is an FHS in each county in England and Wales it is not practicable to list addresses of the secretaries as these change with great frequency. Information regarding branches and their location can be obtained from the Federation of Family History Societies (Administrator: Mrs. P. A. Saul, 31 Seven Star Road, Solihull, West Midlands B91 2BZ). Be sure you send *three* International Reply Coupons and a self-addressed airmail envelope, otherwise you will not rceive a reply.

It will be in your interest to join the Society in the area of your interest. You will get its publications on a regular basis, and you will also be able to have your queries published in its regular newsletter. In addition, the FHS will tell you if anyone else is already researching or tracing your family.

There are also a number of small one-name organizations, and information about them can be obtained from the Guild of One-Name Studies, 15 Cavendish Gardens, Cranbrook, Ilford, Essex 1G1 3EA.

Boyd's Marriage Index

When searching the records of the counties, you should be aware of Boyd's Marriage Index. This is held by the Society of Genealogists, 37 Harrington Gardens, London. It was compiled by the late Percival Boyd between 1925 and 1955, when he died. His manuscripts were bequeathed to the Church of Jesus Christ of Latter Day Saints (the Mormons) on condition that they complete the work. This is being done. Many County Record Offices have copies for their county on their shelves.

There are too many registers to list in this book, but a complete list of parishes which have been listed can be bought from the society above. It is estimated that between fourteen and fifteen per cent of all marriages are included, and between six and seven million names are listed. It is important you realize that *not all* marriages in a county are listed—only those from parishes on which work has been done—and *not all* the marriages in a parish have been indexed. In other words, the Marriage Index is not the answer to all your problems, but if you are reasonably lucky it may be of considerable help.

The counties covered by the Index are listed below; the first column of figures shows the number of parishes which have been included and the second column shows the percentage of the whole number in the county which they represent:

County	Parishes	%	County	Parishes	%
Bedford	8	6%	Leicester	140	51%
Berkshire	13	8	Lincoln	99	15
Buckingham	64	30	Middlesex & London	177	73
Cambridge	170	99	Norfolk	275	38
Cheshire	18	11	Northampton	43	14
Cornwall	206	93	Northumberland	84	73
Cumberland	35	22	Nottingham	161	68
Derby	80	40	Oxford	142	57
Devon	170	34	Rutland	23	38
Dorset	79	27	Shropshire	126	49
Durham	71	69	Somerset	123	24
Essex	381	94	Stafford	4	2
Gloucester	200	47	Suffolk	489	98
Hampshire	107	35	Surrey	69	45
Hereford	6	2	Sussex	57	17
Hertford	48	36	Warwick	30	11
Huntingdon	17	16	Westmorland	13	16
Isle of Wight	28	90	Wiltshire	73	21
Kent	130	32	Worcester	41	17
Lancashire	102	31	Yorkshire	207	24

Please also remember the Pallot Index. This is an index to marriages in London parish registers and covers over 100 parishes. Many parishes in the Greater London area are also now included. A fee is charged for each search and information can be obtained from Achievements Ltd., Northgate, Canterbury, Kent CT1 1BA.

In the following pages the genealogical records available in each County Record Office are listed on a county-by-county basis. For some counties the information is in great detail, in others it is brief. This is because the listing of the various records was supplied by the various County Record Offices (CROs); some went to a great deal of trouble to be of assistance in this book, others were more casual.

You will also find information as to the amount of searching which the various Record Offices are prepared to undertake for you, and whether they charge for this service or not.

Remember that new material is constantly arriving at the various CROs and being catalogued, and it is then available to you. All this takes time, and the detailed listings in this chapter should not be taken as the final word. In the listings of parish registers, for example, the names of the parishes which have donated their registers are complete at this time. However, if the name of a parish in which you are interested does not appear, be sure you check with the CRO to find out if they now have it.

Avon

This county was created from Bath and Bristol, and parts of Somerset and Gloucestershire. There is not yet a County Record Office, and the County Council does not hold material of interest to the ancestor-hunter. Material relating to what is now Avon will be found in the County Record Offices of Gloucestershire and Somerset, and the City Councils of Bath and Bristol:

Family History Societies
There are three Family History Societies covering this area:
Bristol and Avon
Gloucestershire
Somerset and Dorset
(See page 89 for remarks concerning Family History Societies.)

Gloucestershire County Record Office
Worcester Street, Gloucester, GL1 3DW. (Open daily, and on Thursday evenings and Saturday mornings by appointment.)

The staff will make the usual brief search without any charge (except for return postage), but if you need a long or speculative search you will be referred to a record-searcher. (For details of holdings of the Gloucestershire CRO, see page 133.)

Somerset County Record Office

Obridge Road, Taunton TA2 7PU. (Open Monday-Thursday, 0900-1245 hours and 1345-1650 hours; Friday, 0900-1620 hours; Saturday, by appointment, 0915-1215 hours.)

The office will carry out limited searches for postal inquirers without a fixed charge, but invites donations to a fund for buying microfilms, books, and manuscripts. Those requiring long searches will be sent a list of professional researchers. (For details of holdings of the Somerset CRO, see page 189.)

Bristol Record Office

The Council House, Bristol BS1 5TR.

This office holds the following parish registers: Bristol (5), Coalpit Heath, Frampton Cotterell, Northwick, Pilning, and Warmley.

Bath Record Office

The Council House, Bath.

These offices hold the official archives of their respective cities, including apprentice and burgess registers, family and estate records, parish and Nonconformist registers, and Bishop's Transcripts. Short searches will be undertaken and no fee is charged, but donations will be welcome.

Bedford

Family History Society

(See page 89 for remarks concerning Family History Societies.)

County Record Office

County Hall, Bedford MK42 9AP. (Open daily, Monday to Friday.)

The office will undertake, without charge, a brief preliminary search for inquirers by mail—although in future a charge may be made. For longer searches the ancestor-hunter will be sent a list of professional record-searchers.

Parish Registers

All the registers in the Archdeaconry of Bedford (which covers the same area as the county) have been transcribed and indexed up to 1812. About two-thirds of the registers have been published. Those held in the CRO, both originals and microfilm, are listed below: Ampthill, Arlesey, Aspley Guise, Astwick, Barford (Great and Little), Barton, Battlesden, Bedford (Holy Trinity, St. Cuthbert, St. John, St. Leonard, St. Mary, St. Paul, St. Peter), Biddenham, Biggleswade, Billington, Bletsoe, Blunham, Bolnhurst, Bromham, Caddington, Caldecote, Campton, Cardington, Carlton and Chellington, Chalgrave, Clapham, Clifton, Clophill, Colmworth, Cople, Cranfield, Dean, Dunstable, Dunton, Eaton Bray, Eaton Socon, Edworth, Eggington, Elstow, Eversholt, Everton, Eyeworth, Farndish, Felmersham, Flitton, Flitwick, Goldington, Gravenhurst (Upper and Lower), Harlington, Harrold, Hatley Cockayne, Haynes, Heath and Reach, Henlow, Higham Gobion, Hockliffe, Holwell, Houghton Conquest, Hulcote, Husborne Crawley, Kempston (All Saints, Church of the Transfiguration), Kensworth, Keysoe, Knotting, Langford, Leighton Buzzard (All Saints, St. Andrew), Lidlington, Linslade (at Buckinghamshire CRO), Luton (Christchurch, St. Mary, St. Matthew, St. Peter), Magerhanger, Marston Moretaine, Maulden, Melchbourne, Meppershall, Millbrook, Milton Bryan, Milton Ernest, Northill, Oakley, Odell, Pavenham, Pertenhall, Podington, Potsgrove, Potton, Pulloxhill, Ravensden, Renhold, Ridgmont, Riseley, Roxton, Salford, Sandy, Sharnbrook, Shefford, Shelton, Shillington, Silsoe, Souldrop, Southill, Stagsden, Stanbridge, Staughton (Little), Steppingley, Stevington, Stondon (Upper), Stotfold, Streatley, Studham, Sundon, Swineshead, Tempsford, Thurleigh, Tilbrook, Tilsworth, Tingrith, Toddington, Totternhoe, Turvey, Warden (Old), Westoning, Whipsnade, Wilden, Willington, Wilshamstead, Woburn, Woburn Sands, Wootton, Wrestlingworth, Wymington, Yelden.

Also to be found in the CRO are:

Bishop's Transcripts

These—with gaps—cover the period from the seventeenth century up to the 1850s. There are no marriages recorded after 1837.

Nonconformist Registers

There are indexes available for many of these in the CRO. In a number of cases registers are still in the original churches, so check with the CRO. There are microfilms available of the registers in the custody of the Public Record Office, London.

Marriage Licences

These are in the CRO for various periods: 1747-48, 1758-59, 1771-72, 1778-1812. There are a few between 1575 and 1618. A list of the licences since 1812 is in the course of preparation.

Census Returns

The census returns for the county are on microfilm for the period 1841-71.

Wills

Those from the sixteenth century to 1837 are indexed alphabetically on cards. The period from then until 1857 has not yet been done.

Mormon Index

This is an alphabetical list of the baptismal and marriage entries of all but twelve of the Bedfordshire parishes. In all cases the records go up to 1812, and some go to the 1850s. Marriages are not included after 1837.

Cemetery Records

These are microfilm copies of the registers of burial and cremation at Bedford Cemetery for the period 1855-1972. They are indexed.

Miscellaneous

These include parish records; poor law lists; apprenticeship records; land deeds; directories; newspapers; poll books and electoral registers; land taxes (1797-1832); and tithe records. There is also an indexed list of all men between seventeen and fifty-five living in North Bedfordshire in 1803.

Berkshire

Family History Society

(See page 89 for remarks concerning Family History Societies.)

County Record Office

Shire Hall, Reading, Berkshire RG1 3EE. (Open Monday-Wednesday, 0900-1700 hours; Thursday, 0900-1930 hours; Friday, 0900-1630 hours.)

The office will check a specific entry without a fee if a name, a place, and a date are given. Personal searches may be made without charge. More extensive searches will be undertaken for an agreed fee.

Parish Registers

The CRO holds records for the Archdeaconry of Berkshire, which has roughly the same boundaries as the county had before the changes of 1974. This means it also has records of many parishes now in Oxfordshire. The registers held in the CRO are:

Abingdon, Aldermaston, Aldworth, Appleford, Appleton, Arborfield, Ardington, Ashampstead, Ashbury, Aston Tirrold, Aston Upthorpe, Avington, Barkham, Basildon, Baulking, Beech Hill, Beedon, Beenham, Binfield, Bisham, Blewbury, Botley, Bourton, Bracknell, Bradfield, Bray, Braywood, Brightwalton, Brightwell, Brimpton, Buckland, Bucklebury, Burghfield, Buscot, Catmore, Caversham, Cookham Deane, Craddleworth, Challow (East and West), Charney Bassett, Chieveley, Childrey, Chilton, Cholsey, Clewer, Coleshill, Compton, Compton Beauchamp, Coxwell (Great and Little), Cumnor, Denchworth, Denford, Didcot, Donnington, Drayton, Easthampstead, Eaton Hastings, Enborne, Englefield, Faringdon, Farnborough, Fawley, Fernham, Finchampstead, Frilsham, Fyfield, Garford, Garston (East), Goosey, Grazeley, Greenham, Hagbourne, Hampstead Marshall, Hampstead Morreys, Hanney (East and West), Harwell, Hatford, Hendred (East and West), Hinksey (South),* Hinton Waldrist, Hungerford, Hurley, Hurst, Ilsley (East and West), Inkpen, Kingston Bagpuze, Kingston Lisle, Kintbury, Knowl Hill, Lambourn, Leckhampstead, Letcombe Bassett, Letcombe Regis, Littlewick Green, Lockinge, Longcot and Fernham, Longworth, Lyford, Maidenhead, Marcham, Midgham, Milton, Moreton (North and South), Mortimer West End, Moulsford, Newbury (St. John, St. Nicholas), Oare, Padworth, Pangbourne, Purley, Radley, Reading (6 parishes), Remenham, Sandhurst, Shaw-cum-Donnington, Shefford (East and West), Shellingford, Shinfield, Shippon, Shottesbrooke, Shrivenham, Sonning, Sotwell, Sparsholt, Speen, Speenhamland, Stanford Dingley, Stanford-in-the-Vale, Steventon, Stratfield Mortimer (St. John, St. Mary), Streatley, Stubbings, Sulham, Sulhampstead Abbots, Sulhampstead Bannister, Sunningdale, Sunninghill, Sunningwell, Swallowfield, Thatcham, Theale, Tidmarsh, Tilehurst, Uffington, Ufton Nervet, Upton, Wallingford (St. Leonard, St. Mary the More, St. Peter), Wallingford, Waltham (White), Waltham St. Lawrence, Wantage, Warfield, Wargrave, Wasing, Watchfield,

*Deposited in the Bodleian Library, Oxford.

Welford, Wickham (and Hoe Benham), Windsor (All Saints, Holy Trinity, St. Saviours), Windsor (New), Windsor (Old), Winkfield, Winterbourne, Wittenham (Little and Long), Wokingham, Woodhay (West), Woolhampton, Wootton, Yattendon.

In addition, Besselsleigh and Crowmarsh Gifford are held on microfilm.

Marriages

Indexed transcripts of marriages for the following parishes are held in the CRO: Bradfield, Buscot, Hanney (West), Harwell, Hendred (West), Hurst, Ilsley (East), Kingston Lisle, Purley, Reading (St. Lawrence), Ruscombe, Sparsholt, Sulham, Wantage, West Woodhay, Yattendon.

Wills

The position regarding Berkshire wills is a good example of the problems in finding the exact location of a will for a particular place (see Chapter 7, page 71). The CRO has no official collection of wills, although a few have come in from private sources.

The wills proved in the Archdeaconry Court, 1508-1857, are in the Bodleian Library, Oxford. Indexes to these wills are in the CRO. Wills could also be proved in the Bishop's Consistory Court. Until 1836 Berkshire was in the Diocese of Salisbury, so wills proved in the Consistory Court there include many from Berkshire. These are in the Wiltshire Record Office, Trowbridge. Wills proved after 1836, when Berkshire was transferred to the Diocese of Oxford, are in the Bodleian Library, Oxford. Wills proved in the various peculiars are also divided between Trowbridge and Oxford.

Tithes

There are some tithe records and the names mentioned are in the Personal Name Index of the CRO.

Maps

The CRO holds many maps from the sixteenth century and a number of them show the names of property-holders.

Local Records

There is a good collection of these, including Constable's Records (court cases, convictions, etc.); poor law books; apprentice and militia rolls; and civil records of the various parishes.

Census Returns

Microfilms of the 1851 Census are held in the CRO for the city of Reading. These are indexed. Other Berkshire census returns can be found in the Surrey County Record Office, Kingston-on-Thames;

the Wiltshire County Record Office, Trowbridge; and the Central Library, Oxford.

Marriage Licences
The CRO holds a few of these but they are not listed.

Nonconformist Registers
Registers or transcripts are held for a few Quaker Meetings; Baptists (Reading); United Reform (Reading); Catholic (St. James, Reading); and Methodists (Bracknell, Chieveley, Hungerford, Maidenhead, Newbury, Reading).

Bishop's Transcripts
These are in the CRO, Trowbridge, Wiltshire, for the Diocese of Berkshire (pre-1836), and in the Bodleian Library, Oxford, for the Diocese of Oxford (since 1836).

Buckinghamshire

Family History Society
(See page 89 for remarks concerning Family History Societies.)

Buckinghamshire County Record Office
County Hall, Aylesbury, Bucks. HP20 1UA. (Open Monday to Friday, 0900-1715 hours.)

Postal inquiries can be answered only if they do not involve extensive research. When writing, be as precise as possible, and enclose a self-addressed envelope and return postage. No fee is charged. If an extensive search is needed, you will be referred to local record-searchers.

Parish Registers
These come from the Archdeaconry of Buckingham, which used to cover the same area as the pre-1974 county (i.e., it included Slough and neighbouring parishes south to the Thames which have since been transferred to Berkshire). More than sixty-six per cent of the parish registers of the old county are in the Buckinghamshire County Record Office. They are listed below:

Addington, Adstock, Akeley, Ashendon, Aston Abbots, Aston Clinton, Aston Sandford, Astwood, Aylesbury (St. Mary), Aylesbury (Walton), Barton Hartshorn, Beachampton, Beaconsfield, Biddlesden, Bierton, Bledlow, Bledlow Ridge, Bletchley, Boarstall, Bradenham, Bradwell (Old), Brill, Britwell, Broughton, Buckland, Burnham, Cadmore End, Calverton, Chalfont St. Giles, Chalfont St. Peter, Chearsley, Cheddington, Chenies, Chesham Bois, Chetwode, Chicheley, Chilton, Cholesbury, Claydon East, Claydon Steeple, Clifton Reynes, Cold Brayfield, Colnbrook, Cublington, Cuddington, Datchet, Dinton, Dorney, Dorton, Drayton Beauchamp, Dunton, Edgcott, Edlesborough, Ellesborough, Emberton, Eton, Eton Wick, Farnham Royal, Fenny Stratford, Flaundon, Fleet Marston, Foscott, Fulmer, Gawcott, Gayhurst, Granborough, Grendon Underwood, Grove, Haddenham, Halton, Hampden (Great), Hampden (Little), Hardmead, Hardwick with Weedon, Hartwell, Haversham, Hawridge, Hazlemere, Hedgerley, Hillesden, Hitcham, Hoggeston, Horsenden, Horwood (Great), Horwood (Little), Hughenden, Hulcott, Ibstone, Ickford, Iver, Ivinghoe, Kimble (Great), Kimble (Little), Kingsey, Lane End, Langley Marish, Lathbury, Latimer, Lavendon, Leckhamstead, The Lee, Linford (Great), Linford (Little), Linslade, Long Crendon, Loughton, Ludgershall, Maids Moreton, Marlow (Little), Marsh Gibbon, Marston (North), Marsworth, Medmenham, Mentmore, Milton Keynew, Missenden (Great), Missenden (Little), Moulsoe, Mursley, Newport Pagnell, Newton Blossomville, Newton Longville, North Crawley, Oakley, Olney, Oving, Padbury, Penn, Pitchcott, Pitstone, Preston Bissett, Prestwood, Quainton, Radclive, Radnage, Ravenstone, Risborough Monks, St. Leonards, Shabbington, Shenley, Sherington, Simpson, Slapton, Slough St. Mary, Soulbury, Stantonbury, Stoke Goldington, Stoke Hammond, Stoke Mandeville, Stokenchurch, Stoke Poges, Stone, Stony Stratford(2), Stowe, Swanbourne, Taplow, Tattenhoe, Thornborough, Thornton, Tingewick, Turweston, Twyford, Tyringham, Upton-cum-Chalvey, Waddesdon, Walton, Wavendon, Wendover, Westbury, Weston Turville, Weston Underwood, Wexham, Whaddon, Willen, Winchendon (Lower), Winchendon (Upper), Wing, Wingrave, Wolverton(2), Woolstone (Great), Woolstone (Little), Worminghall, Wotton Underwood, Woughton-on-the-Green, Wraysbury, Wycombe West(2).

There are also microfilms held of registers not deposited for the parishes of Buckingham, Denham, Latimer, and Winslow, and modern transcripts held of registers not deposited for the parishes of Bletchley (indexed) and Brickhill Row.

Nonconformist Registers
Microfilm copies of the Buckinghamshire Nonconformist registers

in the Public Record Office, London, are available in the Buckingham County Record Office. They comprise

(a) Registers of Birth or Baptism and Burials for thirty-three congregations of Baptists, Congregationalists, and Wesleyan and Primitive Methodists for the period 1765-1837.

(b) Quaker Registers of Birth, Marriage, and Burial (1656-1837) for the Buckinghamshire Quarterly Meeting, and the Upperside, Leighton, and Buckingham Monthly Meetings.

In addition, a few original post-1837 Nonconformist registers are held in the CRO.

Bishop's Transcripts
In general, these begin about 1600 and continue to 1840, and are in the CRO. There are many gaps.

Census Returns
Microfilm copies of these from 1851 to 1871 are in the County Reference Library, County Hall, Aylesbury—two floors up from the CRO.

Wills
Wills in the Archdeaconry of Buckingham date from 1483 and administrations from 1633. Both are in the CRO. There is an alphabetical index from 1483 to 1858 for wills and from 1633 to 1857 for administrations.

Marriage Licences
The original bonds from 1663 to 1849 are in the CRO and are indexed by name of bridegroom. However, very few exist before 1733.

Newspapers
The CRO holds files of the *Aylesbury News* (*Bucks Advertiser*) from 1836 to 1851. Others are in the County Reference Library.

Miscellaneous
The miscellaneous records—and there are many—include title deeds; manorial records; settlement and apprentice records; quarter sessions reports; and poll books for 1784 (indexed).

Cambridgeshire

Family History Society
(See page 89 for remarks concerning Family History Societies.)

County Record Offices
The "new" county of Cambridge includes the "old" county of Huntingdon. As a result, there is a main County Record Office in Cambridge and a branch one in Huntingdon:

CAMBRIDGE: Shire Hall, Cambridge CB3 0AP. (Open Monday to Thursday, 0900-1245 hours and 1345-1715 hours; Friday, 0900-1245 hours and 1345-1615 hours; also Tuesday, by appointment, 1715-2100 hours.)

HUNTINGDON: Grammar School Walk, Huntingdon PE18 6LF. (Open Monday to Friday, 0900-1700 hours; Saturday, by appointment, 0900-1300 hours.)

The offices will undertake a small amount of research for correspondents and charge a fee after the first hour. For more protracted searches, a list of record agents will be supplied.

Parish Registers
These are divided between the two offices:

CAMBRIDGE:

Abington (Great), Abington (Little), Abington Pigotts, Arrington, Ashley-with-Silverley, Babraham, Balsham, Barnwell, Barrington, Bartlow, Barton, Barway, Bassingbourn-with-Kneesworth, Benwick Bottisham, Bourn, Boxworth, Brinkley, Burrough Green, Burwell, Caldecote, Cambridge (20 parishes), Camps (Castle), Camps (Shudy), Carlton-cum-Willingham, Caxton, Chatteris, Cherryhinton, Chesterton, Chettisham, Cheveley, Childerley, Chippenham, Chishill (Great), Chishill (Little), Christchurch, Clopton, Coates and Eastrea, Coldham, Comberton, Conington, Coton, Cottenham, Coveney, Croxton, Croydon-with-Clopton, Ditton (Fen), Ditton (Wood), Doddington, Downham, Drayton (Dry), Drayton (Fen), Dullingham, Duxford St. John, Duxford St. Peter, Eastrea, Eaton Socon, Elm, Elsworth, Eltisley, Ely (Cathedral, Chettisham, Holy Trinity, Prickwillow, St. Mary, Stuntney), Eversden (Great and Little), Fordham, Fowlmere, Foxton, Friday-bridge, Fulbourn (All Saints, St. Vigor), Gamlingay, Girton, Gore-field, Gransden (Little), Grantchester, Graveley, Grunty Fen, Guyhirn with Ringsend, Haddenham, Hardwick, Harlton, Harston, Haslingfield, Hatley (East), Hatley (St. George), Hauxton, Heydon,

Hildersham, Hinxton, Histon, Horningsea, Horseheath, Ickleton, Impington, Isleham, Kennett, Kingston, Kirtling, Knapwell, Kneesworth, Landbeach, Landwade, Leverington, Linton, Litlington, Little Ouse, Littleport, Littleport St. Matthew, Lode, Lolworth, Longstanton (All Saints, St. Michael), Longstowe, Madingley, Manea, March, March St. John, March St. Mary, March St. Peter, Melbourn, Meldreth, Mepal, Milton, Morden Guilden, Morden Steeple, Murrow, Newmarket, Newton, Newton-by-Wisbech, Oakington-with-Westwick, Orwell, Outwell, Over, Pampisford, Papworth Agnes, Papworth Everard, Parson Drove, Prickwillow, Rampton, Reach, Sawston, Shelford (Great), Shelford (Little), Shepreth, Shingay, Snailwell, Soham, Southea-with-Murrow, Stanground, Stapleford, Stetchworth, Stow-cum-Quy, Stretham, Sutton, Swaffham Bulbeck, Swaffham Prior, Swavesey, Tadlow, Teversham, Thetford, Thorney, Thriplow, Toft, Trumpington, Tydd St. Giles, Upwell, Walton, Waterbeach, Welney, Wendy-with-Shingay, Wentworth, Westley Waterless, Weston Colville, Westwick, Whaddon, Whittlesey (St. Andrew, St. Mary), Whittlesford, Wicken, Wickham (West), Wilbraham (Great and Little), Wilburton, Willingham, Wimblington, Wimpole, Wisbech (St. Augustine, St. Mary, St. Peter), Witchem, Witchford, Wood Ditton, Wratting (West).

HUNTINGDON:

Abbotsley, Abbots Rippon, Alconbury-cum-Weston, Alwalton, Barham, Bluntisham-cum-Earith, Botolph Bridge, Brampton, Brington, Broughton, Buckden, Buckworth, Bury-cum-Hepmangrove, Bythorn, Caldecote, Catworth (Great), Chesterton, Colne, Covington, Denton, Diddington, Earith, Easton, Ellington, Elton, Everton-with-Tetworth, Eynesbury, Farcet, Fenstanton, Fenton, Fletton, Folksworth, Gidding (Great, Little, and Steeple), Glatton, Godmanchester, Grafham, Gransden (Great), Haddon, Hail Weston, Hamerton, Hartford, Hemingford Abbots, Hemingford Grey, Hilton, Holme, Holywell-cum-Needingworth, Houghton, Huntingdon (All Saints, St. Benedict, St. John Baptist, St. Mary), Keyston, Kimbolton, King's Ripton, Leighton Bromswold, Lutton, Molesworth, Morborne, Newton (Water), Offord Cluny, Offord Darcy, Oldhurst, Orton Longueville, Orton Waterville, Paxton (Great and Little), Pidley-cum-Fenton, Ponder's Bridge, Ramsey, Ramsey St. Mary, Raveley (Great), Ripton (Abbots), Ripton (King's), St. Ives, St. Neots, Sapley, Sawtry (All Saints, St. Andrew), Sibson-cum-Stibbington, Somersham, Southoe, Spaldwick, Stanground, Staughton (Great), Steeple Gidding, Stibbington, Stilton, Stow Longa with Little Catworth, Stukeley (Great), Stukeley (Little),

Swineshead, Thurning, Tilbrook, Toseland, Upton-with-Copping-
ford, Upwood with Great Raveley, Warboys, Waresley, Washing-
ley, Water Newton, Weston, Weston (Hail), Weston (Old),
Winwick, Wistow, Woodhurst, Woodston, Woolley, Wyton, Yaxley, Yelling.

Since 1975 the old Soke of Peterborough has been part of
Cambridgeshire, but the registers for that area are in the
Northamptonshire County Record Office, Delapré Abbey,
Northampton NN4 9AW, and are listed below:
Ailsworth, Ashton, Bainton, Barnack, Castor with Milton, Deeping
Gate, Etton, Eye, Glinton, Helpston, Longthorpe, Marholm,
Maxey, Newborough, Northborough, Paston-with-Werrington,
Peakirk, Peterborough (All Saints, Cathedral, St. Barnabas, St.
John Baptist, St. Mark, St. Mary Boongate, St. Paul), Pilsgate, St.
Martin Stamford Baron, Southorpe, Sutton, Thornhaugh, Ufford
with Ashton, Walcot, Wansford, Werrington, Wittering,
Wothorpe.

Bishop's Transcripts
The two record offices hold these for nearly every parish in
Cambridgeshire and Huntingdonshire. They are divided between
the two record offices in the same way as the parish registers.
Roughly, they date from 1604 up to the early 1800s.

Nonconformist Registers
Please bear in mind:
   (a) Independent may have been originally Congregational or
Presbyterian, or may have later become Congregational or Presby-
terian.
   (b) Methodist includes all sects of that church.
   (c) Few registers cover Birth or Baptism, Marriage, and Death or
Burials—usually only one or two of these categories.
Independent: Barrington, Bassingbourn-with-Kneesworth, Bur-
well, Cambridge, Duxford, Eversden (Great), Fordham, Fowlmere,
Fulbourn, Linton, Littleport, Melbourn, Newmarket, Royston, St.
Ives, Sawston, Shelford (Little), Soham, Whittlesey, Wisbech.
Methodist: Alconbury-cum-Weston, Cambridge, Cambridge
(Barnwell), Chatteris, Cottenham, Downham, Ely, Glinton, Helps-
ton, Huntingdon, Isleham, Manea (Circuit), Meldreth, Mildenhall
(Circuit), Newborough, Outwell, Peterborough (Circuit and city
chapels), St. Ives (Circuit), Stanground, Wickhambrook (Circuit),
Wisbech, Woodston.

Baptist: Bluntisham-cum-Earith, Chatteris, Ellington, Gamlingay, Holywell-cum-Needingworth, Isleham, Kimbolton, March, Shelford (Great), Spaldwick, Whittlesey, Wisbech.
Presbyterian: Yaxley.
Irvingite: Cambridge.
Lady Huntingdon's Connexion: Ely.
Moravian: Kimbolton.
Unitarian: Wisbech.
Congregational: Castor, Chesterton, Sawston.
Quaker: Bluntisham-cum-Earith, Brampton, Cambridge, Chatteris, Colne, Ellington, Fenstanton, Godmanchester, Haddenham, Hemingford Abbots, Hemingford Grey, Huntingdon, Littleport, Needingworth, Offord Cluny, Offord Darcy, Ramsey, St. Ives, Somersham, Sutton, Wisbech.

Two final reminders:

1. Methodist Circuits and Quaker Meetings can cover a much wider area than the places mentioned.

2. The above Nonconformist registers are divided between the two CROs at Cambridge and Huntingdon.

Marriage Bonds and Licences
The CRO at Huntingdon holds these for the Archdeaconry of Huntingdon for the period 1663-1883.

Marriage Notice Books (civil marriages)
These only survive for three registration districts in the "old" county of Cambridge. The city of Cambridge is covered for the period 1837-1911; 39 parishes of the district of Chesterton are covered from 1837 to 1932, and 22 parishes of Newmarket are covered from 1838 to 1877. These books are in the Cambridge County Record Office.

Census Returns
These are on microfilm and are held for the period 1841-71 in both offices for the areas served by them.

Wills
Those for the period 1479-1857 for Huntingdon are held in the CRO there. Those for Cambridgeshire for the period 1449-1858, with administrations and inventories, are in the University and Diocesan Archives at Cambridge University. Those for the Isle of Ely are also there. Wills for certain areas transferred out of the county at various periods are in neighbouring record offices; the

exact location for a particular place should be checked with the Cambridge CRO.

Other Records
These include land tax assessments in the two offices; manorial records; estate and family papers; poll and hearth taxes; poll books and electoral lists; and early directories and newspapers.

Cheshire

Family History Societies
There are two Family History Societies serving this area:
Cheshire
North Cheshire
(See page 89 for remarks concerning Family History Societies.)

County Record Office
The Castle, Chester, Cheshire CH1 2DN. (Open Monday-Friday, 0900-1700 hours. Last request for documents is at 1630 hours.)

The office will not undertake lengthy searches, but will refer inquiries to local record-searchers. A specific inquiry with name, date, and place will be dealt with free of charge. It is suggested that, in the case of personal visits to the CRO, you give advance notice, and, if possible, details of the records you intend to search. This will ensure that space is reserved for you, and that the documents are ready for you.

Parish Registers
The following are held by the Cheshire CRO:
Acton, Alderley, Aldford, Altrincham, Alvanley, Ashton upon Mersey, Aston, Audlem, Backford, Barnston with Pensby, Barrow, Bebington, Bidston, Birkenhead (9 parishes), Bosley, Bowdon, Brereton, Bromborough, Bruera, Buglawton, Bunbury, Burleydam, Burton, Burtonwood, Burwardsley, Byley cum Lees, Chadkirk, Cheadle, Chester (11 parishes), Christleton, Church Hulme, Church Lawton, Church Minshull, Claughton cum Grange (Christ Church, St. Michael), Coppenhall, Crewe (Christchurch, St. Paul), Dane Bridge, Daresbury, Davenham, Delamere, Disley, Dodleston, Dunham on the Hill, Eccleston, Farndon, Frodsham, Godley-cum-Newton Green, Goostrey, Grappenhall, Great Budworth, Guilden Sutton, Halton, Handforth, Handley, Hargrave, Hartford, Harthill,

Haslington, Helsby, Heswall, Hoylake, Hyde, Ince, Kelsall, Knutsford, Lache cum Saltney, Latchford St. James, Liscard (Egremont St. John), Little Budworth, Lostock Gralam, Lower Peover, Lower Tranmere St. Luke, Lymm, Macclesfield (Christ Church, St. Michael), Macclesfield Forest with Wildboarclough, Marbury, Marple, Marston, Middlewich, Mobberley, Moreton, Mottram in Longdendale, Nantwich, Neston, New Brighton, New Ferry, Newton Flowery Field, Newton-in-Mottram, Norbury, Northwick, Odd Rode, Over, Over Peover, Plemstall, Pott Shrigley, Poynton, Prenton, Prestbury, Pulford, Rock Ferry, Rostherne, Runcorn, Sandbach, Sandiway, Seacombe, Shocklach, Shotwick, Stalybridge (St. Paul), Stockport, Stoke, Swettenham, Tarporley, Tarvin, Tattenhall, Thurstaston, Tilston, Tranmere St. Paul, Upton (Overchurch), Wallasey, Warburton, Warrington (St. Paul, St. Peter), Waverton, West Kirby, Weston (Runcorn), Weston Point, Whitegate, Wilmslow, Wincle, Winwick, Wistaston, Witton, Woodchurch, Woodford, Woodhead, Wybunbury.

Bishop's Transcripts
These are in the Cheshire CRO and date mainly from the early 1600s, but there are many gaps, particularly pre-1660. They are not indexed. A card-index system shows the dates for which the transcripts survive for each parish.

Nonconformist Registers
The CRO has microfilm copies of all the Cheshire Nonconformist registers in the Public Record Office in London. Registers since 1840 are either in the churches or in the CRO.

Marriage Licences
These are in the custody of the CRO.

Wills and Other Probate Records
Cheshire wills dating back to 1545 and up to 1858 are in the Cheshire CRO. They are indexed. The CRO also has more recent wills from the District Probate Registry dating from 1858 to 1940, with indexes up to 1929.

Census Returns
The office has the complete county on microfilm from 1841 to 1871, and also a single census for the parish of Wybunbury in 1831.

Other Records
These include land tax assessments; family deeds and letters; many printed registers, transcripts, lists, and indexes; early directories and newspapers; and poll books and electoral lists.

Cleveland

This is one of the "new" counties formed from parts of Durham and the North Riding of Yorkshire.

Family History Society
(See page 89 for remarks concerning Family History Societies.)

Cleveland County Archives Department
81 Borough Road, Middlesbrough, Cleveland TS1 3AA. (Open Monday-Thursday, 0900-1300 hours and 1400-1700 hours; Friday, 0900-1300 hours and 1400-1630 hours.)

It is necessary to make an appointment in order to consult documents or microfilm in the Archives Department. The department will carry out short searches for no fee. For longer searches, it will be necessary to make arrangements with a local record-searcher—a list will be supplied.

Parish Registers
The Department does not hold original parish registers for that part of Cleveland which lies in the Diocese of Durham, but only microfilm copies. Originals are in the individual churches or in the Durham County Record Office (County Hall, Durham). The following list of registers held is divided in two—those from the Diocese of York and those from the Diocese of Durham:

YORK: Acklam and Middlesbrough, Boosbeck, Brotton, Dormanstown, Easington, Eston, Kirkleatham, Kirklevington, Linthorpe, Liverton, Loftus, Marske-by-the-Sea, Marton in Cleveland, Middlesbrough (The Ascension, St. Aidan, St. Chad, St. Columba, St. Cuthbert, St. Hilda, St. John, St. Martin, St. Oswald, St. Paul, St. Peter, St. Thomas), Newton under Roseberry, North Ormesby, Ormesby, Redcar, South Bank, Stainton in Cleveland, Thornaby, Upleatham, Wilton, Yarm.

DURHAM: Egglescliffe, Greatham, Grindon, Hartlepool, Long Newton, Redmarshall, Stockton (St. James, St. John, St. Peter, St. Thomas), Stranton, Wolviston.

Nonconformist Registers
Methodist: Records available are concerned with:
Baptisms: Boosbeck, Brotton Circuit, Dormanstown, Eston (and Wilton), Eston (Jubilee Road), Eston (South Bank and Normanby), Eston Chapel, Eston Circuit, Eston Junction, Grangetown, Guisborough Circuits, Lingdale Chapel, Middlesbrough, New Marske, Normanby, Redcar, Saltburn, Skelton, New Skelton, South Bank, Staithes, Stanghow, Stockton, Stokesley.
Marriages: Billingham, Brotton, Eston, Guisborough, Hartlepool, Loftus, Middlesbrough, Normanby, North Ormesby, Redcar, Saltburn, Stockton, Thornaby, Yarm.
Note: Only two of the above registers date back to the nineteenth century—Middlesbrough (1860-86) and Stockton (Brunswick Wesleyan Methodist (1891-1971) and North Terrace Wesleyan Methodist (1897-1955))
United Reformed Church (Congregational and Presbyterian): Linthorpe, Thornaby.
Independent Chapels and Presbyterians: Guisborough, Staithes (Hinderwell), Stockton (High Street), Stockton Green, Stokesley.
Catholic: Hartlepool, High Wrisall (including Friarage, Yarm), Stockton (including Darlington).

Census Returns
Available for Cleveland County for the period 1841-71.

Registers of Electors
These cover Middlesbrough and North Yorkshire back to 1832 (with gaps) and other lists for scattered areas of the county.

Cemetery Records
The Department holds a number of these from Middlesbrough, dating back to 1854.

Miscellaneous
These include Boyd's Marriage Index for Yorkshire and Durham; transcripts of tombstone inscriptions; land taxes; tithe maps and apportionments; and rate books.

Cornwall

Family History Society
(See page 89 for remarks concerning Family History Societies.)

County Record Office
County Hall, Truro, Cornwall TR1 3AY. (Open Tuesday to Thursday, 0930-1300 hours and 1400-1630 hours; Friday, 0930-1300 hours and 1400-1630 hours; Saturday, 0900-1200 hours.)

The office will give advice or will spend up to thirty minutes making a search, if given reasonably specific information (for example, a parish name and the date within a few years of a baptism, marriage, or burial). No lengthy search will be undertaken. No charge is made, but two International Reply Coupons must be sent with your inquiry. The office will list local researchers for you if a protracted search is needed.

Parish Registers
There are approximately 250 parishes in Cornwall, of which 190 have deposited records in the County Record Office; the balance remain in the parishes. Those in the custody of the CRO are listed below:

Advent, Altarnum, Antony, Baldhu, Blisland, Boconnoc, Bodmin, Bolventor, Botus Fleming, Bradock, Breage, Bude Haven, Budock, Buryan, Camborne, Cardinham, Carnmenellis, Chacewater, Charlestown, Colan, Constantine, Cornelly, Creed, Crowan, Cuby, Cury, Davidstow, Duloe, Egloshayle, Egloskerry, Endellion, Feock, Forrabury, Fowey, Germoe, Gerrans, Grade, Gulval, Gunwalloe, Gwennap, Gwithian, Helland, Helston, Hessenford, Illogan, Kenwyn, Kilkhampton, Ladock, Landewednack, Landrake, Landulph, Laneast, Lanhydrock, Lanivet, Lanlivery, Lannarth, Lanreath, Lansallos, Lanteglos by Camelford, Lanteglos by Fowey, Launcells, Launceston, Lawhitton, Lelant, Lesnewth, Lewannick, Lezant, Linkinhorne, Liskeard, Little Petherick (or St. Petroc Minor), Looe, Lostwithiel, Ludgvan, Luxulyan, Mabe, Maker, Manaccan, Marazion, Marhamchurch, Mawgan in Meneage, Mawgan in Pydar, Mawnan, Menheniot, Mevagissey, Michaelstow, Millbrook, Minster, Mithian, Morval, Mount Hawke, Mullion, Mylor, Newlyn, North Hill, North Petherwin, Otterham, Padstow, Par, Pelynt, Pencoys, Pendeen, Penzance (St. Mary), Perranarworthal, Perranuthnoe, Perranzabuloe, Phillack, Philleigh, Pillaton, Porthleven, Poundstock, Probus, Quethiock, Rame, Redruth, Roche, Ruan Lanihorne, Ruan Major, Ruan Minor, St.

Agnes, St. Allen, St. Anthony in Meneage, St. Anthony in Rose-
land, St. Austell, St. Blazey, St. Breock, St. Breward, St. Clement, St.
Clether, St. Columb (Major and Minor), St. Dennis, St. Dominick,
St. Elwyn, St. Enoder, St. Erme, St. Erney, St. Erth, St. Ervan, St.
Eval, St. Ewe, St. Gennys, St. Germans, St. Gluvias, St. Hilary, St.
Issey, St. Ive, St. Ives, St. John, St. Juliot, St. Just in Roseland, St.
Kea, St. Keverne, St. Kew, St. Keyne, St. Levan, St. Mabyn, St.
Martin by Looe, St. Martin in Meneage, St. Mellion, St. Merryn, St.
Mewan, St. Minver, St. Neot, St. Pauls, St. Pinnock, St. Sampson (or
Golant), St. Stephen in Brannel, St. Stephens by Launceston, St.
Stephens by Saltash, St. Thomas by Launceston, St. Tudy, St. Veep,
St. Wenn, St. Winnow, Sancreed, Scilly Isles, Sennen, Sheviock,
Sithney, South Hill, South Petherwin, Stithians, Stokeclimsland,
Stratton, Talland, Temple, Tideford, Tintagel, Torpoint, Towed-
nack, Tremaine, Tresmere, Trevalga, Treverbyn, Trewen, Truro
(St. George, St. John, St. Mary, St. Paul), Tuckingmill, Tyward-
reath, Veryan, Warleggan, Week St. Mary, Wendron, Whitstone,
Withiel, Zennor.

Nonconformist Registers
A small number of nineteenth- and twentieth-century Nonconformist registers are in the Cornwall CRO. No Catholic registers are
held.

Bishop's Transcripts
These are split between the Cornwall and Devon CROs because the
ecclesiastical jurisdiction did not coincide with the county boundaries. An inquiry should be made as to the location of a particular
transcript.

Wills
Wills and administrations of Cornwall from 1600 to 1857 are
available at the CRO. An alphabetical index for 1600-1800 has
been published by the British Record Society and one for 1800-57
is held at the CRO. Probate records for twenty-eight parishes
(peculiars of the Bishop of Exeter) were destroyed in the Second
World War.

Census Returns
Microfilm copies of the Cornwall returns, 1841-71, are held at the
CRO. There is a charge for each reel of film consulted. It is
necessary to make an appointment before any of the above records
can be examined. (Phone Truro 3698.)

The Royal Institution of Cornwall

County Museum and Art Gallery, River Street, Truro (phone Truro 2205), holds some one hundred and twenty Cornish parish registers on microfilm. The majority of them are copies of the original registers held in the CRO, but it has microfilms of the following registers which are *not* in the CRO: Boyton, Cubert, Egloshayle, Madron, Manaccan, Merther, Morvah, Newlyn (East), Newlyn (West), Par, Paul, Pendeen, Poughill, St. Anthony in Meneage, St. Michael Penkivel, St. Stephen in Brannel, Treneglos.

Additional material held by the Royal Institution includes a large reference library; Cornish newspapers 1798-1956; many old photographs; and various manuscript records.

Devon and Cornwall Record Society

Various parish register transcripts and microfilms of pre-1837 Nonconformist registers are available for a fee. They are located at Westcountry Studies Library, Castle Street, Exeter. Secretary: Mr. G. Paley, 7 The Close, Exeter, Devon.

Cumbria

This new county consists of the old counties of Cumberland and Westmorland, plus parts of Lancashire and the North Riding of Yorkshire. There is one County Archivist but there are three County Record Offices: Carlisle, Kendal, and Barrow-in-Furness.
CARLISLE: The Record Office, The Castle, Carlisle CA3 8UR.
KENDAL: The Record Office, County Hall, Kendal LA9 4RQ.
BARROW: The Record Office, Duke Street, Barrow-in-Furness LA14 1XW.
(The offices at Carlisle and Kendal are open Monday-Friday, 0900-1700 hours; and at Barrow on Monday, Tuesday, and Thursday, 1400-1800 hours. Other times by appointment.)

The offices will not undertake lengthy searches, although inquiries of a limited nature will be answered as far as possible. The name of a professional researcher will be supplied on request.

Cumbria Family History Society

(See page 89 for remarks concerning Family History Societies.)

Parish Registers

The parish registers in a few cases date from 1538, but many of them date only from the seventeenth century. Many original registers and all Bishop's Transcripts are in the CROs at Carlisle and Kendal. Many of the registers have been printed and indexed and these are available in the CROs. One valuable printed source, available at the Carlisle office, is the indexed list of irregular Scots "Marriages at Gretna" from 1829 to 1855—the majority of which were of Cumberland people.

The lists of the available parish registers are:

CUMBERLAND:

Addingham, Aikton, Ainstable, Allhallows, Allonby, Alston, Arlecdon, Armathwaite, Arthuret, Aspatria, Bassenthwaite, Beaumont, Beckermet (St. Bridget), Beckermet (St. John), Bewcastle, Bigrigg, Blackford, Bolton, Bootle, Borrowdale, Bowness-on-Solway, Brampton, Bridekirk, Brigham, Bromfield, Brough-by-Sands, Broughton (Great), Buttermere, Caldbeck, Camerton, Carlisle (Christchurch, Holy Trinity, St. Cuthbert, St. James, St. Mary with St. Paul), Castle Carrock, Castle Sowerby, Cleator, Cleator Moor, Clifton, Cockermouth (All Saints and Christchurch), Corney, Cotehill and Cumwhinton, Croglin, Crosby-on-Eden, Cross Canonby, Crosthwaite, Culgaith, Cumrew, Cumwhitton, Currock, Dacre, Dalston, Dean, Dearham, Denton (Nether and Over or Upper), Distington, Drigg, Edenhall, Egremont, Embleton, Ennerdale, Eskdale, Farlam, Flimby, Frizington, Garrigill, Gilcrux, Gilsland, Gosforth, Greystoke, Grinsdale, Haile, Harrington, Hayton (Aspatria), Hayton (Carlisle), Hensingham, Hesket-in-the-Forest, Holme (Eden), Holme (St. Cuthbert), Holme (St. Paul), Holme Cultram, Houghton, Hutton-in-the-Forest, Ireby, Irthington, Irton, Isel, Ivegill and High Head, Keswick, Kirkandrews-on-Eden, Kirkandrews-on-Esk, Kirkbampton, Kirkbride, Kirkland, Kirklinton, Kirkoswald, Lamplugh, Lanercost, Langwathby, Lazonby, Lorton, Loweswater, Maryport, Matterdale, Melmerby, Millom (Holy Trinity), Moresby, Mosser, Muncaster, Mungrisdale, Netherwasdale, Newlands, Newton Arlosh, Newton Reigny, Nicholforest, Orton (Great), Ousby, Penrith (Christ Church), Plumbland, Plumpton Wall, Ponsonby, Raughton Head, Renwick, Rockcliffe, Rosley, St. Bees, St. Johns-in-the-Vale, Salkeld (Great), Scaleby, Scotby, Seascale, Seaton, Sebergham, Setmurthy, Silloth, Skelton, Skirwith, Stanwix, Stapleton, Threlkeld, Thursby, Thwaites, Torpenhow, Uldale, Ulpha, Upperby, Waberthwaite, Walton, Warwick, Wasdale (Nether), Wasdale Head, Watermillock, Waverton, Westnewton, Westward, Wetheral, Whicham, Whitbeck, Whitehaven (Christ Church, Holy Trinity, St. James, St. Nicholas), Wigton, Workington (St. John, St. Michael), Wreay, Wythburn, Wythop.

WESTMORLAND:

Ambleside, Appleby (St. Lawrence, St. Michael), Arnside, Asby (Great), Bampton, Barbon, Barton, Beatham, Bolton, Brougham, Brough-under-Stainmore, Burneside, Casterton, Cliburn, Clifton, Crook, Crosby Garrett, Crosby Ravensworth, Crosscrake, Crosthwaite and Lyth, Dufton, Firbank, Flookburgh, Grasmere, Grayrigg, Hawkeshead, Helsington, Heversham, High Head, Hugill or Ings, Hutton (New and Old), Hutton Roof, Kendal (All Hallows, Holy Trinity, St. George, St. Thomas), Kentmere, Killington, Kirkby Lonsdale, Kirkby Stephen, Kirkby Thore, Langdale, Levens, Long Marten, Longsleddale, Lowther, Lupton, Maller-stang, Mansergh, Mardale, Martindale, Milnthorpe, Morland, Murton-cum-Hilton, Musgrave (Great), Natland, Newbiggin, Newbiggin-on-Lune, Ormside, Orton, Patterdale, Pooley Bridge, Preston Patrick, Ravenstonedale, Rydal, Selside, Shap, Skelsmergh, Soulby, Stainmore, Staveley, Strickland (Great), Swindale, Tebay, Temple Sowerby, Thrimby, Torver, Troutbeck, Underbarrow, Warcop, Windermere, Winster, Witherslack.

LANCASHIRE:

Aldingham, Allithwaite, Askham, Bardsea, Barrow-in-Furness, Blawith, Broughton-in-Furness, Cartmel, Cartmel Fell, Colton, Coniston, Dalton-in-Furness, Dendron, Egton-cum-Newland, Field Broughton, Grange-over-Sands, Haverthwaite, Hawkeshead, Ireleth with Askham, Kirkby Ireleth, Lindal, Lindale, Low Wray, Lowick, Pennington, Rampside, Rusland, Satterthwaite, Sawrey, Seathwaite, Staveley-in-Cartmel, Torver, Ulverston (Holy Trinity), Ulverston (St. Marys), Urswick, Walney, Woodland, Wray.

YORKSHIRE:

Cowgill, Dent, Garsdale, Howgill, Sedbergh.

The above registers are located as follows:
Cumberland: Carlisle CRO.
Westmorland and Yorkshire: Kendal CRO.
Lancashire: Barrow CRO.

Nonconformist

All are located in the Kendal CRO.
Congregational: Kendal, Dent.

Methodist: Kirkby Stephen, Appleby, Tebay Circuit, and Kendal Circuit.
Presbyterian: Kendal.
Unitarian: Kendal.

Wills

The usual probate court was the Consistory Court of Carlisle, and the records are at the Carlisle CRO for the years 1548, 1558-1644, and 1661-1858 (wills, administrations, inventories). There are also copies of wills dating from 1858 to 1940. Indexes are available listing year, name, and parish.

Persons dying in Temple Sowerby, Ravenstonedale, and Docker (in Westmorland) had their wills probated in the Peculiar Courts of these manors, and these are in the Carlisle CRO: Temple Sowerby (1580-1816), Ravenstonedale (1691-1851), Docker (1686-1770).

Wills of persons dying in the Diocese of Chester (the diocese covered the south-west portion of Cumberland and the greater part of Westmorland) from the early sixteenth century to 1858 are in the Lancashire Record Office, Bow Lane, Preston.

Wills of persons dying in the Diocese of Durham (the parish of Alston, with Garrigill and Nenthead in Cumberland, and also Upper Denton before c. 1777) in the period 1540-1857 are in the Prior's Kitchen, The College, Durham.

It occasionally happened that wills were proved in superior courts. This usually occurred when personal property was left in more than one diocese. If it was left entirely in the Province of York (under the jurisdiction of the Archbishop of York), the will may be found among the records at the Borthwick Institute of Historical Research, St. Anthony's Hall, York. If the property was left in the Province of Canterbury (under the jurisdiction of the Archbishop of Canterbury) as well as in the Province of York, or elsewhere in the country outside of York, the will may be found in the Public Record Office, Chancery Lane, London.

Census Returns

Microfilms covering the period 1841-71 are available in each of the three CROs.

Miscellaneous Records

These include many items of value to the ancestor-hunter: manorial records; land tax rolls; tax returns; Protestation Returns (lists of all males over eighteen by parish in 1641); quarter sessions rolls; parish records; poll books; tithe awards; apprenticeship records (particularly Carlisle and Appleby); militia lists; and many early directories dating as far back as 1781.

Derbyshire

Family History Society
(See page 89 for remarks concerning Family History Societies.)

County Record Office
County Offices, Matlock, Derbyshire DE4 3AG.

The new county of Derbyshire consists of the original county, plus a small part of Cheshire. The office is open during the usual office hours.

The office will undertake limited searches, but those requiring a more detailed examination will be referred to local record agents. Owing to a ruling by the Bishop of Derby, photocopies of entries in parish registers cannot be supplied. However, baptismal and marriage certificates can be given on request for a small fee.

Parish Registers
The following are held in the CRO:
Aldercar, Alfreton, Alveston, Ashford, Ault Hucknall, Bakewell, Bamford, Barlborough, Barlow, Barton Blount, Baslow, Beeley, Belper, Blackwell, Bolsover, Boulton, Boylestone, Bradbourne, Brailsford, Brampton, Brassington, Breadsall, Bretby, Brimington, Burbage, Buxton (St. James, St. John), Calke, Calow (Buxton), Castleton, Chellaston, Chelmorton, Chesterfield, Church Broughton, Claycross, Clowne, Crich, Cubley, Dalbury, Dale Abbey, Darley Dale, Denby, Derby (10 parishes), Doveridge, Dronfield, Duffield, Eaton (Little), Eckington, Edensor, Edlaston, Egginton, Elmton, Elton, Elvaston, Etwall, Fairfield, Fenny Bentley, Findern, Foremark, Foston and Scropton, Glossop, Gresley, Hadfield, Hartshorne, Hasland, Hathersage, Hayfield, Hazelwood, Heage, Heanor, Heath, Hognaston, Holbrook, Hope, Horsley, Ilkeston, Ingleby, Kedleston, Kirk (Hallam, Ireton, Langley), Kniveton, Langley Mill and Aldercar, Langwith (Upper), Longford, Long Lane, Longstone (Great and Little), Lullington, Mackworth, Mapleton, Marston on Dove, Marston Montgomery, Matlock (St. Giles), Matlock Bath, Melbourne, Mellor, Middleton by Wirksworth, Monyash, Morley, Morton, Mugginton, Netherseal and

Overseal, Newbold, Newton Solney, Norbury, Normanton (South and Temple), Ockbrook, Osmaston by Ashbourne, Osmaston by Derby, Parwich, Pilsley (by Chesterfield), Pinxton, Pleasley, Radbourne, Repton, Riddings, Rowsley, Sandiacre, Sawley, Scarcliffe, Shardlow, Sheldon, Shirley, Shottle, Smalley, Snelston, Somercotes, South Normanton, Stanton-by-Bridge, Stanton-by-Dale, Stapenhill, Staveley, Sterndale Earl, Stoney Middleton, Sudbury, Sutton-cum-Duckmanton, Sutton on the Hill, Swadlincote, Swarkestone, Taddington, Thorpe, Tibshelf, Ticknall, Tideswell, Tissington, Trusley, Tupton, Walton on Trent, West Hallam, Weston on Trent, Whitfield, Whitwell, Willington, Wingfield (North and South), Winshill, Winster, Wormhill.

Wills and Bishop's Transcripts
As most of Derbyshire was in the Diocese of Coventry and Lichfield, these are held in the Lichfield Joint Record Office, Bird Street, Lichfield, Staffordshire. Those proved for Derbyshire since 1858 are in the Derbyshire CRO.

Nonconformist Registers
Catholic: Holbeck, Mansfield, Spinkhill.
Congregational: Brassington.
Methodist and Wesleyan: Alfreton(C), Ashover, Bakewell, Brimington, Chesterfield, Codnor, Denby, Ilkeston(C), Ironville, Long Eaton, Matlock, Pinxton, Ripley(C), Sandiacre, Winster.
Note: (C) stands for Circuit. This means that a whole district around a central town is included, not just the town itself.
Unitarian: Belper.

Census Returns
Microfilm copies of these for the available four censuses are in the Derby Central Library, The Wardwick, Derby, and in the Local Studies Section of the County Library, County Offices, Matlock, Derbyshire.

Trades Directories
The CRO holds these for the period 1846-1941.

Electoral Registers
The office holds these for the period 1832 to date.

Other Records
These consist of early land tax returns (1780-1832), some directories, and a collection of estate and family papers for a wide area of the county.

Devon

Family History Society
(See page 89 for remarks concerning Family History Societies.)

Devon and Cornwall Record Society
Mr. G. Paley, 7 The Close, Exeter, Devon.

Devon County Record Offices
East Devon: Record Office, Castle Street, Exeter EX4 3PQ.
West Devon: Unit 3, Clare Place, Coxside, Plymouth.

West Devon Area Record Office (Branch)
14 Tavistock Place, Plymouth, Devon PL4 8AN.
   The Devon Record Office will undertake a preliminary search in parish registers and Bishop's Transcripts for a fee. This would normally entail a search for a particular entry for up to ten years, depending on the size of the parish. If a more extensive search is required, the office will provide a list of researchers who will carry out extended searches for a fee.

Parish Registers
Parish registers are held in one or other of the above offices, depending on location.
   The following registers are held in the Devon Record Office, either in its headquarters at Exeter or in its branch office in Plymouth:
EXETER:
Abbots Bickington, Abbotsbury, Abbotskerwell, Allington East, Alphington, Alverdiscott, Alvington (West), Alwington, Arlington, Ashburton, Ashcombe, Ashford, Ashprington, Ashreigney, Ashton, Ashwater, Atherington, Aveton Gifford, Awliscombe, Axminster, Axmouth, Aylesbeare, Bampton, Barnstaple(2), Beaford, Beaworthy, Beer, Belstone, Bere Ferrers, Berry Pomeroy(2), Bickington, Bickington (High), Bickleigh (Tiverton), Bicton, Bideford, Bigbury, Bishop's Nympton, Bishop's Tawton, Bishopsteignton, Blackawton, Blackborough, Bondleigh, Bovey (North), Bovey Tracey, Bow (or Nymet Tracey), Bradfield, Bradford, Bradninch, Bradstone, Bradworthy, Brampford Speke, Branscombe, Bratton

Clovelly, Bratton Fleming, Braunton, Brendon, Brentor, Bride-
stowe, Bridford, Bridgerule, Bridgetown, Brixham(3), Broadclyst,
Broadhembury, Broadhempston, Broadwoodwidger, Brushford,
Buckerell, Buckland (East), Buckland (West), Buckland Brewer,
Buckland Filleigh, Buckland in the Moor, Buckland Tout Saints,
Budeaux (St.), Budleigh (East), Budleigh Salterton, Bulkworthy,
Burlescombe, Burrington, Butterleigh, Butterleigh Cadbury,
Cadeleigh, Calverleigh, Chagford, Challacombe, Chardstock,
Charles, Charleton, Chawleigh, Cheldon, Cheriton Bishop, Cheri-
ton Fitzpaine, Chevithorne, Chivelstone, Christow, Chudleigh,
Churchstow, Churston Ferrers, Clannaborough, Clawton,
Clayhanger, Clayhidon, Clovelly, Clyst St. Lawrence, Clyst St.
Mary, Cockington, Cofton, Colaton Raleigh, Coldridge, Cole-
brooke, Colyton, Combe Pyne, Combe Raleigh, Combe in Teign-
head, Compton Gifford, Cookbury, Cornwood, Cornworthy, Cory-
ton, Cotleigh, Countess Wear, Countisbury with Lynmouth, Cove,
Creacombe, Crediton, Cruwys Morchard, Cullompton, Culmstock,
Dalwood, Dartington, Dartmouth(4), Dawlish(3), Denbury, Devon-
port, Diptford, Dittisham, Doddiscombesleigh, Dolton, Dowland,
Down (East), Down (West), Down St. Mary, Drewsteighnton, Dun-
chideock, Dunkeswell(2), Dunsford, Dunterton, Eggesford,
Ellacombe, Ermington, Exeter(25), Exminster, Exmouth(3), Far-
ringdon, Farway, Feniton, Filleigh, Fitzford, Fremington, Frithel-
stock, Georgeham, Germansweek, Gittisham, Goodleigh,
Gulworthy, Halwell, Halwill, Harberton, Harford, Harpford, Har-
racott, Hartland, Hatherleigh, Heanton Puncharden, Hempston
(Little), Hemyock, Hennock, Highampton, High Bray, Highweek,
Hittisleigh, Hockworthy, Holbeton, Holcombe Burnell, Holcombe
Rogus, Hollacombe, Holne, Holsworthy, Honeychurch, Honiton,
Hooe, Horrabridge, Horwood, Huish, Huish (North), Huish
(South), Huntsham, Huntshaw, Huxham, Iddesleigh, Ide, Ideford,
Ilfracombe, Instow, Ipplepen, Kelly, Kenn, Kennerleigh, Kentis-
beare, Kentisbury, Kenton, Kilmington, Kingsbridge(2), Kings-
kerswell, Kingsnympton, Kingsteignton, Kingston, Kingswear,
Knowstone, Lamerton, Landcross, Landkey, Langtree, Lapford,
Lew (North), Littleham (Bideford), Littleham (Exmouth), Little
Hempston, Loddiswell, Loxbeare, Loxhore, Luffincott, Luppitt,
Luscombe, Lustleigh, Lydford, Lympstone, Lynton, Malborough,
Mamhead, Manaton, Marldon, Martinhoe, Marwood, Marystowe,
Mary Tavy, Meeth, Membury, Merton, Meshaw, Milton (South),
Milton Abbot, Milton Damarel, Modbury, Molton (North and
South), Monk Okehampton, Monkleigh, Monkton, Morchard
Bishop, Morebath, Moreleigh, Moretonhampstead, Musbury,

Nether Exe, Newton Abbot(5), Newton Ferrers, Newton Popple-
ford, Newton St. Cyres, Newton St. Petrock, Newton Tracy, Northam (St. Margaret), Northam (Westward Ho), Northleigh, Nymet
Rowland, Oakford, Offwell, Ogwell (East), Ogwell (West), Otter-
ton, Ottery St. Mary, Paignton, Pancrasweek, Parkham,
Parracombe, Payhembury, Peters Marland, Peter Tavy, Petrock-
stowe, Petton, Pilton, Pimlico, Pinhoe, Plymouth, Poltimore, Pool
South, Portlemouth (East), Poughill, Puddington, Putford (East),
Putford (West), Pyworthy, Rackenford, Rattery, Revelstoke, Rewe,
Ringmore, Roborough, Romansleigh, Rose Ash, Rousdon, St. Giles
in the Wood, Salcombe, Salcombe Regis, Sampford Peverell, Sandford, Satterleigh, Seaton and Beer, Shaldon with Ringmore, Sheb-
bear, Sheepstor, Sheepwash, Sheldon, Sherford, Shillingford St.
George, Shirwell, Shobrooke, Shute, Sidbury, Sidmouth, Silverton,
Slapton, Sourton, Southleigh, Sowton, Spreyton, Starcross, Staver-
ton, Stockland, Stockleigh English, Stockleigh Pomeroy, Stoke
Canon, Stoke Fleming, Stoke Gabriel, Stoke in Teignhead, Stoken-
ham, Stoke Rivers, Stoodleigh, Stowford, Strete, Sutcombe, Swim-
bridge, Sydenham Damerel, Tavistock(3), Tawstock(2), Tawton
(North), Tawton (South), Teigngrace, Teignmouth (East), Temple-
ton, Tetcott, Thelbridge, Thornbury, Thorverton, Thurlestone,
Tipton St. John, Tiverton(4), Topsham(2), Torbryan, Tormoham,
Torquay(8), Torrington (Black), Torwood, Totnes, Townstal, Trent
Ishoe, Trusham, Uffculme(2), Ugborough, Uplowman, Uplyme,
Upottery, Upton, Upton Helions, Upton Pyne, Venn Ottery,
Walkhampton, Warkleigh, Washfield, Washford Pyne, Weare Gif-
ford, Welcombe, Wembworthy, Westleigh, Westward Ho, Whim-
ple, Whitchurch, Whitestone, Widecombe in the Moor,
Widworthy, Willand, Winkleigh, Witheridge, Withycombe
Raleigh, Wolborough, Woodbury, Woodbury Salterton, Wood-
land, Woodleigh, Woolfardisworthy (East), Woolfardisworthy
(West), Worlington (East), Worlington (West), Yarcombe,
Yarnscombe, Zeal Monachorum.

PLYMOUTH:

Allington (East), Bickleigh, Brentor, Brixton, Buckland
Monachorum, Cornwood, Corxton, Dodbrooke (Kingsbridge),
Dunterton, Egg Buckland, Holbeton, Hooe, Horrabridge,
Ivybridge, Lew Trenchard, Lydford, Milton Abbot, Plymouth (28
parishes), Plympton St. Mary, Plympton St. Maurice (or Plympton
Erle), Princetown, Sampford Spiney, Shaugh Prior, Sourton,
Tamerton Foliot, Thrushelton, Walkhampton, Wembury,
Whitchurch, Yealmpton.

Nonconformist Registers

Baptist:
EXETER: Cullompton, Exeter (3 parishes), Honiton.
PLYMOUTH: Plymouth (Ebenezer).

Catholic:
EXETER: St. Nicholas Chapel.

Congregational:
EXETER: Kingsbridge, Tavistock.
PLYMOUTH: Plymouth (5 parishes).

Methodist:
EXETER:

Allington (primitive), Ashburton Circuit (Wesley), Axminster Circuit (Wesley), Barnstaple (Boutport) (Wesley), Barnstaple Circuit, Barnstaple Circuit (Bible Christian), Barnstaple Circuit (Wesley), Barnstaple and Ilfracombe Circuit (Wesley), Bideford (Bridge St.) (Wesley), Bideford Circuit (Bible Christian), Bideford Circuit (Wesley), Bovey (North) (Wesley), Bovey Tracy (Wesley), Bridport Circuit (Wesley), Brixham (Fore St.) (Wesley), Brixham Circuit (Wesley), Buckfastleigh (Wesley), Buckland Brewer (Wesley), Budleigh Salterton Circuit (Wesley), Chagford (Wesley), Christow, Dalwood Circuit (Bible Christian and United Methodist), Dartmouth (4—2 Wesley, 2 Primitive), Dawlish (Primitive), Exeter(7), Exmouth, Hennock (Wesley), Holsworthy Chapel, Holsworthy Circuit (Bible Christian and United Methodist), Honiton (Wesley), Horrabridge (Wesley), Ilfracombe (Wesley), Ipplepen (Wesley), Kingswear (Wesley), Landkey (Wesley), Manaton (Wesley), Molton South Circuit, Moretonhampstead (Wesley), Newton Abbot (Bible Christian and United Methodist), Newton Abbot (Free Methodist), Newton Abbot Circuit (Wesley), Okehampton, Paignton (Bible Christian and United Methodist), Parkham, Plympton St. Mary (United Methodist), Ringsash Circuit (Bible Christian and United Methodist), Sandford, Sticklepath, Stoke in Teignhead (Bible Christian and United Methodist), Tavistock (United Methodist), Tavistock Circuit (Wesley), Teignmouth (Wesley), Teignmouth West (Primitive), Tiverton, Torquay(7), Torrington Circuit (Bible Christian), Torrington Black (Bible Christian and United Methodist), Welcombe (Wesley), Westleigh (Wesley), Wolborough, Woolfardisworthy West (Wesley).

PLYMOUTH:

Brixton (United Methodist), Plymouth(11), Plympton St. Mary (United Methodist), Wembury (Wesley).

Society of Friends (Quakers): At Exeter will be found registers for Eastern Division, including Exeter, Cullompton, Culmstock, Newton Tracey, Topsham. Also separate registers for Culmstock and Exeter (Burials only).

Unitarian: Registers for Lympstone, Tavistock, and Topsham are to be found in Exeter.

Civil Registers

A number of these are in the Exeter office:

(a) Cemetery Registers for Bideford, Cullompton, Exeter (7 cemeteries), Tiverton, and Totnes.

(b) Marriage Notice Books for Axminster, South Molton, and Tiverton.

(c) Poor Law Union Workhouses (Births and Deaths since 1866) for Plympton St. Mary, Tavistock, Tiverton, Torrington.

Bishop's Transcripts

These are all kept in Exeter. Prior to 1812 they are only available on microfilm. Coverage is for the entire Diocese of Exeter, including Cornish parishes for the periods 1598-1675, 1737-40, 1773-1812. Some parishes (Falmouth for example) are complete for the whole period. The transcripts for the years not listed above are in the Cornwall County Record Office, County Hall, Truro, Cornwall TR1 3AY.

After 1812 the transcripts are far less accurate than those for many other dioceses, and they were generally discontinued after 1837.

Marriage Licences

These records are in Exeter. They include registers of licences issued from 1568 to 1876.

Wills

These need special mention because the Exeter Probate Registry was destroyed in 1942 by enemy action during the war. No wills from the period 1532 onwards survived. However, there are published lists of wills between 1568 and 1842 (including "Devon and Cornwall Wills and Administrations 1532-1800" by E. A. Fry, and a smaller list covering some earlier and later dates by Miss O. M. Moger) and these are in the CRO.

The CRO does have certain records which can fill in a little of the missing period:

(a) Inland Revenue Copy Wills (1812-58), which were originally at the Public Record Office, London, but were transferred to Exeter in view of the special circumstances.

(b) A few wills and a large quantity of indexed legal papers from the Exeter Consistory Court relating to wills (sixteenth to eighteenth centuries).

(c) Wills surviving in private collections (indexed).

(d) Wills and Inventories of the Orphans Court of Exeter (1555-1765), and proved in Cockington Manor Court (1540-1623). Neither of these were in the Probate Registry at the time of its destruction.

Note: Wills of Devonians proved in the Prerogative Court of Canterbury are in the Public Record Office, London. Wills of the Peculiar Court of Uffculme are in the Wiltshire County Record Office, County Hall, Trowbridge, Wiltshire BA14 8JG.

Miscellaneous Records

These are also in the Devon CRO and include land tax assessments (1780-1832); voters' lists (1833-1900) for Devon; voters' lists (1833-date) for Exeter; quarter sessions records (1592-1971); and hearth tax rolls (seventeenth century). In addition, there are transportation orders to Australia (1802-54) (these refer to convicts being sent to Botany Bay and other centres) and many private family papers of deeds, histories, estate records, etc. These are partially indexed.

Finally, there is a potentially rich source of information for the descendants of emigrants to other parts of the world. This is a collection of letters from persons of Devon descent living abroad, addressed to Sir Roper Lethbridge, President of the Devonshire Association in 1901. Some of these describe in great detail the origins of the family and the circumstances of the emigration and settlement in a new land.

Westcountry Studies Library

This institution is part of the Devon Library Services, but is close to the Record Office in Exeter and contains genealogical material. It is located in Castle Street, Exeter EX4 3PQ. On the open shelves are early directories and many books of interest to ancestor-hunters. The Devon Censuses are available on microfilm, and there is an index to Devon persons, places, and subjects. The Library houses the collections of the Devon and Cornwall Record Society, including several hundred parish register transcriptions and the Boyd and Fursdon marriage indexes for Devon. The Mormon Computer File Index for Devon and Cornwall is also available.

Dorset

Family History Society
(See page 89 for remarks concerning Family History Societies.)

County Record Office
County Hall, Dorchester. (Open Monday-Friday, 0900-1700 hours.) Appointments are appreciated.

The office will check specific points or make short initial searches (an average of about ten years in a parish register) at no charge. Longer searches will be referred to a local record agent.

Parish Registers
Those held by the CRO are listed below: Affpuddle, Alderholt, Allington, Almer, Alton Pancras, Arne, Ashmore, Askerwell, Athelhampton, Batcombe, Beaminster, Beer Hackett, Belchalwell, Bere Regis, Bettiscombe, Bincombe, Blandford Forum, Blandford St. Mary, Bloxworth, Bothenhampton, Bradford Abbas, Bradford Peverell, Bradpole, Bridport, Broadmayne, Broadway, Broadwindsor, Bryanston, Buckhorn Weston, Buckland Newton, Buckland Newton (Plush), Buckland Ripers, Burleston, Burstock, Burton Bradstock, Canford Magna, Cann, Castleton, Cattistock, Caundle (Bishops, Marsh, Purse, Stourton), Cerne (Nether), Cerne (Upper), Cerne Abbas, Chalbury, Chaldon Herring, Charlton Marshall, Charminster, Charmouth, Cheddington, Chelborough (East and West), Cheselbourne, Chetnole, Chettle, Chickerell, Chideock, Chilcombe, Child Okeford, Chilfrome, Church Knowle, Clifton Maybank, Compton Abbas (Shaftesbury), Compton Valence, Compton West, Coombe Keynes, Corfe Castle, Corfe Mullen, Corscombe, Cranborne, Crichel (More), Dewlish, Dorchester (4 parishes), Durweston, Edmondsham, Enmore Green, Evershot, Farnham, Farrington, Fleet, Folke, Fontmell Magna, Fordington (St. George and West), Frampton, Frome St. Quinton, Frome Vauchurch, Fyehead Neville, Goathill, Godmanstone, Gussage, Halstock, Hammoon, Hamworthy, Handley, Hanford, Haydon, Hazelbury Bryan, Hermitage, Hilfield, Hilton, Hinton Martell, Hinton Parva, Hinton St. Mary, Holnest, Holt, Holwell, Hooke, Horton, Ibberton, Iwerne (Courtney, Minster, Steepleton), Kimmeridge, Kingston, Kingston Magna, Kinson and Ensbury, Knighton (West), Langton Herring, Langton Long Blandford, Langton Matravers, Leigh, Lewcombe, Lillington, Littlebredy, Litton Cheney, Loders, Longbredy, Longburton, Longfleet, Lulworth (East

and West), Lydlinch, Lyme Regis, Lytchett Matravers, Lytchett
Minster, Maiden Newton, Manston, Mapperton, Mappowder,
Margaret Marsh, Marnhull, Marshwood, Melbury (Bubb,
Osmond, Sampford), Melbury Abbas, Melcombe Horsey, Melcombe Regis (Christ Church, St. Mary), Melplash, Milborne St.
Andrew, Milton Abbas, Minterne Magna, Morden, Moreton,
Mosterton, Motcombe, Netherbury, Oborne, Okeford (Child and
Fitzpaine), Orchard (East and West), Osmington, Owermoigne,
Parley (West), Pentridge, Perrott (South), Piddlehinton,
Piddletrenthide, Pilsdon, Pimperne, Poole, Poorton (North), Portisham, Portland, Portland (St. John), Powerstock (West Milton),
Poxwell, Poyntington, Preston, Puddletown, Pulham, Puncknowle, Radipole, Rampisham, Ryme Intrinseca, Salway Ash, Sandford Orcas, Seaborough, Shaftesbury (Holy Trinity, St. James, St.
Peter), Shapwick, Sherborne Abbey, Shillingstone, Shipton Gorge,
Silton, Spetisbury, Stafford (West), Stalbridge, Steeple, Stinsford,
Stock Gaylard, Stockwood, Stoke (East, Wake), Stoke Abbott, Stour
(East, West, Provost), Stourpaine, Stratton, Sturminster (Marshall,
Newton), Sutton Waldron, Swyre, Sydling St. Nicholas, Symondsbury, Tarrant (Keyneston, Rawston, Rushton), Thorncombe,
Thornford, Tingleton, Todber, Toller (Fratrum, Porcorum), Tolpuddle, Trent, Turnerspuddle, Tyneham, Upwey, Walditch, Wareham, Warmwell, Weymouth, Whitcombe, Whitechurch Canonicorum, Wimborne, Wimborne Minster, Winfrith Newburgh,
Winterbourne (Abbas, Anderson, Came, Clenston, Kingston,
Monkton, St. Martin, Steepleton, Stickland, Tomson,
Whitechurch, Zelstone), Winterborne Monkton, Woodlands,
Woodsford, Wool, Woolland, Wootton (Fitzpaine, Glanville,
North), Worth Matravers, Wraxall, Wyke Regis, Wynford Eagle,
Yetminster.

Bishop's Transcripts

These are held in the CRO for the following parishes: Beer Hackett,
Bere Regis, Bishops Caundle, Blandford Forum, Blandford St.
Mary, Chardstock, Chickerell, Corfe Castle, Corfe Mullen,
Edmondsham, Fifehead Neville, Fleet, Gussage St. Michael,
Hawkchurch, Holnest, Horsington (Somerset), Horton, Iwerne
Courtenay, Iwerne Steepleton, Langton Matravers, Longburton,
Lydlinch, Lyme Regis, Pentridge, Piddlehinton, Puddletown, Sandford Orcas, Stinsford, Stourpaine, Sturminster Marshall, Swanage,
Tarrant Hinton, Thorncombe, Thornford, Wambrook, Wootton
(North), Wootton Glanville.

Marriage Indexes

These are held for about sixty parishes, mainly in West Dorset, up to 1812.

Nonconformist Registers

The following original registers or copies are in the CRO:

Catholic: Canford Magna, East Lulworth (Castle), Hampreston and Stapehill, Marnhull, Sopley (Hants), Tichborne (Hants).

Congregational: Christchurch, Dorchester, Wareham, Weymouth (Gloucester St., Hope).

Methodist: Blandford, Bournemouth Circuit, Dorchester Circuit, Poole Circuit, Portland Circuit, Shaftesbury and Gillingham Circuit, Sherborne Circuit, Stour Valley Circuit, Weymouth Circuit, Wimborne Circuit. (Please note that a circuit covered a wide area around the town or district from which it took its name, and not merely the town itself. Many villages were included in each circuit.)

Quaker: Dorset, Hants, and Wilts Meetings (1648-1836), Bridport, Shaftesbury.

Unitarian: Poole, Wareham (latter includes some Congregational entries).

Quarter Sessions

These are records of court sessions held every three months. They cover the period from 1660, with occasional entries as far back as 1625.

Yeomanry and Militia Records

Many of these lists have been lost, but some are on file from 1793.

Tithes

A complete set of Dorset tithe documents is in the CRO and a list is available of the various parishes.

Estate and Family Archives

There is an extensive collection of such papers, and it is indexed under parishes.

Census Returns

Microfilms of the four available censuses for the whole county are in the CRO.

Wills

The CRO holds registered copy wills proved at Blandford for the period 1858-1926 and these are indexed. Pre-1858 wills for Dorset date back to 1383 and are all card-indexed in the office. There are also published indexes to various peculiars whose records are in the CRO. Other peculiars in Dorset are in the card index, but the original wills are in the Wiltshire CRO at Trowbridge.

Other Records
There are early runs of local newspapers; electoral rolls; poll books; and early county directories.

Durham

Family History Society
(See page 89 for remarks concerning Family History Societies.)

County Record Office
County Hall, Durham DH1 5UL. (Open during normal office hours.) The CRO will undertake a limited search of one hour's duration at the standard hourly fee. Requests for more detailed searches will be passed to local record agents. There is no charge for personal searches, but it will be necessary to book an appointment at least twenty-four hours in advance.

The holdings of the CRO include the following:

Parish Registers
Auckland (4 parishes), Aycliffe, Beamish, Bearpark, Belmont, Benfieldside, Billingham, Binchester, Birtley, Bishop Middleham, Bishopton, Bishopwearmouth (Christ Church, Good Shepherd, St. Michael, St. Peter, St. Stephen, St. Thomas), Blackhill, Blanchland (Northumberland), Boldon, Boldon East, Bournmoor, Bowburn, Bowes, Brancepeth, Brandon, Brandon Colliery, Burnopfield, Byers Green, Cassop-cum-Quarrington, Castle Eden, Castleside, Chilton Moor, Chopwell, Cockfield, Collierley, Coniscliffe, Consett, Cornforth, Coundon, Coxhoe, Craghead, Crawcrook, Crook, Croxdale, Dalton-le-Dale, Darlington (Holy Trinity, St. Cuthbert, St. Herbert, St. Hilda, St. James, St. John, St. Matthew, St. Paul), Deaf Hill cum Langdale, Denton, Deptford, Dinsdale, Dunston (Christ Church), Durham (7 parishes), Easington, Ebchester, Edmundbyers, Egglescliffe, Eggleston, Eighton Banks, Eldon, Elwick Hall, Embleton, Eppleton, Escomb, Esh, Evenwood, Fatfield, Fir Tree, Forest and Frith, Frosterley, Fyland's Bridge, Gainford, Gateshead (10 parishes), Gateshead Fell, Greatham, Great Stainton, Greenside, Grindon, Hamsteels, Hamsterley, Hartlepool

(6 parishes), Harton Colliery, Haswell, Haughton-le-Skerne, Haverton Hill, Hawthorn, Heathery Cleugh, Hebburn, Heighington, Hendon (Middle), Hendon (St. Ignatius, St. Paul, St. Polycarp), Herrington, Hetton-le-Hole, Heworth (St. Alban, St. Mary), High Spen, Holmside, Houghton-le-Spring, Hunstanworth, Hunwick, Hylton (North and South), Ingleton, Jarrow, Kelloe, Lamesley, Lanchester, Leadgate, Long Newton, Lumley, Lynesack, Lyons, Marley Hill, Medomsley, Merrington, Middle Hendon, Middleton St. George, Millfield, Monk Hesledon, Monkwearmouth (6 parishes), Muggleswick, Newbottle, New Seaham, Norton (St. Mary), Pallion, Pelton, Penshaw, Pittington, Rainton (East and West), Redmarshall, Romaldkirk, Ryhope, Ryton, Sacriston, Sadberge, St. John's Chapel, Satley, Seaham, Seaham Harbour, Sedgefield, Shadforth, Sherburn, Sherburn Hospital, Shildon, Shildon (New), Shincliffe, Shotton, Silksworth, Sockburn, South Hetton, South Moor, South Shields (8 parishes), Southwick, Spennymoor, Staindrop, Stanhope, Stanley, Startforth, Stella, Stockton (6 parishes), Stranton, Sunderland (Holy Trinity, St. John), Tanfield, Thornley, Thornley (Wolsingham), Tow Law, Trimdon, Tudhoe, Usworth, Washington, Westoe, Whickham, Whitburn, Whitworth, Whorlton, Winlaton, Winston, Witton Gilbert, Witton-le-Wear, Wolsingham, Wolviston.

The following parishes have had their registers indexed up to 1837—some cover Baptisms, Marriages, and Burials, and some only one or two of these categories.

Baptism, Marriage, Burial Indexes: Elwick Hall, Jarrow, Penshaw, Stranton, Whorlton, Winston.

Baptismal Index: Staindrop.

Marriage Register Indexes: Bishopwearmouth, Boldon, Jarrow, Muggleswick, South Shields (St. Hilda), Staindrop, Whitburn.

Marriage Register Indexes for 1813-37 only: Cockfield, Coniscliffe, Darlington, Denton, Egglescliffe, Gainford, Haughton-le-Skerne, Heighington, Hurworth, Long Newton, Middleton St. George, Sadberge, Sockburn, Staindrop, Whorlton, Winston.

Burial Indexes: Sadberge, Staindrop.

Nonconformist Registers
Methodist: These are recorded by circuit, and individual churches are not listed. The circuits included a number of churches within the circuit area, and this area varied over the years. You should consult a Durham map to decide in which circuit or circuits a particular place may be. The circuits held at the CRO are: Barnard Castle, Bishop Auckland, Brandon and Deerness, Chester-le-Street,

Consett, Coxhoe, Crook, Darlington, Durham, Durham Coast and Peterlee, Hartlepool, Seaham, Shildon, Spennymoor and Ferryhill, Stanley, Stockton-on-Tees, Teesdale, Thornley, Weardale, Willington.

The records of the following circuits are held at the Tyne and Wear Archives Department, Newcastle-upon-Tyne: Blaydon, Hetton, Houghton-le-Spring, Jarrow, Ryton and Prudhoe, South Shields, Sunderland North, Sunderland South.

Congregational: Baptisms (records are held for Barnard Castle); Marriages and Baptisms (Ryton, Stockton, Sunderland); Baptisms, Marriages, Deaths (Chester-le-Street, East Boldon, Roker, Sunderland).

Baptist: Hamsterley.

Quaker: Sunderland.

Monumental Inscriptions

Castle Eden, Easington, Elton, Haverton Hill, High Usworth, Long Newton, Penshaw, Ryton, Shildon, West Boldon.

Wills

The CRO does not have custody of wills. All probate material is in the Durham University Library 5, The College, Durham DH1 3EQ.

Bishop's Transcripts

These are also held at the above location.

Census Returns

Microfilms for the four census returns for Durham are held in the CRO.

Directories

The CRO holds *some* nineteenth-century trade directories.

East Sussex

Family History Society

(See page 89 for remarks concerning Family History Societies.)

County Record Office

Pelham House, St. Andrew's Lane, Lewes, East Sussex BN7 1UN. Phone Lewes 5400, ext. 580. (Open from Monday to Thursday 0845-1645 hours; Friday, 0845-1615 hours.)

The office will not undertake research on behalf of members of the public, whether they live in the U.K. or overseas. They will supply a list of record-searchers who are prepared to undertake work in East Sussex.

Parish Registers

Alciston, Alfriston, Arlington, Ashburnham, Barcombe, Battle, Beckley, Beddingham, Berwick, Bexhill St. Peter, Bishopstone, Blatchington (East), Blatchington (West), Bodiam, Bodle St., Brede, Brightling, Brighton (23 parishes), Burwash, Buxted, Catsfield, Chailey, Chalvington, Chiddingly, Chiltington (East), Cross in Hand, Crowborough, Crowhurst, Dallington, Danehill, Dean (East and West), Denton, Ditchling, Eastbourne (7 parishes), Eridge Green, Etchingham, Ewhurst, Fairlight, Falmer, Firle, Fletching, Folkington, Forest Row, Framfield, Frant, Friston, Glynde, Guestling, Guldeford (East), Hadlow Down, Hailsham, Hamsey, Hangleton, Hartfield, Hastings (7 parishes), Heathfield, Heighton (South), Hellingly, Herstmonceux, Hoathly (East), Hollington, Hooe, Hove (7 parishes), Icklesham, Iden, Iford, Isfield, Jevington, Kingston by Lewes, Laughton, Lewes (6 parishes), Litlington, Little Horsted, Lullington, Malling (South), Maresfield, Mayfield, Mountfield, Newhaven, Ninfield, Northiam, Ore (St. Helen), Ovingdean, Patcham, Peasmarsh, Penhurst, Pett, Pevensey, Piddinghoe, Playden, Plumpton, Portslade, Preston, Ringmer, Ripe, Rodmell, Rotherfield, Rottingdean, Rye, St. Leonards, Salehurst, Seaford, Sedlescombe, Selmeston, Southease, Stanmer, Streat, Tarring Neville, Telscombe, Ticehurst, Uckfield, Udimore, Wadhurst, Waldron, Warbleton, Wartling, Westfield, Westham, Westmeston, Whatlington, Whitehawk, Willingdon, Wilmington, Winchelsea, Withyham, Wivelsfield.

Wills

In the CRO are wills and other testamentary records of the Consistory Court for the Archdeaconry of Lewes; of the Peculiar Court of the Bishop of Chichester for the Archdeaconry of Lewes, and the Exempt Deaneries of South Malling and Battle.

Up to 1858 the Archdeaconry Court of Lewes proved wills or granted letters of administration. The area covered all parishes in East Sussex, except for fourteen parishes in South Malling and Battle, and included some parishes now in West Sussex. The wills, or copies, which have survived from the sixteenth century are in the East Sussex County Record Office, and are indexed.

Probate in the Peculiar of South Malling was granted by the Archbishop of Canterbury, and the parishes in that area are

Buxted, Framfield, Glynde, Isfield, Lewes, Mayfield, Ringmer, St. Thomas at Cliff, South Malling, Stanmer, Uckfield, Wadhurst (and Lindfield and Edburton in West Sussex.) Probate in the parish of Battle was granted by the Dean of Battle.

Wills proved in the Prerogative Court of Canterbury are in the Public Record Office, Chancery Lane, London, but indexes are available in the East Sussex CRO. Wills since 1858 can be seen in the District Probate Registry, 28 Richmond Place, Brighton BN2 2NA. An index to wills proved in the Lewes District Probate Court (1858-96) is in the East Sussex CRO.

Census Returns
Microfilms of census returns for 1841-71 for the whole of East Sussex (except for Brighton, which is only held for 1861) are in the East Sussex CRO.

Bishop's Transcripts
Microfilms of these are available in the West Sussex CRO, West Street, Chichester, Sussex PO19 1RN.

Marriage Licences
These and Marriage Bonds are in the West Sussex CRO.

Nonconformist Registers
Some of these registers in the Public Record Office, Chancery Lane, London, have been transcribed and are in the East Sussex County Record Office.

Index of Persons
An index of persons is being built up gradually from the catalogue of documents in the East Sussex County Record Office.
Note: You should also check the genealogical material in the West Sussex County Record Office (see page 207). As you will have seen above, the records of the two Sussex counties overlap in several instances.

Essex

Family History Society
(See page 89 for remarks concerning Family History Societies.)

County Record Office

County Hall, Chelmsford, Essex CM1 1LX. (Open Monday, 1000-2045 hours; Tuesday-Thursday, 0915-1715 hours; Friday, 0915-1615 hours.) An appointment is advised in order that a seat may be reserved and records produced in advance. Phone Chelmsford 67222, ext. 2104.

Some classes of records, relating to the Southend area, are housed in the branch office at Southend Central Library, Victoria Avenue (phone Southend 612621, ext. 49). Inquiries regarding Colchester Borough records should be addressed to the Branch Archivist, Essex Record Office, The Castle, Colchester (phone Colchester 77475).

Limited searches of the records will be made by the offices for a fee. They will only make searches for single entries of specific baptisms, marriages, or burials, except that a search for the baptisms of all children of a named person will be treated as one search. Longer searches will not be done, but a list of record agents willing to do the work on a fee basis will be supplied.

Parish Registers

Abberton, Aldham, Alphamstone, Alresford, Ardleigh, Arkesden, Ashdon, Ashen, Ashingdon,* Aveley, Baddow (Little), Bardfield (Great), Bardfield (Little), Barking, Barkingside, Barnston, Basildon, Beaumont-cum-Moze, Belchamp (Otten and Walter), Benfleet (South),* Bentley (Great and Little), Berden, Berechurch, Bergholt (West), Billericay, Birch, Blackmore, Bobbingworth, Bocking, Boreham, Borley, Bowers Gifford, Bradfield, Bradwell-juxta-Coggeshall, Bradwell-juxta-Mare, Braintree, Braxted (Great and Little), Brentwood, Brightlingsea, Bromley (Little), Broomfield, Broxted, Bulmer, Bulphan, Bumpstead (Helions), Bumpstead (Steeple), Bures (Mount), Burnham, Burstead (Great and Little), Buttsbury, Canfield (Great and Little), Canning Town, Chadwell St. Mary, Chapel, Chelmsford, Chesterford (Little), Chickney, Chignall (St. James and Smealey), Childerditch, Chishall (Great and Little), Chrishall, Clacton (Great and Little), Clavering, Coggeshall (Great and Little), Colchester (12 parishes), Colne (Earls, Wakes, White), Colne Engaine, Copford, Corringham, Cranham, Creeksea, Danbury, Debden, Dedham, Dengie, Doddinghurst, Downham, Dunmow (Great and Little), Dunton, Easter (Good and High), Easthorpe, Easton (Great and Little), Eastwood,* Eisenham, Elmdon, Elmstead, Epping, Fambridge (North and South),* Farnham, Faulkbourne, Feering, Felsted, Fordham, Foulness,* Foxearth, Frating, Frinton, Fryerning, Fyfield, Gestingthorpe, Goldhanger, Gosfield, Greenstead-juxta-Colchester, Greenstead-juxta-Ongar,

Hadstock, Hallingbury (Great), Halstead, Ham (East), Hanningfield (South and West), Harwich, Hawkwell,* Hazeleigh, Hedinghem (Sible), Hempstead, Heybridge, Heydon, Hockley,* Horkesley (Little), Hornchurch, Horndon (East and West), Horndon-on-the-Hill, Ilford, Ilford (Little), Ingatestone, Ingrave, Inworth, Kelvedon, Laindon, Lamarsh, Langdon Hills, Langenhoe, Langford, Langley, Latchingdon-cum-Snoreham, Latton, Laver (High, Little, Magdalen), Lawford, Layer Breton, Layer-de-la-Haye, Layer Marney, Leigh, Leighs (Little), Lexden, Leyton, Lindsell, Liston, Littlebury, Loughton, Maldon, Manningtree, Manuden, Margaretting, Markshall, Mashbury, Mayland, Mersea (East), Merser East, Messing, Mistley, Moreton, Moulsham, Mountnessing, Mucking, Mundon, Netteswell, Nevendon, Norley (Black), Norton (Cold), Norton Mandeville, Oakley (Great and Little), Ockenden (North and South), Ongar (Chipping), Ongar (High), Orsett, Parndon (Great and Little), Pattiswick, Peldon, Pentlow, Pitsea, Pleshey, Purleigh, Quendon, Ramsden Crays, Ramsey, Rawreth,* Rayne, Rettendon,* Rickling, Rivenhall, Rochford,* Roothing (Abbess, Aythorpe, Beauchamp, Berners, High, Leaden, Margaret, White), Roydon, Runwell, St. Lawrence, Saling (Great and Little), Sampford (Great and Little), Sandon, Shalford, Sheering, Shelley, Shellow Bowells, Shoebury (North and South),* Shopland,* Silvertown West, Southminster, Springfield, Stambourne, Stanford-le-Hope, Stanford Rivers, Stansted Mountfitchet, Stapleford Tawney, Stebbing, Steeple, Stifford, Stisted, Stock, Stondon Massey, Stow Maries, Strethall, Sutton,* Takeley, Tendring, Tey (Great, Little, Marks), Thaxted, Theydon (Mount, Garnon), Thorrington, Thundersley,* Thurrock (Grays, West), Tilbury (East and West), Tilty, Tollesbury, Tolleshunt Knights, Toppesfield, Totham (Little), Twinstead, Ugley, Upminster, Vange, Victoria Docks, Wakering (Great),* Walden (Saffron), Waltham (Great and Little), Walthamstow, Wanstead, Warley (Great and Little), Weald (North and South), Wendens Ambo, Wendon Lofts, Wethersfield, Wicken Bonhunt, Wickford, Wickham St. Paul's, Widdington, Widford, Wigborough (Great and Little), Willinggale Doe, Willinggale Spain, Wimbish, Witham, Wivenhoe, Wix, Woodford, Woodham Ferrers, Woodham Mortimer, Woodham Walter, Wrabness, Writtle, Yeldham (Great and Little).

The following parishes were formed in the eighteenth century: Barkingside, Billericay, Canning Town (Holy Trinity, St. Gabriel),

*Those registers marked with an asterisk are now in the Record Office at Southend.

Halstead, Ilford (Great), Moulsham, Silvertown West, Victoria Docks, Woodford Bridge, Woodford Wells, Woolwich (North).

The following parish registers are held on microfilm:
Birchanger, Birdbrook, Brentwood, Elsenham, Hadleigh, Hedingham (Castle), Henham, Holland (Great), Hutton, Kelveden Hatch, Kirby-le-Soken, Maplestead (Great and Little), Middleton, Mile End, Navestock, Nazeing, Newport, Prittlewell, Radwinter, Romford, St. Osyth, Stambridge (Great and Little), Sturmer, Waltham (Holy Cross).

Bishop's Transcripts
These are held for the period 1800-78 (incomplete for both parishes and years, especially 1810-13).

Nonconformist Registers
Roman Catholic: Ingatestone Hall Chapel, Thorndon Hall Chapel.
Quaker: Witham (including Chelmsford and Maldon and area).
Congregational: Baddow (Little), Brentwood, Chelmsford, Epping, Ingatestone, Kelveden, Romford, Roothing (Abbess, Leaden, White), Southend, Stansted Mountfichet, Wakering (Great), Witham.
Methodist: Colchester Circuit, Harwich, Shoeburyness, Southend.

The CRO also holds non-denominational records of the Nonconformist Cemetery, Chelmsford, for 1846-89.

Census Returns
These are complete for the period 1841-71 for the whole county, including those London boroughs which were formerly part of Essex.

Wills
Essex was in the Province of Canterbury and the Diocese of London. It included the archdeaconries of Essex and Colchester, and part of that of Middlesex. A large number of parishes in the county scattered through the three ecclesiastical areas were under the jurisdiction of the commissary court of London. They are all now in the CRO for the period 1400-1858 and are indexed.

Marriage Licences
These cover the period 1665-1851 but are indexed for the grooms only.

Miscellaneous Records
These include Quarter Sessions Rolls (1556-1714), incorporated in the Personal Names Index of the CRO; Poor Law Settlement Papers

(1660-1834), indexed; poll books; electoral registers; and early directories.

Gloucester

Family History Society
(See page 89 for remarks concerning Family History Societies.)

County Record Office
Worcester Street, Gloucester GL1 3DW. (Open daily on weekdays, 0900-1700 hours; Thursday evening and occasional Saturday mornings by appointment.)

Postal inquiries will be answered and short, specific searches made without charge. More extensive searches must be made in person, or by engaging a record-searcher—a list of names will be sent on request.

Parish Registers
Abenhall, Adlestrop, Alderley, Alderton, Aldsworth, Alvington, Amberley, Ampney Crucis, Ampney Down, Ashelworth, Aston Blank, Aston Magna, Awre, Badgeworth, Bagendon, Barnsley, Barnwood, Baunton, Berkeley, Beverstone, Bibury, Bicknor (English), Bisley, Blaisdon, Bledington, Blockley, Boddington, Bourton-on-the-Hill, Bourton-on-the-Water, Brimscombe, Broadwell, Brockworth, Bromsberrow, Brookthorpe, Cam, Cam (Lower), Cerney (South), Charfield, Charlton Kings, Chipping Sodbury, Christchurch, Churchdown, Cinderford, Cinderford St. John, Cirencester, Clearwell, Coaley, Coates, Coleford, Compton Abdale, Coln St. Aldwyns, Coln St. Dennis, Condicote, Corse, Cranham, Cutsdean, Daylesford, Deerhurst, Donnington, Dowdeswell, Driffield, Drybrook, Duntisbourne Rouse, Dursley, Dymock, Eastington, Eastleach Martin, Eastleach Turville, Ebrington, Edgeworth, Elkstone, Elmore, Elmstone Hardwicke, Evenlode, Flaxley, Framilode, Frampton-on-Severn, Fretherne, Frocester, Gloucester (18 parishes), Guiting Power, Guiting Temple, Hampnett, Harescombe, Harnhill, Hartpury, Hasfield, Hatherley Up, Hatherop, Hawkesbury, Hempsted, Hewelsfield, Hill, Horsley, Hucclecote, Huntley, Icomb, Kempley, Kingscote, King's Stanley, Kingswood, Lasborough, Lassington, Lechlade, Leigh, Leonard

Stanley, Longborough, Longhope, Longney, Lower Cam, Lower Lemington, Lydney, Maiseyhampton, Mangotsfield, Marston Maisey, Matson, Mickelton, Minchinhampton, Minsterworth, Miserden, Mitcheldean, Moreton-in-the-Marsh, Nailsworth, Naunton, Newent, Newington Bagpath, Newland, Newnham, Newnton (Long), Nibley (North), Northleach with Eastington, Norton, Notgrove, Nympsfield, Oddington, Oldbury-on-Severn, Owlpen, Oxenhall, Oxenton, Ozleworth, Painswick, Pauntley, Pitchcombe, Quedgeley, Quenington, Randwick, Redmarley, Rendcomb, Rissington (Great and Little), Rissington (Little and Wyck), Rockhampton, Ruardean, Rudford, Saintbury, Salperton, Sandhurst, Sapperton, Saul, Sharpness, Sherborne, Shipton Cliffe, Shipton Sollars, Shorncote, Slaughter (Upper), Sodbury (Old), Somerford Keynes, Staunton (Coleford), Staunton (Ledbury), Staverton, Stinchcombe, Stone, Stonehouse, Stow-on-the-Wold, Stratton, Stroud, Sudeley, Swell (Lower), Swell (Upper), Tetbury, Tewkesbury, Thornbury, Tirley, Todenham, Turkdean, Uley, Upleadon, Upton St. Leonards, Viney Hill, Walton Cardiff, Washbourne (Great), Westbury-on-Severn, Westcote, Westonbirt, Whaddon, Whiteshill, Whitminster (or Wheatenhurst), Willersey, Winstone, Witcombe (Great), Woodchester, Woolaston, Wotton-under-Edge, Wyck Rissington.

Some registers have been lost or damaged by fire (Huntley, Oldbury-on-Severn, Oxenhall), floods (Saul and Minsterworth), or rats (Newland). Losses include all the pre-1813 registers of Woolstone and Harescombe, and of Stanton and Snowshill before 1735.

Some registers for places now in the county of Avon are in the Bristol Record Office (see page 92).

Bishop's Transcripts
These are in the CRO and generally date from 1598, but seven parishes go back to 1569, thirteen to 1570, and several to 1580. In several cases the transcripts have survived and the registers have been lost.

Marriages
The records from the Gloucester Consistory Court are now in the CRO. It is worth noting on the subject of marriages that in the early part of the eighteenth century several Gloucester clergymen specialized in performing marriages, usually without banns or licences. These marriages occurred in Hampnett, Lassington, Newington Bagpath, and Oddington. If you cannot find an expected marriage in the county, it might be worth while searching the registers of these parishes.

The CRO possesses Roe's Marriage Index, which adds to and continues the Gloucester section of Boyd's Marriage Index mentioned earlier in this book.

There is one other peculiarity affecting Gloucester marriages which is worth noting. The Forest of Dean area is on the borders of Monmouthshire and Herefordshire. Many marriages took place in nearby towns over the county border, such as Chepstow and Ross-on-Wye. The area was isolated from the mainstream of life in the county and this led to a number of illegal marriages within the prohibited degrees—which makes ancestor-hunting in the Forest of Dean a very interesting project!

Nonconformist Registers
The originals of these are, of course, in the Public Record Office in London, but the CRO has a number on microfilm and is acquiring more as time goes by.

Personal Names Index
This is well worth checking as an aid to finding an individual, or finding a parish where a number of people with a particular surname may have lived.

Census Returns
The CRO holds census microfilms of the whole county, including some Bristol parishes, for 1851. An index is in the process of completion.

Marriage Licences
These only survive in considerable numbers for 1822 and 1823, but the allegations (statements) made and bonds given in order to obtain a licence exist in full from 1637 to 1837.

Newspapers
The CRO does not hold newspapers, but early issues of many of them are in the Gloucester Public Library, including the *Gloucester Journal* from 1722.

Cemetery Records
Many public burial-grounds were set up in the middle of the last century, and the CRO holds cemetery registers for Gloucester (1857-89), Tewkesbury (1856-66), and some District Councils.

Wills
The Gloucester Probate Registry has deposited in the CRO all wills proved from 1858 to 1941, and they are indexed. Diocesan wills from 1541 to 1858 are in the CRO, and are indexed up to 1800.

Most Gloucestershire wills before 1541 were proved at Worcester and are in the Worcester CRO. Copies of these on microfilm are in the CRO in Gloucester and are indexed.

Miscellaneous Records
The CRO contains a very large quantity of estate and family archives, mainly concerned with property and marriage settlements. There is a personal-names index for these. There are also various tax rolls, court records, and poor law books.

Greater Manchester

Family History Society
(See page 89 for remarks concerning Family History Societies.)

County Record Office
None. The records of this "new" county are in the Lancashire County Record Office, and in the individual boroughs which, with parts of Lancashire and Cheshire, make up the county: Bolton, Bury, Manchester, Oldham, Rochdale, Salford, Stockport, Wigan.

A useful source of information is the Central Library, St. Peter's Square, Manchester M2 5PD. Its holdings include:

Parish Registers
The Library is the record office for the Diocese of Manchester and is receiving a large number of parish registers from the Manchester area. It is not prepared to list these.

Nonconformist Registers
It holds the records of various Nonconformist churches, particularly Methodist. No list can be made available of these.

Other Records
These include a Mormon Index based on baptism and marriage entries in church registers. No information can be given as to the dates and places covered by this. There are also local directories from 1772 to 1969; microfilms of the censuses for Manchester for the years available; and microfilms of many places in Cheshire.

It is regrettable that the CRO is unwilling to provide further information, and it is suggested you write directly to the Archivist, Miss Jean Ayton, at the above address for the information which is normally made available.

Hampshire

Hampshire Genealogical Society
(See page 89 for remarks concerning Family History Societies.)

Hampshire County Record Office
20 Southgate Street, Winchester SO23 9EF. (Open Monday-Friday, 0915-1630 hours.)

The office is not able to undertake lengthy searches for the public, although the County Archivist says they might spend a little more time on inquiries from overseas. In general, they would only be prepared to answer specific questions that might involve checking the registers of a parish for two or three years on either side of an approximate date. No charge is made for such a search. For more extensive searches, you will be referred to a list of professional searchers who will work for you for a fee.

Parish Registers
These are drawn from that part of the Diocese of Winchester lying within the boundaries of the present county of Hampshire—except for the cities of Portsmouth and Southampton and some neighbouring parishes, and the Isle of Wight, all of which have their own record offices. A few parishes on the eastern borders of the county (now in the Diocese of Guildford) are also excluded.

The CRO holds the following registers:

Abbotts Ann, Alresford (Old), Amport, Andover, Ashe, Ashley, Ashmansworth, Avington, Baddesley (North), Barton Stacey, Basing, Basingstoke, Baughurst, Bentworth, Bighton, Binsted, Bishops Sutton, Bishops Waltham, Boarhunt, Boldre, Botley, Bournemouth (St. Peter), Bradley, Bramdean, Bramley, Bramshott, Branagore, Brown Candover, Bullington, Buriton, Bursledon, Calshot, Chawton, Chilbolton, Chilcomb, Chilton Candover, Chilworth, Church Oakley, Clatford (Goodworth), Clatford (Upper), Colmer, Compton, Copythorne, Cornampton, Damerham, Deane, Dogmersfield, Droxford, Dummer, Eastleigh, Easton, Ecchinswell and Sidmonton, Eldon, Eling, Ellisfield, Eversley, Exbury, Exton, Faccombe, Farleigh Wallop, Farnborough, Farringdon, Fawley, Foxcott, Freemantle, Froxfield, Froyle, Fyfield, Goodworth Clatford, Grateley, Greatham, Greywell, Hale, Hambledon, Hartley Wespall, Hawkley, Headbourne Worthy, Hedge End, Highclere, Hinton Ampner, Hursley, Hurstbourne Tarrant, Hyde, Itchen Abbas, Itchen Stoke, Kimpton, Kingsclere, Kingsley, Kings Somborne, Kings Worthy, Knights Enham, Laverstoke, Leckford, Lickenholt, Litchfield, Longparish, Longstock, Mapledurwell, Martin, Maybush, Medstead, Meon (East), Meon (West), Meonstoke, Micheldever, Michelmersh, Milford, Minstead, Monk Sherborne, Monxton, Morestead, Mottisfont, Nately Scures, Nately Up, Newnham, Newton Valence, Newton (Soberton), Northington, Nursling, Nutley, Oakley (Church), Oakley (East), Odiham, Otterbourne, Overton, Ovington, Pamber, Plaitford, Popham, Preston Candover, Priors Dean, Privett, Quarley, Rockbourne, Romsey, Rownhams, Selborne, Shalden, Sherborne St. John, Shipton Bellinger, Shirley, Sholing, Sidmonton, Silchester, Soberton, Somborne (Kings), Somborne (Little), Sopley, Southwick, Southsea, Sparsholt, Steep, Stockbridge, Stoneham (North), Stratfield Turgis, Stratton (East), Sutton (Long), Swanmore, Swarraton, Tadley, Tangley, Timsbury, Tisted (West), Titchfield, Tufton, Tytherley (East), Tytherley (West), Upham, Upper Nately, Upton Grey, Vernham Dean, Waltham (North), Warnborough (South), Weeke, Wellow (East and West), Weyhill, Wherwell, Whitchurch, Whitsbury, Wickham, Wield, Winchester (15), Winchfield, Woodhay (East), Woodmancote, Wootton St. Lawrence.

Parish Registers in typescript (copies)

Abbotts Ann, Aldershot, Alton, Amport, Ashe, Basing, Basingstoke, Baughurst, Bentley, Bentworth, Blendworth, Boldre, Botley, Brading, Bramley, Bransgore, Breamore, Bullington, Burghclere, Bursledon, Calbourne, Candover (Brown), Candover (Preston), Chawton, Chilworth, Christchurch, Church Oakley, Cliddesden, Colmer, Coombe, Corhampton, Crawley, Crondall, Deane, Dibden, Dogmersfield, Dummer, Durley, Eastrop, Eling, Ellingham, Elvetham, Eversley, Ewhurst, Exton, Faccombe, Farnborough, Fordingbridge, Fyfield, Hamble, Hannington, Harbridge, Hartley Maudit, Hartley Wintney, Havant, Hayling (North), Heckfield, Herriard, Highclere, Hinton Ampner, Hound, Hunton, Hurstbourne Priors, Hurstbourne Tarrant, Ibsley, Kingsclere, Knights Enham, Lasham, Laverstoke, Linkenholt, Litchfield and Tufton, Longparish, Long Sutton, Mapledurwell, Martin, Medstead, Meon (West), Meonstoke, Monk Sherborne, Monxton, Nateley (Upper), Nateley Scures, Newnham, Newport, Newtown, Niton, Odiham, Otterbourne, Overton, Pamber, Penton Mewsey, Petersfield, Popham and Woodmancote, Portsmouth (St. Thomas), Priors Dean and Colmer, Ringwood, Rotherwick, Rowner, St. Mary Bourne, Selborne, Sherborne St. John, Sherfield on Lodden, Silchester, Sopley, Southampton (4), Steventon, Stoke Charity, Stoneham,

Stratfield Saye, Stratfield Turgis, Tadley, Tangley, Tufton, Tufton and Bullington, Twyford, Upham, Vernham's Dean, Wallop, Waltham, Warnborough (South), Wellow, Weyhill, Whitchurch, Wield, Winchester (11), Winchfield, Winslade, Wolverton, Wonston, Woodhay (East), Woodmancote, Wootton St. Lawrence, Worldham, Worthy (Kings), Worting, Yateley, Yaverland.

Public Cemeteries
Aldershot, Bournemouth East, Ringwood, Winchester.

Nonconformist Registers
Baptist: Whitchurch.
Congregational: Winchester.
Methodist: Alresford, Andover, Basingstoke, Botley, Broughton, Christchurch, Crondall, Eastleigh, Fareham, Fleet, Greatham, Houghton, Hurstbourne Tarrant, Liss, Michelsever, Petersfield, South Stoneham, Winchester (5 churches).
Society of Friends (Quakers): Alphabetical digest of registers covering the whole of Dorset and Hampshire. (Originals in the Public Record Office, London.)

Bishop's Transcripts
The Hampshire CRO has the great majority of these for the period 1780-1858 but the marriages are not included after 1837.

Census Returns
These are on microfilm in the CRO. If you intend to visit in person to check these, it is advisable to reserve a microfilm-viewer in advance.

Marriage Licences
Those held cover the periods 1607-40, 1669-80, 1689-1837. They are indexed.

Wills and Administrations
The CRO holds all the surviving locally proved wills from c. 1500 to 1858, together with officially registered copy wills from the Winchester District Probate Registry from 1858 to 1941. Indexes are available. Administrations form a separate series from 1561 to 1858.

Land and Property Records
Rating (local tax) lists survive for many places since the seventeenth century. There are also land tax assessments, tithe maps and apportionments, and manorial records. There are many other minor sources, and the CRO should be consulted about these.

Card Index

The CRO has an index of names abstracted mainly from their collection of deeds; it is not comprehensive, but may be very useful.

Hereford and Worcester

As previously mentioned, these two counties were amalgamated in 1974. The two record offices—although now joined under one County Archivist—continue to operate on a separate geographical basis. The holdings of the two offices are therefore shown separately below, but in certain areas it may be necessary for you to deal with both of them.

1. Hereford

Family History Society

(See page 89 for remarks concerning Family History Societies.)

County Record Office

Old Barracks, Harold Street, Hereford HR1 2QX.

As a general rule, this office holds records of the Diocese of Hereford and the old county of Herefordshire. It is prepared to make a brief search in answer to a postal inquiry, but will not undertake protracted research.

Parish Registers

The County Record Office holds some two-thirds of the registers of the parishes in the old county of Hereford. They cover the period 1600-1850, with some earlier and some later than these dates. They are listed below:

Abbeyclose, Aconbury, Acton Beauchamp, Allensmore, Almeley, Ashperton, Aston, Avenbury, Aymestry, Bacton, Ballingham, Bartestree, Bishop's Frome, Bishopstone, Blakemere, Bockleton, Bodenham, Bolstone, Brampton Abbots, Bredenbury, Bredwardine, Bredwardine and Brobury, Breinton, Bridge Sollars, Bridstow, Brilley, Brinsop, Brobury, Brockhampton by Ross, Brockhampton in Bromyard, Bromyard, Bullingham, Burghill,

Burrington, Byford, Byton, Callow, Canon Frome, Castle Frome, Clehonger, Clifford, Clodock and Longtown, Collington, Cradley, Credenhill, Croft, Dewchurch Much, Dewsall, Dilwyn, Dorstone, Doscoed, Downton, Dulas, Eardisland, Eardisley, Eaton Bishop, Edwin Loach, Edwin Ralph, Elton, Evesbatch, Ewyas Harold, Eye, Fawley, Felton, Ford, Fownhope, Garway, Grendon Bishop, Hampton Bishop, Harewood, Hatfield, Hentland, Hereford (Holy Trinity, St. James, St. Martin, St. Nicholas, St. Owen, St. Peter), Holmer, Hope Mansell, Hope under Dinmore, Huntington (Kington), Kenchester, Kenderchurch, Kentchurch, Kilpeck, Kimbolton, Kingsland, Kings Pyon, Kington, Kinnersley, Kinsham, Knill, Laysters, Lea, Leinthall Earls, Leinthall Starkes, Leintwardine, Letton, Leysters, Lingen, Little Birch, Little Cowarne, Little Dewchurch, Little Hereford, Little Marcle, Llancillo, Llangarran, Llangrove, Llangua, Llanrothall, Llanwarne, Lucton, Lugwardine, Lyonshall, Mansell Gamage, Mansell Lacey, Marden, Marstow, Mathon, Michaelchurch on Arrow, Middleton-on-the-Hill, Moccas, Moreton Jeffries, Morton on Lugg, Much Birch, Much Cowarne, Much Marcle, Norton Canon, Ocle Putchard, Old Radnor, Orcop, Pembridge, Pencombe, Pencoyd, Peterstow, Pipe and Lyde, Presteigne, Preston Wynne, Ross, Rowelstone, St. Devereux, St. Weonards, Sarnesfield, Shobdon, Stanford Bishop, Staunton on Arrow, Staunton on Wye, Stoke Edith, Stoke Lacy, Stoke Prior, Stretford, Stretton Grandison, Stretton Sugwas, Sutton St. Michael, Sutton St. Nicholas, Tarrington, Tedstone Wafer, Thornbury, Thruxton, Titley, Tretire with Michaelchurch, Ullingswick, Upton Bishop, Wacton, Walterstone, Wellington, Welsh Newton, Weobley, Westhide, Weston Beggard, Weston under Fenyard, Whitchurch, Whitney-on-Wye, Wigmore, Willersley, Winforton, Withington, Wolferlow, Woolhope, Wormbridge, Wormesley, Yarkhill, Yarpole, Yazor.

Bishop's Transcripts
The CRO holds these for all parishes in the Diocese of Hereford from 1660 to 1850.

Marriage Licences
These are also in the office and cover the period 1662-1910. They are indexed.

Wills
Wills proved and administered within the Diocese from 1540 to 1858 are in the CRO, and are indexed.

Census Returns

Census records for the old county from 1841 to 1871 are on microfilm.

Miscellaneous

These include a large number of estate and family collections, including manorial records, and records of land transfers; parish records, including poor law administration, settlement, removal, and apprenticeship; all records of quarter sessions since 1670; and a number of Hereford city records, including Freemen's Rolls.

2. Worcester

Family History Society

(See page 89 for remarks concerning Family History Societies.)

County Record Office

St. Helen's, Fish Street, Worcester WR1 2HN.

The office will not undertake lengthy genealogical research. An isolated inquiry involving not more than a few minutes' work would be answered and no fee charged. A list of searchers is available.

This office contains the historic archives of Worcestershire and especially Worcester diocesan records; and archives of Nonconformist churches, landed families, lawyers, and commercial companies. The diocesan records include Bishop's Transcripts; wills and administrations; and tithe records. Some of the material is indexed.

The office states it can only list its records very briefly. This limited information is as follows:

Parish Registers

The registers from the Diocese of Worcester, which have been lodged with the CRO, are located in the Shire Hall, Worcester. The balance remain in the original parishes. The registers are on microfilm and persons who intend to search in person are advised to reserve a microfilm-viewer in advance of their visit.

The following information about parish registers held in the CRO has been obtained from other sources:

Abberley, Abberton, Alfrick with Luisley, Alvechurch, Ashton-under-Hill, Astley, Aston Somerville, Badsey, Beckford, Belbroughton, Beoley, Berrow, Besford, Bewdley, Birtsmorton, Bishampton, Bredon, Bredon's Norton, Bretforton, Briclehampton, Broadway, Bromsgrove, Castle Morton, Catshill, Childswickham, Church Honeybourne, Churchill, Claines, Clifton upon Teme, Cofton Hackett, Cookley, Cotheridge, Cradley, Cradley Heath, Croome d'Abitot, Darby End, Defford, Doddenham, Dodderhill, Dormston, Doverdale, Dowles, Droitwich (St. Andrew, St. Nicholas), Droitwich (St. Peter), Dudley, Earls Croome, Eastham, Eckington, Eldersfield, Elmbridge, Elmley Castle, Evesham, Fairfield, Far Forest, Fladbury, Flyford Flavell, Flyford Grafton, Grimley, Hadzor, Hallow, Hanley Castle, Hanley Child, Hanley William, Harvington, Heightington, Hill and Moor, Hill Croome, Hindlip, Hollybush, Holt, Kempsey, Kidderminster, Kington, Knighton on Teme, Knightwick, Leigh with Bransford, Lindridge, Littleton (North and Middle), Littleton (South), Longdon, Luisley, Malvern, Malvern (Great), Martin Hussingtree, Martley, Naunton Beauchamp, Norton and Lenchwick, Norton juxta Kempsey, Oddingley, Ombersley, Orleton, Pedmore, Pendock, Peopleton, Piddle North, Pinvin, Powick, Redditch, Redditch (Astwood Bank, Crabbs Cross), Ribbesford, Rochford, Rock, Salwarpe, Sapey (Lower), Sedgeberrow, Severn Stoke, Shelsley Beauchamp, Shelsley Walsh, Spetchley, Stanford, Stoke Prior, Stone, Stourbridge, Stourport, Strensham, Suckley, Tardebigge, Tenbury, Throckmorton, Tibberton, Upton Snodsbury, Upton upon Severn, Upton Warren, Warndon, Welland White Ladies (Aston), Whittington, Wichenford, Wick, Wickhamford, Witley (Great and Little), Worcester (20 parishes), Wribbenhall, Wyre Piddle.

Bishop's Transcripts
These records from the Diocese of Worcester are in the Worcester Record Office.

Wills
The probate records are arranged in chronological order and consist of nearly 900 boxes. A calendar and name-and-place index, published by the British Record Society, exists for all Worcester probate records from 1451 to 1652. The period 1660-1858 is also indexed at the CRO, as is the later period 1858-1928. The period between 1652 and 1660 is not covered in Worcester because wills were proved in London at that time, under orders from the Commonwealth government.

Note: It is regretted that more detailed information about the Worcestershire records has not been made available by the County Archivist. It is suggested you write directly to Miss Margaret

Henderson, Senior Assistant Archivist, Record Office, Fish Street, Worcester WR1 2HN, and try and obtain the additional information you require.

Hertford

This is one of the few unchanged counties—the boundaries are as they have existed for very many years.

Family History Society
(See page 89 for remarks concerning Family History Societies.)

County Record Office
County Hall, Hertford, Herts. SG13 8DE. (Open 0915-1715 hours, Monday-Thursday; 0915-1630 hours on Friday.) An appointment is not essential, but if you can tell the office you are coming the documents you need will be ready and waiting for you.

The policy with regard to inquiries by mail is that searches of up to two hours' duration will be undertaken for a moderate fee. For longer searches the inquirer will be referred to a professional record-searcher.

Before 1877 Hertfordshire was divided between the two dioceses of London and Lincoln. In that year the Diocese of St. Albans was created. Basically, the county was divided between the Archdeaconry of Middlesex, which came under the ecclesiastical jurisdiction of London, and the Archdeaconry of Huntingdon, which came under Lincoln. Because the county was divided in this way in the past there are many gaps in church records, and this affects both parish registers and wills. However, the CRO has done a superb job of gradually collecting all the miscellaneous records under one roof.

The registers and other records of more than seventy-five per cent of the ancient parishes are now in the CRO, plus a quarter of the forty-odd parishes created since the eighteenth century. Most of those parishes whose registers are not in the CRO are covered by Bishop's Transcripts, so that total coverage of the parishes is almost complete, and certainly better than in any other county. In a few parishes the early registers have been lost, and in others there is the usual gap which occurred during the Commonwealth from 1643 to 1660.

Parish Registers and Bishop's Transcripts

Albury, Aldbury, Aldenham, Amwell (Great), Amwell (Little), Anstey, Apsley End, Ardeley, Arkley, Ashwell, Aspenden, Aston, Ayot St. Lawrence, Ayot St. Peter, Baldock, Barkway, Barley, Barnet, Barnet (East), Bayford, Bengeo (Christ Church), Bengeo (St. Leonards and Holy Trinity), Benington, Berkhamstead, Berkhamstead (Little), Bishop's Stortford (All Saints, Holy Trinity, St. Michael), Bourne End, Bovingdon, Boxmoor, Bramfield, Braughing, Brent Pelham, Broxbourne, Buckland, Bushey, Bushey Heath, Bygrave, Caldecote, Cheshunt, Chipperfield, Chipping Barnet, Chorleywood, Clothall, Codicote, Colney (London), Colney Heath, Cottered with Broadfield, Croxley Green, Datchworth, Digswell, Eastwick, Elstree, Essendon, Flamstead, Flaunden, Frogmore, Furneux Pelham, Gaddesden (Great), Gaddesden (Little), Gilston, Goffs Oak, Gravely with Chivesfield, Hadham (Little), Hadham (Much), Harpenden (St. Nicholas and St. John), Hatfield, Hemel Hempstead (St. Mary, St. Paul), Hertford (All Saints, St. Andrew, St. John), Hertingfordbury, Hexton, High Cross, High Wych, Hinxworth, Hitchin (St. Mary and Holy Saviour), Hockerill, Hoddesdon, Holwell, Hormead (Great), Hormead (Little), Hundon, Ickleford, Ippollitts, Kelshall, Kensworth, Kimpton, King's Walden, Knebworth, Langley (Abbots), Langley (Kings), Langleybury, Layston with Buntingford, Leavesden, Lemsford, Letchworth, Leverstock Green, Lilley, Markyate, Marston (Long), Meesden, Mill End, Munden (Great), Munden (Little), Nettleden, Newnham, Northaw, Northchurch, North Mimms, Norton, Offley, Oxhey, Pelham Brent, Pirton, Potten End, Puttenham, Radlett, Radwell, Redbourn, Reed, Rickmansworth, Ridge, Royston, Rushden, Sacombe, St. Albans (Abbey, Christchurch, St. Michael, St. Peter, St. Stephen), St. Paul's Walden, Sandon, Sandridge, Sarratt, Sawbridgeworth, Shenley, Shephall, Standon, Stanstead Abbotts, Stanstead St. Margarets, Stapleford, Stevenage, Stocking Pelham, Sunnyside, Tewin, Therfield, Thorley, Throcking, Thundridge, Totteridge, Tring, Walkern, Wallington, Waltham Cross, Ware (Christchurch, St. Mary), Wareside, Waterford, Watford (Christ Church, St. Andrew, St. James, St. John, St. Mary, St. Michael), Watton-at-Stone, Welwyn, West Hyde, Westmill, Weston, Wheathampstead, Widford, Wigginton, Willian, Woodhill, Wormley, Wyddial, Wymondley (Great), Wymondley (Little).

Nonconformist Registers (on microfilm)

Independent: Ashwell, Barkway, Berkhamstead, Bishop's Stortford, Braughing, Bushey, Cheshunt, Hadham (Little), Harpenden,

Hatfield, Hemel Hempstead, Hertford, Hitchin, Hoddesdon, King's Langley, Layston with Buntingford, Redbourn, Rickmansworth, St. Albans, St. Paul's Walden, Sandon, Sawbridgeworth, Walkern, Ware (2), Watford, Welwyn.
Wesleyan: Bishop's Stortford, Hemel Hempstead, Hitchin, St. Albans.
Presbyterian: Cheshunt, St. Albans, Ware.
Baptist: Hemel Hempstead, Hitchin, Rickmansworth, St. Albans, King's Walden, Watford.
Apostolic Catholic: Ware.
Lady Huntingdon's Connexion: Cheshunt, Hertford.

Land Tax Assessments

The earliest of these dates back to 1690 for the parishes of Cashio and Dacorum, but the vast majority start in the first half of the eighteenth century. All landowners and their tenants are listed and are filed by parish. They ended in 1832.

Militia Lists

These list all men between the ages of eighteen and forty-five liable for service. Most lists start in 1758 and continue to 1786, except for Braughing and Hertford hundreds, where they do not end until 1801.

Manorial Records and Deeds

These cover transfers of tenancy on large estates when tenants left or died. They are partially indexed.

Poll Books and Registers of Electors

Some of these date back to 1697 and continue to 1832. Since the ballot was not secret, the records show not only who voted but how they voted, and you may have the horror of discovering that you have a Tory or a radical hidden away in your family tree. However, you can always keep quiet about this!

Census Returns

These exist on microfilm for the period 1841-71.

Marriage Index

This covers all marriages before 1837 within the county. It contains records of a quarter of a million marriages, and is of great value to anyone tracing Hertfordshire ancestry.

Wills

These are not all in the CRO and the locations are given below:

Archdeaconry of St. Albans: This covered twenty-two parishes, of which most, but not all, were near St. Albans. Wills from 1415 to 1858 are in the CRO and are indexed.

Archdeaconry of Huntingdon: This covered seventy-six parishes in the county. Wills for the period 1557-1857 are in the CRO and indexed.

Consistory Court of Lincoln: This covered a small number of parishes. The wills for 1320-1652 are in the Lincoln CRO, but there are indexes in the Hertford CRO.

Archdeaconry of Middlesex: This covered twenty-six parishes on the eastern side of the county. The wills for 1538-1857 are at the Chelmsford CRO, but indexes are in the Hertford CRO. (These remarks also apply to the parishes of Bishop's Stortford, Little Hadham, Much Hadham, Little Hormead, and Royston.)

Episcopal Consistory Court of London: There are scattered Hertfordshire wills from this jurisdiction in the Greater London Record Office, but an index for the period 1514-1811 is available in the CRO.

Peculiar Court of the Dean and Chapter of St. Paul's Cathedral: The wills for the parishes of Albury, Brent Pelham, and Furneux Pelham were under the jurisdiction of this court. They are located in the Dean and Chapter Library of St. Paul's Cathedral, London, but the CRO holds an index for the period 1560-1837.

Humberside

This new county consists of Grimsby and Hull, most of the old East Riding of Yorkshire, parts of Lincolnshire, and parts of the old West Riding.

Family History Society

(See page 89 for remarks concerning Family History Societies.)

County Record Office

County Hall, Beverley, Humberside HU17 9BA. (Open Monday-Thursday, 0915-1645 hours; Tuesday, 0915-2000 hours; Friday, 0915-1600 hours.)

It is essential that advance notice be given of an intended visit to the search room, by mail or telephone (0482-867131, ext. 394).

Parish Registers
Aldbrough, Anlaby, Atwick, Bainton, Barmby Marsh, Barmston, Beeford, Bempton, Bessingby, Beswick, Beverley (Minster, St. Mary), Bilton, Bishop Burton, Blacktoft, Boynton, Brandesburton, Brantingham and Ellerker, Bridlington (Christ Church, St. Mary), Brough, Burstwick, Burton Agnes, Burton Fleming, Burton Pidsea, Butterwick, Carnaby, Catwick, Cayton, Cherry Burton, Cloughton, Cottam, Cottingham, Cowlam, Driffied (Great and Little), Drypool, Easington, Eastrington, Ellerker, Elloughton and Brough, Etton, Filey, Flamborough, Folkton, Fordon, Foston on the Wolds, Foxholes, Fraisthorpe, Fridaythorpe, Ganton, Garton in Holderness, Garton on the Wolds, Goxhill, Grindale, Hackness, Halsham, Harpham, Harwood Dale, Hedon, Hilston, Hollym cum Withernsea, Holme on the Wolds, Holmpton, Hornsea, Hotham, Howden, Hull (27 parishes), Humbleton, Hunmanby, Hutton Cranswick, Keyingham, Kilham, Kilnsea, Kilnwick, Kirkburn, Langtoft, Laxton, Leconfield, Leven, Lissett, Lockington, Long Riston, Lowthorpe, Lund, Mappleton, Middleton in the Wolds, Muston, Nafferton, Newington, Newland, Newport, North Cave, North Dalton, North Ferriby, North Frodingham, North Newbald, Nunkeeling, Ottringham, Owthorne with Rimswell, Patrington, Paull, Preston, Reighton, Rise, Roos, Routh, Rowley, Rudston, Ruston Parva, Sancton, Scalby, Scarborough, Sculcoates, Seamer, Sigglesthorne, Skeffling, Skerne, Skidby, Skipsea, Skirlaugh, Sledmere, South Cave, South Dalton, Speeton, Sproatley, Sunk Island, Sutton, Swine, Thixendale, Thorngumbald, Thwing, Tunstall, Ulrome, Walkington, Wansford, Watton, Wawne, Welton with Melton, Welwick, Wetwang, Willerby (Staxton), Winestead, Withernsea, Withernwick, Wold Newton, Wressle.

The following parishes from the old East Riding of Yorkshire are now located in the Borthwick Institute of Historical Research, St. Anthony's Hall, York YO1 2PW:
Burnby, Catton, Esrick, Fangfoss, Hayton, Kilnwick Percy, Langton, Londesborough, Nunburnholme, Rillington, Scrayingham, Shipton Thorne, Skipwith, Stamford Bridge, Stillingfleet, Thorganby, Wheldrake, all parishes of York.

Nonconformist Registers
These include original and microfilmed registers.
Baptist: Beverley, Bishop Burton, Bridlington, Driffield, Great Driffield, Hull, Hunmanby, Kilham, Skidby.
Congregational: Beverley, Beverley (Lairgate), Bridlington, Cottingham, Cowick, Driffield, Elloughton, Goole, Hornsea, Howden,

Hull, Market Weighton, North Frodingham, Skipsea, South Cave, Swanland.

Methodist: The following circuit registers (remember that these cover the surrounding area of each place): Beverley, Bridlington, Driffield, Hornsea, Market Weighton, Pocklington, Snaith, Withernsea. The following individual churches: Beverley, Bewerley, Bridlington, Great Driffield, Hull, Newport, Patrington, Pocklington, Snaith, Swinefleet.

Catholic: Everingham, Holme on Spalding Moor, Hull, Marton, Sancton.

Quaker: Bridlington, Elloughton, Holderness, Holme, North Cave, Owstwick, Pontefract, Welwick. (Also, genealogical notes on several Quaker families in the eighteenth and nineteenth centuries are in the CRO—Belton, Bullivant, Dixon, Holborn, Rheam, Sanderson, Stickney, Turner, West, and Wilson.

Unitarian: Hull.

Unitarian Baptist Society: Hull.

It should be noted at this point that the CRO is the successor to the old East Riding of Yorkshire office and inherited its archives; therefore, the emphasis is still on East Yorkshire and will be for some time to come. Many records for what is now Humberside are still in the Lincoln and Wakefield Record Offices and have not been transferred. Grimsby borough archives are in the area record office there, which is administered by the CRO. Hull has its own record office. However, like other "new" counties, Humberside is in the process of steadily centralizing its records.

Census Returns
Those for the old East Riding are on microfilm in the Beverley Public Library, and those for Hull in the Central Library there.

Bishop's Transcripts; Marriage Bonds; Tithe Awards; Wills
These are in the Borthwick Institute of Historical Research, St. Anthony's Hall, York.

Other Records
Some wills from private archives and the Holderness area manorial court records are in the CRO.

Isle of Wight

County Record Office
26 Hillside, Newport, Isle of Wight PO30 2EB.

The County Record Office holds parish registers for all the island parishes. All baptisms and burials before 1858 and all marriages before 1837 have been card-indexed. In addition, there are holdings of Nonconformist registers. There are also parish rate books.

The CRO has a Consolidated Index which includes, in addition to the registers mentioned above, numerous lists of people from the Poll Tax Records of 1378, the Lay Subsidy of 1522, the Royal Survey of the island in 1559, and the Ship Money Assessment of 1637. The Index contains 360,000 names and is on microfilm.

No records of ecclesiastical courts are held—i.e., no wills, Bishop's Transcripts, marriage licences, etc. These will be found in the Hampshire County Record Office: 20 Southgate Street, Winchester SO23 9EF. (Open Monday-Friday, 0905-1630 hours.)

Brief overseas inquiries will be dealt with by the staff, but all requests involving more than thirty minutes' work will be passed to a local record agent, who will charge a fee.

Kent

Family History Societies
There are three Family History Societies covering this area:
Folkestone
Kent
North West Kent
(See page 89 for remarks concerning Family History Societies.)

County Archives Office
County Hall, Maidstone, Kent ME14 1XQ. (Open Monday-Friday, 0900-1630 hours.)

The office will undertake a short search for a specific entry at no charge. It will not undertake protracted searches, but will send a list of local researchers who are available to do this work for a fee.

Parish Registers

As there is no CRO, these are to be found in five different places and the information is given below:

CATHEDRAL ARCHIVES AND LIBRARY, Canterbury, Kent CT1 2EG:
Acrise, Badlesmere, Barfrestone, Betteshanger, Birchington, Bishopsbourne, Bridge, Buckland, Canterbury (16 parishes), Challock, Charlton, Chartham, Cheriton, Chilham, Chillenden, Chislet, Crundale, Davington, Deal, Doddington, Dover (4 parishes), Eythorne, Folkestone, Fordwick, Godmersham, Goodnestone by Faversham, Goodnestone by Wingham, Graveney, Guston, Hackington, Ham, Hardres (Upper), Hawkinge, Hoath, Hougham, Ickham, Littlebourne, Luddenham, Lydden, Lyminge, Molash, Mongeham (Great), Nackington, Newington-next-Hythe, Nonington, Northbourne, Oare, Ospringe, Otterden, Patrixbourne, Petham, Preston-next-Faversham, Reculver, Ringwood, Ripple, St. Nicholas at Wade, Sandwich (3 parishes), Seasalter, Sevington, Sheldwick, Shoulden, Sibertswold, Staple, Stelling Minnis, Stodmarsh, Stourmouth, Sturry, Swalecliffe, Temple Ewell, Tenterden, Teynham, Thanet, Thanington, Tilmanstone, Walmer (St. Saviour), Walmer St. Mary, Waltham, Westbere, Whitfield, Wickhambreaux, Wittersham, Womenswold, Woodnesborough, Wootton.

GREATER LONDON RECORD OFFICE, The County Hall, London SE1 7PB:
Deptford (5 parishes), Greenwich (5 parishes), Lewisham (2 parishes), Woolwich (10 parishes).

GREENWICH BOROUGH ARCHIVES, Charlton House, Charlton Road, Greenwich, London SE7:
Greenwich (Holy Trinity, St. Luke, St. Paul).

KENT ARCHIVE OFFICE, County Hall, Maidstone, Kent ME14 1XQ:
Addington, Allington, Appledore, Ashford South, Ash-next-Ridley, Aylesford, Barming, Bearstead, Beckenham, Benenden, Bexley, Bickley, Biddenden, Biggin Hill, Bilsington, Birling, Birling (Lower), Blean, Bobbing, Borden, Borstal (Rochester), Boughton Malherbe, Boughton Monchelsea, Boxley, Brabourne, Brasted, Bredhurst, Brenchley, Brenchley (Paddock Moor), Brenzett, Brompton (Old), Brookland, Broomfield, Burham, Burmarsh, Capel, Chalk, Charing, Chart (Little), Chart Sutton, Chatham (3 parishes), Chevening, Chislehurst, Cliffe, Cobham, Cooling, Cowden, Cranbrook, Cray St. Mary, Cray St. Paul, Crockenhill, Cuxton, Darenth, Detling, Ditton, Dover (St. John Mariner), Downe, Dymchurch, Eastchurch, Ebony, Eccles, Elmley, Elm-

stead, Erith, Eynsford, Farleigh (East and West), Farnborough, Farningham, Frindsbury, Frinstead, Frittenden, Gillingham, Grain, Gravesend, Hadlow, Halden (High), Halling, Halstead, Halstow (High and Lower), Harrietsham, Hartley, Hartlip, Harty, Hastingleigh, Hayes, Headcorn, Hever, Higham, Hildenborough, Hinxhill, Hollingbourne, Hoo, Hope, Horsmonden, Horton Kirby, Horton Monks, Hothfield, Hunton, Ifield, Ightham, Ivychurch, Iwade, Kemsing, Kenardington, Keston, Kingsdown, Kingston, Knockholt, Lamberhurst, Langley, Leeds, Leigh, Leybourne, Leysdown, Lidsing, Linton, Longfield, Loose, Luddesdown, Lullingstone, Luton, Maidstone (6 parishes), Malling (East and West), Meopham, Mereworth, Milton-next-Gravesend, Milton-next-Sittingbourne, Minster-in-Sheppey, Murston, Nettlestead, Newington-next-Sittingbourne, Northfleet Rosherville, Offham, Orpington, Otford, Otham, Peckham West, Pembury, Penge, Penshurst, Plaxtol, Pluckley, Postling, Preston-next-Faversham, Queenborough, Ridley, Rochester, Rodmersham, Rolvenden, Romney (Old and New), Ryarsh, Seal, Sellinge, Sevenoaks, Sheerness, Sheerness Garrison, Shoreham, Shorne, Sidcup, Sittingbourne, Smarden, Smeeth, Snargate, Snave, Snodland, Stanford, Stansted, Stockbury, Stoke, Stone-in-Oxney, Stone-next-Dartford, Stowting, Strood, Sundridge, Sutton-at-Hone, Sutton East, Sutton Valence, Swanlet, Swanscombe, Tenterden, Teston, Thurnham, Trottiscliffe, Tudeley, Tunbridge Wells, Upchurch, Upnor, Warden, Warehorn, Wateringbury, Westwell, Wickham (East), Willesborough, Wilmington, Woodchurch, Wouldham.

BOROUGH OF LEWISHAM, 170 Bromley Road, London SE6 2UZ: Deptford (High Street), Lewisham (20 parishes).

Wills

Before 1857, church courts in Rochester and Canterbury proved wills, and the registered copies and original wills have survived from the last years of the fourteenth century. These, together with wills of the Deanery of Shoreham and the parish of Cliffe, are located in the County Archives Office and are indexed. Wills for the county since 1857 are in the District Probate Registry, 28 Richmond Place, Brighton, Sussex BN2 2NA.

Letters of Administration

These were granted to a person to administer the estate of the deceased if no will had been made. Indexed lists of these are in the County Archives Office. They date from the fifteenth century up to 1857.

Marriage Licences
The Canterbury Cathedral Archives and Library have these for the periods 1637-39, 1715-98, 1829-43, and 1897-1909.

Bishop's Transcripts
The transcripts for the Rochester Diocese are in the office, and those for Canterbury in the Cathedral Archives and Library.

Tithe Records
The office has an indexed list of landowners and tenants in each parish in or about the year 1840.

Electoral Records
Poll books listing those who voted in the parliamentary elections from 1713 to 1837 are available.

Census Returns
Microfilm copies of these for Kent from 1841 to 1871 can be examined, by appointment, in the Reference Department, The County Library, Springfield, Maidstone, Kent.

Lancashire

Family History Societies
There are two Family History Societies in this area:
Manchester and Lancashire
Rossendale
(See page 89 for remarks concerning Family History Societies.)

County Record Office
Bow Lane, Preston PR1 8ND. (Open during regular office hours.)
   The office regrets it can do no more for postal inquirers than make a brief search, given exact dates. Those with longer inquiries will be referred to a list of record agents.

Parish Registers
The following registers are held in the Lancashire CRO:
Abram,* Accrington, Adlington (Standish), Admarsh, Ainsworth, Aldingham, Altcar, Altham, Ancoats (All Souls, Christ Church, St. Andrew), Ashton-in-Makerfield,* Ashton-on-Ribble, Ashton-under-Lyne (Christ Church, St. James, St. Peter), Ashworth, Astley, Atherton, Aughton, Bacup, Balderstone, Bamber Bridge, Bardsea,

Barrow-in-Furness, Barton (Preston), Barton-upon-Irwell, Bedford, Belmont, Bentham (Yorks), Bevington, Bickerstaffe, Billinge, Birch (Hopwood), Birch (Rusholme), Bispham, Blackburn (10 parishes), Blackley, Blackpool (Holy Trinity, St. John), Blackrod, Blawith, Bleasdale, Bolton-by-Bolland (Yorks), Bolton-le-Moors (All Saints, Emmanuel, Holy Trinity, St. George, St. John), Bolton-le-Sands, Bootle, Bradshaw, Brathay, Bretherton, Brindle, Broughton (Preston), Broughton East (Cartmel), Broughton-in-Furness, Burnley (St. James, St. John, St. Margaret, Whalley), Burscough, Burtonwood, Bury (St. John, St. Paul, St. Thomas), Carnforth, Cartmel, Cartmel Fell, Caton, Chadderton (St. John, St. Matthew), Chapel-le-Dale (Yorks), Chatburn, Cheetham (St. Luke, St. Mark, St. Thomas), Childwall, Chipping, Chorley (Croston, St. George, St. Peter), Chorlton-cum-Hardy, Chorlton-on-Medlock (All Saints, St. Luke), Church, Church Kirk, Churchtown, Claughton, Clayton-le-Moors, Cleveley, Clifton-with-Salwick, Clitheroe, Cockerham, Cockey Moor, Colne, Colton, Coniston, Copp, Coppull, Croft, Crompton, Crosby (Great), Croston, Culcheth, Dalton (Wigan), Dalton-in-Furness, Darwen (Lower), Darwen (St. Barnabas), Darwen (St. James, St. John, Trinity), Deane, Dendron, Denton (Manchester), Denton (St. Lawrence), Didsbury, Dobcross (Yorks), Douglas, Downham, Dunnerdale, Eccles, Eccleston, Eccleston (Great), Edenfield, Edgehill (St. Catherine, St. Mary, St. Stephen), Egton-cum-Newland, Ellel, Ellenbrook, Elton (All Saints, St. Stephen), Euxton, Everton (St. Augustine, St. Chrysostom, St. George, St. Peter), Farington, Farnworth, Felkirk (Yorks), Fence, Feniscowles, Field Broughton, Finsthwaite, Flixton, Flookburgh, Formby, Friarmere (Yorks), Frodsham (Cheshire), Fulwood, Garstang, Garston, Glasson, Glazebury, Golborne,* Goodshaw, Goosnargh, Gorton, Grange-over-Sands, Grassendale, Great Harwood, Great Marsen, Great Sankey, Gressingham, Grindleton, Haigh, Hale, Halewood, Halliwell (St. Luke, St. Peter), Halsall, Halton, Hambleton, Harpurhey, Harwood, Haslingden, Haverthwaite, Hawkshead, Heapey, Heaton Norris, Heptonstall (Yorks), Hesketh-with-Becconsall, Hey, Heysham, Heywood, Higher Walton, Hindley, Hoghton, Holcombe, Holker (Lower), Hollinfare, Hollinwood, Holme-in-Cliviger, Hoole, Hopwood, Hornby, Horwich, Hulme, Hulton (Little), Huyton, Ingleton and Chapel-le-Dale (Yorks), Ireleth, Inskip, Kirkby, Kirkby Ireleth, Kirkdale (St. Aidan, St. Mary), Kirkham, Knotty Ash, Knowsley, Lancaster (St. Anne, St. John, St. Thomas), Lancho, Lathom (St. James, St. John), Leck, Lees, Leigh, Levenshulme, Leyland, Lindale, Littleborough, Little Hulton, Little Lever, Little Marsden,

Liverpool (30 parishes), Longridge, Longton, Lowick, Lowton, Lund, Lydgate (Yorks), Lydiate, Lytham, Maghull, Manchester (43 parishes), Marton, Mawdesley, Melling, Melling (Halsall), Mellor, Mellor Brook, Middleton, Middleton-in-Lonsdale (Cumbria), Millom (Cumbria), Milnrow, Mitton, Mossley, Mossley Hill, Moss Side, Much Woolton, Nelson, Newburgh, Newchurch-in-Culcheth, Newchurch-in-Pendle, Newchurch-in-Rossendale, Newton Heath, Newton-le-Willows,* North Meols, Oldham (6 parishes), Old Laund Booth, Openshaw, Ormskirk, Oswaldtwistle, Out Rawcliffe, Outwood, Over Darwen, Over Kellet, Overton, Over Wyresdale, Padiham, Parbold, Parr (Holy Trinity, St. Peter), Peel, Pendlebury, Pendleton, Pennington (Leigh), Pennington (Lonsdale), Penwortham, Pilkington, Pilling, Pleasington, Poulton-le-Fylde, Poulton-le-Sands, Poulton-with-Fearnhead, Prescot, Prestbury (Cheshire), Preston (11 parishes), Prestwich, Quernmore, Radcliffe, Rainford, Ramsbottom, Rawtenstall, Ribby-with-Wrea, Ribchester, Ringley, Rivington, Rochdale, Royton, Rufford, Rusholme Birch, Rusland, Saddleworth (Yorks), St. Helens, St. Michaels-on-Wyre, Salesbury, Salford (5 parishes), Samlesbury, Satterthwaite, Sawley, Scarisbrick, Seaforth, Seathwaite, Sefton, Shaw, Shireshead, Silverdale, Skelmersdale, Skerton, Skipton (Yorks), Southport (5 parishes), Speke, Spotland, Stalmine, Stalybridge, Stand, Standish, Stanley, Staveley, Stretford, Sutton, Swinton, Tarleton, Tatham, Tatham Fell, Thornton, Thornton-in-Lonsdale (Yorks), Thurnham, Tockholes, Todmorden, Tonge, Torver, Tosside, Tottington, Toxteth Park (7 parishes), Trawden, Treales, Tuebrook, Tunstall, Tunstead, Turton, Tyldesley, Ulverston, Unsworth, Up Holland, Urswick, Waddington (Yorks), Walkden, Walmersley, Walmsley, Walney, Walton-le-Dale, Walton-on-the-Hill, Wardleworth (St. James, St. Mary), Warrington (All Saints, Holy Trinity, St. Paul), Warton (Amounderness), Warton (Lonsdale), Waterloo, Wavertree (Holy Trinity, St. Mary), Weeton, West Derby, Westhoughton, Whalley, Whiston, Whitechapel, Whitehaven (Cumbria), Whitewell, Whittington, Whittle-le-Woods, Whitworth, Widnes, Wigan,* Windle, Winwick, Withington, Withnell, Woodland, Woodplumpton, Worsley, Worsthorne, Wuerdle, Wyresdale (Over), Yealand Conyers.

The registers marked with an asterisk (plus Bickershaw, Earleston) are in the Wigan Record Office, Town Hall, Leigh WN7 1DY.

Bishop's Transcripts
The CRO holds a great number of these, covering the majority of the parishes in the county.

Marriage Bonds and Licences

Chester marriage bonds up to 1858, including Lancashire south of
the river Ribble (i.e., south of Preston), are in the Cheshire County
Record Office, The Castle, Chester. Lancaster marriage bonds up to
1861 for North Lancashire are in the Lancashire CRO.

Census Returns

Microfilm copies of censuses are *not* kept in the CRO but are
available in local libraries in the county for areas covered by them.

Nonconformist Registers

The holdings in the CRO are extensive—either copies of those
registers deposited in the PRO, London, or originals never sent
there and lodged later with the CRO:

Catholic Registers and Related Records: Accrington, Aighton,
Alston Lane, Ancoats (St. Alban, St. Anne, St. Michael), Appleton,
Ardwick, Ashton-in-Makerfield, Ashton-under-Lyne, Aughton,
Bamber Bridge, Barton (Newhouse), Barton-upon-Irwell, Bedford,
Billinge, Blackbrook, Blackburn (5 parishes), Blackley, Blackrod,
Bolton (4 parishes), Bradford, Brierfield, Brindle, Broughton (Fer-
nyhalgh), Broughton (Higher and Lower), Brownedge, Bryn, Burn-
ley (6 parishes), Burscough, Cheetham Hill, Chipping, Chorley
(South Hill, Weld Bank), Chorlton-cum-Hardy, Chorlton-on-
Medlock (Holy Family, Holy Name), Claughton-in-Amounderness,
Clayton Green, Clayton-le-Moors, Clitheroe, Colne, Cottam, Croft,
Crosby (Great and Little), Crosby Harkirk, Croston, Croxteth, Cul-
cheth, Darwen, Didsbury, Dunkenhalgh, Eccles, Eccleston, Eccles-
ton (Great), Euxton, Failsworth, Fernyhalgh, Formby, Garstang,
Garswood, Gillmoss, Goosnargh, Gorton, Haigh, Harkirk, Hasling-
den, Heaton Norris, Heywood, Hindley, Hollinwood, Hornby,
Hulme, Ince Blundell, Ince-in-Makerfield, Irlam, Kirkby, Kirk-
ham, Lancaster, Lea, Leagram, Lee House, Lees, Leigh, Leighton
Hall, Levenshulme, Leyland, Little Hulton, Liverpool (St. Mary),
Longridge, Longsight, Lowe House, Lydiate, Lytham, Manchester
(37 parishes), Mawdesley, Miles Platting, Mossley, Mowbreck
Hall, Nelson, Netherton, Newhouse, Oldham, Ormskirk, Orrell,
Osbaldeston, Oswaldtwistle, Padiham, Pleasington, Portico, Poul-
ton-le-Fylde, Preston, Rawtenstall, Ribchester, Rishton, Robert
Hall, Rochdale (St. John, St. Patrick), Royton, Rusholme, St.
Helens, Salford (4 parishes), Salwick Hall, Samlesbury, Scarisbrick,
Scorton, Shaw, Singleton, South Hill, Southworth Hall, Standish,
Stonyhurst, Stretford, Swinton, Tatham, Thornley, Thurnham,
Towneley, Ulverston, Urmston, Walton-le-Dale, Warrington,
Weaste, Weld Bank, Westby, Whittle-le-Woods, Widnes, Wigan

(Holy Family, St. John, St. Mary), Willows, Windle, Windleshaw, Woolston, Woolton, Wrightington, Yealand.

Wesleyan: Accrington, Ancoats, Ashton-under-Lyne, Bacup, Barrowford, Barton-on-Irwell, Bedford, Besses o' the Barn, Blackburn, Blackley, Bolton, Brinscall, Burnley, Bury, Cadishead, Chorley, Chorlton, Chorlton-on-Medlock, Clitheroe, Colne, Crumpsall, Darwen, Deane, Droylsden, Eccles, Failsworth, Fence, Flixton, Freckleton, Garstang, Halshaw Moor, Haslingden, Haughton Green, Heaton Norris, Higham, Hoddlesden, Irlam, Lamberhead, Lancaster, Leigh, Levenshulme, Littleborough, Liverpool, Longholme, Manchester, Mellor, Mereclough, Middleton, Nelson, Oldham, Old Laund Booth, Over Darwen, Oswaldtwistle, Padiham, Pendleton, Prescot, Preston, Prestwich, Radcliffe, Rakefoot, Rawtenstall, Rochdale, Rossendale, Rossendale Forest, St. Helens, Salford, Shawforth, Shaw-in-Crompton, Skelmersdale, Southport, Swinton, Tottington, Trawden, Turton, Tyldesley, Ulverston, Unsworth, Walmesley, Wardle, Warrington, Whalley (Colne), Whalley (Trawden), Wigan.

Methodist (including Wesleyan Methodist, Primitive Methodist, New Connexion, United, Trinity, Zion, Ebenezer, etc.): Ashton-under-Lyne, Blackburn, Bolton, Burnley, Bury, Carnforth, Chorley, Colne, Darwen, Eccles, Haslingden, Lancaster, Lees, Liverpool, Manchester, Morecambe, Mossley, Newchurch-in-Rossendale, Overton, Padiham, Pendleton, Preston, Rochdale, Roughlee, Todmorden, Trawden, Warton, Waterfoot.

Independent: Ashton-in-Makerfield, Ashton-under-Lyne, Bamford, Blackburn, Blackley, Bolton, Bretherton, Burnley, Bury, Calderbrook, Chaigley, Chorley, Clitheroe, Cockerham, Colne, Darwen, Eccles, Edgeworth, Farnworth, Forton, Garstang, Goosnargh, Haslingden, Hindley, Horwich, Inglewhite, Kirkdale, Lancaster, Leigh, Liverpool, Manchester, North Meols, Oldham, Pilkington, Prescot, Preston, Rainford, St. Helens, Salford, Southport, Tottington, Toxteth Park, Turton, Walkerfold, Walmersley, Warrington, Westhoughton, Wigan.

Baptist (including Welsh, and Particular): Bacup, Blackburn, Bolton, Burnley, Butterworth, Cloughfold, Colne, Eccles, Hawkshead Hill, Inskip, Lancaster, Liverpool, Manchester, Oldham, Preston, Rochdale, Rossendale, Sabden, Staleybridge, Tottlebank.

New Jerusalemites: Accrington, Middleton, Outwood, Pilkington, Ringley, Salford, Tyldesley.

Congregational: Bolton, Broughton, Droylsden, Edgeworth, Horwich, Liverpool, Manchester, Rainhill, Salford, Southport, Stretford, Ulverston.

Presbyterian (including Scotch Church): Ainsworth, Astley, Blackburn, Blackley, Bolton, Bury, Chorley, Chowbent, Eccles, Failsworth, Gateacre, Lancaster, Liverpool, Manchester, Ormskirk, Padiham, Prescot, Risley, Rivington, Rochdale, Salford, Spotland, Tottington, Turton, Walmsley, Warrington, Winwick.

Unitarian: Bolton, Chorlton-on-Medlock, Croft, Fallowfield, Gorton, Liverpool, Manchester, Newchurch-in-Rossendale, Pilkington, Preston, Rossendale.

Lady Huntingdon's Connexion: Middleton, Preston, Rochdale, Tyldesley, Warrington.

Moravian: Fairfield, Oldham.

Inghamites: Colne, Winewall.

Swedenborgian: Bolton, Salford.

Universalists: Liverpool.

Bible Christians: Manchester, Salford.

Unaffiliated: Accrington, Aighton, Bailey, Birch, Blackburn, Blackpool, Bootle, Chagley, Chipping, Eccles, Hulme, Kirkham, Littleborough, Liverpool, Pendlebury, Pendleton, Rochdale, Worsley.

Society of Friends (Quakers): Colthouse, Crawshawbooth, Fylde, Hardshaw, Hawkshead, Height, Lancaster, Marsden, Oldham, Preston, Rochdale, Rossendale, Swarthmoor, Todmorden, Toxteth Park, Ulverston.

Civil Registration

Occasionally the birth and death registers of individual institutions are deposited in the CRO. This list includes all such records catalogued up to Feburary 1979. It also includes registers of births made under the Vaccination Act, 1871, which in some cases are virtual duplicates of the records of district registry offices.

Also included are the Registrar's Marriage Notice Books for the Lancaster Registration District (i.e., civil records, 1920-54):
Aighton (Workhouse), Arkholme (Vaccination), Blackburn (Hospital), Brierfield (Urban District Council), Broughton, Caton (Vacc.), Clitheroe (Hospital and Workhouse), Earby (UDC), Lancaster (Hospital and Registration District), Preston (Workhouse and Civil Hostel), Tunstall (Vacc.), Walton-le-Dale (UDC), Whitworth (UDC), Wray (Vacc.). The earliest of these records are in 1837 and the latest in 1977; these dates, however, do not apply in each place.

Surname Index

This is the Mormon Microfiche Index and contains 2,182,563 entries—mainly christenings, but also some marriages.

Wills and Probate Records

The original wills of most Lancashire people are kept in the Lancashire Record Office. Before 1858, jurisdiction was in the church courts, and in Lancashire this meant the Diocese of Chester for those living south of the Ribble, and the Archdeaconry of Richmond for those to the north. Indexes from 1545 to 1833 have been printed by the Record Society and are in the CRO. From 1858 onwards wills were proved in a civil court and these are indexed in the CRO for the period 1858-1923. Catholic wills had to be probated among the Quarter Sessions records and a list of these is in the CRO.

Some wills are in other CROs. The parishes of Broughton, Kirkby Ireleth, and Seathwaite in the Deanery of Furness formed a peculiar probate jurisdiction of the Dean and Chapter of York. Original wills are in the Borthwick Institute, York, and indexes are in the Lancashire CRO. There are other wills in Chester and York, but lists of these are in the Lancashire County Record Office.

Other Records

These include quarter sessions records; poll books and electors lists; directories; maps; and newspapers.

Leicester

Family History Society

(See page 89 for remarks concerning Family History Societies.)

County Record Office

57 New Walk, Leicester LE1 7JB. (Open normal office hours, Monday-Friday.)

The office will undertake short searches without charge, but inquiries involving protracted searches will be referred to local researchers.

Parish Registers

These cover most of Leicestershire and about one-half of Rutland (now incorporated in the county):

Ab Kettleby and Holwell, Allexton, Anstey, Appleby, Arnesby, Asfordby, Ashby-de-la-Zouch (Holy Trinity, St. Helen), Ashby Folville with Barsby, Ashby Magna, Ashby Parva, Ashwell, Ayston,

Bagworth, Barkestone, Barlestone, Barrowden, Barrow upon Soar, Barwell, Beeby, Belgrave (St. Michael, St. Peter), Belton (Leicester), Belton (Rutland), Bitteswell, Blackfordby, Blaston (St. Michael and St. Giles), Bottesford, Branston, Braunston, Braunstone, Brentingby, Bringhurst and Drayton, Brooke, Brooksby, Broughton Astley, Bruntingthorpe, Burley, Burrough on the Hill, Burton Lazars, Burton Overy, Caldecott, Carlton Curlieu, Catthorpe, Claybrooke, Cold Newton, Cold Overton, Coleorton, Congerstone, Cossington, Coston, Cotesbach, Cottesmore, Countesthorpe, Crance, Croxton (South), Croxton Kerrial, Dalby on the Wolds, Desford, Diseworth, Dishley and Thorpe Acre, Donington le Heath, Drayton, Dunton Bassett, Earl Shilton, Eastwell, Eaton, Edith Weston, Edmondthorpe, Egleton, Ellistown, Enderby, Evington, Fenny Drayton, Fleckney, Foston, Foxton, Freeby, Frisby on the Wreake, Gaddesby, Garthorpe, Gaulby, Glenfield, Glooston, Goadby Marwood, Great Bowden, Great Easton, Great Glen, Great Stretton, Grimston, Groby, Gumley, Hallaton, Hambleton, Harby, Harston, Hathern, Hemington, Hinckley (Holy Trinity, St. Mary, St. Paul), Hoby, Holt, Horninghold, Hose, Hoton, Hugglescote, Humberstone, Hungarton, Husbands Bosworth, Ibstock, Ilston on the Hill, Kegworth, Ketton, Keyham, Kilby, Kilworth (South), Kimcote and Walton, Kings Norton, Kirby Bellars, Kirby Muxloe, Kirkby Mallory, Knighton, Knipton, Knossington, Langham, Langton (East and West), Laughton, Leicester (19 parishes), Leire, Little Bowden, Lockington and Hemington, Loddington, Long Clawson, Long Whatton, Loughborough, Lowesby and Cold Newton, Lubenham, Luffenham (South), Lutterworth, Lyddington, Lyndon, Manton, Market Bosworth, Market Harborough, Markfield, Measham, Medbourne cum Holt, Melton Mowbray, Misterton, Morcott, Mountsorrel (Christchurch, St. Peter), Mowsley, Muston, Narborough, Newbold Verdon, Newton Harcourt, Newton Linford, Normanton, Normanton le Heath, North Kilworth, North Luffenham, Norton (East), North juxta Twycross, Oadby, Old Dalby, Orton on the Hill, Osgathorpe, Owston, Packington, Peatling Magna, Peatling Parva, Peckleton, Pickwell, Plungar, Prestworld, Queniborough, Quorn, Ragdale, Ratby, Ratcliffe Culey, Ratcliffe on the Wreake, Rearsby, Redmile, Rotherby, Rothley, Saddington, Saltby, Sapcote, Saxby, Saxelby, Scraptoft, Seaton, Shackerstone, Shangton, Sharnford, Shawell, Shearsby, Sheepy Magna, Shepshed, Sibson, Skeffington, Snarestone, Somerby, Sproxton, Stanford upon Avon, Stapleford, Stathern, Stockerston, Stoke Dry, Stoke Golding, Stonesby, Stoney Stanton, Stretton en le Field, Stretton Parva, Swannington, Swepstone, Swinford, Swithland, Theddingworth, Thornton, Thorpe Acre, Thorpe Arnold cum Brentingby, Thorpe Langton, Thrussington, Thurcaston, Thurlaston, Thurmaston, Tilton on the Hill, Tinwell, Tugby, Tur Langton, Twycross, Twyford, Uppingham, Waltham on the Wolds, Walton, Wardley, Wartnaby, Whetstone, Whissendine, Whitwick (St. George, St. John), Wigston Magna, Willoughby Waterleys, Wing, Wistow and Newton Harcourt, Withcote, Witherly, Woodhouse Eaves, Wyfordby, Wymeswold, Wymondham.

Bishop's Transcripts
There are some transcripts available for every parish in the old county of Leicestershire. (Those for the old county of Rutland are in the Northamptonshire CRO, but copies are in the Leicestershire CRO.) Coverage is not very good as there is very little recorded before 1700 or after 1812.

Nonconformist Registers
These are available for a good many areas of the county. Most include baptisms or births, some have marriages as well, and only a few record deaths or burials.
Baptist: Arnesby, Barrowden, Blaby, Castle Donington, Diseworth, Fleckney, Hinckley, Kegworth, Kilby, Leicester (4 chapels), Long Whatton, Loughborough, Market Harborough, Morcott, Oakham, Quorndon, Rothley, Shepshed, Sileby, Syston, Thurlaston, Woodhouse Eaves.
Congregational: Bardon Park, Caldecott, Great Easton, Kibworth, Leicester, Wigston Magna, Wymondham.
Independent: Ashby-de-la-Zouch, Earl Shilton, Hinckley, Ketton, Kibworth, Leicester (3 chapels), Loughborough, Lutterworth, Market Bosworth, Market Harborough, Melton Mowbray, Newton Burgoland, Oakham, Sheepy Magna, Ullesthorpe, Uppingham, Wigston Magna.
Presbyterian: Ashby-de-la-Zouch, Bardon Park, Hinckley, Leicester, Loughborough, Mountsorrel, Narborough, Wigston Magna.
Methodist: Leicester, Oakham.
Wesleyan Methodist: Anstey, Ashby-de-la-Zouch, Burbage, Castle Donington, Claybrooke, Great Glen, Griffydam, Hinckley, Leicester, Loughborough, Market Harborough, Medbourne, Melton Mowbray, Mountsorrel, Sileby, Syston.
Primitive Methodist: Coleorton, Hinckley, Ibstock, Leicester, Loughborough, Melton Mowbray, Whitwick.
United Methodist: Charley, Kegworth, Loughborough, Quorndon.

Society of Friends (Quakers): Branston, Hinckley, Leicester, Old Dalby.
Roman Catholic: Hinckley, Leicester.
Dissenters (not specified): Ashby-de-la-Zouch, Foxton (entered in the parish registers of these two places).
New Jerusalemites: Loughborough.

Census Returns
Microfilm copies of these for the period 1841-71 are held in the CRO. They are indexed by parish.

Wills
Probate records from 1494 to 1941 are held in the CRO. They are indexed in one form or another for the whole period.

Marriage Licences and Bonds
Those held in the CRO cover the period 1570-1891.

Miscellaneous
These include early directories; quarter sessions records, 1675-1974; education records dating from the 1870s; and many family collections from the oldest families in Leicestershire and Rutland (except for the collections of the Duke of Rutland, which remain in his possession).

Lincoln

Family History Society
(See page 89 for remarks concerning Family History Societies.)

Spalding Gentlemen's Society
N. Simson, The Museum, Spalding. (In spite of the name, this is an Historical Society!)

County Record Office
The Castle, Lincoln, Lincolnshire LN1 3AB. (Open Monday-Friday, 0930-1645 hours.)
  The office will make a short search in a specific area for an overseas inquirer, but will charge a fee for this—check with the CRO for the exact amount. Longer searches will also be undertaken for a quoted fee after the nature of the search is known.

Parish Registers

Addlethorpe, Aisthorpe, Alford, Algarkirk, Allington, Althorpe, Alvingham, Amcotts, Anderby, Anwick, Apley, Asgarby by Spilsby, Ashby by Partney, Ashby de la Launde, Ashby West, Aslackby, Asterby, Aswarby, Aswardby, Aubourn with Haddington, Aunsby, Authorpe, Aylesby, Bardney, Barkston, Barkwith East, Barkwith West, Barlings, Barnetby, Barnoldby le Beck, Barrow on Humber, Barton on Humber (St. Peter), Bassingham, Baston, Baumber, Beckingham, Beesby, Belton by Grantham, Benington in Holland, Bennington (Long) with Foston, Benniworth, Bicker, Bigby, Billingborough, Bilsby, Binbrook (St. Gabriel, St. Mary), Biscathorpe, Blyton, Bolingbroke, Bonby, Boothby Graffoe, Bottesford, Boultham, Bourne, Braceborough, Bracebridge, Braceby, Bradley, Branston, Brattleby, Brauncewell, Brigg, Brigsley, Brinkhill, Brocklesbury, Broxholme, Bucknall, Burgh on Bain, Burton by Lincoln, Buslingthorpe, Butterwick (West), Cadney, Caenby, Caistor, Cammeringham, Candlesby, Canwick, Careby, Carlby, Carlton (Castle), Carlton (South), Carlton le Moorland, Carlton Scroop, Cawkwell, Caythorpe, Chapel St. Leonard, Claxby by Alford, Claxby by Normanby, Claxby Pluckacre, Clee, Cleethorpes (St. Peter), Clixby, Coates (Great), Coates (North), Coates by Stow, Cockerington (North), Coleby, Corby Glen, Corringham, Covenham (St. Bartholomew, St. Mary), Cowbit, Cranwell, Creeton, Crowland, Crowle, Croxby, Croxton, Cumberworth, Cuxwold, Dalby, Dalderby, Deeping West, Dembleby, Denton, Digby, Doddington (Pigot), Donington in Holland, Donington on Bain, Dorrington, Dunston, Eagle, Eastville, Edenham, Edlington, Elkington (North), Elkington (South), Elsham, Enderby (Bag), Enderby (Mavis), Enderby (Wood), Evedon, Ewerby, Faldingworth, Farforth with Maidenwell, Farlesthorpe, Fenton, Fillingham, Firsby, Fishtoft, Fiskerton, Folkingham, Fosdyke, Foston, Fotherby, Frampton, Friesthorpe, Friskney, Frithville, Frodingham, Fulbeck, Fulstow, Gainsborough, Gautby, Gayton le Marsh, Gayton le Wold, Gedney, Gedney Hill, Glentham, Glentworth, Goltho with Bullingham, Gosberton, Goulceby, Goxhill, Grainthorpe, Grasby, Greatford (with Willsthorpe), Greetwell, Grimoldby, Grimsby (Great), Grimsby (Little), Grimsby (St. Barnabas), Gunby (St. Nicholas), Hacconby, Haceby, Hackthorn, Hagnaby, Hagworthingham, Hainton, Hale (Great), Haltham on Bain, Halton (West), Halton Holegate, Hameringham, Hannah with Hagnaby, Hanworth (Potter), Hareby, Harlaxton, Harmston, Harpswell, Harrington, Hatton, Haugham, Hawerby with Beesby, Haxey, Healing, Heapham, Heckington, Hemingby, Hemswell, Heydour,

Hibaldstow, Hogsthorpe, Holbeach, Holton Beckering, Holton le Moor, Holywell, Honington, Horbling, Horsington, Howsham, Humberton, Hundleby, Huttoft, Hykeham (North and South), Immingham, Ingham, Ingoldmells, Ingoldsby, Irby on Humber, Irnham, Keddington, Keelby, Kelsey (North), Kelsey (South—St. Mary, St. Nicholas), Kelstern with Calcethorpe, Kettlethorpe, Kingerby, Kirkby (East), Kirkby on Bain, Kirkby Underwood, Kirkby with Osgodby, Kirmington, Kirmond le Mire, Kirton in Holland, Kirton Lindsey, Kyme (South), Laceby, Langton by Horncastle, Langton by Partney, Langton by Wragby, Laughton, Leasingham with Roxholme, Lenton (or Lavington), Leverton, Limber (Great), Lincoln (16 parishes), Lissington, Louth (Holy Trinity, St. James, St. Michael), Ludborough, Luddington, Ludford, Lusby, Lutton, Mablethorpe, Maltby le Marsh, Markby, Marshchapel, Martin by Horncastle, Marton, Melton Ross, Messingham, Metheringham, Midville, Miningsby, Minting, Moorby, Morton by Bourne, Moulton, Mumby, Navenby, Nettleham, Nettleton, Newton (Wold), Newton by Folkingham, Newton by Toft, Newton on Trent, Nocton, Normanby by Spital, Normanby le Wold, Normanton, Norton (Bishop), Ormsby (North), Osbournby, Owersby, Owmby by Spital, Owston Ferry, Oxcombe, Partney, Pickworth, Pilham, Ponton (Great and Little), Quadring, Quarrington, Raithby with Hallington and Maltby, Raithby by Spilsby, Ranby, Rand, Rasen (Middle and West), Rauceby (North and South), Redbourne, Reepham, Reston (North and South), Revesby, Riby, Rigsby, Riseholme, Rothwell, Roughton, Rowston, Ruckland, Ruskington, Saleby, Saltfleet (All Saints, St. Clement, St. Peter), Sausthorpe, Saxby by Owmby, Saxilby, Scamblesby, Scampton, Scarle (North), Scartho, Scothern, Scotter, Scremby, Scrivelsby with Dalderby, Searby, Sedgebrook, Sempringham, Sibsey, Sixhills, Skegness (St. Clement, St. Matthew), Skellingthorpe, Skendleby, Skidbrook, Skillington, Skinnand, Sleaford (New), Snarford, Snelland, Snitterby, Somercotes (North), Somersby, Sotby, Spanby, Spilsby, Spittlegate, Spridlington, Springthorpe, Stainby, Stainfield, Stainton (Market), Stainton by Langworth, Stallingborough, Stapleford, Steeping (Little), Stenigot, Stewton, Stickford, Stixwould, Stoke Rochford with Easton, Stow St. Mary, Stragglethorpe, Strubby, Sturton (Great), Sudbrooke, Sutterby, Sutterton, Sutton Bridge (or St. Matthew), Sutton in the Marsh, Swallow, Swarby, Swaton, Swayfield, Swinderby, Swineshead, Swinhope, Swinstead, Syston, Tathwell, Tattershall, Tealby, Temple Bruer, Tetford, Theddlethorpe (All Saints, St. Helen), Thimbleby, Thoresway, Thorganby, Thornton by Horncastle, Thornton Curtis, Thornton le Moor,

Thorpe on the Hill, Threckingham, Thurlby by Bourne, Toft next Newton, Torksey, Torrington (East), Torrington le Moor, Torrington West, Tothill, Trusthorpe, Uffington, Ulceby (nr. Grimsby), Usselby, Utterby, Waddingham, Waddington, Waddingworth, Wainfleet (All Saints), Wainfleet (St. Mary), Walcot by Folkingham, Walesby, Waltham, Welby, Well, Wellingore, Welton by Lincoln, Welton le Wold, Westborough, Weston, Whaplode, Whaplode Drove, Wickenby, Wilksby, Willingham, Willingham (Cherry), Willingham by Stow, Willoughby (Scot), Willoughby (Silk), Willoughby in the Marsh, Wilsford, Winthorpe, Wispington, Witham, Withcall, Withern, Woodhall (Old), Woolsthorpe, Wootton, Worlaby by Brigg, Worlaby by Louth, Wrangle, Wrawby by Brigg, Wyberton, Wyham cum Cadeby, Wyville, Yarborough.

Nonconformist Registers

A large number of Methodist baptismal and marriage registers have now been deposited. Most date from the mid-nineteenth century, although there are a few of earlier date. In the beginning there was usually a baptismal register for each circuit, but gradually individual chapels started their own registers. Although several chapels were licensed for marriages, only a few unofficial "registers" survive for the period before 1900. Many registers covering the period up to the present decade are also in the CRO, but only the early ones are listed here:

Barton on Humber, Caistor and Laceby, Cleethorpes, Epworth, Gainsborough, Goxhill, Grantham, Grimsby, Gringley on the Hill (Notts), Holton le Clay, Horncastle, Kirton End, Lincoln, Louth, Market Rasen, Messingham, Saltfleet, Sleaford, Spilsby, Ulceby, Wainfleet, Waltham, and the Boston, Grimsby, Lincoln, and Scunthorpe Circuit, and the Coningsby, Lincoln North, and Scunthorpe Circuit.

It is important to remember that the chapels in many of the above places also served nearby villages, so check your map!

Bishop's Transcripts

These are in the CRO and are divided into two series: 1562 to 1812 and 1813 to the 1830s. Not all parishes still exist and there are many gaps in the others.

Mormon Computer File Index

Baptismal entries, plus a certain number of marriages, are indexed on microfilm.

Wills

To find a Lincolnshire will or administration there are printed lists from 1320 to 1652, a typescript index for 1660-1700, and manuscript indexes up to 1857. Wills from that time up to 1874 are in the District Probate Registry and are indexed. Administrations are in the CRO, with many Inventories attached, and these, too, are indexed.

Marriage Licences

A full transcript of Marriage Licences and Bonds from 1574 to 1846 is available in the CRO, together with registers of Marriage Licences from 1837 to 1954.

Miscellaneous

Other records in the Lincoln CRO include civil records of several areas; a large library containing a great number of genealogical works, including parish registers; voters' lists (Lindsey, 1832 to this date, and Kesteven, 1832-65); family pedigrees; and school records.

London

Family History Societies

There are five Family History Societies covering this area:
Central Middlesex
North Middlesex
West Middlesex
Waltham Forest
East London
(See page 89 for remarks concerning Family History Societies.)

Record Offices

Greater London Record Office, 40 Northampton Road, Clerkenwell, London EC1. This office holds a great many records of all kinds relating to Greater London, which includes within its area territory which was at one time in Essex, Kent, Surrey, and Middlesex. Regrettably, the Head Archivist is not prepared to provide any information about the holdings. No searches will be made for postal inquirers, however specific. No information will be given from the records. I suggest, therefore, that you write directly to Miss J. Coburn, Head Archivist, at the above address and see what information you can abstract. I believe that personal callers are better treated, but cannot guarantee this.

Historical Societies

There are many local historical societies scattered across Greater London. It is not possible to list all their addresses, but you should be able to obtain the address of a particular one by writing to the Public Library in the district—that address will be sufficient. The Historical Societies of which I am aware are:

Barking, Barnes, Barnet, Beddington and Carshalton, Bexley, Brentford and Chiswick, Camden, Chingford, City of London, Clapham, Ealing, East London, Edmonton, Enfield, Fulham, Greenwich and Lewisham, Hammersmith, Hampton Hill, Harpenden, Hatch End and Pinner, Hayes and Harlington, Hendon, Holborn, Hornsey, Hounslow, Islington, Kensington, Kingston-upon-Thames, Lamorbey and Sidcup, Lewisham, Merton and Morden, Mill Hill and Hendon, Norbury, Northolt, Orpington, Paddington, Romford, Ruislip and Northwood, St. Marylebone, St. Pancras, Southall, Stanmore, Edgware and Harrow, Sunbury and Shepperton, Surbiton, Twickenham, Upminster, Uxbridge, Walthamstow, Wandsworth, Wanstead, Wembley, West Drayton.

Two things for you to remember:

1. These are *historical* societies and not genealogical. Usually such societies have a committee or a group interested in genealogy, but this is not always the case.

2. Be sure you enclose two International Reply Coupons and a self-addressed airmail envelope; otherwise you will not get a reply.

A final word: a superb source of information about the *City* of London and, to a lesser degree, other parts of the county is the Guildhall Library, Aldermanbury (see page 63).

Merseyside

This new county consists of Liverpool, Bootle, Southport, and St. Helen's, plus parts of Lancashire and Cheshire. There is no County Record Office, and records are held in the individual cities, and in the County Record Offices of Cheshire and Lancashire.

Family History Societies
There are five Family History Societies serving the new county of Merseyside:
Liverpool
Cheshire
North Cheshire
Manchester and Lancashire
Rossendale
(See page 89 concerning Family History Societies.)

Liverpool Record Office
William Brown Street, Liverpool L3 8EW. Its holdings include the following:

Parish Registers
There are the registers of nearly eighty local parishes in the Record Office.

Nonconformist Registers
These are mainly Methodist and date from 1837 onwards. There are also some Quaker and Jewish registers. A fairly recent development is that the Catholic Archbishop of Liverpool has instructed the Catholic clergy to deposit their pre-1900 registers in the Record Office, and this is now being done.

Miscellaneous
The holdings of the LRO also include cemetery records from 1825; apprentice books; workhouse records; early newspapers from 1756; directories from 1766; probate indexes; many manorial and family records; census returns from 1841; and poll books.

Norfolk

Family History Society
(See page 89 for remarks concerning Family History Societies.)

County Record Office
Central Library, Norwich, Norfolk NR2 1NJ. (Open Monday to Friday, 0900-1700 hours; Saturday, 0900-1200 hours. Special arrangements can be made for not more than three documents to be made available for use in the Central Library when it is open and the CRO is closed.)

The office will undertake short, specific searches for a small fee; those needing longer searches will be referred to a list of record agents.

Parish Registers

Alburgh, Aldborough, Alderford, Alpington, Antingham, Arminghall, Ashby St. Mary, Ashby with Oby, Ashmanhaugh, Ashwellthorpe, Attleborough, Attlebridge, Aylmerton, Baconsthorpe, Bacton, Banningham, Barford, Barmer, Barnham Broom, Barningham (North), Barsham (North and East), Barton Bendish (St. Andrew), Barton Bendish (St. Mary), Barton Turf, Bawburgh, Bawdeswell, Baythorpe, Bedingham, Beechamwell, Beeston next Mileham, Beeston Regis, Beeston St. Lawrence, Beetley, Beighton, Belaugh, Bessingham, Besthorpe, Bexwell, Billingford, Billockby, Bilney (East), Bintry, Bircham (Great, Newton, and Tofts), Bixley, Blickling, Blofield, Blo Norton, Bodham, Bodney, Booton, Boughton (Ely), Bracon Ash, Bradenham (East and West), Bradfield, Bramerton, Brampton, Brancaster, Brandiston, Braydeston, Bressingham, Bridgham, Briston, Broome, Brundall, Brunstead, Buckenham (St. Nicholas and Old), Burgh next Aylsham, Burgh St. Margaret, Burlingham (St. Andrew and St.Edmund), Burlingham St. Peter, Burnham Deepdale, Burnham Norton, Burston, Buxton, Bylaugh, Caistor-on-Sea, Caistor St. Edmund, Cantley, Carbrooke, Carleton (East, Forehoe, Rode), Carleton St. Peter, Castle Rising, Caston, Catton, Cawston, Cley, Clippesby, Cockley Cley, Colby, Colton, Corpusty, Costessey, Coston, Cranwich, Cranworth, Cressingham (Great and Little), Crimplesham (Ely), Cringleford, Crostwick, Crostwight, Crownthorpe, Croxton, Denton, Denver, Dereham (East and West), Didlington, Dilham, Diss, Ditchingham, Downham Market, Dunston, Dunton, Earlham, Easton, Eaton, Eccles, Edgefield, Edingthorpe, Elmham (North), Elsing, Felbrigg, Felmingham, Felthorpe, Feltwell (St. Mary, St. Nicholas), Fersfield, Filby, Fincham (St. Martin, St. Michael), Fleggburgh, Flordon, Fordham, Forncett St. Mary, Forncett St. Peter, Foulden, Foxley, Framingham Earl, Freethorpe, Frettenham, Fritton, Fundenhall, Garboldisham, Garveston, Gateley, Gayton, Gayton Thorpe, Gimingham, Gissing, Gooderstone, Gresham, Griston, Guestwick, Guist, Gunton, Hackford, Halvergate, Hanworth, Hapton, Hardingham, Hardwick, Hargham, Harleston, Harling (East and West), Hassingham, Haveringland, Haynford, Hedenham, Heigham (St. Bartholomew, St. Philip), Helhoughton, Hellington, Hemblington, Hempnall, Hempstead by Holt, Hempstead with Eccles, Hethel, Hethersett, Hevingham, Heydon, Hickling, Hilborough, Hilgay, Hockering, Hockwold, Hoe, Holme Hale, Holt, Honing, Honingham, Horsey, Houghton next Harpley, Hoveton St. John, Hoveton St. Peter, Hunstanton, Hunworth, Ickburgh, Intwood with Keswick, Irstead, Itteringham, Kenninghall, Ketteringham, Kimberley, Knapton, Lakenham, Lammas (Little Hautbois), Langford, Larling, Lessingham, Lexham (East), Limpenhoe, Lingwood, Lopham (North and South), Lyng, Lynn (St. Margaret, St. Nicholas), Lynn (West), Marlingford, Marsham, Matlaske, Mautby, Melton (Little), Methwold, Metton, Mileham, Morley St. Botolph, Morley St. Peter, Morningthorpe, Morton on the Hill, Moulton St. Mary, Mundesley, Mundford, Neatishead, Necton, Needham, Newton by Castle Acre, Newton Flotman, Northwold, Norwich (32 parishes), Oby, Oulton, Oxborough, Oxnead, Panxworth, Paston, Plumstead (Great and Little), Plumstead by Holt, Poringland, Postwick, Quidenham, Ranworth, Raynham (East, South, West), Redenhall with Harleston, Reedham, Reepham with Kerdiston, Ridlington, Ringland, Rockland All Saints, Rockland St. Mary, Rockland St. Peter, Rollesby, Roudham, Roughton, Rudham (East and West), Runcton (North), Runhall, Runham, Runton, Rushall, Ruston (East), Salle, Salthouse, Saxlingham Nethergate and Thorpe, Saxthorpe, Scarning, Sco Ruston, Scottow, Scoulton, Sculthorpe, Shelfanger, Shelton, Shimpling, Shingham, Shipdam, Shotesham (All Saints, St. Mary with St. Martin), Shouldham, Shouldham Thorpe, Shropham, Skeyton, Sloley, Smallburgh, Snetterton, Snettisham, Snoring (Great and Little), Southacre, Southburgh, Southery, South Walsham (St. Lawrence, St. Mary), Southwood, Sparham, Sprowston (St. Mary and Margaret, St. Cuthbert), Stalham, Stanfield, Stanford, Stanhoe with Barwick, Starston, Stoke Holy Cross, Stokesby with Herringby, Stow Bardolph, Stradsett, Stratton St. Mary, Stratton St. Michael (with St. Peter), Stratton Strawless, Strumpshaw, Suffield, Sustead, Swafield, Swainsthorpe, Swannington, Swanton Abbot, Swardeston, Syderstone, Tacolneston, Tasburgh, Tatterford, Tattersett, Taverham, Themelthorpe, Thetford (St. Cuthbert, St. Mary, St. Peter), Thompson, Thorpe Abbotts, Thorpe Episcopi (next Norwich), Thorpe Hamlet (St. Leonard, St. Matthew), Thorpe Market, Threxton, Thrigby, Thurgarton, Thurne with Ashby and Oby, Thuxton, Tilney All Saints, Titchwell, Tittleshall with Godwick, Tivetshall St. Margaret, Tivetshall St. Mary, Tofts (West), Topcroft, Tottington, Trimingham, Trowse, Trunch, Tuddenham (East), Tuddenham (North), Tunstall, Tunstead, Tuttington, Twyford, Upton, Walton West, Weasenham (All Saints, St. Peter), Weeting, Wellingham, Wereham, Westacre, Weston Longville, Whitwell, Wickhampton,

Wicklewood, Wilby, Wilton, Winch (West), Winfarthing, Witch-ingham (Great), Witchingham (Little), Witton by Blofield, Witton by North Walsham, Woodbastwick, Wood Dalling, Wood Norton, Wood Rising, Woodton, Worstead, Wramplingham, Wreningham, Wroxham, Wymondham, Yarmouth (Great)(St. Nicholas), Yax-ham, Yelverton with Alpington.

The following registers in Suffolk are also in the CRO:
Barnby, Blundeston with Flixton, Carlton Colville, Cove (North), Fritton, Gisleham, Gunton, Kessingland, Kirkley, Lound, Lowes-toft (St. John), Mutford, Rushmere.

Nonconformist Registers
Some microfilm copies are held of the Norfolk registers in the PRO, plus a few later original registers.

Transcripts
In Norfolk there are two types of trancripts, Archdeacon's and Bishop's. Before 1812, transcripts were sent by the parishes to the Archdeacons for six years out of every seven, the seventh being a Bishop's Visitation year. From 1813 all returns were made to the Bishop. The two series run from 1600 to 1838, with gaps, and are in the CRO.

Marriage Licences
Many of these are in the CRO at intermittent intervals over a period from 1557 to 1915.

Nonconformist Registers
There are a few copies of registers lodged with the Public Record Office in London in 1837, plus a few originals acquired since then by the CRO. There are records of Quaker Meetings for Norfolk and Norwich from 1613 to 1836, and for Cambridge and Huntingdon from 1631 to 1837.

Wills
The CRO holds wills of the Norwich Consistory Court from 1370 to 1857 with some gaps. They are indexed. Wills proved from 1857 to 1941 are also indexed and in the CRO. There are very good records, too, of administrations and inventories from the early sixteenth century.

Census Returns
There is a microfilm copy of the 1851 return for Norwich.

Land Tax

The CRO holds land tax returns on a parish basis (with some missing) for the period 1767-1832.

Deeds and Manorial Records

If you know the parish from which your ancestor came, these records may be useful in providing additional information.

Other Records

The CRO has registers of freemen of the city of Norwich from 1317 and of the city of Great Yarmouth from 1429. In order to engage in trade it was necessary to be a freeman, and to be a freeman it was necessary to be the son of a freeman. If this strikes you as rather restrictive, you are not alone!

There are also voters' lists from 1830, poll books from 1702, and directories for Norfolk from 1836, Norwich from 1783, Great Yarmouth from 1863, and King's Lynn from 1846.

Northamptonshire

Family History Society

(See page 89 for remarks concerning Family History Societies.)

County Record Office

Delapré Abbey, Northampton NN4 9AW. (Open Monday, Tuesday, Wednesday, Friday, 0915-1300 hours and 1400-1645 hours; Thursday, 0915-1300 hours and 1400-1945 hours; Saturday, 0900-1215 hours.)

Postal inquiries are answered as to types of records available, but research is not undertaken. If possible, specific questions will be answered as time permits. Inquiries as to the existence of registers will be answered. An inquiry as to the existence of a will can also be answered, provided the period in which the will may have been proved is narrowed down to a few years. The reason for the latter restriction is that there is no alphabetical index to the wills except for a brief period (1510- 1652). Otherwise, names of researchers familiar with the office and its records will be supplied. A fee will be charged, but this is a direct matter between the inquirer and the researcher.

Parish Registers

Abington, Abthorpe, Addington (Great and Little), Alderton, Apethorpe, Arthingworth, Ashby St. Ledgers, Ashley, Ashton, Aynho, Badby, Barnack, Benefield, Billing (Great and Little), Blakesley, Blatherwycke, Boddington, Boughton, Bozeat, Brackley, Bradden, Brafield, Brampton Ash, Braunston, Braybrooke, Brington, Brixworth, Brockhall, Broughton, Bulwick, Burton Latimer, Byfield, Caldecote, Canons Ashby, Carlton (East), Castor, Catesby, Chacombe, Charwelton, Chelveston, Chipping Warden, Church Brampton, Clapton, Clay Coton, Clipston, Cogenhoe, Cold Ashby, Cold Higham, Collingtree, Corby, Corby (Sts. Peter and Andrew), Cosgrove, Cotterstock, Cottingham, Courteenhall, Cranford (St. Andrew and St. John), Cransley, Creaton, Crick, Culworth, Dallington, Daventry, Deanshanger, Deene, Denford, Denton, Desborough, Dingley, Dodford, Draughton, Duddington, Duston, Earls Barton, Easton Maudit, Easton Neston, Easton on the Hill, Ecton, Edgcote, Etton, Evenley, Everdon, Eydon, Eye, Farndon (East), Farthinghoe, Fawsley, Faxton, Flore, Fotherinhay, Furtho, Glapthorne, Glendon, Glinton, Grafton Regis, Grafton Underwood, Greatworth, Grendon, Gretton, Guilsborough, Gunton, Haddon (East), Haddon (West), Hannington, Hardingstone, Hardwick, Hargrave, Harlestone, Harpole, Harrington, Harringworth, Harrowden (Great and Little), Hartwell, Haselbeech, Hellidon, Helmdon, Helpston, Hemington, Heyford, Higham Ferrers, Hinton, Holcot, Holdenby, Horton, Houghton (Great), Houghton (Little), Irchester, Irthlingborough, Isham, Islip, Kelmarsh, Kettering, Kilsby, Kingscliffe, Kings Sutton, Kislingbury, Lamport, Laxton, Lilbourne, Little Houghton, Loddington, Long Buckby, Lowick, Luddington, Maidwell, Marholm, Marston St. Lawrence, Marston Trussell, Maxey, Mears Ashby, Middleton Cheney, Milton Malsor, Moreton Pinkney, Moulton, Naseby, Nassington, Newnham, Newton Bromswold, Northampton (All Saints, Christ Church, Far Cotton St. Mary, St. Edmund, St. Giles, St. Katharine, St. Peter, St. Sepulchre), Northborough, Norton, Oakley (Great and Little), Old, Orlingbury, Orton, Oundle, Overstone, Oxendon (Great), Passenham, Paston, Pattishall, Paulerspury, Peakirk, Peterborough (St. Barnabas, St. John, St. Mark, St. Mary, St. Paul), Piddington, Pitsford, Plumpton, Polebrook, Potterspury, Preston Capes, Preston Deanery, Pytchley, Quinton, Radstone, Raunds, Ravensthorpe, Ringstead, Roade, Rockingham, Rothersthorpe, Rothwell, Rushden, Rushton, Scaldwell, Sibbertoft, Silverstone, Slapton, Slipton, Southwick, Spratton, Stanwick, Steane, Stoke Albany, Stoke

Bruerne, Stoke Doyle, Stowe Nine Churches, Strixton, Sudborough, Sulgrave, Sutton, Sywell, Tansor, Thenford, Thornhaugh, Thorpe Malsor, Thorpe Mandeville, Thrapstone, Titchmarsh, Towcester, Twywell, Ufford, Upton (Northampton), Upton (Peterborough), Wadenhoe, Wakerley, Walgrave, Wansford, Wappenham, Warkton, Warkworth, Warmington, Watford, Weedon Bec, Weedon Lois, Weldon, Welford, Wellingborough, Welton, Weston by Welland, Weston Favell, Whittlebury, Wicken, Wilbarston, Wilby, Winwick, Wittering, Wollaston, Woodford (Thrapston), Woodford Halse, Wood Newton, Wootton, Yardley Hastings, Yarwell, Yelvertoft.

Nonconformist Registers

Note: Methodist Circuit Registers usually cover the surrounding villages as well as the town on which the circuit was based.

Baptist: Aldwinckle, Blisworth, Braunston, Burton Latimer, Desborough, Earls Barton, Gretton, Grimscote, Hackleton, Haddon (West), Kettering (Carey), Kettering (Fuller), Kings Sutton, Kislingbury, Middleton Cheney, Northampton, Ravensthorpe, Ringstead, Roade, Thrapston, Towcester, Weedon Lois, and Weston.

Congregational: Ashby St. Ledgers, Castor, Flore, Northampton (King's Head Lane, Primrose Hill, Victoria Road), Weldon, Welford, Wilbarston, Wollaston, Yelvertoft.

United Reformed: Brackley, Brigstock, Byfield, Creaton, Crick, Daventry, Kettering, Kilsby, Long Buckby, Newnham, Northampton (Castle Hill and Commercial Street), Old, Oundle, Peterborough, Potterspury and Yardley Gobion, Rothwell, Towcester, Weedon and Flore, Wellingborough, Yardley Hastings.

Moravian: Woodford Halse.

Quaker: Bugbrooke and Northampton Monthly Meeting, Wellingborough Monthly Meeting.

Methodist: Boughton, Brackley, Braunston, Brixworth, Crick, Daventry, Denford, Desborough, Eye, Finedon, Glinton, Helpston, Higham Ferrers, Kettering (Bath Road and Rockingham Road), Kettering Circuit, Newborough, Northampton (Circuit), Northampton (Gold St., Grafton St., Horsemarket, Kingsley Park, Queen's Road, Regent Square, Scarletwell St.), Peterborough (Circuit), Peterborough (Boroughbury, Cobden St., Midland Road, Newark, New Road, Stanground, Wesley Hall and Hampden Road, Wentworth St.), Raunds, Raunds (Circuit), Rushton, Silverstone, Towcester (Circuit), Wellingborough (Circuit), Welton (Circuit), Yaxley.

Unitarian: Northampton.

Bishop's Transcripts

For this diocese, Bishop's Transcripts survive only from the early eighteenth century and usually end between 1860 and 1880.

Wills

The diocese is divided into two for probate purposes:
    North:Peterborough Consistory Court
    South:Northampton Archdeaconry Court
Wills are in the custody of the CRO and are indexed.

Miscellaneous Documents

These date back to 1100 and cover all aspects of the life of the county and of the people living in it: charters, rolls, deeds, letters, diaries, files, minutes, ledgers, accounts, maps, inventories, etc. There are General Card Indexes of subjects, places, and persons containing over 250,000 entries.

The CRO also has maps, guides, and various booklets on sale, and a list of these will be sent on request.

Census Returns

The CRO holds the following microfilms:
    1851:The whole of Northamptonshire and the Soke of Peterborough.
    1861:Northampton registration district only.
    1871:The same as 1851.

Directories

The earliest is 1784 but the entries (which are very brief) only cover Daventry, Kettering, Northampton, Peterborough, Thrapston, Towcester, and Wellingborough.

Marriage Licences

There are some in the custody of the CRO.

Northumberland

Family History Society

(See page 89 for remarks concerning Family History Societies.)

County Record Office

Melton Park, North Gosforth, Newcastle-upon-Tyne NE3 5QX. (Open Monday, 0900-2100 hours; Tuesday-Thursday, 0900-1700 hours; Friday, 0900-1630 hours.)

The office will search its records for a fee of about $10 per thirty minutes. For more complicated or protracted searches you will be referred to a list of local researchers.

Parish Registers

The following, together with copies, constitute practically one hundred per cent of the county parish registers:

Allendale (St. Cuthbert, St. Peter), Alnham, Alnwick, Alston, Alwinton, Amble, Ancroft and Haggerston Castle, Ashington, Bamburgh, Beadnell, Bedlington, Belford, Bellingham, Benwell (St. Aidan, St. James), Berwick-upon-Tweed, Birtley, Blanchland, Blyth (St. Cuthbert, St. Mary), Bolam, Branxton, Byrness, Bywell (St. Andrew, St. Peter), Cambo, Cambois, Carham, Chatton, Chevington, Chillingham, Chollerton, Corbridge, Cornhill, Corsenside, Cramlington, Cullercoats, Dinnington, Doddington, Earsdon, Edlingham, Eglingham, Ellingham, Elsdon, Falstone, Felton, Ford, Garrigill, Gosforth, Greenhead, Greystead, Halton, Haltwhistle, Hartburn, Haydon Bridge, Hebburn, Heddon-on-the-Wall, Holy Island, Howick, Howick Panns, Humshaugh, Hunstanworth, Ilderton, Ingram, Jesmond, Killingworth, Kirkharle, Kirkhaugh, Kirknewton, Kirkwhelpington, Knarsdale, Kyloe, Lambley, Lesbury, Longbenton, Longframlington, Longhirst, Long Horsley, Longhoughton, Lowick, Matfen, Meldon, Mitford, Monkseaton, Morpeth, Nenthead, Netherwitton, Newbrough, Newcastle-upon-Tyne (22 parishes), Norham, North Shields, Ovingham, Ponteland, Rennington, Rock, Rothbury, St. John Lee, Scotswood, Scremerston, Seghill, Shilbottle (St. James), Shotley, Simonburn, Slaley, Stamfordham, Stannington, Sugley, Thorneyburn, Throckington, Tweedmouth, Tynemouth, Tynemouth (Christ Church), Ulgham, Walker, Wallsend (St. Luke), Warden, Wark, Whalton, Whittingham, Whittonstall, Whorlton, Widdrington, Willington, Wooler.

Bishop's Transcripts

These are held in the Department of Palaeography and Diplomatic, University of Durham, Durham.

Census Returns

Copies of the returns for the available years are on microfilm in the CRO.

Nonconformists

The CRO holds few original registers, but transcripts or microfilms of the majority of the pre-1838 registers are available. Presbyterianism was particularly strong in the county and more information about individual churches, their subsequent history, and their records can be obtained from the United Reformed Church History Society, 86 Tavistock Place, London WC.

Wills

Up to 1858, wills were proved in the church court for the area in which the deceased held property, and before 1858, wills for the county (excluding Hexhamshire and Thockrington) will be found in the Department of Palaeography and Diplomatic, University of Durham, Durham. Wills (and Bishop's Transcripts) for the two peculiars mentioned are in the Borthwick Institute, Peasholme Green, York YO1 2PW.

The CRO has transcripts and abstracts of wills and administrations for part of the York diocese, including Hexhamshire, and for the Durham diocese, relating to the county of Northumberland, for the period 1500-1810, with indexes. In addition, the office has an original register of Hexham wills from 1694 to 1707.

For the period 1858-1941 the CRO holds copies of wills of persons dying in Northumberland and Newcastle-upon-Tyne.

Marriage Bonds

The originals from 1590 to 1815 are in the Department of Palaeography and Diplomatic, but the CRO holds microfilm copies.

Nominal Lists

The CRO holds manuscript and printed lists of people who lived in the county, but they are not complete. It should be noted that Bedlingtonshire, Norham, and Islandshire were in the county of Durham until 1844, so records of these areas may be in the Durham CRO, County Hall, Durham.

Tithes

The CRO holds this list of all owners and occupiers for the period 1840-50.

Monumental Inscriptions

There are lists of these copied from gravestones in churchyards and inscriptions in churches, but they are not complete.

Boyd's Marriage Index

This is an alphabetical index to marriages in seventy-three per cent of the parish churches in the county from 1538 to 1812. The original is held by the Society of Genealogists, but microfilm copies are in the CRO.

Land Tax Assessments

These cover the period 1748-1831 and list landowners and tenants within parishes.

Militia Returns

These run from 1762 to 1798, within parishes, and list men liable for military service. There are also muster rolls of the county volunteers for the Napoleonic Wars period.

Electoral Registers and Poll Books

These list persons voting, or able to vote, in local and parliamentary elections. The registers cover the period 1832-1974 and the books from 1698 to 1852.

Readdie's Marriage Index

This is an alphabetical index to all the marriage registers in North Northumberland from 1813 to 1837.

Other Records

These include Hearth Tax Returns (1664) and Protestation Returns for 1642 (Berwick and Morpeth only). The latter list all adult males who took an oath to defend the Protestant religion. There are also county directories from the early nineteenth century and many family trees and pedigrees of landed families. These are either in the CRO or in the Central Library, Newcastle-upon-Tyne.

Finally, there is the Mormon Index. This is an alphabetical list of names extracted from microfilmed copies of baptisms and marriages in the parish and Nonconformist churches in the county. It runs from the mid-1500s up to the mid-1800s. It must be emphasized that it is incomplete, as not all parishes and churches are included.

North Yorkshire

Family History Society

(See page 89 for remarks concerning Family History Societies.)

County Record Office

County Hall, Northallerton, North Yorkshire DL7 8AD. An appointment *must* be made before visiting the CRO—phone Northallerton (0609) 3123, ext. 455. (Open Monday-Thursday,

0900-1650 hours; Wednesday, 0900-2050 hours; Friday, 0900-1620 hours.)

The office will undertake genealogical searches for a fee, which should be negotiated directly.

Parish Registers

Ainderby Steeple, Aislaby, Aldborough (Boroughbridge), Aldfield, Allerston, Ampleforth, Appleton Wiske, Arkendale, Arkengarthdale, Arncliffe with Halton Gill, Askrigg, Aysgarth, Ayton (Great), Bagby, Baldersby, Barton (St. Cuthbert, St. Mary), Bedale, Bellerby, Bentham (High), Bilsdale, Bilton (Knaresborough), Birkby, Bishop Thornton, Bolton Abbey, Bolton cum Redmire, Bolton on Swale, Boroughbridge, Bransdale cum Farndale, Brignall, Brompton (Northallerton), Brompton by Sawdon, Broughton in Craven, Burneston, Burnsall, Burton in Lonsdale, Burton Leonard, Byland (Old), Carlton in Cleveland, Catterick, Chapel-le-Dale, Clapham, Cleasby, Cold Kirby, Consitone, Copgrove, Coverham, Cowthorpe, Cowton (East, North, South), Crakehall, Crathorne, Croft, Cropton, Cundall, Dacre, Danby, Danby Wiske, Deighton, Downholme, Dunsforth, Easby, Ebberston, Edstone, Egton, Ellerburn, Eryholme, Eskdaleside-cum-Ugglebarnby, Faceby, Farnham, Felixkirk, Finghall, Forcett, Fylingsdale, Gargrave, Giggleswick, Gilling (Richmond), Gilling (Ryedale), Glaisdale, Goathland, Goldsborough, Green Hammerton, Greenhow Hill, Grinton, Grosmont, Hampsthwaite, Hardraw, Harlsey (East), Harome, Hartwith, Hauxwell, Hawes, Hawnby, Hawsker, Helmsley, Hinderwell, Hipswell, Hornby, Horsehouse, Horton-in-Ribblesdale, Hubberholme, Hudswell, Hunsingore, Husthwaite, Hutton Bonville, Hutton Buscel, Hutton Magna, Hutton Rudby, Ingleby Arncliffe, Ingleby Greenhow, Ingleton, Kettlewell, Kilburn, Kildale, Kilvington (South), Kirby Fleetham, Kirby in Cleveland, Kirby Knowle, Kirby Malham, Kirby Malzeard, Kirby Misperton, Kirby Moorside, Kirby on the Moor, Kirby Ravensworth, Kirby Sigston, Kirby Wiske, Kirkdale, Kirk Deighton, Kirk Hammerton, Kirklington, Langton (Great), Lastingham, Leake, Leathley, Leeming, Levisham, Leyburn, Linton in Craven, Lockton, Long Preston, Lunds, Lythe, Manfield, Markington, Marrick, Marske in Swaledale, Marton cum Grafton, Marton in Craven, Masham, Melsonby, Middleham, Middlesmoor, Middleton (by Pickering), Middleton on Leven, Middleton Tyas, Muker, Newton upon Rawcliffe, Nidd, Normanby, Northallerton, Nun Monkton, Nunnington, Osmotherly, Oswaldkirk, Otterington (North and South), Ouseburn (Great and Little), Pateley Bridge, Patrick Brompton, Pickering, Pickhill, Ramsgill, Redmire, Richmond, Ripley, Ripon (Cathedral, Holy Trinity), Roecliffe, Rokeby, Rosedale, Rounton (East and West), Roxby, Ruswarp, Rylstone, Salton, Sandhutton and Carlton Miniott, Sawley, Scawton, Scruton, Seamer (near Stokesley), Sessay, Settle, Sharow, Silton (Over), Sinnington, Skelton cum Newby, Skipton in Craven (Christ Church, Holy Trinity), Skipton on Swale, Smeaton (Great), Snainton, Sneaton, Sowerby, Spennithorne, Spofforth, Stainley (South), Stainton in Cleveland (Chapel of Thornaby, St. Paul), Stallingbusk, Stanwick St. John, Staveley, Stokesley, Stonegrave, Tanfield (West), Thirkleby, Thirsk, Thormanby, Thornton Dale, Thornton in Craven, Thornton in Lonsdale, Thornton le Street, Thornton Steward, Thornton Watlass, Topcliffe, Wath, Welbury, Wensley, Westerdale, Whitby (Dunsley, St. Hilda, St. John, St. Mary, St. Michael, St. Ninian), Whixley, Whorlton in Cleveland, Winksley, Witton (East and West), Worsall, Wycliffe, Wykeham, Yafforth.

Other North Yorkshire parishes with records in the Borthwick Institute of Historical Research, Peasholme Green, York YO1 2PW, are:

Acaster Malbis, Acomb, Alne, Amotherby, Appleton le Street, Askham Bryan, Askham Richard, Barlby, Barton le Street, Bilborough, Bilton in Ainsty, Birdsall, Birkin, Bishopthorpe, Bolton Percy, Bossall, Brafferton, Brandsby, Brayton, Bulmer, Burythorpe, Buttercrambe, Carlton juxta Snaith, Cawood, Church Fenton, Copmanthorpe, Coxwold, Crambe, Crayke, Dalby, Drax, Dringhouses, Dunnington, Easingwold, Elvington, Escrick, Farlington, Foston, Fulford, Grimston (North), Haxby, Healaugh, Helmsley (Gate, Upper), Helperthorpe, Hemingbrough, Heslerton (West), Heslington, Holtby, Hovingham, Huntington, Husthwaite, Huttons Ambo, Kirby Grindalythe, Kirby Wharfe, Knapton, Langton, Malton (Old), Malton (St. Leonard, St. Michael), Marston (Long), Marton cum Moxby, Monk Fryston, Moor Monkton, Myton on Swale, Naburn, Newton Kyme, Newton upon Ouse, Norton, Ormesby, Osbaldwick, Overton, Poppleton (Nether), Raskelf, Riccall, Rillington, Rufforth, Ryther, Sandhutton, Saxton, Scampston, Scrayingham, Selby (Abbey, St. James), Settrington, Sherburn, Sherburn in Elmet, Sheriff Hutton, Shipton by Beningborough, Skelton (near York), Skipwith, Slingsby, Stillingfleet, Stillington, Stockton on the Forest, Strensall, Sutton on the Forest, Tadcaster, Terrington, Thorganby, Thormanby, Thorpe Bassett, Warthill, Weaverthorpe, Westow, Wharram le Street, Wharram

Percy, Wheldrake, Whenby, Whitwell on the Hill, Wigginton, Wighill, Wintringham, Wistow, Yedingham, York (27 parishes).

Other registers are in the custody of the Leeds Archives Department, Sheepscar, Leeds LS7 3AP:
Allerton Mauleverer, Arncliffe, Carlton in Craven, Denton, Pannal.

Other registers are in the Humberside CRO, County Hall, Beverley, HU17 9BA:
Butterwick, Cayton, Cloughton, Folkton, Foxholes, Ganton, Hackness, Harwood Dale, Hunmanby, Muston, Reighton, Scalby, Seamer (near Scarborough), Willerby.

Other registers are in the West Yorkshire CRO, Newstead Road, Wakefield, WF1 2DE:
Kirk Smeaton, Womersley.

Wills, Probate Records, Bishop's Transcripts
All of these records are in the Borthwick Institute (address above).

Census Returns
The CRO holds these for the county for 1851 on microfilm.

Deeds
The Register of Deeds for the period 1736-1970 is in the CRO.

Land Tax
These returns in the CRO are incomplete between 1719 and 1832, but complete for 1785.

Other Records in the CRO
Freeholders Register (1788); Poll Books (1807-35); Electoral Registers (1832-75); Quarter Sessions Records (1651-1833); Manor Court Rolls (1677 onwards); and an extraordinary collection of municipal records (freemen's lists, apprenticeships, muster rolls, etc.) and manorial court records.

Nottinghamshire

Family History Society
(See page 89 for remarks concerning Family History Societies.)

County Record Office

County House, High Pavement, Nottingham, Nottinghamshire NG1 1HR. (Open Monday, 0900-1645 hours; Tuesday, 0900-1915 hours; Wednesday and Thursday, 0900-1645 hours; Friday, 0900-1615 hours.)

Owing to the large number of genealogical inquiries received in the office, the staff are only able to undertake limited and specific searches of records. For lengthy searches inquiries will be referred to a list of local record agents.

Parish Registers

Adbolton, Alverton, Annesley, Annesley Woodhouse, Arnold, Askham, Aslockton, Aspley, Attenborough, Auckley, Austerfield, Averham, Awsworth, Babbington Moor, Bagthorpe, Balderton, Barnby in the Willows, Barnby Moor, Barnstone, Barton in Fabis, Basford, Basingfield, Bathley, Bawtry, Beckingham, Beesthorpe, Beeston, Belle Eau Park, Bellhouse Grange, Besthorpe, Bestwood Park, Bevercotes, Bilborough, Bilby, Bilhaugh, Bilsthorpe, Bingham, Bleasby, Blidworth, Blyth, Bole, Bolham, Bothamsall, Boughton, Bradmore, Bramcote, Brinsley, Broadholme, Broughton Sulney, Broxtowe, Budby, Bulcote, Bulwell, Bunny cum Bradmore, Calverton, Carburton, Car Colston, Carlton, Carlton in Lindrick, Carlton on Trent, Carrington, Caunton, Caythorpe, Chilwell, Cinderhill, Clayworth, Clifton, Clipston, Clipstone, Clumber, Coates, Coddington, Colston Bassett, Colwick, Cossall, Costock, Cotgrave, Cotham, Cotmoor, Cottam, Cromwell, Cropwell Bishop, Cropwell Butler, Cuckney, Dallington, Darlton, Daybrook, Dunham, Eakring, East Bridgford, East Drayton, Easthorpe, East Leake, East Markham, East Stoke, Eastwood, Eaton, Edingley, Edwalton, Edwinstowe, Egnanton, Elkesley, Elston, Elston Chapel, Elton, Epperstone, Everton, Farndon, Farnsfield, Felley, Fenton, Finningley, Fiskerton, Flawborough, Flawford, Fledborough cum Woodcoates, Flintham, Fulwood, Gamston (near Nottingham), Gamston (near Retford), Gateford, Girton, Glapton, Gleadthorpe, Gonalston, Gotham, Goverton, Granby, Grassthorpe, Greasley, Greaveslane, Grimston, Gunthorpe, Habblesthorpe, Haggonfield, Halam, Halloughton, Harby, Hardwick, Harwell, Harworth, Haughton, Hawksworth, Hawton, Haywood Oaks, Headon cum Upton, Hexgreave, Hickling, Hockerton, Hodsock, Holbeck, Holme, Holme Pierrepont, Hoveringham, Hucknall Huthwaite, Hucknall Torkard, Hyson Green, Kelham, Kersall, Keyworth, Kilton, Kilvington, Kimberley, Kingston on Soar, Kinoulton, Kirkby

Hardwick, Kirkby in Ashfield, Kirkby Woodhouse, Kirklington, Kirton, Knapthorpe, Kneesall, Lambley, Lamcote, Laneham, Langar, Langford, Langold, Laxton, Lenton, Linby, Lindhurst, Littleborough, Little Carlton, Little Drayton, Little Gringley, Littleworth, Lound, Lowdham, Mansfield (St. Lawrence, St. Peter), Mansfield Woodhouse, Manton, Maplebeck, Markham Clinton, Marnham, Martin, Mattersey, Meering, Milnthorpe, Milton, Misson, Misterton, Moorgate, Moorhouse, Moreton, Morton, Netherfield, Nether Langwith, Nettleworth, Newark (Christchurch, St. Leonard, St. Mary Magdalene), New Basford, New Radford, Newstead, Newthorpe, Newton, Normanton (near Southwell), Normanton in Elkesley, Normanton on Soar, Normanton on Trent, Normanton on the Wolds, Nornay, North Clifton, North Collingham, North Leverton, North Muskham, North Scarle, North Wheatley, North Wilford, Norton Cuckney, Norwell, Norwell Woodhouse, Nottingham (27 parishes), Nuthall, Oldcoates, Ollerton, Ompton, Ordsall, Osberton, Osmandthorpe, Ossington, Owthorpe, Oxton, Papplewick, Park Leys, Perlethorpe, Pleasley Hill, Plumtree, Radford (near Worksop), Radford All Souls, Radcliffe on Trent, Radford St. Michael, Radford St. Peter, Radley, Ragnall, Ranby, Ranskill, Ratcliffe, Rayton, Rempstone, Retford St. Saviour, Rolleston, Ruddington, Rufford, Salterford, Saundby, Saxondale, Scaftworth, Scarrington, Scofton, Screveton, Scrooby, Selston, Serlby, Shelford, Shelton, Shireoaks, Sibthorpe, Skegby, Skegby (Marnham), Sloswick, Sneinton (St. Christopher, St. Luke, St. Philip, St. Stephen), Sookholme, South Carlton, South Clifton, South Collingham, South Leverton, South Muskham, South Retford, South Scarle, South Wheatley, Spalford, Stanford on Soar, Stanton on the Wolds, Stapleford, Staunton, Staunton Chapel, Staythorpe, Stoke Bardolph, Stokeham, Strelley, Sturton le Steeple, Styrrup, Sutton, Sutton Bonington (St. Anne, St. Michael), Sutton cum Lound, Sutton in Ashfield, Sutton on Trent, Sutton Passeys, Swanston, Syerston, Teversal, Thoresby, Thorney, Thoroton, Thorpe next Newark, Thrumpton, Thrumpton on Ordsall, Thurgarton, Tilne, Tithby, Tollerton, Torworth, Toton, Treswell, Trowell, Tuxford, Underwood, Upper Broughton, Upton, Walesby, Walkeringham, Wallingwells, Warsop, Watnall, Welbeck, Welham, West Bridgford, West Burton, West Drayton, Westhorpe, West Leake, West Markham, Weston, West Retford, West Stockwith, West Thorpe, Widmerpool, Wigsley, Wilford, Willoughby, Willoughby in Walesby, Willoughby in the Wolds, Wimpton, Winthorpe, Wiseton, Wiverton, Wollaton, Woodborough, Woodcoates, Woodhouse, Woodhouse Hall, Woodthorpe, Wysall, Zouch.

Nonconformist Registers
These may be original or microfilmed.
Baptist: Kirby Moorhouse, Mansfield (Stockwell Gate), Nottingham (Broad St., Friar Lane, George St.), Old Basford, Sutton Bonington, Sutton in Ashfield, Wymeswold (and East Leake).
Presbyterian: Mansfield, Nottingham (High Pavement), Selston.
Catholic: Nottingham (St. Johns).
Congregational or Independent: East Retford, Hyson Green, Keyworth, Mansfield, Moorgreen, Newark, Nottingham (Castle Gate, Friar Lane, St. James), Ranskill, Sutton-in-Ashfield, Worksop.
Methodist: Calverton, East Retford, Hyson Green, Mansfield, Newark, New Basford, Nottingham, Old Radford, Oxton, Ruddington, Worksop Bridge.
Inghamite: Bulwell.

Bishop's Transcripts
These are located in Southwell Minster, but microfilm copies are in the CRO. It should be noted that there are many missing years in the transcripts.

Census Returns
The CRO holds the 1851 Census on microfilm. There are other years (1841, 1861, and 1871) at the Local Studies Library in Nottingham.

Marriage Licences
The CRO does not hold any, but some are in the custody of the Department of Manuscripts at Nottingham University.

Wills and Administrations
The CRO holds these for the county for the sixteenth to twentieth centuries. There are also some wills for Nottinghamshire located in the Borthwick Institute, St. Anthony's Hall, York.

Other Records
These include Nottingham Cemetery Records from 1837 to 1918; Poor Law Papers for some parishes; and early newspapers and directories.

Oxfordshire

Family History Society
(See page 89 for remarks concerning Family History Societies.)

County Record Office
County Hall, Oxford, Oxfordshire OX1 1ND. (Open Monday-Thursday, 0900-1300 hours and 1400-1700 hours; Friday, 0900-1300 hours and 1400-1600 hours.)

The office will not undertake any search of its records without payment of a fee in advance. Anything which involves more than an hour's work will be referred to professional record agents.

The parish registers previously in the Bodleian Library are now in the CRO.

Census Returns
No information has been divulged about these but it is assumed that the CRO must have them on microfilm.

Registers of Electors
These are available from 1832 in the CRO but are not indexed.

Other Records
Those in the CRO include Inclosure Awards and Maps; Land Tax Assessments (1785-1832); Quarter Sessions files (1687-1832); and various private and family records.

Wills
The Bodleian Library holds the following: Bishop of Oxford's Court (1516-1857); Archdeacon of Berkshire (1508-1857); and Peculiars (1550-1858).

Bishop's Transcripts
These are in the Bodleian Library and cover Oxfordshire parishes from 1720.

It is regretted that it has not been possible to obtain more information than this about Oxfordshire records. The following list of the parish registers held in the Bodleian Library has been obtained from another source, and the author is grateful for the kind co-operation of the person concerned:

Adwell, Albury, Alkerton, Alvescot, Ambrosden, Ardley, Asthall, Asthalleigh, Aston North, Aston Rowant, Baiscote, Bampton, Bampton Aston, Banbury, Banbury South, Barford (St. John, St. Michael), Beckley, Begbroke, Benson, Berrick Salome, Bicester, Binsey, Bix, Bladon, Bletchingdon, Bodicote, Bourton (Great),

Britwell Salome, Brize Norton, Broughton, Broughton Poggs, Bucknell, Cassington, Caversfield, Chalgrove, Charlsbury, Charlton on Otmoor, Chastleton, Checkendon, Chesterton, Chiselhampton, Churchill, Clanfield, Claydon, Clifton Hampden, Cogges, Combe, Compton (Little), Cornwell, Cottisford, Cowley (St. James, St. Luke), Cropredy, Crowell, Crowmarsh Gifford, Cuddesdon, Culham, Cuxham, Deddington, Dorchester, Drayton (St. Leonard), Duns Tew, Easington, Elsfield, Enstone, Epwell, Ewelme, Eynsham Fritwell, Fewcott, Fifield, Finmere, Forest Hill, Fringford, Gasrington, Glympton, Godington, Goring, Hailey with Crawley, Hampton Gay, Hampton Poyle, Hanwell, Hardwick, Harpsden, Haseley (Great), Headington, Heyford (Upper and Lower), Heythrop, Holton, Hook Norton, Horspath, Idbury, Ipsden, Islip, Kencot, Kiddington, Kidlington, Kingham, Kirtlington, Langford, Launton, Leigh (South), Lewknor, Littlemore, Mapledurham, Marsh Baldon, Marston (New), Merton, Middleton Stoney, Milton-under-Wychwood, Minster Lovell, Mixbury, Mollington, Mongewell, Nettlebed, Newington, Newington (South), Newton Purcell, Noke, Northleigh, Northmoor, Nuneham Courtenay, Oddington, Oxford (23 parishes), Piddington, Pishill, Pyrton, Rollright (Great and Little), Rotherfield Greys, Rotherfield Peppard, Rousham, Salford, Sandford St. Martin, Sarsden, Shenington, Shifford, Shiplake, Shipton-on-Cherwell, Shipton-under-Wychwood, Shirburn, Shorthampton, Shutford, Sibford, Somerton, Souldern, Stadhampton, Standlake, Stanton Harcourt, Steeple Aston, Steeple Barton, Stoke (Lyne), Stoke (North), Stoke Row, Stoke Talmage, Stonesfield, Stratton Audley, Swalcliffe, Swerford, Swinbrook, Syncombe, Tadmarton, Taynton, Tetsworth, Tew (Great), Thame, Toot Baldon, Towersey, Warborough, Wardington, Waterperry, Waterstock, Watlington, Wendlebury, Westcote Barton, Weston (South), Weston-on-the-Green, Wheatfield, Wheatley, Widford, Witney, Witsey (Holy Trinity), Woodeaton, Woodstock, Wootton, Wroxton, Yarnton.

Shropshire (Salop)

Family History Society
(See page 89 for remarks concerning Family History Societies.)

County Record Office
Shirehall, Abbey Foregate, Shrewsbury, Shropshire SY2 6ND.
(Open Monday and Thursday, 0900-1240 hours and 1320-1700
hours; Friday, 0900-1240 hours and 1320-1600 hours.)

The office is prepared to do twenty minutes of searching without
charge, and after that a fee will be quoted on an hourly basis. It will
also supply a list of local record agents whose fees appear to be
lower than those charged by the CRO.

Parish Registers
The following registers are held by the CRO:
Acron Scott, Adderley, Albrighton (Shifnal), Ashford Carbonell,
Astley Abbotts, Aston Burnell, Atcham, Barrow, Benthall, Berring-
ton, Betton Strange, Billingsley, Bishop's Castle, Bolas Magna,
Boningale, Boraston, Bridgnorth, Bromfield, Broseley, Burford,
Burwarton, Calverhall, Cardeston, Cardington, Caynham, Chel-
marsh, Cheswardine, Chetton, Chetwynd, Child's Ercall, Church
Aston, Church Preen, Church Stretton, Cleobury Mortimer, Cleo-
bury North, Clive, Cockshutt, Condover, Coreley, Cound, Criftins,
Culmington, Dawley (Magna and Parva), Diddlebury, Donington,
Dudleston, Easthope, Eaton Constantine, Eaton-under-Heywood,
Edgmond, Edgton, Edstaston and Wem, Ellesmere, Fitz, Ford,
Frodesley, Glazeley with Deuxhill, Great Bolas, Great Ness, Great
Wollaston, Greete, Habberley, Hanwood, High Ercall, Highley,
Hinstock, Holdgate, Hope, Hope Bagor, Hope Bowdler, Hopesay,
Hordley, Hughley, Ightfield, Kinlet, Kinnerley, Knockin, Lee Bot-
wood, Lee Brockhurst, Leighton, Little Ness, Llanymynoch, Long-
don on Tern, Longford, Longnor, Loppington, Loughton, Ludford,
Ludlow, Lydham, Madeley, Mainstone, Malinslee, Market Dray-
ton, Melverley, Middleton in Chirbury, Middleton Scriven, Monk-
hopton, Monteford, More, Moreton (Oswestry), Moreton Chapel,
Moreton Corbet, Moreton Say, Much Wenlock, Munslow, Mynd-
ton, Nash, Neen Savage, Neen Sollars cum Milson, Newport,
Newtown (Wem), Norbury, Norton in Hales, Oldbury, Onibury,
Oswestry, Oxon and Shelton, Petton, Pitchford, Pontesbury, Prees,
Preston Gubbalds, Quatford, Quatt Malvern, Ratlinghope, Rich-
ard's Castle, Rodington, Ruyton Towne, Saint Martin, Selattyn,
Shawbury, Shelton and Oxon, Shelve, Shifnal, Shipton, Shrawar-
dine, Shrewsbury (Holy Trinity, St. Chad, St. Giles, St. Julian, St.
Mary, St. Michael), Sidbury, Silvington, Smethcott, Snead, Stanton
(Long), Stanton Lacey, Stanton on Minsheath, Stapleton, Stirch-
ley, Stockton, Stoke on Tern, Stokesay, Sutton (Shrewsbury), Sut-

ton Maddock, Tasley, Tong, Tugford, Upton Cressett, Waters
Upton, Wellington, Welshampton, Wem, Wentnor, Westbury,
Weston Lullingfield, Weston Rhyn, Wheathill, Whitchurch, Whit-
tington, Whitton, Willey, Wistanstow, Wollaston (Alderbury or
Alberbury), Wollaston Chapelry, Wombridge, Woolstaston, Wor-
field, Worthen, Wroxeter, Yockleton.

Other Records

These include wills since 1858; quarter sessions records; parish
records; poor law records; manor court rolls and accounts; land
records; leases and title deeds; family papers and letters; surveys;
and maps.

The County Record Office actually holds far more material than
many other CROs, yet probably has a far smaller staff. Archives are
often low on the priority list when the County Council prepares its
annual budget, but Shropshire appears to be an extreme case.

Shrewsbury County Library

Local Studies Section, Castle Gates, Shrewsbury, Shropshire.

The following registers are held in the Shrewsbury County
Library:

Parish Registers: Alberbury, Battlefield, Bitterley, Cardeston, Halford, Milson, Neen Sollars, Pulverbatch, Shrewsbury (Abbey,
Albrighton, Holy Cross and St. Giles), Stowe, Uffington.

Roman Catholic: Acton Burnell, Mawley Hall, Newport, Plowden,
Shrewsbury.

Baptist: Bridgnorth, Minsterley, Shrewsbury.

Wesleyan: Clee Hill, Ditton Priors.

Quaker: Broseley, Shrewsbury.

Presbyterian: Wem.

Independent: Broseley, Church Pulverbatch, Clive, Dodington,
Dorrington, Ellesmere, Llanyblodwell, Ludlow, Lyth Hill, Market
Drayton, Minsterley, Oldbury, Oswestry, Shrewsbury (High Street
and Swan Hill), Wem, Whitchurch, Whixall.

Methodists: Coalbrookdale, Dawley, Ironbridge, Ludlow, Madeley, Newport, Peaton Strand, Prees Green, St. Georges, Shrewsbury, Wellington, Wrockwardine.

Census Returns

These are not in the CRO but in the Shrewsbury County Library
mentioned above.

The County Library has a collection of family pedigrees and
histories, and the Mormon Index for the county.

Bishop's Transcripts and Wills

These records are not in the Library or the CRO. Those for the Lichfield Diocese are in the Lichfield Joint Record Office, Bird Street, Lichfield, and those for the Hereford Diocese are in the Hereford Record Office, The Old Barracks, Harold Street, Hereford.

Somerset

Family History Society

(See page 89 for remarks concerning Family History Societies.)

County Record Office

Obridge Road, Taunton, Somerset TA2 7PU. (Open Monday to Thursday, 0900-1245 hours and 1345-1650 hours; Friday until 1620 hours; Saturday, by appointment, 0915-1215 hours.)

This is one of the few almost unchanged counties, losing only a part of the old county to the new county of Avon (mainly the Bath area). The office will carry out limited searches for overseas inquiries without a fixed charge, but will invite donations to a fund for buying microfilms, books, and manuscripts.

Parish Registers

The following is a list of original registers and copies held by the CRO:

ORIGINAL REGISTERS: Aisholt, Alford, Aller, Angersleigh, Ansford, Ashbrittle, Ashcott, Ash Priors, Axbridge, Babcary, Babington, Backwell, Badgworth, Bagborough (West), Banwell, Barrington, Barrow (North and South), Barrow Gurney, Barton St. David, Barwick, Bath (Abbey, St. Barnabas, St. James, St. Mary), Bathealton, Bathford, Bawdrip, Beercrocombe, Berkeley, Berrow, Bickenhall, Bicknoller, Biddisham, Bishops Hull, Bishops Lydeard, Bishops Sutton, Blackford, Bleadon, Bradford-on-Tone, Bratton Seymour, Brean, Brent (East), Bridgwater (Holy Trinity, St. John, St. Mary), Broadway, Brockley, Brompton Ralph, Brompton Regis, Broomfield, Brushford, Bruton, Buckland (Dinham and West), Buckland St. Mary, Burnham-on-Sea, Burrington, Burrowbridge, Burtle, Butcombe, Butleigh, Cadbury (North and South), Camel (Queen and West), Camerton, Cannington, Carhampton, Castle Cary, Catcott, Chaffcombe, Chapel Allerton, Chard, Charlcombe,

Charlinch, Charlton (Adam, Horethorne, Macrell), Cheddon Fitzpaine, Chedzoy, Chelvey, Cheriton (North), Chewton Mendip, Chillington, Chilthorne Domer, Chilton (Polden and Trinity), Chinnock (East), Chinnock (Middle), Chipstable, Chiselborough, Churchill, Churchstanton, Clandown, Clapton-in-Gordano, Clatworthy, Claverton, Cleeve, Clevedon, Cloford, Combe (Florey and Hay), Combe St. Nicholas, Combwich, Compton (Dundon, Martin, Pauncefoot), Congresbury, Corfe, Corston, Corton Denham, Cossington, Cothelstone, Cranmore (East and West), Creech St. Michael, Crewkerne, Cricket (Malherbie and St. Thomas), Croscombe, Crowcombe, Cucklington, Cudworth, Culbone, Curland, Curry Mallet, Curry Rivel, Cutcombe, Dinder, Dinnington, Ditcheat, Dodington, Donyatt, Doulting, Dowlish Wake, Downhead, Draycott, Drayton, Dulverton, Dunkerton, Durleigh, Durston, Easton-in-Gordano, Edington, Elm, Elworthy, Emborough, Englishcombe, Enmore, Exford, Exton, Farleigh Hungerford, Farrington Gurney, Fiddington, Fitzhead, Fivehead, Flax Bourton, Foxcote, Furnham (Chard), Glastonbury (St. Benedict, St. John), Goathurst, Godney, Greinton, Halse, Ham (High), Hardington, Hardington Mandeville, Harptree (East and West), Haselbury Plucknett, Hatch (West), Hatch Beauchamp, Hawkridge, Heathfield, Hemington, Hewish St. Ann, Hillfarrance, Hinton (Blewett, Charterhouse, St. George), Holcombe, Holford, Holton, Hornblotton, Horrington (East), Horsington, Huish (Champflower, Episcopi), Huntspill (East), Hutton, Ilchester, Ilminster, Isle Brewers, Keinton Mandeville, Kenn, Kewstone, Keynsham, Kilmersdon, Kilton, Kilve, Kingsdon, Kingstone, Kingston St. Mary, Kingston Seymour, Kingweston, Kitnor, Kittisford, Knowle (St. Giles), Langford Budville, Langport, Langridge, Leighland, Leigh-on-Mendip, Lilstock, Limington, Locking, Long Ashton, Long Load, Long Sutton, Lopen, Lovington, Luxborough, Lydeard St. Lawrence, Lydford (East and West), Lyncombe (St. Mark), Lyng, Maperton, Mark, Marston Bigot, Marston Magna, Martock, Meare, Mells, Merriott, Middlezoy, Midsomer Norton, Milverton, Minehead, Misteron, Monksilver, Monkton (West), Monkton Combe, Moorlinch, Muchelney, Nailsea, Nettlecombe, Newton (North, St. Loe), Northover, Norton (Fitzwarren, Malreward, St. Philip), Norton-sub-Hamdon, Nynehead, Oake, Oare, Oaulton, Odcombe, Orchard Portman, Othery, Otterford, Otterhampton, Paulton, Pawlett, Pendomer, Pennard (East and West), Penselwood, Perrott (North), Petherton (South), Pilton, Pitminster, Pitney, Podymore Milton, Porlock, Portbury, Portishead, Priddy, Puckington, Puriton, Puxton, Pylle, Quantoxhead (East and West),

Raddington, Radstock, Rimpton, Rodden, Rode, Rodney Stoke, Ruishton, Runnington, St. Decumans, St. Michaelchurch, Saltford, Sampford (Arundel and Brett), Seavington (St. Mary, St. Michael), Shapwick, Shepton Beauchamp, Shepton Mallet, Shipham, Skilgate, Somerton, Spaxton, Staple Fitzpaine, Staplegrove, Stawell, Stawley, Stockland Bristol, Stocklinch (Magdalen, Ottersay), Stogumber, Stogursey, Stoke (North, South, St. Gregory, St. Mary, St. Michael), Stoke Pero, Stoke-sub-Hamdon, Stowell, Stowey (Nether, Over), Stratton-on-the-Fosse, Street, Stringston, Sutton Mallet, Swainswick, Swell, Tatworth (Chard), Taunton (Holy Trinity, St. Andrew, St. James), Tellisford, Templecombe, Thorne Coffin, Thorne St. Margaret, Thornfalcon, Thurlbear, Thurloxton, Tickenham, Timberscombe, Timsbury, Tintinhull, Tolland, Treborough, Trull, Twerton, Ubley, Uphill, Upton, Walcot (St. Andrew, St. Swithin), Walton, Walton-in-Gordano, Wambrook, Wayford, Weare, Wellington (All Saints), Wellow, Wells (St. Cuthbert, St. Thomas), Wembdon, Westbury, Weston All Saints, Weston-in-Gordano, Weston-super-Mare, Westonzoyland, Whatley, Wheathill, Whitelackington, Whitestaunton, Wick St. Lawrence, Widcombe (St. Thomas), Williton, Wilton, Wincanton, Winsford, Winsham, Witham Friary, Withiel Florey, Withycombe, Withypool, Wiveliscombe, Wookey, Woolavington, Woolley, Wootton (North), Worle, Wrington, Writhlington, Wyke Champflower, Yarlington, Yatton, Yeovil Marsh, Yeovilton.

HANDWRITTEN COPIES: Aller, Ansford, Banwell, Bath (Abbey, St. James, St. Michael), Bathampton, Batheaston, Beercrocombe, Bicknoller, Bleadon, Brent Knoll, Broadway, Bruton, Burnett, Cadbury (North), Castle Cary, Chard, Charlton Mackrell, Chipstable, Combe Florey, Corfe, Cricket St. Thomas, Donyatt, Doulting, Emborough, Evercreech, Frome, Glastonbury (St. John), Hatch (West), Hatch Beauchamp, Horsington, Ilminster, Ilton, Isle Brewers, Kilmersdon, Kingstone, Kingston St. Mary, Kingweston, Kittisford, Langridge, Long Ashton, Long Load, Lullington, Minehead, Norton Fitzwarren, Orchardleigh, Orchard Portman, Penselwood, Petherton (North), Pitcombe, Pitminster, Raddington, Radstock, Rode, St. Michaelchurch, Shepton Montague, Shipham, Stogumber, Stoke (North), Stowell, Stowey, Street, Swainswick, Thurloxton, Timsbury, Trull, Twerton, Wedmore, Wellington, Weston All Saints, Weston-super-Mare (St. Johns), Wilton, Woolley.

MICROFILMS OF ORIGINAL REGISTERS: Abbots Leigh, Ansford, Cadbury (North and South), Crewkerne, Edington, Huntspill, Martock, Meare, Mells, Minehead, Moorlinch, Portishead, Ruishton, Seaborough, Stawell, Sutton Mallet, Taunton St. Mary, Thornfalcon, Wambrook, Wayford, Wells (St. Cuthbert), Wraxall, Wrington, Yeovil.

Bishop's Transcripts
There are many of these dating back to the sixteenth century, but there are gaps and many parishes are missing. They are in the CRO and indexes are available.

Nonconformist Registers
All the Somerset registers in the PRO, London, have been micro-filmed for the CRO. In addition, they have a number of original registers from various places:
Methodist: *Baptisms*: Bridgwater, Catcott, Dunster, North Pether-ton, Watchet, Williton, Woolavington; *Marriages*: Taunton; *General*: Wellington.
Baptist: Isle Abbots.
Congregational: Bishops Lydeard, Milverton, Nunney (Trudox-hill), Winsham (burials).

Union Workhouses (Registers of Births and Deaths)
Axbridge, Bedminster, Bridgwater, Chard, Clutton, Dulverton, Frome, Keynsham, Langport, Shepton Mallet, Taunton, Welling-ton, Wincanton, Yeovil.

Census Returns
These are held on microfilm for 1851 and 1871 for the whole county.

Wills
The original Somerset wills were destroyed by bombing in the Second World War. The Estate Duty copy wills (1812-57) have been transferred from the PRO to the CRO and have been indexed. The original manuscript collections of the Rev. Frederick Brown (from which six volumes of wills have been published) are also in the CRO, together with a card index.

Marriage Bonds
These cover the period 1574-1899 but are only indexed for 1675-1755.

Quarter Sessions Rolls
These are in the CRO from 1603 to 1620 and 1660 to 1720, and are indexed by personal name.

Other Records

These consist mainly of private and estate deposits, including manorial rolls, lists of tenants and workers, etc., and they can be of considerable value to ancestor-hunters. If you have an ancestor who worked on a particular estate in Somerset, you should write to the County Archivist for more detailed information.

South Yorkshire

Family History Societies

There are two Family History Societies in this area:
Doncaster
Sheffield and District
(See page 89 for remarks concerning Family History Societies.)

County Record Office

Cultural Activities Centre, Ellin Street, Sheffield S1 4PL. (Open Monday-Thursday, 0900-1700 hours; Friday, 0900-1600 hours.)

The office welcomes inquiries from overseas and is willing to do short specific searches at no charge. If general searching is required, a record agent should be employed.

Parish Registers

The CRO holds no original registers but has a certain number on microfilm and printed transcripts of some others (including the Sheffield registers for 1560-1719). The office also holds an index of marriages for the period 1754-1813 and burials for 1754-66, both for Sheffield.

However, a number of South Yorkshire registers are held in Doncaster and Sheffield:

DONCASTER ARCHIVES DEPT, KING EDWARD ROAD, BALBY, DONCASTER DN4 ONA:

Adlingfleet, Adwick on Dearne, Armthorpe, Balby, Barnby Dun, Brampton Bierlow, Burghwallis, Cowick, Doncaster, Ellington, Fenwick, Goole, Hatfield, Hickleton, Hook, Jump, Kirk Bramwith, Loversall, Marr, Melton on the Hill, Mexborough, Rawcliffe, Rossington, Skelbrooke, Snaith, Sprotborough, Stainforth, Stainton, Swinefleet, Sykehouse, Thurnscoe, Tickhill, Wadworth, Warmsworth, Wentworth, Wombwell

SHEFFIELD CITY LIBRARIES, SURREY STREET, SHEFFIELD S1 1XZ:

Beighton, Braithwell, Hooton Roberts, Sheffield (all parishes)

Nonconformist Registers
The CRO holds on microfilm all pre-1837 registers for the county. These are, of course, copies of the ones sent to the Public Record Office, London, in 1837.

Bishop's Transcripts
These are also on microfilm for the county.

Census Returns
These are held for the period 1841-71. There is an alphabetical index for the 1851 Census for Sheffield.

Wills
The CRO holds no pre-1858 wills. These are at the Borthwick Institute, St. Anthony's Hall, Peasholme Green, York YO1 2PW. They do hold a list of wills from 1858 up to 1928.

Other Records
There are early directories for the Sheffield area, and poll books, voters' lists, early histories, etc.
Note: The South Yorkshire CRO, like the other offices for "new" counties, is gradually acquiring items of genealogical interest as and when funding is available.

Staffordshire

Family History Society
(See page 89 for remarks concerning Family History Societies.)

Staffordshire County Record Office
County Buildings, Eastgate Street, Stafford, Staffordshire ST16 2LZ. (Open Monday-Thursday, 0900-1300 hours and 1400-1700 hours; Friday, 0900-1300 hours and 1400-1630 hours.)
  Generally speaking, the ecclesiastical records held in the Staffordshire County Record Office are those of the Archdeaconry of Stafford, which came under the authority of the Diocese of Lichfield. The office does not undertake protracted genealogical searches but refers inquirers to a list of record agents who are available for genealogical research.

Lichfield Joint Record Office

Bird Street, Lichfield WS13 6PN. (Open Monday-Friday, 1000-1715 hours.) The ecclesiastical records here are those of the Diocese of Lichfield. It is a branch of the CRO.

William Salt Library

This is a branch of the CRO and is located in Eastgate Street, Stafford. (Open Tuesday-Thursday, 0930-1245 hours and 1345-1700 hours; Friday, 0930-1245 hours and 1345-1630 hours; Saturday, 0930-1300 hours.) The Library contains a collection of printed works relating to local history, printed parish registers, and early local newspapers.

Parish Registers

STAFFORDSHIRE CRO: Abbots Bromley, Acton Trussell, Alrewas, Alsagers Bank, Alstonfield, Alton, Armitage, Ashley, Audley, Bagnall, Barlaston, Baswich, Beckbury, Betley, Biddulph, Bilston (St. Leonard), Bilston (St. Mary), Blithfield, Blore, Blore Ray, Blurton, Blymhill, Bobbington, Bradeley, Brown Edge, Bucknall cum Bagnall, Burslem (St. John, St. Paul), Bushbury, Butterton, Calton, Cannock, Cannock (Heath Hayes), Cauldon, Caverswall, Chapel Chorlton, Cheadle, Chebsey, Cheddleton, Chesterton, Church Eaton, Clifton Campville, Cobridge, Codsall, Colwich (Great Haywood), Coppenhall, Croxden, Darlaston (St. George), Darlaston (St. Lawrence), Dilhorne, Draycott in the Moors, Drayton Bassett, Dresden, Dunstall, Dunston, Easington, Eccleshall (Cotes Heath), Edingale, Elfrod, Ellaston, Ellenhall, Enville, Etruria, Farewell, Fradswell, Gailey, Gayton, Gnosall, Goldenhill, Gratwich, Great Wyrley, Grindon, Hanbury, Hartshill, Haughton, Haywood (Great), Heath Hayes, Hednesford, Hints, Hollington, Ilam, Ipstones, Keele, Kingsley, Kingstone, Kinver, Lapley, Leek, Leigh, Longdon, Longnor, Longton (St. James), Longton (St. John), Madeley, Maer, Marchington, Marston, Mayfield, Meerbrook, Milwich, Moreton, Mow Cop, Moxley, Newborough, Newcastle (Porthill, St. George, St. Giles), Newchapel, Norbury, Normacot, Northwood, Ogley Hay with Brownhills, Okeover, Oulton, Patshull, Pattingham, Pelsall, Penkridge, Penn, Quarnford, Quarry Bank, Ranton, Rocester, Rugeley, Rushton Spencer, Sandon, Sedgley, Seighford, Shareshill, Sheen, Shenstone, Stafford (Castlechurch, Christ Church, St. Chad, St. Mary, St. Paul, St. Thomas), Stafford (St. John), Standon, Stoke Milton, Stoke-on-Trent, Stone, Stowe, Stretton, Tatenhill, Tettenhall, Tettenhall Wood, Thorpe Constantine, Tittensor, Tividale, Tixall, Trysull,

Tunstall (Christchurch, St. Chad, St. Mary), Tutbury, Walsall (St. George, St. John, St. Mark, St. Paul), Walsall Wood, Wednesbury, Wednesfield, Weston, Weston under Lizard, Wetton, Whitgreave, Whitmore, Willenhall (St. Stephen), Wilnecote, Wolstanton, Wolverhampton (Christ Church, St. George, St. James, St. Luke, St. Mary, St. Matthew, St. Peter, St. Stephen), Wood Green, Wychnor, Uttoxeter, Yoxall.

LICHFIELD JOINT RO: Lichfield (St. Chad, St. Mary, St. Michael). WILLIAM SALT LIBRARY (printed copies or manuscript transcripts—only listed if they are not included in the above lists): Adbaston, Barlaston, Biddulph, Bloxwich, Bradley in the Moors, Bramshall, Brewood, Burton on Trent, Cauldon, Chebsey, Draycott in the Moors, Dudley St. Edmund, Eccleshall, Ellenhall, Endon, Forton, Great Barr, Hamstall Ridware, Hanley, High Offley, Himley, Keele, Maer, Mavesyn Ridware, Mucclestone, Newchapel, Norton in the Moors, Penn, Pipe Ridware, Ranton, Rowley Regis, Rushall, Sedgley, Swynnerton, Tamworth, Tipton, Trentham, Walsall (St. Matthew), Waterfall, Weeford, West Bromwich, Willenhall St. Giles, Wolstanton, Wombourne.

Note: The William Salt Library also holds Catholic registers for Chillington, Creswell, Walsall, and Wolverhampton.

Nonconformist Registers
The CRO holds a number of these, but at present a list is not available.

Bishop's Transcripts
These are in the Lichfield Joint RO and the earliest date from the 1660s, although a few go back much earlier.

Wills
These are in the Lichfield Joint RO. They begin in 1521 but few exist before 1534, and not all are indexed.

Marriage Licences
These are also at Lichfield but are not completely indexed.

Census Returns
Microfilms of census returns for Staffordshire for 1841-71 are in the CRO. It is necessary to reserve a microfilm viewer in advance of your visit.

Miscellaneous
There are a vast number of other ecclesiastical records in the Lichfield Joint RO, but I suggest you leave these until you have exhausted all other sources of information.

Suffolk

Family History Society
(See page 89 for remarks concerning Family History Societies.)

County Record Office
County Hall, Ipswich, Suffolk IP4 2JS, and School Hall Street, Bury St. Edmunds IP33 1RX. The present county consists of Ipswich, West Suffolk, and most of East Suffolk. The division of records in the two CROs reflects the area covered by the old counties. (Open Monday-Thursday, 0900-1715 hours; Friday, 0900-1615 hours; Saturday, 0900-1300 hours. These times apply to both offices.)

The two offices will undertake limited searches; for example, a search would be made of the registers of a parish for ten years to check the existence of a marriage and any subsequent baptisms. If a longer search is required, such as extracting all entries for a particular surname, then the inquirer will be referred to a local record agent.

Parish Registers
Almost all the registers of the Suffolk parishes are in the custody of the CROs, either as originals or on microfilm. Details of the division of these between the two offices is given below.

BURY ST. EDMUNDS: Acton, Alpheton, Ampton, Ashfield (Great), Assington, Bardwell, Barnardiston, Barnham, Barningham, Barrow, Barton Mills, Beyton, Bradfield, Bradfield Combust, Bradley (Great and Little), Brandon, Brent Eleigh, Brettenham, Brockley, Bures, Bury St. Edmunds (3 parishes), Cavendish, Cavenham, Chedburgh, Chelsworth, Chevington, Clare, Cockfield, Coney Weston, Cornard (Great, Little), Cowlinge, Culford, Dalham, Denham (near Bury), Denston, Depden, Drinkstone, Edwardstone, Elmswell, Eriswell, Euston, Exning, Fakenham Magna, Felsham, Flempton-cum-Hengrave, Fornham, Freckenham, Gazeley, Gedding, Glemsford, Groton, Hargrave, Haverhill, Hawkedon, Hawstead, Hepworth, Herringswell, Hesset, Higham Green, Hinderclay, Hitcham, Honington, Hopton, Hundon, Hunston, Icklingham, Ingham, Ixworth, Ixworth Thorpe, Kedington, Kettlebaston, Lackford, Lakenheath, Langham, Lavenham, Lawshall, Lidgate, Livermere (Great and Little), Market Weston, Melford (Long), Milden, Mildenhall, Monks Eleigh, Newmarket, Newton by Sudbury, Norton, Nowton, Ousden, Pakenham, Poslingford, Preston, Rattlesden, Rede, Risby, Rougham, Rushbrooke, Santon Downham, Sapiston, Saxham (Great and Little), Shimpling,

Somerton, Stanningfield, Stansfield, Stanstead, Stanton, Stoke-by-Clare, Stowlangtoft, Stradishall, Sudbury, Thelnetham, Thorpe Morieux, Thurlow (Great and Little), Thurston, Timworth, Tostock, Troston, Tuddenham, Waldingfield (Great and Little), Walsham-le-Willows, Wangford, Wattisfield, Westley, West Stow, Whelnetham (Great and Little), Whepstead, Wickhambrook, Withersfield, Woolpit, Wordwell, Worlington, Wratting (Great and Little).

IPSWICH: Akenham, Aldeburgh, Alderton, Aldham, Aldringham, Ashbocking, Ashfield, Athelington, Bacton, Badley, Barham, Barking, Barsham, Barton (Great), Battisford, Bawdsey, Baylham, Bealings (Great and Little), Beccles, Bedfield, Benacre, Benhall, Bentley, Bergholt East, Betstead, Bildeston, Blakenham (Great and Little), Blaxhall, Blyford, Blythburgh, Boulge, Boxford, Boxted, Boyton, Braisworth, Bramfield, Bramford, Brampton, Brandeston, Brantham, Bredfield, Bricet (Great), Brightwell with Foxhall, Brome, Bromeswell, Bruisyard, Brundish, Bucklesham, Bungay, Burgate, Burgh, Burstall, Butley, Buxhall, Campsea Ashe, Capel St. Mary, Carlton, Carlton Colville, Charsfield, Chattisham, Chediston, Chelmondiston, Chillesford, Chilton, Coddenham, Combs, Cookley, Copdock, Cornard (Little), Cotton, Cove (North and South), Covehithe, Cransford, Cratfield, Creeting, Cretingham, Crowfield, Culpho, Dallinghoo, Darsham, Debach, Debenham, Denham, Dennington, Dunwich, Easton, Ellough, Elmsett, Erwarton, Eye, Eyke, Falkenham, Farnham, Felixstowe, Finborough (Great and Little), Finningham, Flixton, Flowton, Framlingham, Framsden, Fressingfield, Freston, Friston, Fritton, Frostenden, Gisleham, Gislingham, Glemham (Great and Little), Gosbeck, Grundisburgh, Hacheston, Hadleigh, Halesworth, Harkstead, Harlestone, Hartest, Hasketon, Haughley, Helmingham, Hemingstone, Hemley, Henley, Henstead with Hulver, Heveningham, Higham St. Mary, Hintlesham, Holbrook, Hollesley, Holton (St. Mary, St. Peter), Homersfield, Hoo, Horham, Hoxne, Huntingfield, Iken, Ilketshall, Ipswich (17 parishes), Kelsale, Kentford, Kenton, Kersey, Kesgrave, Kessingland, Kettleburgh, Kirton, Knoddishall, Layham, Leiston with Sizewell, Letheringham, Levington, Lindsay, Linstead (Magna and Parva), Marlesford, Martlesham, Mellis, Melton, Mendham, Mendlesham, Metfield, Mettingham, Mickfield, Middleton cum Fordley, Monewden, Mutford, Nacton, Naughton, Nayland, Nedging, Nettlestead, Newbourn, Newton (Old), Oakley, Occold, Offton with Little Bricett, Onehouse, Orford, Otley, Palgrave, Parham, Peasenhall, Pettaugh, Pettistree, Playford, Polstead, Raydon, Redgrave, Redisham (Great and Little),

Redlingfield, Rendham, Rendlesham, Reydon, Rickinghall (Superior and Inferior), Ringsfield, Ringshall, Rishangles, Rumburgh, Rushmere (Ipswich), Saxmundham, Saxstead, Semer, Shadingfield, Shelland, Shelley, Shipmeadow, Shotley, Sibton, Snape, Soham (Earl and Monk), Somersham, Sotherton, Sotterley, Southelmham (6 parishes), Southolt, Southwold, Spexhall, Sproughton, Sternfield, Stoke Ash, Stoke-by-Clare, Stoke-by-Nayland, Stonham (Aspall and Parva), Stonham Earl, Stoven, Stowmarket, Stowupland, Stradbroke, Stratford (St. Andrew, St. Mary), Stuston, Stutton, Sudbourne, Sweffling, Swilland, Syleham, Tannington, Tattingstone, Theberton, Thorington, Thorndon, Thornham (Magna and Parva), Thrandeston, Thwaite St. George, Trimley, Tuddenham, Tunstall, Ubbeston, Ufford, Uggleshall, Walberswick, Waldringfield, Walpole, Walton, Wangford, Wantisden, Washbrook, Wattisham, Wenham (Great and Little), Westerfield, Westhall, Westhorpe, Westleton, Weston, Wetherden, Wetheringsett with Brockford, Weybread, Whatfield, Wherstead, Whitton cum Thurlestone, Wickham Market, Wickham Skeith, Wilby, Willisham, Wingfield, Winston, Wisset, Wissington, Withersdale, Witnesham, Wixoe, Woodbridge, Woolverstone, Worlingham, Worlingworth, Wortham, Wrentham, Wyverstone, Yaxley, Yoxford.

Note: Other parishes, in Suffolk until 1975, were transferred to Norfolk, and their registers are in the Norfolk Record Office, Central Library, Norwich, Norfolk NOR 57E.

Quarter Sessions Records

These are held at Ipswich for the whole county. Judicial records exist from 1639 but other records, such as land tax returns, are missing. There is also a set of prison records from 1802 to 1870 which gives details of transportation of convicts overseas. If your Suffolk emigrant ancestor had his passage paid overseas, you may find him here!

Nonconformist Registers

It is regretted that no information could be obtained about these, but it is likely that the CROs hold microfilm copies of registers which were surrendered to the General Registry in 1840 and are now in the Public Record Office, London. I suggest that you try to obtain information about them from the County Archivist. He is busy writing a book about the genealogical records of the county and perhaps he will include information about the Nonconformist registers.

Bishop's Transcripts
These are available at both record offices for the archdeaconries of Suffolk and Sudbury. They date from 1560 but are not complete for all parishes.

Wills
These are indexed from 1444 to 1941, for the Archdeaconry of Suffolk to 1857 and for the Ipswich Probate Registry since that date. If a testator held property in two archdeaconries, the will was proved in the consistory court (Norwich for West Suffolk until 1837 and then Ely until 1857). Wills proved in Norwich are in the Norfolk CRO and those for Ely in the Cambridge University Library.

Administrations
The CRO has the original administration bonds for the Archdeaconry of Sudbury for the period 1544-1858.

Marriage Licences
The CRO holds these for the Archdeaconry of Sudbury for 1683-1839. There are some records of earlier licences for 1577-93, 1606-11, and 1660 onwards which have been indexed by the CRO.

Probate Inventories
Those in the CRO cover the period 1573-77 and 1640-1818. They have been listed and indexed by place, name, and occupation.

Census Returns
These are available on microfilm for the years 1851-71.

Tithe Apportionments and Maps
Those for the parishes of the Archdeaconry of Sudbury are at the Bury office, and those for the Archdeaconry of Suffolk at Ipswich.

Marriage Index
This is on microfilm for the whole county for the period 1538-1837. It is indexed.

Churchyard and Monumental Inscriptions
These have been copied for most Suffolk parishes and are indexed and on microfilm in the CRO.

Pedigrees and Biographies
There are a great many of these available for Suffolk families and individuals. Be sure you check for your own family before you go any further. You never know how lucky you may be!

Cemetery Records
Early records from the mid-1800s are available for Bury, Haverhill, and Sudbury at the Bury St. Edmunds office, and for Ipswich at the CRO there.

Directories and Local Newspapers
The earliest Suffolk directory held is that from 1844, and early newspapers include the *Ipswich Journal* from 1720.

Surrey

Family History Societies
There are two Family History Societies in this county:
East Surrey
West Surrey
(See page 89 for remarks concerning Family History Societies.)

County Record Office
County Hall, Kingston-upon-Thames, Surrey KT1 2DN. Branch Office: Guildford Muniment Room, Castle Arch, Guildford, Surrey GU1 3SX. *Kingston*: Monday-Wednesday and Friday, 0930-1645 hours; Thursday, 1345-1645 hours; Saturday, by appointment only, 2nd and 4th of month, 0930-1230 hours. *Guildford*: Tuesday to Friday, 0930-1230 hours and 1345-1645 hours; Saturday, by appointment only, 1st and 3rd of month, 0930-1230 hours.)

The division of responsibility between the two CROs in Surrey should be explained. Guildford holds records of the Borough of Guildford, church records of the Diocese of Guildford, and other records for south-west Surrey. Kingston holds county and civil parish records, church records of the Diocese of Southwark, and other records from north and east Surrey. Each office will gladly advise on the holdings of the other.

The office will make brief searches without charge—usually to inform the inquirer whether or not there are records which might be useful, and not to search those records. Names of record agents will be supplied.

Parish Registers
These are from the dioceses of Guildford and Southwark, and are either original registers, manuscript transcripts, or microfilm:
Abinger, Albury, Aldershot (St. Michael), Alford, Ash, Ashstead,

Banstead, Barnes, Beddington, Betchworth, Bisley, Bookham (Great, Little), Buckland, Byfleet, Camberley, Capel, Carshalton, Caterham, Chaldon, Charlwood, Cheam Common, Chelsham, Chertsey (St. Peter), Chessington, Chiddingfold, Chipstead, Chobham, Clandon (East), Clandon (West), Claygate, Cobham (St. Andrew), Coldharbour, Compton, Coulsdon (St. John), Cove (Hants), Cove (RAF Farnborough), Cranleigh, Crondall (Hants), Crookham (Hants), Crowhurst, Dorking (St. Martin, St. Paul), Dunsfold, Effingham, Egham (St. John), Elstead, Englefield Green, Epsom (Christchurch, St. Martin), Esher (St. George), Ewell (St. Mary), Ewhurst, Farleigh, Farnborough (Hants), Farnham, Felbridge, Fetcham, Fleet (Hants), Frensham, Frimley, Gatton, Godalming (Sts. Peter and Paul), Godstone, Guildford (Christ Church, Holy Trinity, St. Luke, St. Mary, St. Nicholas), Ham, Hambledon, Hascombe, Haslemere, Hawley (Hants), Headley (Hants), Headley with Box Hill, Holmwood, Horley, Horne, Horsell, Horsley, Kingston-upon-Thames (All Saints, St. Luke), Kingswood, Leatherhead, Leigh, Limpsfield, Lingfield, Malden, Merrow, Merstham, Merton (St. James, St. Mary), Mickleham, Milford, Mitcham (Christ Church, St. Olave, St. Paul, St. Peter), Molesey East (St. Mary, St. Paul), Molesey West (St. Peter), Morden, Mortlake, Newdigate, Nork, North Sheen, Nutfield, Ockham, Ockley, Okewood, Ottershaw, Oxted, Peperharrow, Petersham, Pirbright, Puttenham, Pyrford, Raynes Park, Redhill (St. John, St. Matthew), Reigate (St. Mary Magdalene), Richmond (Holy Trinity, St. John, St. Mary Magdalene), Ripley, Rowledge, St. Martha, Salfords, Sanderstead, Seale, Send, Shalford, Shere, Shottermill, Stoke D'Abernon, Stoke next Guildford, Surbiton (St. Andrew, St. Mark), Sutton (St. Barnabas, St. Nicholas), Tandridge, Tatsfield, Thames Ditton, Thursley, Titsey, Walton on Thames, Walton on the Hill, Wanborough, Warlingham, Westcott, West End, Weybridge, Wimbledon (All Saints, Christchurch, Holy Trinity, St. Andrew, St.Luke, St. Mary), Windlesham, Wisley, Witley, Woking (St. John the Baptist, St. Peter), Woldingham, Woodmansterne, Worplesdon, Wotton, Wyke. (There are also printed registers for Godalming, Oakwood Chapel, Putney, Wandsworth.)

The Minet Library, Lambeth, also has parish register transcripts for a number of Surrey parishes, which supplement the CRO holdings. Information can be obtained from the Lambeth Archives Department, Minet Library, 52 Knatchbull Road, London SE5 9QY.

Nonconformist Records

Most of these records are from the present century. There are a few exceptions:

Methodist: Sutton (1868-1960) and Walton on Thames (1871-1934).

United Reform (Congregational): Thames Ditton (1837-64), Wimbledon (1893-1947).

Note: These Nonconformist registers are baptismal only.

County Records

These are more comprehensive than usual, owing to certain oddities in Surrey's history. From the sixteenth century to 1889, the county was administered by its Court of Quarter Sessions, and the records survive from 1659.

The Court was responsible not only for legal matters but also for the local government of the county. In 1889 a County Council was created and the Quarter Sessions ceased to have administrative responsibility. All its records are in the CRO.

Other Records

The CRO holds records of many family estates; out-of-date records from solicitors, including land transfers, manorial records, and title deeds; and tithe apportionments and maps. However, many wills, Bishop's Transcripts, and marriage bonds and licences are in the Greater London Record Office, The County Hall, London SE1 7PB. For information about this office see page 166.

The Surrey CRO has about five hundred lists of Surrey records held elsewhere, either in Record Offices or in private hands, and will gladly advise on the location of records which it does not itself hold.

Tyne and Wear

This "new" county includes parts of Northumberland and Durham plus Gateshead, Newcastle-upon-Tyne, South Shields, Sunderland, and Tynemouth.

Family History Society

(See page 89 for remarks concerning Family History Societies.)

County Record Office
Archives Department, Blandford House, West Blandford Street, Newcastle-upon-Tyne NE1 4JA. There is a branch office at the Local Studies Centre, Howard Street, North Shields NE30 1LY.
NEWCASTLE: Monday, 0845-1715 hours; Tuesday, 0845-2030 hours; Wednesday to Friday, 0845-1715 hours.
NORTH SHIELDS: Monday, Thursday, Friday, 0900-1300 hours and 1400-1700 hours; Tuesday, 0900-1300 hours and 1400-1900 hours; Wednesday, 0900-1300 hours.

The offices will carry out a brief and specific search—only, for example, a date of birth or baptism, with the inquirer providing name, parish, and date to within two or three years. There is no charge for this at present. If further information is required, a list of local record agents will be provided.

Parish Registers
These are available on microfilm: Benwell, Byker, Cullercoats, Earsdon, Elswick, Hetton le Hole, Houghton-le-Spring, Jesmond, Killingworth, Lamesley, Longbenton, Newburn, Newcastle (16 parishes), North Shields, Penshaw, South Shields (2 parishes), Sunderland (7 parishes), Tynemouth, Usworth, Walker (Christ Church, St. Christopher), Wallsend (St. Luke, St. Peter), Washington, West Rainton, Willington Quay.

Marriage Licences
None are held in the CRO; reference should be made to the CROs of Durham and Northumberland.

Bishop's Transcripts
Those for the area are in the Department of Palaeography and Diplomatic, University of Durham, South Road, Durham DH1 3LE.

Wills
There are a few pre- and post-1858 probate records but no probate collection as such. Here, again, refer to the CROs of the two counties mentioned above.

Newspapers
There are runs of local newspapers from Jarrow, but the best collection is in the Newcastle Central Library, Princess Square, Newcastle-upon-Tyne NE99 1MC.

Nonconformist Registers

The following are held in the CRO:

Methodist (original baptismal registers, including various sects): Blaydon Circuits (including Blaydon, Gateshead, Swalwell), Brunswick Circuit (including Brunswick, Bulman, Copland Place, Gosforth, Hood Street, Killingworth, Seaton Burn, West Moor), Heaton and Wallsend Circuit, Hetton le Hole Circuit (including East Rainton, Hetton, Houghton le Spring, Moorsley, Murton, Newbottle, North Biddick, Philadephia), Newcastle Circuit (Blenheim Street, New Road, St. Lawrence), Newcastle West Circuit (Beaumont, Bell's Close, Benwell Bond, Dunn Street, Elswick Road, Gloucester Street, Lemington, Newburn, Paradise, Park Road, Scotswood, Throckley, Westgate Hill, Westmoreland Road), North Shields and Whitley Bay Circuit (North Shields), Ryton and Prudhoe Circuit (Mickley Square), South Shields Circuit (Baring Street, Frederick Street, Queen Street, Reay Street, South Shields, Victoria Road, West Harton, Zion), Sunderland Circuit (Deptford, Pallion, Southwick, Sunderland), Whickham. In addition to the above circuits there are registers from Hazlerigg.

Quaker: Allendale, Benfieldside, Newcastle and Gateshead, North Shields, Sunderland.

Presbyterian: Sunderland.

Roman Catholic: Newcastle (St. Andrew) for indexed marriages.

Unitarian: Newcastle, Sunderland.

United Reform: Newcastle.

There are also microfilms of Newcastle registers deposited in the PRO, London, in 1837 and these include Independent, Baptist, Swedenborgian, Methodist, Wesleyan, United Secessionist, Congregational, and Presbyterian registers.

Census Returns

These are held on microfilm for the whole county for the period 1841-71.

Other Records

There are no manorial collections, but the CRO holds many land records, including deeds, leases, maps, rentals, and estate records; poll books; and directories.

Cemetery Records

These record grave spaces and burials in Newcastle General Cemetery from 1834 to 1968. Eight cemeteries are covered by the records: All Saints, Ballast Hills, Byker, Elswick, Heaton, Newcastle, St. Andrew, St. John, and St. Nicholas.

Guilds and Freemen

These records run from 1696 to 1830 for apprenticeships, and include Guild and Freemen's Rolls from 1409 to 1974. Records of the Tyne Keelmen contain lists of men employed by the various skippers, mainly in the eighteenth century.

Warwickshire

Family History Society

Now served by West Midland Family History Society.
(See page 89 for remarks concerning Family History Societies).

County Record Office

Priory Park, Cape Road, Warwick CV34 4JS. (Open Monday-Friday, 0900-1300 hours and 1400-1730 hours; Saturday, 0900-1230 hours.)

The office will answer questions about the records but will not undertake research for genealogists. Those wishing to have research done must do it themselves by visiting the CRO or make their own arrangements with a professional record agent from a list which will be supplied.

Parish Registers

Alcester, Alderminster, Allesley, Alne (Great), Alveston, Ansley, Ansty, Arley, Arrow, Ashow, Astley, Aston Cantlow, Atherstone, Atherstone-on-Stour, Attleborough, Austrey, Baddesley Clinton, Baddesley Ensor, Baginton, Balsall (Temple), Barcheston, Barford, Barston, Barton on the Heath, Baxterly, Bearley, Baudesert, Bedworth, Berkswell, Bickenhill, Bidford on Avon, Billesley, Bilton, Bilton (New), Binley, Binton, Birdingbury, Bourton on Dunsmore, Brailes, Brinklow, Brownsover, Bubbenhall, Budbrooke, Bulkington, Burmington, Burton Hastings, Caldecote, Charlecote, Cherington, Chesterton, Churchover, Claverdon, Clifford Chambers, Clifton upon Dunsmore, Coleshill, Combroke, Compton (Fenny), Compton (Long), Compton Verney, Compton Wynyates, Corley, Coton (Chilvers), Coughton, Coundon, Coventry (All Saints, Christ Church, Holy Trinity, St. John Baptist, St. Mark, St. Mary Magdalene, St. Michael, St. Peter, St. Thomas), Cubbington, Curdworth, Dassett (Avon), Dassett (Burton), Dunchurch, Eastern Green, Elmdon, Ettington, Exhall (near Alcester), Exhall (near Coventry), Farnborough, Fillongley, Foleshill, Foleshill St. Paul,

Frankton, Gaydon and Chadshunt, Grafton (Temple), Grandborough, Grendon, Halford, Hampton in Arden, Hampton Lucy, Harborough Magna, Harbury, Hardwick (Priors), Hartshill, Haseley, Haselor, Hatton, Henley in Arden, Hillmorton, Honiley, Honington, Hunningham, Idlicote, Ilmington, Itchington (Bishops), Itchington (Long), Kenilworth, Keresley with Coundon, Kineton, Kingsbury, Kinwarton, Kirby (Monks), Knowle, Ladbroke with Radbourne, Lapworth, Lawford (Church) with Kings Newnham, Leamington Hastings, Leamington Priors, Leamington Priors (The Good Shepherd, Holy Trinity, St. Alban, St. Mark, St. Mary, St. Paul), Lightthorne, Lillington, Loxley, Mancetter, Marston (Butlers), Marston (Lea), Marston (Priors), Marston (Sicca), Marton, Merevale, Meriden, Middleton, Milverton, Moreton Morrell, Morton Bagot, Napton-on-the-Hill, Newbold-on-Avon, Newbold-on-Avon (Long Lawford), Newbold Pacey, Newton Regis, Norton Lindsey, Nuneaton, Nuthurst cum Hockley Heath, Offchurch, Oldberror, Orton (Water), Oxhill, Packington (Great and Little), Packwood, Pillerton Hersey, Pillerton Priors, Polesworth, Preston Bagot, Preston on Stour, Quinton, Radford Semele, Radway, Ratley, Rowington, Rugby, Rugby (Holy Trinity, St. Matthew), Ryton-on-Dunsmore, Salford Priors, Seckington, Sherbourne with Fulbrook, Shilton, Shipston on Stour, Shotteswell, Shuckburgh (Lower), Shustoke, Shustoke (Bentley), Shuttington, Snitterfield, Solihull, Southam, Spernall, Stivichall, Stockingford, Stockton, Stoke, Stoneleigh, Stretton-on-Dunsmore, Stretton-on-Fosse with Ditchford, Studley, Studley (Holy Ascension), Styvechale (Mappleborough Green), Sutton Coldfield, Sutton-under-Brailes, Tachbrook (Bishops), Tanworth, Tidmington, Tredington, Tysoe, Ufton, Walsgrave-on-Sowe, Wappenbury, Warmington, Warton, Warwick (All Saints, St. Mary, St. Nicholas, St. Paul), Wasperton, Weddington, Weethley, Wellesbourne, Weston under Wetherley, Westwood, Whatcote, Whitacre (Over), Whitchurch, Whitnash, Willey, Willoughby, Wilmcote, Wishaw, Withybrook, Wolfhampcote, Wolford, Wolston, Wolverton, Wolvey, Wootton (Leek), Wootton Wawen, Wormleighton, Wroxhall, Wyken, Wyken (Holy Cross).

The parish registers of the Birmingham churches are in the City Reference Library.

The CRO also holds indexed copies of the following registers: Allesley, Aston, Beaudesert (Henley Parish), Bentley (Shustoke Parish), Birmingham (St. Martin), Curdworth, Edgbaston, Gaydon and Chadshunt, Knowle, Radway, Rowington, Shustoke, Stratford-on-Avon, Weddington, Wolfhampcote, Wootton Wawen, Wroxall.

In addition, it holds a published book of Warwickshire marriages for the following parishes:
Anstey, Atherstone-on-Stour, Bishops Tachbrook, Bourton-on-Dunsmore, Butler's Marston, Charlecote, Ettington, Fenny Compton, Halford, Hatton, Honington, Idlicote, Leamington Priors, Long Compton, Priors Hardwick, Snitterfield, Temple Grafton, Whitchurch.

Bishop's Transcripts
There are none in the Warwickshire CRO. They are in the Diocesan Record Offices at Lichfield and Worcester, between which dioceses Warwickshire was formerly divided.

Wills and Probate Records
The same remarks apply.

Original Nonconformist Registers
These do not include deaths or burials. The undermentioned are in the CRO:
Methodist: Harbury, Leamington, Nuneaton.
Congregational: Leamington Spa, Long Compton, Southam, Warwick.
Baptist: Warwick.
Unitarian: Warwick.
Quaker: In the CRO there are records of burials in Warwick between 1660 and 1879, and indexes of births and burials compiled from the registers of quarterly meetings in the county (plus Leicester and Rutland), covering the period 1623-1837.
Roman Catholic: Brailes Catholic Chapel registers from 1778 to 1912.

Other Records
These include early newspapers from 1806; poll books; directories; maps; quarter sessions records; hearth and land tax records; estate and family papers; early maps; and microfilm census returns.

West Midlands

This is a "new" county formed from small parts of the counties of Staffordshire, Warwickshire, and Worcestershire, plus the whole of Birmingham, Coventry, Dudley, Solihull, Walsall, Warley, West Bromwich, Wolverhampton.

There is no County Record Office, so genealogical inquiries should be sent to the particular library covering the area in which you are interested. The details of each of these in the seven metropolitan districts are given below:

Family History Society
(See page 89 for remarks concerning Family History Societies.)

1. Coventry

Coventry City Record Office
Room 220, Broadgate House, Coventry. (Open Monday-Thursday, 0845-1645 hours; Friday, 0845-1615 hours; Saturday, 0845-1200 hours. Appointments are advisable, and are essential on Saturdays.)

The office will do research as requested by mail inquiries from overseas. However, searchers with complicated inquiries are advised to use the services of professional record-searchers; a list of them is available at the Record Office. No fees are charged by the office for the limited searching they do.

Parish Registers
These are in the Warwickshire CRO, Cape Road, Priory Park, Warwick. None are in the Coventry Record Office.

Other Records
Those held include Index of Admissions to the Freedom of the City of Coventry (1722-1934); Registers of Enrolments of Apprentices (1781-1963); Census Returns for the area (1841-71); Trade Directories (1874-1960); Registers of Electors (1877-1980); Coventry Primitive Methodist Circuit records (nineteenth and twentieth centuries); registers of thirteen Methodist churches, the Longford Baptist Church (nineteenth century), and the Unitarian Meeting House, Coventry (eighteenth to twentieth centuries).

2. Sandwell

This area includes the public libraries in West Bromwich, Wednesbury, Warley, and Tipton:

West Bromwich Central Library
High Street, West Bromwich B70 8DZ. Holds parish registers of All Saints, West Bromwich. Diocesan records at Lichfield Joint Record Office. Does not hold any Noncomformist registers.

Wednesbury District Library
Walsall Street, Wednesbury. The parish registers are still in the custody of the Vicar of St. Bartholomew, and the diocesan records are at the Lichfield Joint Record Office. The Nonconformist records include some documents from Camp Street, Ridding Lane, and Vicar Street Methodist churches in the nineteenth century and later.

Warley District Library
High Street, Smethwick B66 1AB. Holds some parish registers. The diocesan records are in the Birmingham Reference Library and the Warwickshire Record Office.

Tipton District Library
Victoria Road, Tipton. Holds registers for the Tipton parishes. Other parish records are still at St. Martin's Church, and the diocesan records are in the Lichfield Joint Record Office. There are some local Methodist church registers for the nineteenth century.

Opening hours for all of the above libraries are: Monday and Friday, 0900-1900 hours; Tuesday and Wednesday, 0900-1800 hours; Thursday and Saturday, 0900-1300 hours.

3. Solihull

Central Library
Homer Road, Solihull B91 3RG. The library does not employ an archivist and has very little archival material. Warwickshire CRO is the main place of deposit for Solihull records.

4. Walsall

Central Library

Lichfield Street, Walsall WS1 1TR. (Open Monday-Friday, 0930-1900 hours; Saturday, 0930-1700 hours.) The staff will search census returns and directories, but for anything more complicated the inquirer will be referred to local record agents.

Most Walsall parish registers are still in the original churches; others are in the Staffordshire CRO and the Lichfield Joint Record Office. There are some Nonconformist registers in the library, including Darlaston, Walsall, and Bloxwich Methodist Circuits, and one Baptist, one Presbyterian, and one Congregational church register from Walsall. The library does have microfilms of the Nonconformist registers for the area sent to the PRO in London in 1837.

The library also has census returns on microfilm for the period 1841-71 for the area.

5. Wolverhampton

Central Library

Snow Hill, Wolverhampton WV1 3AX. (Open Monday-Friday, 1000-1900 hours; Saturday, 1000-1700 hours.) The staff will carry out limited searches without charge, but the inquirer will be referred to professional record-searchers for lengthy research.

The main genealogical holdings of the library are:

Nonconformist Registers

A few are held from local Methodist churches in Wolverhampton.

Wills

There are some original wills and some indexed transcripts. There is an index to all wills proved in the Royal Peculiar of Wolverhampton; originals are in the Lichfield Joint Record Office.

Directories

These are held from 1770 to the present day and work is being done on an index. There are also rate (tax) books (1777-1829) and electoral registers (1852 onwards, but with gaps).

Census Returns

These are held on microfilm for Wolverhampton for the period 1841-71.

Newspapers

There are files of local newspapers from 1789 onwards, but they are not indexed. However, there is an index of births, marriages, and deaths in the personal announcement columns of the *Staffordshire Advertiser* (1795-1820).

Note: Walsall, Wolverhampton, and parts of Dudley and Sandwell were in the county of Staffordshire until 1974. As a result, the County Record Office has substantial holdings of material for this whole area.

Birmingham, Coventry, Solihull, and Smethwick were in Warwickshire until 1974, and consequently many records for these places are in the Warwickshire County Record Office.

6. Dudley

Archives and Local History Department

3 St. James Road, Dudley DY1 1HR. (Open Monday to Friday, 0900-1900 hours; Saturday, 0900-1700 hours.) This department covers the area of Amblecote, Brierly Hill, Cosely, Dudley, Halesowen, Sedgeley, and Stourbridge.

It is recognized as the Diocesan Record Office for the rural deaneries of Dudley and Himley. It holds parish registers for Sedgeley, and Methodist Circuit records for Stour Vale, Dudley, Hasbury and Halesowen, Stourbridge and Brierley Hill—all for the nineteenth and twentieth centuries. It has some duplicates of Methodist marriage registers, some from two Baptist churches, and others from two Unitarian churches.

7. Birmingham

Public Library

Birmingham B3 3HQ. (Open during normal office hours.) The usual amount of time given to answering queries is about thirty minutes, but more may be given to overseas inquirers. Any queries that are too long and complicated will be referred to local researchers, who will negotiate a fee directly with the inquirer.

The library holds most of the parish registers for the city of Birmingham; an obituary index for the period 1741-1860; local censuses for the available years; city directories from 1767; electoral rolls from 1838; rate (tax) books for 1736 onwards; the Mormon Index to parish registers for Warwickshire; copies of Birmingham wills from 1858 to 1929; and also large collections of papers (including title deeds and manorial records) deposited by local landed families and lawyers.

West Sussex

Family History Society
(See page 89 for remarks concerning Family History Societies.)

County Record Office
County Hall, Chichester, West Sussex PO19 1RN. (Open Monday-Friday, 0915-1230 hours and 1330-1700 hours.)

The present policy of the office is to make a short, single search from an initial inquiry either free or at a nominal charge. Longer or succeeding inquiries are referred to local record agents.

Parish Registers
These may be available as originals, Bishop's Transcripts, manuscript transcripts, or on microfilm:
Albourne, Alciston, Aldingbourne, Aldrington, Alford, Alfriston, Amberley, Angmering, Appledram, Ardingly, Arlington, Arundel, Ashburnham, Ashington, Ashurst, Balcombe, Barcombe, Barlavington, Barnham, Battle, Beckley, Beddingham, Beeding (Upper and Lower), Bepton, Bersted (South), Berwick, Bexhill (3 parishes), Bignor, Billingshurst, Binderton, Binsted, Birdham, Bishopstone, Blatchington (East and West), Bodiam, Bodle Street, Bognor, Bolney, Bosham, Botolphs, Boxgrove, Bramber, Brede, Brightling, Brighton (6 parishes), Broadwater, Broadwater Down, Burgess Hill, Burpham, Burton, Burwash, Burwash Weald, Bury, Buxted, Capel, Catsfield, Chailey, Chalvington, Chichester (10 parishes), Chiddingly, Chidham, Chiltington (East and West), Chithurst, Clapham, Clayton, Climping, Coates with Burton, Cocking, Coldwaltham, Colgate, Compton, Coombes, Copthorne, Cowfold,

Crawley, Crawley (West), Crawley Down, Crowborough, Crowhurst, Croydon, Cuckfield, Dallington, Danehill, Dean (East, Chichester), Dean (East, Lewes), Dean (West, Chichester), Dean (West, Lewes), Denton, Dicker (Upper), Didling, Ditchling, Donnington, Dorking, Duncton, Durrington, Earnley, Eartham, Easebourne, Eastbourne (8 parishes), Eastergate, Ebernoe, Edburton, Egdean, Elsted, Eridge Green, Etchingham, Ewhurst, Fairlight, Falmer, Felpham, Fernhurst, Ferring, Findon, Firle (West), Fishbourne (New), Fittleworth, Fletching, Flimwell, Folkington, Ford, Forest Row, Forestside, Framfield, Frant, Friston, Huntington, Glynde, Goring, Graffham, Greatham, Grinstead (East and West), Groombridge (New), Guestling, Guldeford (East), Hadlow Down, Hailsham, Hammerwood, Hampshire (Sussex entries in Hampshire Registers, 1540-1941), Hamsey, Hangleton, Hardham, Hartfield, Harting, Hastings (7 parishes), Haywards Heath, Heathfield, Heene, Heighton (South), Hellingly, Henfield, Heyshott, Highbrook, High Hurst Wood, Hoathly (East and West), Hollington, Hooe, Horsham, Horsted (Little), Horsted Keynes, Houghton, Hove (5 parishes), Hunston, Hurstmonceux, Hurstpierpoint, Icklesham, Iden, Ifield, Iford, Iping, Isfield, Itchenor (West), Itchingfield, Jevington, Keymer, Kingston by Lewes, Kingston by Sea, Kingston Gorse, Kirdford, Kirdford Plaistow, Lancing, Laughton, Lavant (East, Mid), Lavington (West), Lewes (7 parishes), Linch, Linchmere, Lindfield, Litlington, Littlehampton, Lodsworth, London (Sussex entries from London parishes, 1541-1837), Lullington, Lurgashall, Lyminster, Ladehurst, Malling (South), Marden (East, North, Upper), Maresfield, Mark Cross, Mayfield, Merston, Middleton, Midhurst, Milland, Mountfield, Mundham (North), Netherfield, Newhaven (alias Meeching), Mewick, Newtimber, Ninfield, Northchapel, Northiam, Nuthurst, Nutley, Ockley, Ore, Oving, Ovingdean, Pagham, Parham, Patcham, Patching, Peasmarsh, Penhurst, Pett, Petworth, Pevensey, Piddinghoe, Playden, Plumpton, Polegate, Poling, Portfield, Portslade, Poynings, Preston (East), Preston (Hove), Pulborough, Pyecombe, Racton, Ringmer, Ripe, Rodmell, Roffey, Rogate, Rotherfield, Rottingdean, Rudgwick, Rumboldswhyke, Rusper, Rustington, Rye, Salehurst, Sayers Common, Seaford, Sedlescombe, Selham, Selmeston, Selsey, Shermanbury, Shipley, Shoreham (New), Shoreham (Old), Sidlesham, Singleton, Slaugham, Slindon, Slinfold, Sompting, Southease, Southwater, Southwick, Stanmer, Staplefield, Stedham, Steyning, Stoke (North and South), Stoke (West), Stonegate, Stopham, Storrington, Stoughton, Streat, Sullington, Sutton, Tangmere, Tarring (West), Tarring Neville, Telscombe, Terwick,

Thakeham, Thorney (West), Ticehurst, Tidebrook, Tillington, Tortington, Treyford-cum-Didling, Trotton, Tuxlith, Twineham, Uckfield, Udimore, Upwaltham, Wadhurst, Walberton, Waldron, Warbleton, Warblington, Warminghurst, Warnham, Warningcamp, Wartling, Washington, Westbourne, Westfield, Westham, Westhampnett, Westmeston, Whatlington, Wiggonholt cum Greatham, Willingdon, Wilmington, Winchelsea, Wisborough Green, Wiston, Withyham, Withyham Hamlet, Withyham St. John, Wittering (East and West), Wivelsfield, Wivelsfield Hamlet, Woodmancote, Woolavington, Woolbeging, Worth, Worthing (Christchurch, St. George, St. Paul), Yapton.

Nonconformist Registers
Catholic: Arundel, Brockhampton, Burton, Crawley, Easebourne, Midhurst, Slindon.
Methodist: These include United, Wesleyan, Bible Christian and Primitive registers from Aldingbourne, Bognor, Brighton, Chichester, Emsworth, Fishbourne (New), Horsham, Itchenor (West), Littlehampton, Nutbourne, Nyetimber, Pagham, Rye, Selsey, Sidlesham, Stanstead, Stoughton, Walberton, West Wittering, Worthing.
Independent Calvinist: Billingshurst, Chichester, Rudgewick, Wisborough Green and Loxwood.
Congregational: Bosham, Chichester, Hastings, Hurstmonceux, Rye.
Lady Huntingdon's Connexion: Wivelsfield.
Baptist: Chichester, Rye.
Quaker: Horsham (1866-87), Ifield (1865-67), Lewes (1865-1901), Rottingdean (1865-1901).

Census Returns
These are held on microfilm for the whole of the county for the period 1841-71.

Marriage Licences
The CRO holds these for the period 1575-1945.

Index of Emigrants and Transportees
This covers the period 1778-1874 and is published by the CRO in a booklet.

Wills
The CRO holds probate records for the Archdeaconry of Chichester and the peculiars within it (roughly the present county) for the years 1481-1858.

Vaccination Registers

These apply to the following places and cover a period from about 1853 to 1872: Appledram, Bognor, Donnington, Fishbourne (New), Hunston, Merston, North Mundham, Pagham, Preston (Brighton), Rumboldswhyke.

The Public Print-Out

This is an index of baptisms and marriages taken from the microfilms of parish registers, and supplemented with details from Bishop's Transcripts and other transcripts and microfilms. When the project is completed it will be indexed on a parish-by-parish basis.

The Computer File Index

This, like the print-out above, is a product of the Mormon Church. The two will eventually be merged into one index for the county. The CFI contains 200,000 names at present.

Monumental Inscriptions (Tombstones)

Many of these have been copied throughout the county from some fifty-two parishes, and the lists are in the CRO.

Other Records

The CRO holds large quantities of estate and family papers; municipal council records and minutes; school registers; cemetery registers; apprenticeship records; poll books and electoral lists; directories; and early newspapers.

West Yorkshire

Family History Society

None. However, there is the Yorkshire Archaeological Society, and its Family History Section, which is quite outstanding. Its main holdings are family and estate collections, plus a number of transcripts of parish registers. The address is Claremont, Clarendon Road, Leeds LS2 9NZ, which houses both the library and the archives of the Society. The secretary of the Family History Section is Mrs. J. Hanson, 109 Kitson Hill Road, Mirfield, West Yorks WF14 9OS. The headquarters is open on Monday, Thursday, Friday, 0930-1700 hours; Tuesday and Wednesday, 1400-2030 hours; Saturday, 1st and 3rd in each month, 0930-1700 hours. It is closed on every Monday that follows an open Saturday.)

County Record Office

Registry of Deeds, Newstead Road, Wakefield, West Yorks WF1 2DE. (Open Monday-Thursday, 0900-1700 hours; Friday, 0900-1600 hours, or later by arrangement.)

The office is prepared to answer, free of charge, genealogical inquiries of a limited nature, but cannot undertake extensive searches. In the latter case, inquirers will be provided with a list of professional record-searchers, together with details of parish and Nonconformist registers held in the CRO.

Parish Registers

Ackworth, Almondbury, Altofts, Alverthorpe, Armitage Bridge, Badsworth, Barkisland, Barnsley, Batley (All Saints, St. Thomas), Birchencliffe, Birkenshaw-with-Hunsworth, Birstall, Bradley, Brighouse, Brotherton, Brownhill, Carlinghow, Castleford, Cawthorne, Chapelthorpe, Cleckheaton, Clifton, Coley, Copley, Crofton, Crossland Moor, Cross Stone (Todmorden), Cumberworth, Dale, Darrington, Darton, Denby, Dewsbury, Dodworth, Drighlington, Earlsheaton, East Ardsley, Elland, Emley, Farnley Tyas, Featherstone, Ferry Fryston, Flockton with Denby Grange, Gawthorpe and Chickenley, Gildersome, Golcar, Gomersal, Greetland, Halifax (Haley Hill All Souls), Halifax (St. John), Halifax Claremount (St. Thomas), Hanging Heaton, Hartshead, Heath, Hebden Bridge (St. James, St. John), Heckmondwike, Hemsworth (Holy Trinity, St. Helen), Heptonstall, Hightown, Holmbridge, Holmfirth, Horbury, Huddersfield (5 parishes), Illingworth, Kellington, King Cross (Halifax), Kirk Sandall, Kirk Smeaton, Knottingly, Lepton, Lightcliffe, Lindley, Linthwaite, Liversedge, Lockwood, Longwood, Luddenden, Luddenden Foot, Marsden, Midhope, Milnsbridge, Mirfield, Monk Bretton, Mount Pellon (Halifax), Mytholmroyd, Netherthong, Newsome, Norland, Normanton, Northowram, Outwood, Paddock, Penistone, Pontefract, Rastrick (St. John, St. Matthew), Ripponden with Rishworth, Royston, Salterhebble, Sandal, Scissett, Sharlston, Shelley, Shepley, Silkstone, Skelmanthorpe, Southowram, Sowerby, Sowerby Bridge, Stainland, Staithwaite, Thornhill, Thurgoland, Thurstonland, Todmorden (Christ Church, St. Mary Harley Wood), Upperthong, Wakefield (Cathedral, 4 parishes), Walsden, Warmfield, Warley, West Vale, Whitwood, Whitwood Mere, Womersley, Woodhouse (Huddersfield), West Scammonden, Woodkirk, Wragley.

In addition to the above, a number of West Yorkshire registers are held at other locations in the county:

BORTHWICK INSTITUTE OF HISTORICAL RESEARCH, ST. ANTHONY'S HALL,
YORK YO1 2PW

Ancaster Malbis, Appleton Roebuck, Chapel Haddesley, Monk Friston, Poppleton (Upper and Nether), Rushcliffe

LEEDS CITY LIBRARY, CHAPELTOWN ROAD, SHEEPSCAR, LEEDS LS7 3AP

Addingham, Allerton Bywater, Armley, Carleton in Craven, Harewood, Harrogate, Leeds (all parishes), Methley, Pannal, Potternewton, Thornton, Wortley, Wrangthorn, Yeadon.

BRADFORD ARCHIVES DEPT., PRINCE'S WAY, BRADFORD BD1 1NN

Bradford (all parishes), Haworth, Ilkley, Keighley, Kildwick, Queensbury, Riddlesden, Shipley, Silsden.

Methodist Registers

Ackworth, Adwalton, Akroyden, Allerton Bywater, Altofts, Baildon, Batley, Beal, Berry Brow, Birkenshaw, Birstall, Bowling, Bradford, Carlton, Castleford, Chickenley, Churwell, Cleckheaton, Crigglestone, Crofton, Crow Edge, Darrington, Denby Dale, Dewsbury, Drighlington, Earlsheaton, Eccleshill, Farnley Tyas, Featherstone, Ferry Bridge, Frizinghall, Gawthorpe, Glass Houghton, Gomersal, Hade Edge, Hanging Heaton, Hartshead, Hartshead Moor, Heckmondwike, Hepworth, Hinchliffe Mill, Holmfirth, Honley, Hopetown, Horbury, Horbury Junction, Huddersfield, Keighley, Kippax, Knottingley, Little Smeaton, Liversedge, Lofthouse, Loscoe, Manningham, Methley, Mirfield, Morley, Netherthong, New Sharlston, Normanton, Oakenshaw, Ossett Common, Ossett Green, Oulton, Outwood, Ouzlewell Green, Overton, Pontefract, Rothwell, Scholes, Sharlston Common, Shepley, Shipley, South Elmshall, Staincliffe, Thornhill, Tong, Wakefield, Westgate Hill, Whitwood, Woodlesford.

Mormon Index

The CRO holds the Mormon microfiche index to the Yorkshire parish registers. It contains baptism and marriage entries from many Anglican and Nonconformist registers up to about 1850. Remember that not all churches are included.

Census Returns

The CRO holds microfilm copies of the census enumeration books for 1851.

Register of Deeds

This covers the period 1704-1970 and contains five million abstracts of property transactions. It has a name index and a place index for the periods 1704-87 and 1885-1923.

Wills since 1858
The CRO holds records of these up to 1928.

Other Records
These include electoral registers from 1840 to 1974 for the county constituencies (not for the cities); and the records of the West Riding Quarter Sessions (1637-1971).

Wiltshire

Family History Society
(See page 89 for remarks concerning Family History Societies.)

County Record Office
County Hall, Trowbridge, Wiltshire BA14 8JG. (Open Monday to Friday, 0900-1230 hours and 1330-1700 hours; Wednesdays until 2030 hours.)

The office charges no fee for a short, specific search, but inquirers asking, for example, for all references to a particular name will be referred to local researchers working for a fee.

Parish Registers
The following original registers are held in the CRO:
Aldbourne, Alderton, Allington, Alton Barnes, Alvediston, Amesbury, Ansty, Ashley, Ashton (Steeple), Ashton (West), Ashton Keynes, Avebury, Baverstock, Beechingstoke, Bemerton, Berwick Bassett, Berwick St. John, Bishopstone (N. Wilts), Bishopstone (Salisbury), Bishopstrow, Blunsdon (Broad), Blunsdon (St. Andrew), Boscombe, Box, Boyton, Bradford-on-Avon, Bradley (Maiden), Bradley (North), Bremhill, Bremilham, Brinkworth, Britford, Bromham, Broughton Gifford, Bulford, Burbage, Burcombe, Buttermere, Calstone Wellington, Cannings (All), Cannings (Bishop), Chalfield (Great), Chalke (Bower), Chalke (Broad), Chapmanslade, Charlton St. Peter, Cherhill, Cheverell (Great), Cheverell (Little), Chicklade, Chilmark, Chilton Foliat, Chippenham (St. Andrew), Chippenham (St. Paul), Chirton, Chisledon, Chitterne All Saints, Chitterne St. Mary, Cholderton, Christian Malford, Chute, Clyffe Pypard, Codford St. Mary, Codford St. Peter, Colerne, Collingbourne Ducis, Collingbourne Kingston, Compton Bassett, Compton Chamberlayne, Coombe Bissett, Corsham, Corsley, Coulston (East), Cricklade St. Mary, Cricklade St. Sampson, Crudwell, Dauntsey, Derry Hill, Deverill (Brixton), Deverill (Hill),

Deverill (Kingston), Deverill (Longbridge), Deverill (Monkton), Devizes (St. James), Devizes (St. John), Devizes (St. Mary), Dilton, Dilton Marsh, Dinton, Donhead St. Andrew, Donhead St. Mary, Downton, Draycot Cerne, Draycot Foliat, Easton Royal, Eaton (Castle), Ebbesbourne Wake, Edington, Eisey, Enford, Erlestoke, Etchilhampton, Everleigh, Farley, Fifield Bavant, Figheldean, Fisherton Anger, Fisherton Delamere, Fosbury, Fovant, Foxham, Foxley, Froxfield, Fugglestone (St. Peter), Fyfield, Garsdon, Grafton (East), Grittleton, Ham, Hannington, Hardenhuish, Harnham (East), Heddington, Heytesbury, Heywood, Highway, Highworth, Hilmarton, Hilperton, Hindon, Hinton (Broad), Hinton (Little), Holt, Homington, Horningsham, Huish, Huish-with-Oare, Hullavington, Idmiston, Imber, Keevil, Kellaways, Kennett (East), Kington St. Michael, Knook, Knoyle (East), Lacock, Landford, Langford (Little), Langford (Steeple), Langley Burrell, Latton, Laverstock, Lavington (Market), Lavington (West), Lea and Cleverton, Leigh, Leigh Delamere, Liddington, Limpley Stoke, Littleton Drew, Luckington, Lydiard Millicent, Lydiard Tregoze, Lyneham, Maddington, Malmesbury (Abbey Church, St. Mary, St. Peter and St. Paul), Manningford Abbots, Manningford Bruce, Marden, Marlborough (St. Mary, St. Peter), Melksham, Mere, Mildenhall, Milston, Milton Lilbourne, Minety, Neston, Netherhampton, Nettleton, Newnton (North), Newton Tony, Norton, Nunton, Oaksey, Odstock, Ogbourne St. Andrew, Ogbourne St. George, Orcheston St. George, Orcheston St. Mary, Overton, Patney, Pertwood, Pewsey, Porton, Potterne, Poulshot, Preshute, Purton, Ramsbury, Rodbourne Cheney, Rollestone, Rowde, Savernake, Seend, Semington, Semley, Shalbourne, Sherrington, Sherston Magna, Shrewton, Somerford (Little), Sopworth, Stanton Fitzwarren, Stanton St. Bernard, Stanton St. Quinton, Staverton, Stert, Stockton, Stoke (Limpley), Stourton, Stratford-sub-Castle, Stratford Tony, Stratton St. Margaret, Sutton Benger, Sutton Mandeville, Sutton Veny, Swallowcliffe, Swindon (Christchurch, St. John, St. Mark, St. Paul), Teffont Evias, Teffont Magna, Tilshead, Tisbury, Tockenham, Tollard Royal, Trowbridge (Holy Trinity St. Thomas, St. Stephen, Studley St. John), Trowbridge St. James, Tytherton Kellaways, Upton Lovell, Upton Scudamore, Urchfont, Wanborough, Warminster (Christ Church), Warminster (St. John), Westbury, Westwood, Whaddon, Whiteparish, Wilcot, Wilsford, Wilton, Wingfield, Winsley, Winterbourne Bassett, Winterbourne Dauntsey, Winterbourne Earls, Winterbourne Gunner, Winterbourne Monkton, Wishford

(Great), Woodborough, Wootton Bassett, Wootton Rivers, Worton, Wraxall (North and South), Wroughton, Wylye, Yatesbury. *Note*: The Salisbury Registers (Fisherton Anger, St. Edmund, St. Martin, St. Thomas) are at the Council House, Bourne Hill, Salisbury.

The CRO does not hold original registers for the following but has them on microfilm:
Atworth, Axford, Bramshaw, Bratton, Brokenborough, Castle Combe, Chittoe, Christian Malford, Dean (West), Devizes (St. Mary), Ditteridge, Edington, Fittleton, Hankerton, Hannington, Hilperton (burials), Marston (South), Netheravon, Salisbury Cathedral, Seagry, Trowbridge (burials), Westport (St. Mary), Wilcot, Yatton Keynell.

The CRO does not hold original registers for the following, but has them in a printed edition: Wilsford and Lake.

The registers of some former Wiltshire parishes are held in other Record Offices:

Gloucester CRO: Shorncote, Somerford Keynes.

Hampshire CRO: Damerham, Martin, Plaitford, Wellow, Whitsbury.

Bishop's Transcripts
Between fifty and sixty of these are in the CRO.

Nonconformist Registers
Congregational: Devizes, Donhead St. Mary, Heytesbury, Salisbury, Trowbridge.
Baptist: Chapmanslade, Devizes, Rushall, Southwick, Trowbridge.
Methodist: Market Lavington Primitive Methodist Station, Marlborough Methodist Circuit, Marlborough Wesleyan Circuit, Salisbury Circuit, Salisbury Primitive Methodist Station, Salisbury United Methodist Free Church Circuit, Salisbury Wesleyan Circuit, Trowbridge (Manvers Street), Trowbridge and Bradford Methodist Circuit, Trowbridge Wesleyan Circuit, Wilton Primitive Methodist Station.
Independent: Trowbridge (Silver Street).
Society of Friends (Quaker): North Somerset and Wiltshire Monthly Meetings.

Marriage Licences
The CRO holds abstracts of these for the period 1683 to the early nineteenth century. There are also some scattered ones dating back to 1615.

Wills

There were a number of different ecclesiastical jurisdictions in Wiltshire but the CRO holds manuscript indexes to all the wills proved in the various courts. The CRO also holds copies of wills proved from 1858, when the probate registry took over from the church, up to 1928.

Census Returns

The CRO holds a microfilm of the 1851 Census, and can obtain microfilm of the other available years if at least ten days' notice is given.

Taxation Records

There are incomplete hearth tax records; land tax assessments from 1780 to 1832; and published tax returns for the county for 1545 and 1576.

Tithe Awards

An almost complete set is in the CRO.

Library

There is a very extensive library available for visitors—donations, please! It contains a mass of general information about the county which is of great value to ancestor-hunters.

Newspapers

The earliest of those available in the CRO dates from the mid-eighteenth century. For example, they have the *Salisbury Journal* on microfilm from March 1746.

Protestation Returns, 1641

The protestation in support of the Protestant religion was made by all men aged eighteen and up. For Wiltshire they exist for the *hundreds* (i.e., sections of a county) of Cawden and Cadworth, Underditch, Chalke, and part of Branch and Dole, i.e., only parts of the south-eastern border of the county. The originals are in the Record Office of the House of Lords, but printed copies are in the CRO.

Miscellaneous

Other available records include apprenticeships; land deeds; manorial records; estate surveys and rentals; parish records such as poor law administration; family and professional papers; court records; and a large collection of diocesan records. (However, Salisbury Cathedral records are in the custody of the Chapter Clerk, Bishops Walk, The Close, Salisbury.)

Worcester

See under *Hereford and Worcester*

10
WELSH COUNTIES

As I discussed in the chapter on English counties, major changes were made in the Welsh and English county boundaries in 1974. Therefore, when you are looking for a county, it is important to know which areas it now incorporates.

The changes in Wales were more drastic than in England. Certainly from an administrative point of view the reduction in the number of counties makes sense, but to a lover of history the disappearance of the old names is a pity! Below is a list of the new counties.

Note: CBC indicates the County Borough Council. The name of the county town and seat of government is shown in brackets.

CLWYD: Flintshire, most of Denbighshire, part of Merioneth (Mold)

DYFED: Cardiganshire, Carmarthenshire, Pembrokeshire (Carmarthen)

GWENT: Newport CBC, most of Monmouthshire, part of Breconshire (Newport)

GWYNEDD: Anglesey, Caernarfonshire, most of Merioneth, part of Denbighshire (Caernarfon)

MID-GLAMORGAN: Merthy Tydfil CBC, parts of Breconshire, parts of Glamorgan, parts of Monmouthshire (Cardiff)

POWYS: Montgomeryshire, Radnorshire, most of Breconshire (Llandrindod Wells)

SOUTH GLAMORGAN: Cardiff CBC, parts of Glamorgan, parts of Monmouthshire (Cardiff)

WEST GLAMORGAN: Swansea CBC, parts of Glamorgan (Swansea)

There are certain fundamental differences between the genealogical sources available in Wales and those in England. Generally speaking, the Welsh records do not go back as far. You may find it difficult to trace the Welsh branches of your family back as far as the English lines can be identified. Secondly, apart from those records in the Welsh County Record Offices, all documents and lists are centralized in the National Library of Wales. Exceptions are documents kept in the Public Record Office in London.

Perhaps the most noticeable difference is the widespread use of patronymics in Wales as opposed to the fixed surnames of England. An example is to be found in a property grant in 1683, when the witnesses were given as Griffith *Lewis*, son of *Lewis* John William, and Harry *David*, son of *David* John Rees. Gradually the Welsh adopted the English system, but the change occurred over a long period. The tendency was for surnames to be used most commonly by the higher classes of society, and along the English border. In the western areas of Wales patronymics were still in use in the early nineteenth century. One result of this gradual development is the limited number of different surnames in Wales. Another is the existence of many surnames beginning with B or P, such as Bowen (from Ab Owen, the son of Owen) and Powell (from Ap Howell). Married women were often referred to by their maiden names, i.e., Jennett Bennett, wife of David Thomas Rees Prees, in a grant in 1683.

Wales is regarded as a mainly Nonconformist country but only a minority of the population were Nonconformists until well into the nineteenth century. Even if people left the Anglican Church to join a chapel, they were slow to break all ties with the parish church. In rural areas, chapels were often not licensed for marriages and did not have their own burial-grounds.

National Library of Wales
This is located at Aberystwyth, Dyfed, Wales SY23 3BU. The office does not undertake general research into family history and genealogy on behalf of those inquiring by mail. You will be referred to their list of professional researchers. However, the office will undertake very limited searches without fee; for example, checking dates in parish registers or Bishop's Transcripts, or looking for wills over limited periods.

Parish Registers
Four hundred parishes have already lodged their registers in the National Library, and more are coming in all the time. Parish registers in Wales do not often date back before 1660.

Bishop's Transcripts
As you know, these are copies of the parish registers which were sent once a year to the Bishop by the local Anglican clergyman. The earliest transcripts in the National Library date from 1662, but there are many gaps. In the Diocese of Llandaff, for instance, there are only a few before 1723. There are hardly any for the eighteenth century for the archdeaconries of Cardigan and St. Davids. The

transcripts stop at varying dates in the middle or at the end of the nineteenth century. Transcripts of marriages generally stopped in 1837, because of the compulsory civil registration of marriages which was instituted in that year.

Marriage Licences and Bonds
These records cover the eighteenth and nineteenth centuries, and the first thirty years of the twentieth century. It should be borne in mind, however, that only one person in ten was married by licence.

Nonconformist Registers
Many of these are in the Public Record Office in London. Some were not deposited and others were copied before they were sent there. Items from both these categories are in the National Library. In addition, lists of members and contribution books of particular chapels are available, and can provide much information for the ancestor-hunter.

Church Newspapers
The National Library has a number of these monthly publications (usually published by individual chapels), which contain entries of birth, marriage, and death.

Wills
Wills were proved in ecclesiastical courts until 1858. All those proved in Welsh courts are in the Library. An index for Welsh wills on a county basis for the greater part of the eighteenth century is available in the Library. The probate records there cover the whole of Wales, with the exception of fifteen border parishes which were in the Diocese of Hereford; as well, seventeen English parishes which came under Welsh jurisdiction are included.

The original wills generally start around 1600, and some copy wills for St. Asaph and Brecon date back to 1565 and 1570 respectively. There are indexes available for most of the probate records in the Library. In view of the Welsh patronymic naming system, all the earlier indexes (except Llandaff) are arranged either in chronological order, or, in the case of St. Asaph, in alphabetical order under Christian name. A surname card index has been completed for St. Asaph for 1729-1820, and further card indexes are being prepared for other areas.

In 1858 the probate of wills was transferred to the civil courts. The National Library has the custody of copy wills from five probate registries covering the whole of Wales (except for Montgomeryshire) and also Herefordshire. Indexes are available for varying periods for four of the five registries: Carmarthen, Hereford, Llandaff, and St. Asaph. No index is yet available for Bangor.

Copies of all wills proved in the district registries are kept at Somerset House, London, and are indexed. Copies of the index are also available in district registries.

Tithe Records
The maps and apportionment schedules for the whole of Wales are in the National Library. They are indispensable in establishing the location of farms and other estate holdings in the country in 1840. A few of the account books covering the payment of tithes have survived. These are of value since they may show the approximate date when a person ceased to pay tithes, which was probably at the time of death.

Estate and Personal Papers
They include land records, letters, account books, and title deeds. There is a general card index.

Pedigree Books
There are many family trees and family histories in the Library, in the form of published books, manuscript family histories, or rough notes of researchers.

Legal and Administrative Records
A great accumulation of material comes under this heading. Great Sessions and Quarter Sessions of the courts are covered, together with jury lists, coroners' inquests, rate books, education records, etc.

The above notes are a rough guide to the holdings of the National Library of Wales. The records are so detailed and growing so rapidly that a personal visit or the services of a researcher familiar with the Library are almost essential for anyone tracing Welsh ancestors.

Welsh Counties

County Record Offices in Wales hold large collections of parish registers, but some will be at the National Library of Wales, Aberystwyth. Welsh County Record Offices hold no diocesan records—all of those are in the National Library. Records of Nonconformist denominations may be found in County Record Offices and in the National Library.

Clwyd

This new county was formed from the old county of Flint, most of Denbighshire, and part of Merioneth.

Family History Society
(See page 89 for remarks concerning Family History Societies.)

County Record Office
The Old Rectory, Hawarden, Deeside, Clwyd CH5 3NR. (Open Monday-Friday, 0845-1700; Friday, 0845-1630 hours.)

The office will undertake a very limited amount of research on specific questions (for example, looking up one or two entries in a parish register where place and approximate year are known) free of charge. Persons asking for more help than this are given the names of local record agents who each negotiate their fees privately.

There is an area record office at 46 Clwyd Street, Ruthin LL15 1HP.

Parish Registers
The following are held in the Clwyd County Record Office:
FLINTSHIRE PARISH REGISTERS AT HAWARDEN: Bagillt, Bangor, Bistre, Bodel Wyddan, Bodfari, Bronington, Broughton, Brynford, Buckley, Caerwys, Cilcain, Connah's Quay, Cwm, Dyserth, Ffynnongroew, Flint, Greenfield, Gwaenysgor, Gwernaffield, Halkyn, Hanmer, Hawarden, Holywell, Hope, Llanasa, Llanfynydd, Meliden, Mold (St. John), Mostyn, Nannerch, Nercwys, Northop, Overton, Penley, Pontblyddyn, Prestatyn, Rhuddlan, Rhydymyn, Rhyl (Holy Trinity, St. Ann, St. Thomas), St. Asaph, Shotton, Trelawnyd, Tremeirchion, Treuddyn, Whitford, Worthenbury, Ysceifiog.

DENBIGHSHIRE PARISH REGISTERS AT RUTHIN: Abergele, Berse, Betws-yn-Rhos, Broughton, Brymbo, Bryneglwys, Brynymaen, Bylchau, Cerrigydrudion, Chirk, Clocaenog, Colwyn, Colwyn Bay, Denbigh, Efenechtyd, Eglwysbach, Erbistock, Erryrys, Esclusham, Gresford, Gwersyllt, Gwytherin, Gyffylliog, Henllan, Llanarmon Dyffryn Ceiriog, Llanarmon Mynydd Mawr, Llanarmon-yn-iâl, Llanbedr

Dyffryn Clwyd, Llanddoget, Llanddulas, Llandegla, Llandrillo-yn-Rhos, Llandyrnog, Llanelian-yn-Rhos, Llanfair Dyffryn Clwyd, Llanfair Talhaearn, Llanferres, Llanfihangel Glyn Myfyr, Llanfwrog, Llangadwaladr, Llangedwyn, Llangernyw, Llangollen, Llangwm, Llangwyfan, Llangynhafal, Llannefydd, Llanrhaeadr-ym-Mochnant, Llanrhaeadr-yng-Nghinmerch, Llanrhydd, Llanrwst, Llansanffraid Glan Conway, Llansanffraid Glynceiriog, Llansannan, Llansilin, Llantysilio, Llanychan, Llanynys, Llay, Llysfaen, Marchwiel, Minera, Nantglyn, Pentrefoelas, Penycae, Pontfadog, Rhosddu, Rhosllanerchrugog, Rhosymedre, Rossett, Ruabon, Ruthin, St. George, Southsea, Towyn, Trefnant, Trofarth, Wrexham, Ystbyty Ifan.

MERIONETH PARISH REGISTERS AT RUTHIN (on microfilm): Betws Gwerfil Goch, Corwen, Gwyddelwern, Llandrillo-yn-Edeyrnion, Llangar, Llansanffraid Glyndyfrdwy.

Note: The originals are in the Gwynedd County Record Office (Dolgellau Branch: Cae Penarlâg, Dolgellau LL40 2YB).

Nonconformist Registers

Most of the Flintshire registers are held in the Hawarden office, and most of the Denbighshire ones in the Ruthin office. There are exceptions to this, and there is some duplication. The registers of places listed are either original registers or microfilm copies.

RUTHIN

Calvinistic Methodist: Aberchwiler, Abergele, Brymbo, Bryneglwys, Bwlchgwyn, Cefn Meriadog, Cerrigydrudion, Coedpoeth, Denbigh, Derwen, Efenechtyd, Eglwysbach, Glyntraean, Henllan, Llanarmon Dyffryn Clwyd, Llandyrnog, Llanelian, Llanelidan, Llanfair Dyffryn Clwyd, Llanfair Talhaearn, Llanferres, Llangernyw, Llangollen, Llangynhafal, Llannefydd, Llanrhaeadr-yng-Nghinmerch, Llanrwst, Llansanffraid Glanconway, Llansannan, Llantysilio, Llysfaen, Nantglyn, Pentrefoelas, Rhosllanerchrugog, Ruabon, Ruthin, Wrexham, Ystbyty Ifan (Bethel and Capel Mawr).
Independent: Abergele, Brymbo, Cerrigydrudion, Denbigh, Erbistock, Llangwm, Llangynhafal, Rhosllanerchrugog, Rhosymedre, Ruabon, Wrexham, Ystbyty Ifan.
Methodist: Brymbo, Cefn, Chirk, Wrexham.
Wesleyan: Cefn, Denbigh, Llangollen, Llanrwst, Ruabon, Ruthin, Wrexham.
Baptist: Llanfwrog, Llannefydd, Llansannan, Penycae, Wrexham.
Congregational: Llangollen, Llanrwst, Llansilin.

Presbyterian: Wrexham.

HAWARDEN

Calvinistic Methodist: Bagillt, Caerwys, Cilcain, Dyserth, Flint, Halkyn, Holywell, Leeswood, Llanasa, Mold, Nannerch, Newcwys, Northop, Rhosesmor, Rhuddlan, St. Asaph, Treuddyn, Whitford, Ysceifiog.

Independent: Bagillt, Buckley, Cilcain, Holywell, Hope, Mold, Nannerch, Rhesycae, Trelawnyd, Whitford.

Methodist: Bistre, Buckley, Caergwrle, Connah's Quay, Hawarden, Mold and Buckley.

Wesleyan: Holywell.

Baptist: Rhuddlan.

Congregational: Holywell, Rhuddlan, St. Asaph, Waen.

Presbyterian: Rhuddlan, Trelawnyd, Waen.

The Ruthin office also holds microfilms of Calvinistic Methodist registers from the following places in Caernarvonshire: Betws-y-Coed, Caerhun,Conway, Dolwyddelan, Llandudno, Llangwstennin, Llanrhychwyn, Penmachno, Trefriw. It also has on microfilm the registers of the Calvinistic Methodist chapel at Corwen in Merioneth.

Bishop's Transcripts
These are in the National Library of Wales, but a list of St. Asaph records is available in the CRO.

Civil Registration
Addresses of local registry offices are:

ALYN AND DEESIDE: Council Offices, Hawarden

COLWYN: 67 Market Street, Abergele

DELYN: Count Court, Park Lane, Holywell

GLYNDŴR: Station Road, Ruthin

RHUDDLAN: Morfa Hall, Church Street, Rhyl

WREXHAM MAELOR: 23 Chester Street, Wrexham

Wills
Most parishes in Flintshire and Denbighshire were in the Diocese of St. Asaph, but there were exceptions: a number of Denbighshire parishes were in the Diocese of Bangor; a few parishes in both counties were in the Diocese of Chester; Hawarden was a peculiar, exempt from church jurisdiction; and Penley was in the Diocese of Lichfield until 1920.

Most probate records are in the National Library of Wales, the following being a brief account:

CONSISTORY COURT OF ST. ASAPH: Original wills, administrations, and inventories (1557-1858) and register copy wills (1565-1709). A microfilm copy of the latter is available in the Hawarden office of the CRO.

CONSISTORY COURT OF BANGOR: Original wills, administrations, and inventories (1635-1858) and register copy wills (1790, 1851-58).

CONSISTORY COURT OF CHESTER: Original wills, administrations, and inventories for Welsh people only (1546-1858). A list of these up to 1825 is available at the CRO at Hawarden.

PECULIAR COURT OF HAWARDEN: Original wills, administrations, and inventories (1554-1858).

Note: Wills of persons holding land in more than one diocese were proved in the Prerogative Court of Canterbury. These records are in the Public Record Office, Chancery Lane, London.

Since the centralized probate system came into law in 1858 there has been the Principal Probate Registry in London and a number of district registry offices throughout the country. The office covering North East Wales, at St. Asaph, was closed in 1928, and its original wills, dating from 1858 to 1928, are now held in the Bangor Sub-Registry Office, Garth Road, Bangor, and the register copies in the National Library. The Chester District Registry Office, 17 Cuppin Street, Chester, holds original wills from 1858, and copies with indexes are in the Cheshire County Record Office, The Castle, Chester.

Census Returns

Microfilm copies for the period 1841-71 are held in the Hawarden office for Flintshire, and in the Ruthin office for Denbighshire. There are occasional gaps, particularly in 1861, and the whole of the Wrexham area is missing from the 1841 returns. However, an original manuscript return of 1841 for most of Wrexham town is held at Ruthin.

Directories

The CRO at Hawarden holds directories for Flintshire towns for 1828-9, 1835 (all of North Wales), 1841, 1856, 1868, 1874, 1886 (Flintshire and Denbighshire particularly detailed), 1889-90 (all of North Wales), and 1912. The office at Ruthin has the following for Denbighshire: 1818-20, 1829 (Wrexham only), 1830, 1835, 1840 (all of North Wales), 1844, and then at regular intervals until the end of the century.

Miscellaneous

Other records held in the Clwyd offices include books about the counties, listing the more important inhabitants and dating back to the 1680s; some Catholic records for Holywell; poor law records; school registers from the mid-nineteenth century; taxation records for Flintshire and Denbighshire in the respective offices as far back as 1544; quarter sessions records; and a personal name index compiled from all listed collections of family and estate archives. Electoral registers as far back as 1832 for Flintshire are at Hawarden, and from the same date for Denbighshire at Ruthin.

Dyfed

This "new" county was formed from Cardigan, Carmarthen, and Pembroke. The three original record offices continue as before and there has been little unification of records. The addresses of the three offices are:

CARDIGAN: Swyddfa'r Sir, Marine Terrace, Aberystwyth, Dyfed SY23 2DE.

CARMARTHEN: County Hall, Carmarthen, Dyfed SA31 1JP.

PEMBROKE: The Castle, Haverford West, Dyfed SA61 2EF.

All the offices are open Monday-Thursday, 0900-1645 hours; Friday, 0900-1615 hours; Saturday (Carmarthen and Pembroke by appointment), 1st and 3rd of each month. The staff will undertake limited searches but inquirers needing a general search will be referred to local record agents.

Parish Registers

CARDIGAN: Almost all the parish registers for this section of Dyfed are in the National Library of Wales. The office does hold the registers of Henfynyw and Llanddewi Aberarth.

CARMARTHEN: Abergorlech (Llanybyther), Abernant, Ammanford (All Saints, St. Michael), Bettws, Brechfa, Brynamman, Burry Port, Carmarthen (St. David, St. Peter), Castelldwyran, Cilycwm, Cilymaenilwyd, Cwmamman, Cyffig, Cymllynfell, Dafen, Eglwys-Cymmin, Eglwys-Fair-a-Churig, Felinfoel, Gwaencaegurwen, Gwynfe (Llangadock), Henllan Amgoed, Kidwelly, Laugharne, Llanarthney, Llanboidy, Llandawke, Llanddarog, Llanddeusant, Llanddowror, Llandeilo-fawr, Llandissilio, Llandybie, Llandyfeisant, Llanedy, Llanelli (6 parishes), Llanfair-ar-y-Bryn, Llanfallteg, Llanfihangel (Abercowin, Aberythych, ar-Arth, Cilfargen, Rhos-y-Corn), Llanfynydd, Llangadog, Llangain, Llangan, Llangathen, Llangendeirne, Llangennech, Llanglydwen, Llangunnor, Llangyndeyrn, Llangynin, Llanilwch, Llanllawddog, Llanpumpsaint, Llansadwrnen, Llanwinio, Llwynhendy, Manordeilo, Marros, Meidrim, Merthyr, Myddfai, Newchurch, Pembrey, Pendine, Pontyates, Pontyberem, St. Clears, St. Ishmaels, Talley, Trelech a'r Bettws, Whitland.

PEMBROKE: Amroth, Boulston, Brawdy, Carew, Clarbeston, Clynderwen, Cosheston, Crunwere, Ford, Freystrop, Granston, Gumfreston, Haroldston St. Issells, Haroldston West, Hasguard, Haverfordwest (St. Martin, St. Mary, St. Thomas), Hayscastle, Herbrandston, Hodgeston, Johnston, Lambston, Lampeter Velfrey, Lamphey, Lawrenny, Letterston, Llandeloy, Llandissilio, Llanfair Nantygof, Llanfallteg, Llanfyrnach, Llangan, Llangwm, Llanreithan, Llanstadwell, Llanwnda, Llanychlwydog, Loveston, Manorbier, Manorowen, Marloes, Martletwy, Mathry, Milford Haven, Minwear, Monkton and Hundleton, Morfil, Mynachlogddu, Narberth, Nash with Upton, New Moat, Newport, Newton North, Nolton, Pembroke Dock, Penally, Pontfaen, Robeston Wathen, Roch, Rosemarket, Rudbaxton, St. Brides, St. Elvis, St. Florence, St. Ishmaels, St. Lawrence with Ford, St. Nicholas, Siebech, Spittal, Steynton, Talbenny, Tenby, Treffgarne, Uzmaston, Walton West, Whitchurch (Solva), Yerbeston.

Census Returns
These are held on microfilm for the complete "new" county for the available years, and are located in Cardigan and Pembroke (not in Carmarthen).

Wills
These and other probate records are in the National Library of Wales. However, the printed indexes for Carmarthen from 1858 to 1928 are in the Carmarthen office. These are indexed up to 1923.

Tithe Records
These are available for some parishes in Carmarthen for the period 1837-48 and are in the CRO there.

Directories
All offices hold early directories dating back in some cases to 1875.

All three offices, particularly Carmarthen, hold good collections of family papers and records, which either have been donated or are on permanent loan. Cardigan has the PRO Nonconformist registers on microfilm, and also petty session records from 1889 to 1976.

Glamorgan

The Record Office of the "new" county of Glamorgan serves the three counties of West, Mid, and South Glamorgan. Limited research will be undertaken for a fee.

Family History Society of South Wales
(See page 89 for remarks concerning Family History Societies.)

Glamorgan Record Office
County Hall, Cathays Park, Cardiff, Glamorgan CF1 3NE. (Open Monday-Friday, 0900-1700 hours; Friday, 0900-1630.)

Parish Registers
Those held in the Glamorgan County Record Office are:

DIOCESE OF LLANDAFF: Aberavon, Aberpergwm, Afan Vale, Baglan, Briton Ferry, Cadoxton-juxta-Barry, Cadoxton-juxta-Neath, Caerau with Ely, Caerphilly (Bedwas and Eglwysilan), Canton (St. John), Cardiff (St. Dyfrig, St. John, St. Mary, St. Samson, St. Stephen), Cilybebyll, Cogan, Coity, Coychurch, Crynant, Dowlais, Eglwysbrewis, Eglwysilan, Ewenny, Flemingston, Gabalfa, Gelligaer, Gileston, Glyncorrwg, Hirwaun (Aberdare and Penderyn), Lavernock, Lisvane, Llanbethian, Llancarfan, Llandaff, Llanddewi Rhondda (Llanwonno), Llandough-juxta-Cowbridge, Llangan, Llangynwyd, Llanharan, Llanharry, Llanishen, Llansawel, Llantrithyd, Llwynderw, Marcross, Merthyr Mawr, Michaelston-le-pit, Monknash, Nolton, Penarth, Penarth (All Saints), Penrhiwceiber, Pentyrch, Penyfai, Peterston-super-Ely, Peterston-super-Montem, Pyle and Kenfig, Radyr, Resolven, Roath, Roath (St. German), St. Andrews Major, St. Athan, St. Bride's Major, St. Bride's-super-Ely, St. Georges-super-Ely, St. Hilary, St. Lythan's, St. Mary Church, St. Mary Hill, St. Nicholas, Skewen, Sully, Tondu, Treharris (St. Cynon and St. Matthias), Wenvoe, Whitchurch, Wick, Ystradyfodwg, Ystradyfodwg (St. David, St. Peter).

West Glamorgan Area Record Office, County Hall, Swansea SA1 3SN

DIOCESE OF SWANSEA AND BRECON: Abercrave, Callwen, Clydach, Coelbren, Gowerton, Kilvey, Landore, Llangennith, Llangiwg,

Llangiwg (Pontardawe, St. Peter), Llangyfelach, Llansamlet, Llan-
samlet (Glais, St. Paul), Loughor, Manselton, Nicholaston, Oxwich,
Penclawdd, Pendoylan, Penllergaer, Penmaen, Penmarc, Penrice,
Port Eynon, Porthkerry, Reynoldston, Rhossili, St. John-juxta-
Swansea, Sketty, Swansea (Christ Church, Holy Trinity, St. Gabriel,
St. James, St. Jude, St. Luke, St. Mark, St. Mary, St. Matthew, St.
Nicholas, St. Nicholas-on-the-Hill, St. Peter (Cockett), St. Thomas),
Ystalyfera, Ystradfellte, Ystradgynlais.

Nonconformist Registers
The County Record Office holds a number of these, but it is
regretted a list of them is not at present available.

Census Returns
The CRO holds a complete set of microfilms of these for the period
1841-71 for the whole of Glamorgan.

Wills
These are in the National Library of Wales.

Miscellaneous Records
These include quarter sessions records from the sixteenth century;
borough and local council archives; family and estate archives.

Cardiff Library Archives
The archives accumulated by the former Cardiff City Library are
now under the care and administration of the CRO.

Gwent

This "new" county includes Newport, most of Monmouthshire,
and part of Breconshire.

Family History Society
(See page 89 for remarks concerning Family History Societies.)

County Record Office
County Hall, Cwmbran NP4 2XH. (Open Monday-Thursday, 0900-
1700 hours; Friday, 0930-1600 hours.) Inquiries from overseas are
answered without charge, but if any research from original documents is involved, the inquirer will be asked for the standard fee for
one hour's work. This fee will include photocopies of entries.
Further research can be done on the same basis.

Parish Registers

Abercarn, Abergavenny (Holy Trinity, St. Mary), Abersychan, Bassaleg, Bedwas, Bedwellty, Bettws, Bishton, Blaenafon, Bryngwyn, Brynmawr, Caerwent, Caldicot, Chapel Hill, Chepstow, Christchurch (Newport), Cwmyoy, Devauden, Ebbw Vale (Beaufort, Christchurch, Cwm St. Paul), Fleur-de-Lys, Garndiffaith, Goetre, Goldcliff, Griffithtown, Henllas, Itton, Kilgwrrwg, Langstone, Liswerry (Newport), Llanarth, Llandenny, Llandewi Rhydderch, Llandogo, Llanelly, Llanfapley, Llanfihangel (Crucorney, Gobion, Iuxta Rogiet, Llantarnam, Pontymoel, Ystern Llewern), Llanfrechfa, Llangattock iuxta Usk, Llanhilleth, Llanishen, Llanmartin, Llansantffraed, Llanthony, Llantillio Crossenny, Llanvaches, Llanwenarth, Magor, Malpas, Mamhilad, Mitchel Troy, Monmouth (Overmonnow, St. Mary, St. Thomas), Mounton, Mynyddislwyn, Nash, Newbridge, Newchurch, Newport (All Saints, Holy Trinity, St. John Evangelist, St. Mark, St. Matthew, St. Paul, St. Woolos), Oldcastle, Penalt, Penhow, Penmaen (Oakdale), Penrhos (Penrose), Penterry, Pontnewynydd, Portskewett, Raglan, Redwick, Rhymney, Risca, Roggiett, St. Arvans, St. Pierre, Shirenewton, Tintern, Tredegar (St. George), Trelleck Grange, Trevethin, Undy, Whitson, Wilcrick, Wolvesnewton.

Tithes

These records exist for about sixty parishes for the period 1840-60.

Personal Name Index

This is based on most records held by the CRO, except parish records, and covers the period up to 1870.

Electoral Registers

These are on file since 1832.

Other Records

These include a large number of estate and family records, not only of landed estates, but also of old families in the area. Many lawyers have also deposited their early records which cover leases, deeds, land transactions, mortgages, etc.

Gwynedd

This "new" county incorporates the "old" counties of Anglesey, Caernarvonshire, most of Merioneth, and part of Denbighshire.

Family History Society

(See page 89 for remarks concerning Family History Societies.)

County Record Office

County Offices, Caernarfon LL55 1SH. There are three area record offices:

CAERNARFON: County Offices, Shirehall Street, Caernarfon LL55 1SH

DOLGELLAU: Cae Penarlâg, Dolgellau LL40 2YB

LLANGEFNI: Shirehall, Llangefni LL77 7TW

(*Caernarfon*: Monday-Friday, 0930-1230 hours and 1330-1730 hours; Wednesday until 1900 hours; Friday until 1600 hours. *Dolgellau*: Monday-Friday, 0930-1300 hours and 1400-1630 hours. *Llangefni*: Monday-Friday, 0930-1630 hours.)

The above offices are repositories for the original counties of Caernarfon, Merioneth, and Anglesey respectively.

It is regrettable that the County Archivist is not prepared to supply to the public any information whatever about the records he holds in custody. It is suggested you write directly to him—Bryn R. Parry—at the Caernarfon address above and ask for any information you need.

The following information about parish registers held in the three offices above has been obtained from other sources:

LLANGEFNI RECORD OFFICE: Aberffraw, Bodewryd, Bodwrog, Cerrigceinwen, Coedana, Gwredog, Henegglwys, Llanalgo, Llanbabo, Llanbedrgoch, Llanbodrig, Llanddanialfab, Llanddona, Llanddyfnan, Llandeusant, Llandrygarn, Llandysilio, Llanedwen, Llanerchymedd, Llaneugrad, Llanfachraeth, Llanfaetnlu, Llanfairmathafarn-Eithaf, Llanfairynghornwy, Llanfechell, Llanffinan, Llanfigael, Llanfihangel (Dinsylwy, Tre'r Beirdd, Ysceifiog), Llanflewyn, Llanfrwrog, Llangadwaldr, Llangaffo, Llangefni, Llangeinwen, Llangoed, Llangristiolus, Llangwyfan, Llangwyllog, Llanidan, Llanrhuddlad, Llanrhwydrus, Llansadwrn, Llantrisant, Llanwenilwyfo, Llanynghenedl, Llechcynfarwy, Newborough, Penmon, Penmynydd, Penrhosllugwy, Pentraeth, Rhodogeidio, Trefdraeth, Tregaiain, Trewalchmai.

DOLGELLAU RECORD OFFICE: Aberdyfi, Betws Gwerful Goch, Corwen, Ffestiniog, Frongoch, Llanaber, Llanbedr, Llandanwg, Llandecwyn, Llanderfel, Llandrillo, Llanegryn, Llanelltyd, Llanfachreth, Llanfair, Llanfihangel-y-Pennant, Llanfihangel-y-Traethau, Llanfor, Llangar, Llangelynnin, Llansantffraid Glyn Dyfrdwy, Llanycil, Maentwrog, Pennal, Penrhyndeudraeth, Tallyllyn, Trawsfynydd, Tywyn.

CAERNARFON RECORD OFFICE: Abererch, Bangor (St. Mary),

Bethesda (Glanogwen), Betws Garmon, Betws-y-Coed, Bodfuan, Bryncross, Caerhun, Capel Curig, Carnguwch, Ceidio, Clynnog Fawr, Dolwyddelan, Dwygyfylchi, Edern, Llanbeblig, Llanbedrog, Llanbedr-y-Cennin, Llanberis, Llanddeiniolen, Llandegai, Llandudno, Llandudwen, Llandwrog, Llanfaelrhys, Llanfairfechan, Llanfair-is Gaer, Llanfihangel Bachellaeth, Llangwynadl, Llaniestyn, Llanllechid, Llannor, Llanrhos, Llanrhychwyn, Llanstumdwy, Llanwnda, Nefyn (St. David, St. Mary), Penliech, Penmachno, Penrhos, Pentir, Pistyll, Rhiw, Trefriw, Tudweiliog.

Powys

This county includes the "old" counties of Montgomery, Radnor, and most of Brecon. There is no County Record Office and no County Archivist.

The County Library, Cefnllys Road, Llandrindod Wells LD1 5LD, is at present setting up an archives collection. The library does not hold any parish registers—those for the area are either in the National Library of Wales, or in the original churches. It does hold census records on microfilm for four years for the three old counties mentioned above.

This is the only county in Wales without a County Record Office.

Family History Society
(See page 89 for remarks concerning Family History Societies.)

The Welsh Language
You must remember the country is officially bilingual. As you go further back—particularly in the north of the country—you may find some knowledge of Welsh essential. There is a good dictionary available (English-Welsh and Welsh-English). It is Y GEIRIADUR MAWR by H. Meurig and W.O. Thomas (1981). I doubt if it is readily available through inter-library loan, but it can be bought from the Welsh Bookshop, 329 Queenston St., St. Catharine's ON L2P 2X8, Canada.

11

SCOTLAND

Local government was reorganized in Scotland in 1974, just as it was in England and Wales, and many old counties disappeared, or had their boundaries changed. The mainland of Scotland is now divided into nine Regional Councils, and there are three Island Authorities for Orkney, Shetland, and the Western Isles.

The new areas are given below:

CENTRAL REGIONAL COUNCIL: Clackmannan, most of Stirling, parts of Perth and West Lothian. The Central Regional Archives are in Spittal Street, Stirling FK8 1DY.

DUMFRIES AND GALLOWAY: Dumfries, Kirkcudbright, Wigtown. The archives are in the Regional Library, Ewart Library, Catherine Street, Dumfries DG1 1JB.

FIFE: The old county of Fife. Archives are located in the Dunfermline District Library, 1 Abbot Street, Dunfermline KY12 7NL; the Dunfermline Museum, Viewfield, Dunfermline; the Central Library, War Memorial Gardens, Kirkcaldy; the Kirkcaldy Museum and Art Gallery, Kirkcaldy; the Hay Fleming Library, St. Andrews, Fife.

GRAMPIAN: Aberdeen, Kincardine, Banff, most of Moray. The Grampian Regional Archives are in the Department of Law and Administration, Woodhill House, Ashgrove Road West, Aberdeen AB9 2LU. Other archives are in the Aberdeen City Archives, Town House, Aberdeen AB9 2BH, and the North East Scotland Library, 14 Crown Terrace, Aberdeen AB9 2BH.

HIGHLAND: Caithness, Nairn, Sutherland, most of Inverness, most of Ross and Cromarty, parts of Argyll, parts of Moray. The Regional Council is located in The Castle, Inverness. There are archives in the Inverness Burgh Library, Inverness.

LOTHIAN: Edinburgh, East Lothian, most of Midlothian and West Lothian. Archives are located in the Edinburgh City Archives, City Chambers, Edinburgh EH1 1YJ, and the West Lothian Library, 66 Marjoriebanks Street, Bathgate.

STRATHCLYDE: Glasgow, Bute, Dunbarton, Lanark, Renfrew, Ayr, most of Argyll, part of Stirling. The Regional Archives are in the

City Chambers, Glasgow G2 1DU. Other archives are in the Argyll and Bute District Council Archives, Kilmory, Lochgilphead PA31 8RT, and the following public libraries in the region:

Bearsden and Milngavie: Brookwood, Drymen Road, Bearsden G61 3RJ

Clydebank: Dumbarton Road, Clydebank G81 1XH

Cumnock and Doon Valley: Bank Glen, Cumnock KA18 1PH

Dumbarton: Strathleven Place, Dumbarton G82 1BD

Eastwood: Capelrig House, Newton Mearns G77 6NH

Glasgow: Mitchell Library, North Street, Glasgow G3 7DN

Hamilton: 98 Cadzow Street, Hamilton ML3 6HQ

Inverclyde: Watt Monument, Greenock

Kilmarnock and Loudon: Dick Institute, Elmbank Avenue, Kilmarnock KA1 3BH

Kyle and Carrick: 12 Main Street, Ayr KA8 8EB

Lanark: Lindsay Institute, Hope Street, Lanark ML11 7NH

Monklands: (Coatbridge) Academy Street, Coatbridge ML5 3AT; (Monklands) Wellwynd, Airdrie ML20 A6

Motherwell: Hamilton Road, Motherwell ML1 3BZ

Renfrew: High Street, Paisley PA1 2BB

Rothesay: Stuart Street, Rothesay

Strathkelvin: Camphill Avenue, Kirkintilloch

TAYSIDE: Dundee, Angus, Kinross, most of Perth. The archives are in the Dundee District Archives, City Square, Dundee; the Arbroath Library, Hill Terrace, Arbroath DD11 1AH; the Dundee City Library, Albert Square, Dundee DD1 1DB; the Perth and Kinross District Library, Sandeman Library, Perth; the Perth Museum and Art Gallery, George Street, Perth PH1 5LB.

BORDERS: Berwick, Peebles, Roxburgh, Selkirk, part of Midlothian. The Regional Council is located at Newtown St. Boswells. Archives are in the following public libraries in the region:

Duns: 49 Newton Street, Duns

Ettrick and Lauderdale: (Galashiels) Lawyer's Brae, Galashiels TD1 3JR; (Selkirk) Ettrick Terrace, Selkirk TD7 4LE

Roxburgh: (Hawick) Bridge Street, Hawick TD9 9QT; (Kelso) Bowmont, Kelso TD5 7JH; (St. Boswells) St. Boswells TD6 0AG

ORKNEY: The Orkney Islands. Archives are in the Orkney Library, Laing Street, Kirkwall, Orkneys.

SHETLAND: The Shetland Islands. Archives are in the Council offices, 93 St. Olaf Street, Lerwick, Shetlands.

WESTERN ISLES: Public Library, Stornoway, Isle of Lewis.

Note: Since many Scottish counties are named after the county town, it should be pointed out that names above such as Aberdeen,

Banff, and Inverness refer to the whole county, and not just to the county town.

In Scotland, the county reorganization was not followed by the creation of County Record Offices, as in England and Wales.

Generally speaking, the archives held by the Regional Councils are records of the city in which the Council is located, and other records throughout the Council area remain in local Council offices and libraries. I can only assume County Record Offices were not set up because Scotland is a small country, and also because so many of the old records are centrally located in Edinburgh.

Family History Societies

There are now several of these in Scotland and they are listed below. The current addresses of the various secretaries can be obtained from the Scottish Association of Family History Societies (Miss Lillian Malcolm, Hon. Secretary, 4 Loftus Road, Downfield, Dundee, DD3 9TE).

Aberdeen and N.E. Scotland
Borders
Dumfries & Galloway
Glasgow & West Scotland
Highland
Tay Valley
Troon & District

General Register Office

New Register House, Edinburgh EH1 3YT. (Open Monday-Thursday, 0930-1630 hours; Friday, 0930-1600 hours.)

If a search for a particular event is likely to prove too time-consuming because of the lack of identifying detail, or if the search to be made is a general one (i.e., to trace a family tree), the staff cannot undertake the task. The inquirer must undertake the search personally or arrange for someone to search on his behalf. A list of record agents will be supplied. Please note that accommodation in the search room is limited and your accommodation cannot be guaranteed without prior reservation.

The main records fall into three categories—civil registration (births, marriages, deaths, still-births, and adoptions); censuses; and parish registers. Full copies of the entries from any of the above records can be obtained for a fee.

Civil Registration

The records of civil registration are filed and indexed, and are located in the New Register House in the custody of the Registrar General for Scotland. Civil registration started in 1855 in Scotland—eighteen years later than in England and Wales. Earlier, the registration of baptisms, marriages, and burials was solely the responsibility of the Church authorities, just as it was south of the border.

From the point of view of genealogy, the 1855 civil registration forms were magnificent. Unfortunately, the wealth of information demanded and received took so much effort to record that in subsequent years fewer questions were asked. However, let us be very grateful for 1855. In that golden year the following details appeared on the various certificates:

Birth

The name, sex, year, date of month, hour of birth, and place of birth (if in lodgings, so stated) of infant; father's name, rank, profession or occupation, age, birthplace, and date and place of marriage; other children, both living and dead; mother's name and maiden name, age, and place of birth; the signature of her father, or other informant, and residence if not in the house where the birth occurred; when and where the birth was registered.

(If you find an ancestor born in 1855, congratulations! But if not, try checking from your own information if a brother or sister was born in that year. If so, get a copy of the birth certificate so you can get all the details. The same advice applies to marriages and burials.)

Marriage

The date and place of the marriage; the present and normal residence of the bride and groom; the age, rank, profession or occupation of both parties, and, if related, the relationship between them both; the status of each (i.e., whether widower or widow, details of the previous marriages, if any, and details of the children of such marriages); the birthplaces, and the dates and places of registration of the births of the bride and groom; the name, rank, profession or occupation of each of the four parents; and the date and place of the registration of the marriage.

Death

The name, sex, age, place of birth, rank, profession or occupation of the deceased; the length of time of residence in the district where death occurred; name, rank, profession or occupation of both parents; if the deceased was married, the name of the wife, the names and ages of children in order of birth, both living and dead; the year, date, and hour of death; the place of death, the cause, and how long the final illness lasted; the name of the doctor attending, and the date on which he last saw the deceased; the burial place and the name of the undertaker; the signature of the informant and his relationship, if it existed, to the deceased; and the date and place of registration.

You will see at once how much more information was given than in the English and Welsh registrations and how useful all the additional facts can be. Even the years from 1856 to 1860 omit from the birth certificate only the age and place of birth of the parents, and details of their marriage and other children. In 1861 the date and place of the parents' marriage was restored. Quite often in the death certificates some of the questions could not be answered because the informant had no detailed knowledge of the early life of the deceased.

OPR Index
The LDS Church is now indexing all the parish registers on a county basis. The OPR, as the index is called, will be made available immediately each county is copied.

Births, Marriages, and Deaths of Scottish subjects outside Scotland
There are a number of records which may be of use in this area of ancestor-hunting:

Marine Register of Births and Deaths (from 1855): Certified returns received from the Registrar General for Shipping and Seamen with respect to births and deaths on British-registered merchant vessels at sea, if the child's father or the deceased person was a Scottish subject.

Air Register of Births and Deaths (from 1948): Records of births and deaths in any part of the world in aircraft registered in the United Kingdom, where it appears that the child's father or the deceased person was usually resident in Scotland.

Service Records (from 1881): These include the Army Returns of Births, Marriages, and Deaths of Scottish persons at military stations abroad during the period 1881-1959; the Service Departments Registers which, since 1 April 1959, have recorded these events outside the United Kingdom relating to persons normally resident in Scotland who are serving in or are employed by H.M. Forces, including the families of members of the Forces; and certified copies of entries relating to marriages solemnized outside the United Kingdom by army chaplains since 1892, where one of the persons is described as Scottish and at least one of the parties is serving in H.M. Forces.

War Registers (from 1899): There are three registers: South African War (1899-1902), which records the deaths of Scottish soldiers; First World War (1914-19), which records the deaths of Scottish persons serving as warrant officers, non-commissioned officers, or men in the army, or as petty officers or men in the Royal Navy; and Second World War (1939-45), which consists of incomplete returns of the deaths of Scottish members of the armed forces.

Consular Returns (from 1914): Certified copies of registrations by British consuls relating to persons of Scottish descent or birth. Records of births and deaths from 1914, marriages from 1917.

Registers of Births, Marriages, and Deaths in Foreign Countries (1860-1965): Records compiled by the GRO until the end of 1965. It relates to the births of children of Scottish parents, and the marriages and deaths of Scottish subjects. The entries were made on the basis of information supplied by the persons or relations concerned and after consideration of the evidence of each event.

Census Returns

The Registrar General holds the records of the censuses in the General Record Office. These have taken place every ten years since 1841 (with the exception of 1941), and the records from 1841 to 1891 are open for public search. They are in the form of enumerators' books and are not indexed. The actual dates were: 7 June 1841; 31 March 1851; 8 April 1861; 3 April 1871; 4 April 1881; 5 April 1891.

For a fee, the staff will supply a copy of a particular entry with all the details of persons in the house, ages, etc. You will, of course, have to supply at least a surname, and an exact address. A general search of a particular area will not be undertaken unless it is a very small place; otherwise, you will be referred to a record agent who will quote you a fee. The LDS Church has now microfilmed the census returns for the years 1841–91.

Parish Registers

My discussion of parish registers will refer to the Presbyterian Church, since that is the national church of Scotland. Generally speaking, the registers of the Episcopal Church in Scotland (the equivalent of Anglican) and the Catholic Church are in the original churches. However, more detailed information about the exact location of a particular register can be obtained by writing to the archives of the church:

EPISCOPAL CHURCH IN SCOTLAND: Theological College, Rosebery Crescent, Edinburgh.

SCOTTISH CATHOLIC ARCHIVES: Columba House 16 Drummond Place, Edinburgh EH3 6PL.

There is some evidence that parish registers were first kept in the fourteenth century, but none of them have survived. In 1552 the General Provincial Council of Scotland ordered that each parish should keep a register which should record baptisms and marriages, but this was observed by only a few parishes. The earliest register in the custody of the office contains baptisms and the proclamation of banns for the parish of Errol, in Perth, from the year 1553, but the records are far from complete. For some parishes the earliest registers date from the early nineteenth century, and for other parishes no registers have survived.

In 1616 the newly formed Church of Scotland issued an edict that every member church should keep a record of baptisms, marriages, and deaths, but few of the parishes took any action. In fact, only twenty-one parishes kept registers before 1600, and thirty-five did not start them until 1801. Very few of the registers in Scotland have ever been printed and published, or even transcribed in manuscript. However, you should check with the Registrar General's Library as to which of their registers are indexed, and also with the Scottish Central Library, Edinburgh, and the public library in the place in which you are interested. There is no complete and up-to-date list of which Scottish registers have been indexed.

If by chance your ancestors came from Selkirk, you are lucky. All the entries of baptism in the registers of the six parishes of this county (Ettrick, Galashiels, Kirkhope, Roberton, Selkirk, and Yarrow) have been listed and indexed up to 1854.

Generally speaking, the registers are in good condition and, except for the earliest entries, quite legible. The registers that are in the best state of preservation and that began in the early years are, generally speaking, in the large cities and towns. Of course, there is variation in the amount of information supplied. Some contain the barest facts; others go into greater detail. Some contain all sorts of miscellaneous information about the parish and the presbytery, while others contain unexplainable gaps. It must be remembered that Scotland saw two major rebellions, in 1715 and 1745, and a number of minor ones. It also endured bloodthirsty religious strife with the subsequent burning of several churches and their registers in the name of the Lord!

It is a tremendous advantage for the ancestor-hunter that when Scottish civil registration started in 1855, all the old registers were brought to Edinburgh. There are over four thousand volumes from over nine hundred parishes.

One fascinating aspect of the registers, particularly in the Border counties, is the wealth of social comment by the minister or the session clerk. The sins of the congregation (when discovered) are set out in some detail. All those brought before the *kirk* (church) session and found guilty of adultery and fornication are clearly named and their sins are listed in full. Standards of morality were so rigid that even a married couple producing a child eight months after the marriage were called before the session to explain the reason why. I found an account of one such inquisition in a register of a Dumfries parish. The unhappy young couple had to swear they had had no carnal knowledge of each other prior to the marriage, and eight of their relatives and neighbours had to give supporting evidence. The minister and the elders then deliberated for two hours and decided that the fact that the child had arrived only eight months after the marriage was an act of God.

The ministers were equally vicious when an illegitimate child was born. Their Christian principles were strong enough to allow the child to be baptised, but the entries were very specific, making the child's bastard origins quite clear.

There is another area in which Scots parish registers are unique. Under Scots law, hand-festing was recognized. This was the custom whereby a man and a woman could hold hands over water (usually on a bridge) and declare themselves man and wife. This was legally recognized by the state but was a source of worry to the God-fearing ministers of the kirk, who regarded the whole idea as sinful in the extreme. Great pressure was brought to bear on the hand-fested couple to get married in the church, and thus you will find entries of such marriages with mention of the fact that a clandestine, or irregular, marriage had taken place previously. If there were children of the irregular marriage, they were usually baptised at the same time as their parents' church wedding! I remember seeing such an entry in a Kirkcudbright register—eleven children were baptised at the same time, so obviously the parents had resisted all pressures to sanctify their hand-festing over a considerable number of years!

So far as a baptism is concerned, the usual entry in a Scots register shows the maiden name of the mother and usually the names of the godparents or sponsors—generally called witnesses. The general practice was to appoint two men and one woman for a boy, and one man and two women for a girl. Having told you what the "usual" entry contains, I must also say there are frequent exceptions. In fact, you will often find that the minister has only recorded the name of the father—the woman's role in the birth being apparently unimportant!

In marriages the registers record the proclamation of the banns, and in many cases that is all that is recorded. The marrige itself is not specifically mentioned, although one assumes it did actually take place. Often the banns were published in two places if the prospective bride and groom came from separate parishes. In that case, the register of one parish simply stated the banns had been read, whereas in the parish where the wedding was held it also stated that the marriage had taken place. The marriage proclamations, or banns, gave the name of the father of the bride, but the name of the father of the groom was mentioned more rarely.

For some reason Scots ministers often showed no great interest in recording burials, and these records are less complete than those of baptism and marriage. Frequently, though the burial was not mentioned, it was recorded in the registers that a payment had been made for the use of the "mortcloth". This cloth belonged to the parish and was loaned for burials. It was removed from the body at the moment of interment. Tombstones are not as valuable a source of information as in England and Wales because two hundred years ago in Scotland many people were buried without headstones. The Scottish Genealogical Society and its members have been copying inscriptions from tombstones, and manuscript lists of these can be found in local libraries. In many of these cases the copying was done just before the tombstones were removed and piled in a corner of the graveyard. A great deal of this removal is taking place in Scotland, so that graveyards can be completely sodded and the cost of cutting the grass reduced.

If you do not find a particular entry under a particular parish, you should also consult the Register of Neglected Entries (1801-54). This is in the GRO and is a record of births, marriages, and deaths *proved* to have occurred in Scotland between 1801 and 1854 but not entered in the parish registers.

Scottish Record Office

P.O. Box 36, H.M. General Register House, Edinburgh EH1 3YY; and West Register House, Charlotte Square, Edinburgh EH2 4DF. (Open Monday-Friday, 0900-1645 hours; Saturday, 0900-1230 hours, Historical Search Room only.)

The staff will not undertake detailed research or make transcripts of documents but are always glad to advise on the use of the records and to answer specific inquiries or requests for photocopies, provided that sufficient information is given for the documents to be easily identified. The main sources of genealogical information available in the SRO are:

Records of Wills

Scottish testaments were originally the responsibility of the Church. After the Reformation the Church courts were abolished and replaced by the commissary courts, which were set up to deal with wills. The commissariots, as they were called, were abolished in 1876 when the responsibility for proving wills was transferred to the sheriff courts. The commissariot districts usually matched the boundaries of the dioceses of the pre-Reformation bishops. They were set up in 1563 and were thirteen in number. As time went by, they were increased to twenty-two.

None of the commissariot records are complete, but they have been indexed up to 1800 by the Scottish Record Society, and copies can be found in the Central Library in Edinburgh and in district libraries. The Edinburgh Commissariot covered the whole country (rather like the Prerogative Court of Canterbury in England), whereas the other commissariots only covered their particular district.

In addition to the Commissariot records, the GRO holds details of wills proved in the sheriff courts after 1823. Various indexes which will determine the existence of a will are available for consultation. Registers of Deeds (Books of Council and Session) exist from 1554 and are indexed from 1770, and for some unconnected earlier periods.

When examining Scots testaments it is important to know that in Scotland only movable property could be left by testament. Landed property descended by certain fixed laws. This means that in cases where the testator's landed property exceeded in appraised value his movable property, he would be described as *debita excedunt bona* (debts exceed the assets).

When the testator was survived by a widow and children, the movable estate was automatically divided into three—one *terce* (a third) would go to the widow, one terce to the children, and one terce could be left by the testator to anyone he wished. The inventory of the movable property was attached to the will, and this is useful in telling you something about the standard of living of your ancestor.

Because only movable property could be left by testament, and the disposal of landed property was controlled, there was not such a great need for a will as there was in England and Wales, and so wills in Scotland are consequently more rare.

I am grateful to my friend Walter Reid, Writer to the Signet, for the following definition of the Scots Law of Succession:

1. HERITAGE AND MOVABLES: There is no such thing in Scots law as "real property". Land, things attached to land (buildings), and certain rights in land are known as heritage or heritable property as distinct from movable property, which includes cash, shares, etc.

2. TESTATE AND INTESTATE SUCCESSION: As you know, if people die without making a will, their property passes to their survivors according to the rules of intestate succession. If they make a will, it will regulate the succession to part of the estate; a surviving wife and surviving children will have no claim to the rest of it. They can only exercise these rights by giving up any legacy contained in the will, and may elect to accept a legacy rather than exercise their rights.

3. THE LAW BEFORE AND AFTER THE SUCCESSION ACT OF 1964: The system before 1964 dictated that property was automatically inherited by the oldest child, i.e., the law of primogeniture. The 1964 Act ended this system and introduced important reforms in the law of succession. The simplest way of looking at the mechanics of succession is to look separately at the positions before and after the new Act.

Pre-1964 Intestate Succession

(a) HERITAGE: Essentially males were preferred to females, the eldest to the youngest, descent to ascent; there could be no succession through the mother; in ascending the rule of the eldest first was reversed; women in the same degree took jointly. For example, A's heirs were: his eldest son, failing whom, *his* son and so on, failing whom A's second son and descendants and so on through A's sons, failing whom A's daughters, failing whom A's younger brother, failing whom his younger brother's sons, failing whom his other younger brothers and issue, failing whom A's immediately older brother and so on upwards, failing whom A's sister, failing whom A's father, failing whom his father's younger brother and so on. After father and collaterals came the paternal grandfather and his collaterals. The mother and her relatives were completely excluded.

(b) MOVABLES: All those in the same degree of proximity to the intestate succeeded, and if one of that degree had predeceased the intestate, then his or her children took the parent's place, providing that the grade which succeeded was not more remote than brothers and sisters of the intestate. The father, failing whom the mother, took one-half where the succession fell to collaterals. The mother's relatives were excluded. The heir to the testate estate could share in the movable succession only if he collated or threw into a common stock the heritage to which he had succeeded.

The surviving spouse had overriding rights in the deceased's estate, known as *legal rights*: the husband had a *jus relicti* of one-third of his wife's movables (half if there were no children) and a life interest in her heritage, called *courtesy*; the wife was entitled to one-third (half if there were no children) of her husband's movables as *jus relictae* and a life interest, or terce, of one-third of all his heritage. The children also had legal rights, known as *legitim* (formerly known as the bairn's part). They were entitled to a third, or if neither parent survived, to a half of the movable property.

Pre-1964 Testate Succession
The surviving spouse and surviving children had the same legal rights as in intestate succession. The result was that a married man with children could dispose with absolute freedom of one-third of his movable property and two-thirds of his land, unless the spouse and children elected to accept a testamentary provision in satisfaction of their legal rights. So far as the estate passed under the will, there was no distinction between heritage and movables.

Post-1964 Intestate Succession
There is no longer any difference in the law of succession between real estate and movable property. The order of succession is:

1. children of the deceased, including adopted children;
2. if they are dead, their children;
3. if none, then brothers and sisters of the deceased's parents or their children;
4. if none on the father's side, then the same on the mother's;
5. if none, then the next nearest relative on either the father's or the mother's side.

The legal rights of jus relicti, jus relictae, and legitim remain, payable from the movable estate. In addition, the surviving spouse now has important overriding rights, known as *prior rights* in intestacy, to the deceased's dwelling house and contents, and to a cash payment, which is made from the heritage and movable property in proportion to the respective amount of each. These rights take priority over legal rights. The result is that in very many cases of intestacy the surviving spouse takes the whole estate.

Post-1964 Testate Succession

The surviving spouse and surviving children have the same legal rights as in the case of intestacy but the surviving spouse has no prior rights. As was the case before 1964, the surviving spouse and surviving children have to choose between their legal rights and any provision under the will.

Finally, a word or two about the location of present-day wills. They can be recorded for preservation with either the Keeper of the Registers at Register House, Edinburgh, or the Sheriff Clerk of a county. Wills so recorded remain in the hands of the recorder. Wills lodged with applications for confirmation (i.e. probate) are normally recorded with the Sheriff Clerk of the district in which the deceased last resided. In the latter case the original will is returned to the executor, a copy being retained by the Sheriff Clerk for record purposes. At certain intervals sheriff court records, including wills, are sent to the Keeper of the Registers. The date of transfer varies from court to court. At present the average date of transfer appears to be about 1968. Copies of a will can be obtained from the Keeper or the Sheriff Clerk holding either the original or the copy. The sheriff court charges a fee for a search, and this is restricted to a period of five years from the date of death.

The sheriff court districts are located as follows: Aberdeen, Airdrie, Alloa, Arbroath, Ayr, Banff, Cupar, Dingwall (and Tain), Dumbarton, Dumfries, Dundee, Dunfermline, Dunoon (and Oban, Campbeltown, Rothesay), Edinburgh (and Peebles), Elgin, Falkirk, Forfar, Glasgow, Greenock, Haddington, Hamilton, Inverness (and Lochmaddy, Stornoway, Fort William, Portree), Jedburgh (and Duns), Kilmarnock, Kirkcaldy, Kirkwall (and Lerwick), Lanark, Linlithgow, Paisley, Perth, Peterhead, Selkirk, Stirling, Stranraer (and Kirkcudbright), Stonehaven, Wick (and Dornoch).

Legal Terms

There are certain legal terms under Scots law which differ from those of England and Wales, and some definitions are given below:

COMMISSARIOT: The district within the jurisdiction of a commissary court.

COMMISSARY: A person who held authority to exercise jurisdiction on behalf of an archbishop or a bishop. In Scotland the title continued to be used after church authority was abolished.

COMMISSARY COURT: One of the courts which took over jurisdiction from the ecclesiastical courts.

CONFIRMATION: The completion of probate of an estate by the executors.

INVENTORY: A list of personal and household goods left by the deceased, together with their appraised value.

PERSONALTY: Personal property, as opposed to real or landed property.

SHERIFF COURT: The court with jurisdiction over the estate of anyone dying within its district. There are several such districts in each modern sheriffdom. Its chief official, the sheriff clerk, has custody of current testamentary records, and also of those since 1823 which have not been handed over to the Scottish Record Office.

SHERIFFDOM: An administrative area incorporating several counties and sheriff-court districts.

TESTAMENT: Normally this is the same as a will, but in Scotland it is a document which excludes realty (heritable property).

WARRANTS: Usually the drafts from which the entries in the register were made up, but sometimes including the original wills.

Records of Land

Those in the custody of the SRO include Registers of Sasines; Retours and Service of Heirs; Registers of Deeds; and Registers of Tailzies:

Registers of Sasines

Land registration in Scotland depends on the existence of the notary public—an office originating in Roman times. The most important class of notarial instruments is the sasine. The idea that the sasine of land should be recorded by a notary started in Scotland in the fourteenth century. The notary's record of transactions of land was preserved in a book. It therefore became the custom that the sasine must be proved by writing, and the notary became the chief agent in doing this. The registers in which the notaries preserved the record of their actions became known as the protocol books, and the earliest of these still in existence dates back to the early sixteenth century. The SRO holds over two hundred of these books. In 1599 the Register of Sasines and Reversions (redemption of mortgages on land) was established, and Scotland was divided into seventeen districts for this purpose. In seven of these, a major portion of the records survive. The register was abolished in 1609 but eight years later the General and Particular Registers of Sasines were instituted. The General Register was available for sasine of land anywhere in Scotland and the Particular Register recorded lands in a particular district. The registers were put under the control of the Lord Clerk Register and form a complete record of land transactions from then until the present day. As land usually descended from one generation to another within a family, these records are invaluable for genealogical research.

The word *sasine* comes from "seize". To be seized of land means to possess it. A similar word appeared in English medieval law— the Assize of Novel Disseisin, which gave occupiers of land some protection against attempts to evict them.

There is no such thing as "a" sasine. "Taking sasine" was the ceremony by which a man became the legal owner of land, a ceremony which was recorded in documents known as Instruments of Sasine in the Sasine Register, which was established in 1617. Eventually the recording of these writs replaced the ceremony as a means of transferring ownership.

The ceremony was the actual handing over on the land itself of earth and stone or other symbols of land by the seller to the buyer. We have a copy of a record of sasine involving an ancestor of my wife's in 1739. It is too long and boring to quote in full, but the conclusion explains the ceremony—"to the said Alexander Telfer...by delivering to the said William Laidly for and in the name of the said Alexander Telfer of earth and stone of the ground of the said lands of Gareland and a penny money for the said garent.... these things were done upon the ground of the said lands of Gareland betwixt the hours of two and three in the afternoon."

Nearly all the land in Scotland is held on a feudal, not a freehold, basis. That is to say, it is held either directly or indirectly from the Crown. The Sasine Register is a register of all deeds transmitting feudal interests in land. Leases have no place in the feudal system, and were not recorded in the register until 1857. By that time a system of granting long leases instead of extending the feudal chain had grown up to a restricted extent in certain areas. The Registration of Leases Act of 1857 recognized this fact and allowed leases for thirty-one years or more to be so recorded in the register.

No one can have a complete title to feudal property unless the title is recorded in the register, and nothing is recorded in the register which does not transmit a feudal right. I have read that the registration of non-feudal rights in Scotland is voluntary. This is quite wrong and is probably the result of confusion between the Sasine Register and another register known as the Books of Council and Session. This latter register is for people who simply want, on a voluntary basis, to record deeds for preservation.

The registers which really concern the ancestor-hunter are those dating between 1617 and about 1900. These consist of:

1. The old General Register of Sasines (1617-1868) contained in 3779 volumes.

2. The Particular Register of Sasines for the various counties which covers the same period.

3. The New General Register which began in 1869 and continues to the present day. It is kept in county divisions. This is in over 50,000 volumes.

Note: Indexes are available from 1781 and also to parts of the older registers.

Retours and Services of Heirs

These record succession to heritable property from 1545. Abstracts have been printed to 1699. When lands were handed over to an heir, the procedure was for a brieve to be issued from chancery. This ordered the sheriff of the county to empanel a jury to discover what lands the deceased owned at death, and whether the person claiming them was the true heir. The verdict was sent back or "retoured" to chancery and preserved in a "respond book".

Registers of Deeds

These are among the most valuable records in Scotland for the genealogist. They contain all the deeds which have a clause consenting to their registration and preservation. Almost anything may be recorded in the registers. There are three series: the first, in 627 volumes, covers the period 1554 to 1657; the second runs from 1661 to 1811 and is in 959 volumes; the third, from 1812, is indexed. The earlier series is also partly indexed and this work is still proceeding. The sorts of things covered in these registers include an agreement between neighbours over the diversion of a burn, records of the building of churches and schools, records of apprenticeships, trade, and marriage contracts, and even copies of correspondence.

Registers of Tailzies

These cover all entails and disentails of property from 1688 to date. They are indexed from 1688 to 1904.

Register of Hornings, Inhibitions, and Adjudications

This is of lesser value because it is not indexed, but it may be of help in some instances. The word *horning* originated in a curious way many centuries ago. A creditor was able to obtain legal satisfaction against a debtor who had refused to obey a court order to pay his just debts. He could have him denounced as a rebel against the king by having a messenger of arms give three blasts on a horn. After this the debtor's goods were held by the Crown against the claim of the creditor. The register covers the period 1610 to 1902 and is in 1289 volumes.

The other records at the SRO which are of interest because they list individuals include hearth tax and poll tax records compiled in the 1690s on a parish and county basis, listing people under the names of farms and villages; taxation schedules, not indexed; valuation rolls; kirk session records; some Nonconformist and Catholic registers and photocopies; estate records and archives of landed families. The Letters of Inhibition prevented a debtor avoiding his just debts by disposing of his property to others.

There are also records of the acts of the Lords of the Council in civil cases; the exchequer rolls; the accounts of the Lord High Treasurer; the registers of the Privy Council; the Register of the Great Seal; the Register of the Privy Seal; burgh and barony records; regality records. (A barony was lands held from the Crown and a regality was an area of jurisdiction granted by the Crown.) Finally, there are the rolls of the cess tax. This was a special tax levied in the seventeenth and eighteenth centuries to raise funds for the support of troops. Some of these rolls are in the SRO and others are in the archives of the major cities and towns.

There are various organizations in Scotland which can be of great help to you:

The Scots Ancestry Research Society

3 Albany Street, Edinburgh EH1 3PY. This is a non-profitmaking organization. It exists to help people of Scottish blood to trace information about their ancestors in Scotland. It was established in 1945 and since then the Society has investigated more than 50,000 inquiries from people of Scottish descent. I will not quote fees in these days of inflation, but they are reasonable in comparison with the costs of employing commercial companies.

The Scottish History Society

c/o The Department of History, University of Aberdeen, Aberdeen AB9 2UB. The Society is primarily an historical society not concerned with genealogical matters, but it publishes a number of books and booklets which provide information of value to ancestor-hunters. A list of publications can be obtained from the above address.

The Scottish Records Association

c/o The Archivist, The University, Glasgow GI2 8QQ. This organization issues information about the various places in Scotland where national, regional, and district archives can be found.

The Scottish Genealogy Society

Miss J. P. S. Ferguson, M.A., A.L.A., 21 Howard Place, Edinburgh EH3 5JY. The aims of the Society are to promote research into family history and to undertake the collection and publication of genealogical material. The Society does not undertake research for ancestor-hunters but will supply a list of record agents. Membership is reasonable, and if you are of Scots descent I urge you to join. I should mention that the Hon. Secretary, Joan Ferguson, is the author of *Scottish Family Histories held in Scottish Libraries* and *Scottish Newspapers held in Scottish Libraries*—two invaluable books.

One of the current projects of the Chairman of the Council of the Society, Donald Whyte, F.H.G., F.S.A., is the production of a book listing Scottish emigrants to Canada. When this is published, it will be a companion to his other book about emigration to the United States. Another member is working on a similar book about pre-1855 emigrants to Australia and New Zealand. The addresses of these two people are given below—they will welcome information about Scots emigrants for inclusion in their books:

Mr. Donald Whyte, 4 Carmel Road, Kirkliston, West Lothian.

Mr. Duncan McNaughton, 28 Pitbauchlie Bank, Dunfermline.

One of the major projects of the Society is the publication of books of Monumental Inscriptions (wording on tombstones) for various districts of Scotland. As you know, tombstones often contain information which is not obtainable anywhere else. The books cover the pre-1855 period and include all legible inscriptions for the areas covered. A number of the books are out of print, and for up-to-date information as to which ones are available you should write to Miss Ferguson at her address given above. Be sure you send the usual two International Reply Coupons and a self-addressed airmail envelope.

The Clan System

No genealogical guide for ancestor-hunting in Scotland would be complete without a short explanation of the clan system. Contrary to popular belief, not all Scots belong to a clan. The clan system has its roots in the Highlands and was never part of the life in the central part of the country or in the Lowlands.

The Highland Line, which divided Scotland into the Highlands and the Lowlands, ran from Dumbarton in the west in a northeasterly direction almost as far as Aberdeen. There it turned north and then west, passing south of Inverness, and then headed north to a point midway between Cape Wrath and John o'Groats. Everything north and west of the line was considered Highland. The word *clan* simply means "kin", and far back in history the Highlanders grouped themselves around the leading landowner of the district. He provided them with protection against marauding bands of robbers from other areas, and they, in turn, provided him with a strong force of fighting men to enable him to expand his estates or his sphere of influence. In many cases they were related to him; in others, they simply adopted his name.

The chiefs of the clans were soon known by the name of their estates, so there was Cameron of Lochiel, MacNeil of Barra, Macdonald of Keppoch, and so on. A Highlander living on the estate of the chief of Clan Cameron never adopted the servile approach of the Englishman under similar circumstances. There was no bowing and scraping, no pulling the forelock—he stood straight and addressed his clan chief as "Lochiel". All the emphasis within the clan was not on land, but on the blood connection between the chief and the clansmen.

The death of the clan system was the unsuccessful Rising of 1745 when Prince Charles (Bonnie Prince Charlie) tried to regain the throne for his father, the exiled James III. His defeat at the battle of Culloden, and the subsequent killing of the clansmen and the execution of many of the chiefs, also destroyed the system itself.

Any vestiges which still remained disappeared in the later years of the Highland Clearances. This was when the chiefs found they could live an easy social life in Edinburgh, supported by the raising of sheep on their lands. The clansmen were ejected from their land and the ties of sentiment and blood and service were broken.

In the Lowlands there was the same grouping of tenants around the local great landlords—the Scotts, the Maxwells, the Douglases, the Hamiltons—but this grouping was based on land tenure and not on kinship or service.

The differences between Highlanders and Lowlanders went deep and were largely racial. The Highlanders were descended from the Celts, and the Lowlanders were of Saxon and Teutonic origin.

The great concentration of one surname in a particular district—such as the Campbells in Argyll and the MacIntoshes south of Inverness, around Moy, does not make ancestor-hunting very easy for people of Highland descent. There was not only duplication of surnames but duplication of first names as well. If there were four Alexander Stewarts in a village at one time, it was no problem *then* because they would be Black Alexander, Alexander the Red, Lang Alexander, and Wee Alexander. This was helpful in those days, but it creates difficulties now. However, if your name happens to be McKenzie or Stewart or a similar common Highland name, do not assume that your ancestors emigrated from the part of Scotland associated with that name—they could have left that area centuries ago. There are more Campbells in the Glasgow telephone directory than there are in the whole of Argyll!

12

IRELAND (EIRE AND NORTHERN IRELAND)

At the start it must be said that it is harder to trace ancestors in Ireland than it is in the other parts of what used to be called the British Isles. This is because of a major disaster affecting many of the records needed by the genealogist.

In 1922 the Public Record Office in the Four Courts Building, Dublin, was taken over by one side during the Civil War. Previously, the British government, then in control of Ireland, had ordered all the Church of Ireland parish registers to be lodged in the building for "safety" during the Troubles. (The order did not apply to the Catholic or the Presbyterian Church, or to other Protestant sects.) Some of the Church of Ireland registers were not sent to Dublin, and some of those that were had been copied first. The registers were placed in the Four Courts Building, which already housed all the wills and the census returns, and a few months later it came under fire. The records of Ireland were used to barricade the windows, the place caught fire, and everything went up in flames.

Since then, the Public Record Offices of both Eire and Northern Ireland have managed to collect a great deal of what is called "substitute" or "secondary" material. For example, all lawyers in the two sections of Ireland were asked to search their files and dusty deed-boxes for wills, which were then photocopied. Other vital documents surfaced in estate and family collections.

So searching is hard, but by no means impossible. I know one man who spent three weeks in Ireland last year—having done his homework before he went so that he knew exactly where every record was—and in that time he traced his father's side back to 1795 and his mother's to 1640. The first side was Catholic and the other Protestant.

An Irish surname may be borne by a great number of people—Murphy, Kennedy, O'Brien, and so on—so be sure you have some details about your ancestor besides a surname before you start searching in Ireland.

Since the partition of the country in 1922 the records have been partitioned to a great degree also. However, this has not been possible to do in every case, and there is some overlapping. If you are ancestor-hunting in Eire, you may well find you have to search records in Belfast, and vice versa.

Before you start your hunt in Ireland it is wise to become familiar with the various divisions of the country, because many of the records are based on these divisions—provinces, counties, baronies, parishes (civil or religious), townlands, and poor law unions:

PROVINCES: The four provinces of Ireland—Ulster, Leinster, Munster, and Connaught—take their names from four of the ancient kingdoms of Ireland—Uladh, Laighean, Mumha, and Connacht.

COUNTIES: Twelve counties were created in 1210 by King John, and others followed in the reigns of Mary I and Elizabeth I. There are thirty-two counties in the whole of Ireland, of which six are in Northern Ireland and the rest in Eire.

BARONIES: This division goes back into the mists of early Irish history and is based on Gaelic family holdings. There are three hundred and twenty-five baronies in all Ireland. They were turned into civil divisions by the English in the nineteenth century for the purpose of land valuation.

PARISHES: These are of two kinds—ecclesiastical and civil. The civil parish was used for land valuations, was usually smaller than the ecclesiastical one, and often had a different name. There are about two and half thousand ecclesiastical parishes in the whole country.

TOWNLANDS: This is a small rural section of a parish. Its average area is three hundred and fifty acres. There are just over sixty thousand of these townlands in all Ireland.

POOR LAW UNIONS: In 1838 the whole country was divided into districts, or Unions, in which the local rate-payers were made financially responsible for the care of all the poor or starving people in the area. In the years of the great potato famines the numbers of people involved were considerable. It was the pressure from local people unwilling to bear the cost which led to mass emigration. Paupers and their families would often have their passages overseas paid by local subscription, on the cold-blooded calculation that this would be cheaper than supporting them indefinitely by local taxes. The fact that the emigrants might starve or die on the long voyage, and had no jobs waiting for them overseas, did not enter into the calculations.

The Poor Law Union covered an average area of ten miles' radius from the Poor House, which was usually located in a market town.

Eire

First, make sure you have read all about the great fire of 1922 and the consequent destruction of records. Second, be sure you have absorbed all the details of the various civil and ecclesiastical divisions of Ireland. Without this information you will not know where to look or why you are looking.

You will have to search many unusual records in Eire to find your ancestors. In England and Wales everything is straightforward—civil registration, censuses, church registers, wills, and the superb network of County Record Offices; in Scotland it is almost as good. In Eire many of these sources no longer exist, or, if they still do, they are incomplete and disordered.

However, do not give up hope—the luck of the Irish will be with you!

First, you must have the name of a place to start, preferably a townland or a parish. A county is not enough to open up all sources of information to you. If you have no specific knowledge about an exact place, but have a vague family story about a vague general area—"Father always said he thought his father said we came from somewhere in the Galway area"—try a letter to a local newspaper. If you can't find out its name, it doesn't matter—just write to The Editor, The Weekly Newspaper, Killarney; or, in a big city, to The Editor, The Daily Newspaper, Cork. Your letter is fairly certain to be published. Write something along the lines of the suggested letter in Chapter 2. Some of the newspapers in Eire which are known to be very co-operative in publishing *short* letters of inquiry are:

The Irish Independent, Dublin
The Irish Press, Dublin
The Irish Times, Dublin
The Cork Examiner, Cork
The Anglo-Celt, Cavan
The Clare Champion, Ennis
The Donegal Democrat, Ballyshannon
The Impartial Reporter, Enniskillen

The Kerryman, Tralee
The Leitrim Observer, Carrick-on-Shannon
Sligo Champion, Sligo

If you know the name of the place but cannot find it on a map or in a gazetteer in a local library, you should write to the Place Names Commission, Phoenix Park, Dublin, and they will tell you where it is. You must give them a rough idea of the location, if you know it, because many Irish place-names are duplicated. If you can tell them "It's near Cork" or "It's on the sea on the southwest coast," this will be helpful.

You may also find it worth while to buy a six-inches-to-the-mile Ordnance Survey map covering the area of a particular village. You can buy them for about a pound from the Government Publications Sales Office, GPO Arcade, Dublin. It is simpler to send a sterling draft from a bank than a P.O. money order. Eire has some very complicated foreign exchange regulations now, and if you buy a P.O. money order it has to be payable to the Eire government, who, in turn, send a cheque to the addressee. This rigmarole does not apply to bank drafts.

Now let us talk about the various centres of information in Eire and the records which they hold. They help to fill in the gaps caused by the 1922 Four Courts fire.

Public Record Office of Ireland
Four Courts, Dublin. The Public Record Office does not as a rule carry out any detailed searches, but if complete details such as full names and exact addresses and dates are supplied, the records will be consulted without charge (except for a small fee for a photocopy of the particular entry). Inquiries which require a prolonged search will be referred to the Genealogical Office, Dublin Castle (see later entry).

Census Returns
A census was taken every ten years from 1821, but only those for 1901 and 1911 survive completely. The returns for each townland or street give the names, ages, occupations, and religion of everyone in the house, together with place of birth.

There are some scattered returns from the censuses of 1821, 1831, 1841, and 1851 covering parts of the counties of Antrim, Derry, and Fermanagh in Northern Ireland, and Cavan, Cork, Galway, King's, Meath, and Waterford in Eire. Do not expect too much from these as there are only a few parishes involved. Most have been copied by the LDS Church.

The Primary Valuation

(also known as Griffith's Valuation)

This was a survey of land and property carried out between 1847 and 1865 for the purpose of assessments for tax purposes; specifically, local taxes to support poor law administration. There is a printed book for each Poor Law Union showing names of *occupiers* of land and buildings. Most have been copied by the LDS Church.

The Tithe Applotment Books

These record a survey of a different kind carried out between 1823 and 1837 to determine the amount of tithe payments made to the established church. The records give the names of occupiers of land. Remember that everyone had to pay tithes to the Church of Ireland, even if they were Catholics or Nonconformists.

Both of these surveys may help to take the place of the missing census returns. The LDS Church has copies.

Wills

Before 1858 wills had to be proved in the Diocesan Courts of the Church of Ireland—*all* wills, not just those of the members of the church. These wills were destroyed in the fire, but the indexes are in the Public Record Office. Where a person had property in more than one diocese, his will was proved in the prerogative court. *Abstracts* of all wills so proved between 1536 and 1810 are contained in the Betham Papers. A copy of the printed Index to the Prerogative Wills of Ireland 1536-1810 is available in the PRO.

Since 1858, wills have been proved in district registries or in the principal registry in Dublin. The PRO holds an index to these, and this shows the name and address of the deceased, the value of the estate, the date of death, and the name and address of the executor(s). All wills proved since 1904 and copies of most wills proved in district registries since 1858 are also available.

Wills and other probate records have often been found in family and estate papers, and in lawyers' records. A separate index to these is available and is kept up to date.

Marriage Bonds

These were documents obtained to guarantee there was no just impediment to a marriage by licence. As with other records, they did not survive the fire, but the indexes did and are in the PRO. They only cover certain areas for certain periods, and are listed below:

Armagh, 1727-1845; Cashel and Emly, 1664-1807; Clogher, 1711-1866; Cloyne, 1630-1867; Cork and Ross, 1623-1845; Derry (five only); Down, Connor, and Dromore, 1721-1845; Dublin, 1672-1741; Elphin, 1733-1845; Kildare, 1790-1865; Killala and Achonry, 1787-1842; Killaloe, 1719-1845; Kilmore and Ardagh, 1697-1844; Limerick, 1827-44; Meath, 1665, 1702-1845; Ossory, Ferns and Leighlin, 1691-1845; Raphoe, 1710-55, 1817-30; Tuam, 1769-1845; Waterford and Lismore, 1649-1845.

Note: It must be remembered that the use of marriage bonds and licences was usually confined to the upper classes. If your ancestors were prominent landowners, you may well find information in the above records; if your ancestors were scratching out a precarious existence in a shanty on the edge of a bog in Connemara, be prepared for a disappointment.

Religious Censuses

These took place in 1766, when the local rector of the Church of Ireland was instructed to list heads of households as either Protestant or Catholic. The originals were nearly all lost in the 1922 fire, but some transcripts and extracts had been made previously. Both the few originals and the copies are in the PRO. These refer to parishes in the dioceses of Armagh(39), Cashel and Emly(21), Clogher(8), Cloyne(62), Connor(4), Cork and Ross(4), Derry(10), Down(1), Dublin(4), Ferns and Leighlin(1), Fromore(1), Kildare(4), Kilmore and Ardagh(7), Limerick(1), Ossory(1), Raphoe(3), and Waterford(1).

Remember that a number of the dioceses straddled what is now the partition line between Eire and Northern Ireland and you will find details of the counties included in each diocese a few pages further on.

Indexes

Many different types of records in the PRO have been indexed and these should be checked early in your search, as they may take you directly to the entry you want. The more unusual the surname, the more successfully you will be able to use the indexes.

Quit Rents

These records were transferred to the PRO in 1943 from the original government departments. They date from the seventeenth century and include information about land revenues; land surveys (1654-56); forfeited estates; and other Crown Land transactions.

There are many other genealogical records in the PRO, such as family histories and trees; lists of inhabitants of various places; lists of freeholders and electors; petitions; and records of town and parish councils.

The Office of the Registrar General

8 Lombard Street East, Dublin 2. This office contains records of births, marriages, and deaths from 1 January 1864. Protestant marriage records started on 1 April 1845. It is open Monday-Friday, 0930-1700 hours, and facilities are available for you to do your own research. Those inquiring by mail will be charged a small fee. General searches will not be undertaken by the staff, and you will be referred to the Genealogical Office, Dublin Castle. A search will be made if sufficient information is supplied, i.e., names in full, and date and place of the event. In the case of a birth, it is advisable to supply the names of the parents, in view of the duplication of names in Eire. (The LDS Church has microfilmed and indexed entries from 1845 to 1920.)

The Genealogical Office

2 Kildare Street, Dublin 2. This office is open Monday-Friday, 0930-1700 hours. It is a state agency under the jurisdiction of the Ministry of Education and incorporates the former Ulster Office of Arms. The office has custody of very large collections of family histories and trees dating back to Norman times. Bear in mind that the majority of these pedigrees refer to families of high social standing.

Among the records held by the Genealogical Office are:

Wills

Abstracts of the Prerogative Wills of Ireland by Sir William Betham, mainly seventeenth to nineteenth centuries. Also a collection known as the Eustace Will Abstracts covering a similar period.

Obituaries

These have been extracted from Irish newspapers from the seventeenth and eighteenth centuries, and refer mainly to prominent citizens or important landowners.

Prerogative Marriage Licences

These cover the period 1600-1800 and are indexed by diocese.

Freeholders

These rolls cover the following counties and years, but are not complete:

NORTHERN IRELAND: Armagh, 1753; Fermanagh, 1788.

EIRE: Clare, 1829; Donegal, 1761-75; Kilkenny, 1775; Limerick,

1776, 1829; Longford, 1830-36; Meath, 1755-90; Queen's, 1758-75; Roscommon, 1780; Tipperary, 1775-76; West Meath, 1761.

Directories
The office holds directories for 1809 for Cork, Limerick, and Waterford.

Marriage Licences and Bonds
These are held for the dioceses of Dublin and Ossory (Co. Kilkenny) for periods during the seventeenth and eighteenth centuries.

Militia Lists
All Protestant males between sixteen and sixty were liable for call-up in the militia, and Officers lists are held for 1761 for the counties of Cork, Donegal, Dublin, Kerry, Limerick, Louth, Monaghan, Roscommon, and Tipperary.

Other Records
There are also hearth money rolls (taxes); lists of freemen of the city of Dublin; poll taxes; army lists, 1746-72; and indexed records of Grants of Arms in all Ireland from 1552.

The Genealogical Office will undertake research for an agreed fee. If you wish to take advantage of its services, you should write, giving full details of your problems, and ask for an estimate of the cost of a detailed search. However, the Office stresses two major points: (a) There is a two-year waiting list for research, and (b) research is not easy because most people of Irish blood scattered around the world are descended from emigrants who left Ireland in large numbers about 100 to 150 years ago and may be unlisted in any public record.

The National Library of Ireland
Kildare Street, Dublin. The various major sources of genealogical information held at this library are:

Pedigrees
The holdings include a considerable number of family trees and histories. Most of them, as usual in Ireland, refer to well-established and well-known families.

Directories
These include the Dublin City Directory from 1751; a Directory of Ireland, 1846 and 1879; Landowners of Ireland, 1878; Belfast Almanacs from 1770; Cork Directory, 1787.

Counties

On a county basis the following miscellaneous information is on file:

CORK: Statistical Survey, eighteenth and nineteenth centuries.

DERRY: Book of Plantation, 1609.

DONEGAL: Poll of Electors, 1761.

DOWN: Estate Rolls, eighteenth century.

DUBLIN: City Voters List, 1832; History of Dublin (City) Guilds.

GALWAY: Town Rate Book of Loughrea, 1854 and 1887.

LEITRIM: Estate Rentals, 1844.

LIMERICK: County and Estate Maps, 1747; Limerick (city) Assembly Book, eighteenth century.

LONGFORD: Cromwellian settlement of the county.

MAYO: Strafford's Survey.

MEATH: County Freeholders List, 1775.

WEXFORD: Miscellaneous Quit Rents.

Royal Irish Academy

19 Dawson Street, Dublin. This organization holds a great deal of genealogical material:

The Books of Survey and Distribution

These are seventeenth-century records of land transactions, and the following counties of Eire are covered (the Northern Ireland counties are listed in the next section):

Vol. 1: Dublin, Wicklow, Carlow

Vol. 2: Wexford, Kildare

Vol. 3: King's and Queen's (Offaly and Leix)

Vol. 4: Kilkenny

Vol. 5: East Meath, Louth

Vol. 6: West Meath, Longford

Vol. 7: Tipperary (Part 1)

Vol. 8: Tipperary (Part 2)

Vol. 9: Cork (Part 1)

Vol. 10: Cork (Part 2)

Vol. 11: Waterford

Vol. 12: Limerick

Vol. 13: Kerry

Vol. 14: Cavan, Monaghan

Vol. 15: Donegal

Vol. 16: Leitrim, Sligo, Mayo

Clare, Galway, and Roscommon are missing. All volumes are indexed.

Genealogical Collections

The collections of the Academy are very large, well organized, and catalogued. Much of the information is indexed.

Public Documents

These include a printed list of Freeholders for Co. Tipperary in 1776 and Strafford's Survey of Co. Mayo 1635-37, showing ownership of the land *before* Plantation.

The Academy staff is prepared to undertake limited searches. If you visit in person, you should bring with you a letter of introduction from a librarian who knows you. This is because of the valuable nature of the early records and genealogical manuscripts dating back to the Middle Ages.

Trinity College

Dublin. The Manuscripts Room holds several volumes of genealogies collected in the seventeenth century and extensive genealogies (descents) in the Irish language. Other useful sources include lists of names in heraldic and ecclesiastical manuscripts and in military and civil lists; a collection of deeds; extracts from Dublin parish registers; and records of Trinity College's own history. Printed catalogues of the manuscripts exist, and there is a typescript guide to those that are of Irish genealogical interest.

Registry of Deeds

Henrietta Street, Dublin. (Open daily, 1000-1600 hours.) Practically all the land records of all Ireland are lodged here, and many date back to 1708. The deeds cover such subjects as leases, business transactions, land transfers, marriage licences, and wills. Two indexes, one under surnames and the other under place names, exist for this massive collection.

Basically, the Irish land records are very similar to the sasines of Scotland. Over 800,000 deeds are listed up to 1833. They have all been copied into registers, so there is no need to refer to the original unless you want to see the actual signature of your ancestor. There is no point in listing the counties in the one hundred volumes, but typical titles are:

Vol. 29: County Kildare, 1739-1810
Vol. 73: County Louth, 1738-1810
Vol. 95: County Antrim, 1828-1832

The State Paper Office

Birmingham Tower, Dublin Castle. This houses government records from the Chief Secretary's Office and includes a great deal of specialized material which may or may not be applicable to your ancestors! The records include criminal index books, registers of convicts sentenced to transportation overseas, the 1798 Rebellion papers, Fenian and Land League records, and details of evicted tenants.

Some valuable information is still held by individual churches.

Church Registers

Catholic: The original registers are in the original churches and date back to about 1820, with some much earlier and some much later. They are available on microfilm in the National Library of Ireland, Kildare Street, Dublin.

Church of Ireland: The majority of these registers up to 1870 are in the PRO, but some remain in the original churches. In addition, the PRO has copies of other surviving registers, and a number of *extracts* from registers. These latter are not complete—they may cover only a particular period of time, or only baptisms, or marriages, or burials. Full information can be obtained from the PRO.

Presbyterian: The following registers are still with the original churches—except those marked with an asterisk. These are in the custody of the Presbyterian Historical Society, Church House, Fisherwick Place, Belfast, Northern Ireland:

Note: In Ireland, Co. stands for County, just as in England and Wales "-shire" means "the county of".

CO. CAVAN: Bailieborough, Ballyjamesduff, Bellasis, Cavan, Clones, Cootehill, Seafin.

CO. CORK: Bandon, Cork, Lismore, Queenstown.

CO. DONEGAL: Ballindrait, Ballylennon, Ballyshannon, Bucrana, Burt, Carnone, *Carrigart, Convoy, Crossroads, Donegal, Donoughmore, Dunfanaghy, Fannet, Knowhead, Letterkenny, Monreagh, Moville, Newtowncunningham, Ramelton, Raphoe, Rathmullan, St. Johnstown, Trenta.

CO. DUBLIN: Dublin.

CO. GALWAY: Galway.

CO. KERRY: Tralee.

CO. LEITRIM: Carrigallen, Drumkeeran, *Killeshranda.

CO. LEIX: *Mountmellick.

CO. LIMERICK: Limerick.

CO. LONGFORD: Corboy, Longford, Tully.

CO. LOUTH: Corvalley, Drogheda, Dundalk.

CO. MAYO: Ballina, Killala.

CO. MONAGHAN: Ballyalbany, Ballybay, Ballyhobridge, Broomfield, *Cahans, Castleblayney, Clontibret, Corlea, *Crieve, Derryvalley, Drumkeen, *Frankford, *Glennan, Middletown, Newbliss, Scotstown, Stonebridge.

CO. SLIGO: Sligo.

CO. WATERFORD: Waterford.

CO. WEST MEATH: Carlow.

CO. WEXFORD: Wexford.

CO. WICKLOW: Bray.

There are other specialized sources of information which will be of great value to some of you, but not to all:

Huguenots: Many of these French Protestant refugees came to Ireland from France some three hundred and more years ago. Most of them settled in Dublin, and the poplin business was begun there by Huguenots. There were four Huguenot churches in Dublin. Their registers for the period 1680-1830 have been printed by the Huguenot Society in London, England, and copies are in the Genealogical Office in Dublin. There were smaller settlements developed in such places as Co. Leix (Queen's County), and in Kilkenny, Limerick, and Cork.

Quakers: The Society of Friends established themselves in Ireland in 1654. Fortunately, the Society has always attached great value to the preservation of records. Registers of birth, marriage, and death for the provinces of Munster, Leinster, and Connaught, dating from the mid-1600s, are in the Historical Library at 6 Eustace Street, Dublin. There are also six volumes of Quaker wills from the seventeenth and eighteenth centuries. Finally, in the library you will also find a great many Quaker family trees, several diaries and journals of early Irish Quakers, and copious correspondence. There is also some information about the Quaker emigration to Pennsylvania between 1682 and 1750.

Records relating to the province of Ulster are held in the Friends' Meeting House, Lisburn, Co. Antrim. These include records of Meetings at Antrim, Ballinderry, Ballyhagen, Ballymoney, Coleraine, Cootehill, Hillsborough, Lisburn, Lurgan, Oldcastle, and Rathfriland.

Palatines: A little-known immigration *into* Ireland was that of religious refugees from the Palatinate area of Germany. Some eight hundred and fifty of them landed at Dublin in 1709. (Many more emigrated to the Americas, where they settled in Pennsylvania.) Those remaining in Ireland settled mainly in Limerick and Kerry, and even today many non-Irish and probably German surnames can be found in those areas. There is a privately printed book which deals with the history of some two hundred Irish Palatine families, and details of this will be found in the Bibliography at the end of the book.

Other sources of information for Irish records:

IRISH GENEALOGICAL RESEARCH SOCIETY: F. Payton, Glenholme, High Oakham Road, Mansfield, Nottinghamshire.

SOCIETY OF GENEALOGISTS: 14 Charterhouse Buildings, London EC1M 7BA. Early Irish directories: Dublin, 1761-1904; Limerick (City), 1769; Cork, 1787; Leinster Province, 1788; Co. Clare, Co. Tipperary, Co. Limerick (all 1788).

There is now an Irish Family History Society with small groups in a number of counties. For detailed and up-to-date information write to Michael Egan, Convent View, Tullamore, Co. Offaly, Eire. (be sure to enclose two International Reply Coupons).

Finally, here is a list of counties and the dioceses with jurisdiction within them:

CARLOW: Leighlin
CAVAN: Ardagh, Meath, Kilmore
CLARE: Killaloe, Kilfenora, Limerick
CORK: Cork, Ross, Cloyne, Ardfert
DONEGAL: Clogher, Derry, Raphoe
DUBLIN: Dublin
GALWAY: Clonfert, Elphin, Killaloe, Tuam
KERRY: Ardfert
KILDARE: Dublin, Kildare
KILKENNY: Leighlin, Ossory
LAOIS OR LEIX (QUEEN'S): Dublin, Kildare, Leighlin, Ossory
LEITRIM: Ardagh, Kilmore
LIMERICK: Cashel, Emly, Killaloe, Limerick
LONGFORD: Armagh, Meath
LOUTH: Armagh, Clogher
MAYO: Killala, Achonry, Tuam
MEATH: Armagh, Kildare, Kilmore, Meath
MONAGHAN: Clogher
OFFALY (KING'S): Clonfert, Kildare, Killaloe, Meath, Ossory
ROSCOMMON: Ardagh, Clonfert, Elphin, Tuam
SLIGO: Ardagh, Elphin, Killala
TIPPERARY: Cashel, Killaloe, Waterford, Lismore
WATERFORD: Waterford, Lismore
WESTMEATH: Ardagh, Meath
WEXFORD: Dublin, Ferns
WICKLOW: Dublin, Ferns, Leighlin

Many of the above records have been copied by the LDS Church.

As you will know by now you have to look in many places when you are ancestor-hunting in Eire. In Dublin alone you have to visit the Registrar General, the Public Record Office, the Genealogical Office, the Registry of Deeds, the Royal Irish Academy, at least three libraries, and probably the headquarters of the particular denomination in which you are interested.

My original advice about not going overseas until you have sat down and done your homework applies particularly to Ireland. The records are so scattered and their condition is so bad in places that you have double the normal amount of searching to do as compared with neighbouring areas. It can be done, and done very successfully, but you do need patience and determination. Good luck!

Northern Ireland

This part of Ireland is referred to as Northern Ireland rather than Ulster because the ancient province of that name contained more than the present six counties of Northern Ireland—the other Ulster counties are in Eire.

Public Record Office of Northern Ireland

This is the main source of genealogical records in Northern Ireland and is hereinafter referred to as PRONI.

The main holdings of the office (at 66 Balmoral Avenue, Belfast BT9 6YN) are:

Church Registers

There are three main denominations involved—Church of Ireland (the equivalent of the Church of England), Presbyterian, and Catholic.

The Church of Ireland was required to keep parish registers from 1634 but the law was not strictly enforced and there are many gaps in surviving registers. In addition, many were lost over the years, and many more were destroyed in the Four Courts fire in 1922.

The office has copies or originals of all the Church of Ireland registers which survive; of all existing Catholic registers for the original nine counties of Ulster; and of many Presbyterian registers. There are more Presbyterian registers in the original churches, and a few in the custody of the Presbyterian Historical Society.

Lists of surviving registers appear at the end of this chapter and are based on the latest available information from official and ecclesiastical sources in Northern Ireland.

The Quakers (Society of Friends)

The Quakers kept good records of births, marriages, and deaths of their members from the mid-seventeenth century and copies are in PRONI. Further information about Quaker records can be obtained from the Society of Friends Historical Library, 6 Eustace Street, Dublin, Eire.

Wills and Other Testamentary Records

As in England and Wales, wills were proved or probated in the diocesan courts, unless goods or land were held in more than one diocese. In that case they were probated in the Prerogative Court of the Archbishop of Armagh. The church jurisdiction ended in 1858 when a civil Court of Probate was established.

The original wills were lost in the 1922 fire, but copies of the indexes survive for most of the wills, and they give the name and location of the testator and the date of probate.

The original civil wills from 1858 to 1900 were also lost in the fire, but the district probate registries at Armagh, Belfast, and Londonderry kept copies of wills probated for the original nine counties of the Province of Ulster, i.e., for the present six counties plus Donegal, Monaghan, and Louth.

Original wills from 1900 to 1959 are in PRONI for the six counties and Donegal, and can be copied for a fee. Wills from 1960 to date are in the Probate and Matrimonial Office, Royal Courts of Justice, Belfast BT1 3JF, and copies may be purchased. Wills of deceased persons formerly resident in the Londonderry area may be in the District Probate Registry, Bishop Street, Londonderry, which is now the only District Registry in Northern Ireland. Wills are retained in these two offices for twenty years and are then transferred to PRONI.

Pre-1858 wills still turn up occasionally in collections of family papers or in lawyers' records, and these additional ones are listed in the personal-name index of PRONI. Another source of good information there is the Burke Collection, which contains details of 16,000 wills and 5,000 grants of administration, all prior to 1800, in forty-two volumes. However, bear in mind that these apply in the main to people of wealth and high social standing.

It must also be remembered that if a person did not make a will, there may have been a Grant of Intestacy. This gives some information about the deceased, and the indexed Grants are in PRONI.

The indexes to pre-1858 wills in the office relate to a diocese and not to a county. The following dioceses cover the Northern Ireland counties, but it is only a rough guide, as there were many exceptions and variations:

ARMAGH: Co. Armagh and south Co. Derry

CLOGHER: south Co. Tyrone, Co. Fermanagh

CONNOR: Co. Antrim

DERRY AND RAPHOE: north Co. Derry, north Co. Tyrone

DOWN: north Co. Down

DROMORE: south Co. Down

Census Returns

In 1740, the Irish Parliament in Dublin ordered a return of all Protestant householders. A few censuses for the area now known as Northern Ireland survived, and are in PRONI. In 1766 the Church of Ireland clergymen were told to make a return of Protestants and Catholics in their parishes. All the originals were destroyed, but copies of a few of the lists are in PRONI.

Censuses were taken on a regular basis from 1821, but almost all those for the period 1821-51 were lost in the Four Courts fire in 1922, and those from 1861 to 1891 were destroyed in error at a later date.

The scattered returns which do survive from the earliest period are:

1821, Co. Fermanagh: Aghalurcher, Derryvullen.

1831, Co. Derry: Aghanloo, Agivey, Arboe, Ballyaghran, Banagher, Finlogan, Glendermot, Killowen, Macosquin, Tamlaght, Templemore, Termoneeny.

1841, Co. Fermanagh: Currin.

1851, Co. Antrim: Aghagallon, Aghalee, Ballinderry, Ballymoney, Carncastle, Craigs, Donaghy, Grange, Killead, Kilwaughter, Larne, Rasharkin, Tickmacrevan.

1851, Co. Fermanagah: Drumheeran.

The Census returns are closed for 100 years in PRONI (from the date of enumeration) but the returns for 1901 and 1911 may be inspected in the Public Record Office in Dublin.

Civil Registration

In Ireland the compulsory registration of births, marriages and deaths did not start until 1 January 1864. However, Protestant marriages were recorded from 1 April 1845. The records are in the General Register Office, 49 Chichester Street, Belfast BT1 4HL.

Tithe Applotment Books (1823-37)

The tithe was a tax on agricultural land (originally a tenth of the produce) which was paid by occupiers of *all* religious denominations to the Church of Ireland. In 1823 it was replaced by a cash payment by landowners. The amount due was based on a special survey. The records were arranged by civil parish and townland in what are known as Tithe Applotment Books. Compiled between 1823 and 1837, these are in PRONI for 242 of the 273 parishes surveyed in Northern Ireland. The records give the name of the landholders and the acreage.

Militia and Yeomanry Muster Rolls

All *Protestant* males between sixteen and sixty were liable for service in the militia. The records in PRONI are for 1630 and 1631, plus an additional list for 1642 and 1643 for Co. Down only. There are also some records of Yeomanry and Regular Army units between 1741 and 1804.

Valuation Records

These are lists of people occupying lands and houses and are available from 1830 onwards. The valuation for the period 1848-64—known as Griffith's Valuation—has been printed and is available in PRONI in thirty volumes. It is arranged by counties, and within counties by Poor Law Unions, and within these by parishes.

There were twenty-seven Poor Law Unions in Northern Ireland:

CO. ANTRIM: Antrim, Ballycastle, Ballymena, Ballymoney, Belfast, Larne, Lisburn.

CO. ARMAGH: Armagh, Lurgan.

CO. DERRY: Coleraine, Londonderry, Magherafelt, Newtown (Limavady).

CO. DOWN: Banbridge, Downpatrick, Kilkeel, Newry, Newtownards.

CO. FERMANAGH: Enniskillen, Irvinestown, Lisnakea.

CO. TYRONE: Castlederg, Clogher, Cookstown, Dungannon, Omagh, Strabane.

Marriage Bonds

These were issued by the bishops of the Church of Ireland. The originals were destroyed in the 1922 fire but indexes are in PRONI. The names of the bride and bridegroom are given, and the date of the bond. The indexes are:

1. Marriage Bonds, 1625-1857

2. Grants of Probate, Intestacy, and Marriage Licences, 1595-1857
3. Diocese of Armagh, 1727-1845
4. Diocese of Clogher, 1709-1866
5. Diocese of Down, Connor, and Dromore, 1721-1845

Hearth Money, Subsidy, and Poll Tax Records

These are lists of persons paying taxes and are of particular value to ancestor-hunters interested in the seventeenth century. The Hearth Money Rolls list people, parish by parish, who paid a tax of two shillings on each hearth. The tax was collected over areas known as "Walks", which were based on a town—the Walk covered a large area around and in the place named.

The Subsidy Rolls list the nobility, clergy, and laity who paid a grant to the King. The name and parish of each person is given. The Poll Tax lists people who paid a tax on each person over twelve years old living in a house.

The originals of all the above were destroyed in 1922, but PRONI holds copies.

Voters, Poll, and Freeholders Records

These are lists of people actually voting in an election, or entitled to vote. They survive for some places and periods, and are arranged on a county basis:

CO. ANTRIM: 1776
CO. ARMAGH: 1753, 1813-39, 1851
CO. DERRY: 1813, 1832, 1868
CO. DOWN: 1789, 1790, 1813-21, 1824, 1830
CO. FERMANAGH: 1747, 1788, 1796-1802
CO. TYRONE: 1796 (Dungannon Barony only)
BELFAST: 1832-37

Landed Estate Records

Many records of the big private estates are in PRONI, but generally speaking it will be the Rent Rolls which will be of genealogical interest to you.

Poor Law Records

These are the records of the Boards of Guardians who administered the poor law in Ireland from 1838 to 1948. Each Poor Law Union was named after the chief town in an area, and often crossed county boundaries. These are in the office and may well be of great interest to you, since a very high percentage of the Irish population was starving and destitute in the early part of the last century.

Emigration Records

The law did not require that lists of emigrants from Ireland be kept. There are some isolated lists in PRONI—names of emigrants to America from 1804 to 1806; shipping agents' papers (J. & J. Cooke) listing passengers sailing from Londonderry for the United States and Canada in the period 1847-71. This latter list gives names, ages, and place of residence. In addition, PRONI has microfilmed the names of some 45,000 people landing in U.S. ports between about 1847 and 1871—mainly Baltimore, Boston, and Philadelphia. These are being indexed at present.

There are also some parish records from about 1830 to 1840 which list names of people leaving Co. Antrim and Co. Derry for overseas.

Tombstones

There are over a thousand graveyards in Northern Ireland, and it is estimated that nearly half have been recorded by the Ulster Historical Foundation. Copies of these lists are in PRONI.

Personal Names Card Index

If you have no idea where your ancestors came from in Northern Ireland, you can check the distribution of a particular surname by looking at Index cards to the 1830 Tithe Applotment Books. These have been compiled by PRONI and give the name of the payer, the amount paid, and the size of the farm or smallholding. They are listed by townland.

Royal Irish Academy

This is located at 19 Dawson Street, Dublin, Eire, and contains a great deal of genealogical information. Most of it applies to Eire and was listed on pages 267-8. However, it also has several records of value to ancestor-hunters in Northern Ireland:

The Books of Survey and Distribution

These are seventeenth-century records of land transactions, and the following Northern Ireland counties are included:
Vol. 14: Tyrone, Fermanagh
Vol. 15: Antrim, Armagh, Derry, Down
The volumes are indexed.

Emigration Lists

These are lists of persons who emigrated between 1833 and 1835 from various parishes in Co. Derry to the United States and Canada. The parishes are Aghadowey, Aghanloo, Agivey, Arboe, Ardtrea,

Ballyaghran, Ballynascreen, Ballyrashane, Ballyscullion, Ballywillin, Balteagh, Banagher, Bovevagh, Clondermot, Coleraine, Desertlyn, Desertmartin, Desertoghill, Drumechose, Dunbo, Dungiven, Errigal, Kilcronaghan, Kildollagh, Killowen, Kilrea, Magilligan, Yallaght Finlagan.

Family Pedigrees
There is a considerable collection of these, but only a few refer to the six northern counties.

The Academy staff is prepared to undertake very limited searches of records. If you are visiting the Academy in person, you should bring with you a letter of introduction from a librarian. This is simply because of the valuable nature of many of the early records, such as "The Great Book of Lecan" and other genealogical manuscripts dating back to the Middle Ages.

The following organizations in Northern Ireland and in England can be of great help to the ancestor-hunter:

The Federation for Ulster Local Studies
Secretary: Brian Turner, B.A., Knockbawn, Knocknadona, Lisburn, Co. Antrim.

This organization was founded in 1975 and now consists of thirty-six historical societies from each of the nine original counties of Ulster, with a combined membership of 7,000. These societies are not primarily concerned with genealogy, although interest is developing rapidly. However, many individual members are genealogists. If you have difficulties in a particular area, it is worth while to write to the Secretary and ask to be put in touch with a local society in the area of your interest. Be sure you send the usual self-addressed airmail envelope and *two* International Reply Coupons.

Ulster Historical Foundation
66 Balmoral Avenue, Belfast BT9 6NY. This body was set up in 1956 as the Ulster-Scot Historical Society to give assistance to descendants of Ulster people who were tracing their ancestors.

It is located very conveniently in the same building as the Public Record Office of Northern Ireland (PRONI). The services of the Foundation are available on a fee basis. You must be prepared to pay at least fifteen pounds for an initial search, and this is non-returnable. An average search and report may cost £75 and there is no guarantee of success. If the inquirer cannot give a precise location, such as city, village, townland, or parish (a county is not sufficient), and religion, it is unlikely a search can be made. In any case, there is likely to be a waiting period of at least six months before a search can be started.

In addition to its primary purpose of carrying out searches, the Foundation is also publishing a Gravestone Inscription Series of books which can give unique information to the genealogist. Because of the 1922 fire, and the generally poor condition of the remaining registers, a tombstone may well be the only record of someone's existence before civil registration started in 1864. Eighteen volumes have been published for graveyards in Co. Down, and a further eight will be needed to complete the recording of all pre-1900 inscriptions in the county. The series has now been extended to Co. Antrim with the publication of the first volume for that county. Transcribers are at work in the other four counties.

The Foundation has also published three books of general history:

Ulster Emigration to Colonial America 1718-1715 by R. J. Dickson.

The Scots Migration to Ulster in the Reign of James I by M. Perceval-Maxwell.

Essays in Scotch-Irish History by M. Jones.

The Ulster Genealogical and Historical Guild

This is an offshoot of the Ulster Historical Foundation and is located at the same address. Its aim is to promote public knowledge of and interest in Ulster genealogy, and to build up a collection of books, manuscripts, and transcripts of genealogical material. Subscribers are invited to donate copies of their family records so they may be deposited in PRONI.

The Guild is also compiling an alphabetical list of names of families being researched. This will be a complete record of Ulster genealogical work in progress, and will be updated annually.

The Presbyterian Historical Society of Ireland

Church House, Fisherwick Place, Belfast BT1 6DW.

This Society is not a major genealogical source, since its records are concerned primarily with ministers of the church. However, they have up-to-date information about the location of a particular parish register. Inquirers will be given the name of the minister of the Presbyterian church in the area in which they are interested.

Any inquiry must be accompanied by a self-addressed airmail envelope, two International Reply Coupons, and five pounds. However, many of the registers have now been copied by the LDS Church.

Belfast Library and Society for Promoting Knowledge

Linen Hall Library, 17 Donegall Square North, Belfast BT1 5GD.

The unique collections of this Society consist of nearly a hundred manuscript notebooks written by R. W. H. Blackwood, containing a great deal of important material about Co. Down families; and an Index to Births, Marriages, and Deaths in the *Belfast News Letter*, 1738-1800. For most of this period this was the only newspaper in the northern part of Ireland. There is also a very good collection of published family histories of Northern Ireland interest.

The Society will do some searching, as the Blackwood collection is roughly indexed. However, you must send the usual enclosures, and a small donation to the Library for the purchase of books will be very welcome.

John McCabe, Ulster Family Research Service, Site 3, Stonebridge End, Lisburn, Co. Antrim.

This is a fee-base organization of which I have no personal experience, but a number of people have praised its efficiency and reasonable fees.

Society of Friends

If you have Quaker ancestry, the resources of this organization will be invaluable to you. Fortunately, the Quakers have always paid great attention to records and record-keeping. The Society was established in Ireland in 1654 and registers of births, marriages, and deaths have been maintained from that time. There are two addresses in Ireland with which you must deal:

The Friends Meeting House

Lisburn, Co. Antrim. This office holds the registers for the various Meetings in the original Province of Ulster (nine counties). These registers include those of Meetings at Antrim, Ballinaderry, Ballyhagen, Ballymoney, Coleraine, Cootehill, Hillsborough, Lisburn, Lurgan, Oldcastle, and Rathfriland.

The Historical Library of the Society

6 Eustace Street, Dublin. This contains the registers and records for the other three provinces of Ireland, and also six volumes of wills dating back to the seventeenth century, plus many family trees of members, and a number of diaries and journals of early Quakers.

One final word: the division of Quaker records between Dublin and Belfast points out the need for a careful check of the Dublin records even though your ancestors came from one of the present six counties of Northern Ireland. Be sure you read about the records of Eire at the beginning of the chapter. For example, the Genealogical Office, Dublin Castle, has Co. Down wills for the period 1646-1858; it has a Belfast Directory for 1809; and it has Militia Lists for Co. Derry, Co. Down, and Co. Tyrone for 1761.

To repeat, the country may be partitioned, but many of the records are not divisible.

Church Registers

The following Northern Ireland registers exist in the form of originals or copies made before 1922. They are either in the original church or in PRONI (Public Record Office of Northern Ireland). The latter office has copies of all Church of Ireland registers, some Catholic, and some Presbyterian. Since no up-to-date list is available, it will be necessary for you to contact the church or the PRONI to find out the location.

Catholic

CO. ANTRIM: Ahoghill, Antrim, Armoy, Ballintoy, Ballyclare, Ballymacarrett, Ballymoney and Derrykeighan, Belfast (St. Joseph, St. Malachy, St. Mary, St. Patrick, St. Peter), Braid (Ballymena), Carnlough, Carrickfergus, Culfeightrin (Ballycastle), Cushendall, Cushendun, Derryaghy, Duneane (Toomebridge), Dunloy (Cloughmills), Glenarm, Glenavy and Killead, Greencastle, Kirkinriola (Ballymena), Larne, Loughuile, Portglenone, Portrush, Ramoan (Ballycastle), Randalstown, Rasharkin, Tickmacrevan (Glenarm).

CO. ARMAGH: Aghagallon and Ballinderry (Lurgan), Armagh, Ballymacnab (Armagh), Ballymore and Mullaghbrac (Tandragee), Creggan (Crossmaglen), Derrynoose (Keady), Drumcree (Portadown), Forkhill, Killeavy (Bessbrook), Kilmore (Rich Hill), Loughgall, Loughgilly, Seagoe, Shankill (Lurgan), Tynan.

CO. DERRY: Ballinderry, Ballynascreen, Ballyscullion (Bellaghy), Banagher, Coleraine, Cumber (Claudy), Desertmartin, Drumechose (Limavady), Dungiven, Errigal, Faughanvale, Glendermot (Waterside, Derry), Kilrea, Maghera, Magherafelt, Magilligan, Moneymore, Templemore (Derry), Termoneeny.

CO. DOWN: Aghaderg (Loughbrickland), Annaclone, Ardkeen, Ballygalget (Portaferry), Ballynahinch, Ballyphilip, Banbridge, Bangor, Bright (Ardglass), Clonallon (Warrenpoint), Clonduff (Hilltown), Donaghmore, Downpatrick, Dromara, Dromore, Drumaroad (Castlewellan), Drumbo, Drumgath (Rathfriland), Drumgooland (Upper and Lower), Dunsford, Kilbroney (Rostrevor), Kilclief and Strangford, Kilcoo (Rathfriland), Loughinisland,

Maghera and Bryansford (Newcastle), Magheralin, Moira, Mourne, Newcastle, Newry, Newtownards inc. Comber and Donaghadee, Saintfield (Downpatrick), Saul and Ballee, Tullylish, Tyrella and Dundrum.

CO. FERMANAGH: Aghalurcher (Lisnakea), Aghaveagh, Carn (Belleek), Cleenish, Culmaine, Devenish, Enniskillen, Galloon, Inishmacsaint, Irvinestown, Roslea, Tempo.

CO. TYRONE: Aghaloo, Ardboe, Ardstraw (Cappagh), Ardtrea, Badoney, Ballinderry (Cookstown), Ballyclog, Beragh, Camus (Strabane), Cappagh, Clogher, Clonfeacle (Moy), Clonoe (Coalisland), Desertcreat, Donaghcavey (Fintona), Donaghedy, Donaghhenry (Coalisland), Donaghmore, Dromore, Drumglass (Dungannon), Drumragh (Omagh), Eglish (Dungannon), Errigal Keeran (Ballygawley), Kildreas, Kileeshil (Tullyallen), Kilskerry (Trillick), Leckpatrick (Strabane), Lissan (Cookstown), Longfield, Pomeroy, Termonamongan, Termonmaguirk (Carrickmore), Urney.

Note: Many of the above registers do not start before 1840, some start in 1820, and only Armagh, Creggan, and Camus date back before 1800. In addition, not all registers list all three events—baptism, marriage, and burial.

Church of Ireland

CO. ANTRIM: Aghalee, Ahoghill (Ballymena), Antrim, Ballinderry, Ballintoy (Ballycastle), Ballyclug, Ballymacarrett, Ballymena, Ballymoney, Ballynure, Ballysillan, Belfast (10 parishes), Carnamoney, Carrickfergus, Craigs (Belfast), Derryaghy (Lisburn), Derrykeighan, Drummaul (Randalstown), Dunluce (Bushmills), Dunseverick (Bushmills), Finvoy (Ballymoney), Glenarm, Glenavy, Glynn (Larne), Inver (Larne), Lambeg, Layde (Cushendall), Lisburn (Blaris), Magheragall (Lisburn), Muckamore (Antrim), Skerry, Stoneyford, Templecorran, Templepatrick, Whitehouse (Belfast).

CO. ARMAGH: Aghavilly (Armagh), Annaghmore (Loughgall), Ardmore, Armagh, Ballymore (Tandragee), Ballymower (Whitecross), Camlough (Newry), Creggan (Crossmaglen), Derrynoose (Armagh), Drumbanagher (Newry), Drumcree (Portadown), Eglish (Moy), Grange (Armagh), Keady, Kilcluney (Markethill), Killylea, Loughgall, Loughgilly (Markethill), Milltown (Magheramoy), Mullavilly (Tandragee), Newtownhamilton, Sankill, Tartaraghan (Loughgall), Tynan.

CO. DERRY: Ballinderry, Ballyeglish (Moneymore), Ballynascreen, Banagher (Derry), Castledawson, Clooney, Coleraine, Cumber (Claudy), Desertlyn (Moneymore), Desertmartin, Drumechose

(Limavady), Dungiven, Glendermot, Kilcronaghan (Tubbermore), Killowen (Coleraine), Kilrea, Learmount (Derry), Londonderry, Maghera, Magherafelt, Tamlaghard (Magilligan), Tamlaghfinlagan, Tamlaght (Portglenone), Termoneeny (Castledawson), Woods Chapel.

CO. DOWN: Aghaderg (Loughbrickland), Annalong (Castlewellan), Ardkeen, Ballee (Downpatrick), Ballyculter (Strangford), Ballyhalbert (Kircubbin), Ballyphilip (Portaferry), Ballywalter (Newtownards), Bangor, Clonduff (Hilltown), Comber, Donaghadee, Donaghcloney, Downpatrick, Drumballyroney (Rathfriland), Drumbeg (Lisburn), Drumbo (Lisburn), Drumgooland, Dundonald, Gilford, Hillsborough, Holywood, Inch, Innishargy, Kilbroney (Rostrevor), Kilcoo, Killaney, Killinchy, Kilmood, Kilmore, Knocknamuckley (Gilford), Knockbreda (Belfast), Loughlin Island, Magheralin, Moira, Moyntags (Lurgan), Newcastle, Newry, Saintfield, Seagoe, Seapatrick (Banbridge), Tullylish (Banbridge), Tyrella (Clough), Warrenpoint.

CO. FERMANAGH: Aghadrumsee (Clones), Aghalurcher (Lisnakea), Aghaveagh (Lisnakea), Belleek, Bohoe (Enniskillen), Clabby (Fivemiletown), Coolaghty (Kesh), Derryvullen (Enniskillen), Devenish (Ballyshannon), Drumkeeran (Kesh), Galloon, Inishmacsaint, Killesher (Enniskillen), Mullaghafad (Scotstown), Magheracross, Magheraculmoney (Kesh), Maguiresbridge, Tempo, Trory (Enniskillen).

CO. TYRONE: Arboe (Cookstown), Ardtrea (Cookstown), Badoney (Gortin), Ballyclog (Stewartstown), Brackaville, Caledon, Camus, Cappagh, Carnteel (Aughnacloy), Clonfeacle (Dungannon), Derg, Derrylorgan (Cookstown), Desertcreat (Cookstown), Donaghedy (Strabane), Donaghhenry (Dungannon), Donaghmore (Castlefin), Drumglass (Dungannon), Drumragh (Omagh), Edenderry (Omagh), Errigal (Garvagh), Findonagh (Donacavey), Fivemiletown, Kildreas (Cookstown), Killyman (Dungannon), Kilskerry (Enniskillen), Lissan (Cookstown), Sixmilecross, Termonamongan (Castlederg), Tullyniskin (Dungannon), Urney (Strabane).

Note: Most of the above registers date from about 1750 onwards. Only a few date back to the seventeenth century—Derryaghey (Lisburn), Sankill, Londonderry, Comber, Magheralin, Seagoe, and Drumglass.

Presbyterian

CO. ANTRIM: Antrim, Armoy, Ballycarry, Ballycastle, Ballyeaston (Ballyclare), Ballylinney (Ballyclare), Ballymacarrett (Belfast), Ballymena, Ballymoney, Ballynure, Ballysillan, Ballywillan (Portrush), Belfast (Fisherwick, Rosemary), Boardmills (Lisburn), Broughshane, Buckna, Carnmoney, Carrickfergus, Castlereagh, Cliftonville, Cloughwater, Connor (Ballymena), Crumlin, Cullybackey, Donegore (Templepatrick), Drumbo (Lisburn), Dundonald (Belfast), Dundron (Belfast), Finvoy (Ballymoney), Gilnahurk (Belfast), Glenarm, Glenwherry (Ballymena), Grange (Toomebridge), Kilraught, Larne, Loughmourne, Lylehill, Moss Side, Portrush, Raloo (Larne), Randalstown, Rasharkin, Templepatrick, Tobberleigh.

CO. ARMAGH: Ahorey, Armagh, Bessbrook, Cladymore, Clare (Tandragee), Cremore, Donacloney (Lurgan), Gilford, Keady, Kingsmills (Whitecross), Knappagh, Lislooney, Loughgall, Lurgan, Markethill, Mountnorris, Newmills (Portadown), Newtownhamilton, Portadown, Poyntzpass, Richill, Tandragee, Tullyallen, Vinecash (Portadown).

CO. DERRY: Ballykelly, Banagher, Boveedy (Kilrea), Castledawson, Coleraine, Crossgar (Coleraine), Cumber (Claudy), Derrymore, (Limavady), Derry, Draperstown, Drumechose (Limavady), Dunboe (Coleraine), Dungiven, Faughanvale (Eglinton), Garvagh, Gortnessy (Derry), Killaigh (Coleraine), Kilrea, Lecompher, Limavady, Maghera, Magherafelt, Magilligan, Moneymore, Portstewart.

CO. DOWN: Anaghlone (Banbridge), Anahilt (Hillsborough), Annalong, Ardaragh (Newry), Ballydown (Banbridge), Ballygilbert, Ballygraney (Bangor), Ballynahinch, Ballyroney (Banbridge), Ballywalter, Banbridge, Bangor, Carrowdore (Greyabbey), Clarkesbridge (Newry), Clonduff (Banbridge), Clough (Downpatrick), Cloughey, Comber, Conlig, Donaghadee, Downpatrick, Dromara, Dromore, Drumbanagher (Derry), Drumgooland, Drumlee (Banbridge), Edengrove (Ballynahinch), Glastry, Groomsport, Hillsborough, Kilkeel, Killinchy, Killyleagh, Kilmore (Crossgar), Kirkcubbin, Leitrim, Lissera, Loughagherry (Hillsborough), Loughbrickland, Magherally (Banbridge), Millisle, Mourne, Newry, Newtownards, Portaferry, Raffrey (Crossgar), Rathfriland, Rostrevor, Saintfield, Scarva, Seaforde, Strangford, Tullylish (Gilford), Warrenpoint.

CO. FERMANAGH: Enniskillen, Lisbellaw, Pettigo.

CO. TYRONE: Albany, Ardstraw, Aughataire (Fivemiletown), Aughnacloy, Ballygawley, Ballygoney (Cookstown), Ballynahatty (Omagh), Ballyreagh, Brigh, Carland, Castlederg, Cleggan (Cookstown), Clenanees (Castlecaulfield), Clogher, Coagh, Cookstown, Donaghedy (Strabane), Drumquin, Dungannon, Edenderry (Omagh), Eglish (Dungannon), Fintona, Gillygooly (Omagh), Gor-

tin, Leckpatrick (Strabane), Minterburn (Caledon), Moy, Newmills
(Dungannon), Omagh, Orritor (Cookstown), Pomeroy, Sandholes
(Cookstown), Strabane, Urney (Sion Mills).

Note: Many of the above registers do not start before 1820, and
only a few date back to the eighteenth century, including some
early ones which go back to the 1600s—Antrim, Dundonald,
Ballykelly, Portaferry.

13

THE ISLE OF MAN AND THE CHANNEL ISLANDS

The Isle of Man

The Isle of Man is located in the Irish Sea, almost exactly equidistant from England, Ireland, and Scotland. It is not a part of the United Kingdom, but is a Crown possession which is largely self-governing. It was first conquered by the Vikings in 800, and during the next four centuries they controlled the island and its Celtic inhabitants. The King of Norway sold it to the King of Scots in 1266. It was later seized by Edward I of England, and then belonged to a succession of English noblemen until the Crown took it over in 1609.

The government is the Tynwald Court, which consists of an upper house called the Council and a lower house called the House of Keys. It is one of the oldest parliaments in the world—probably second only to that of Iceland.

Civil Registration
The compulsory registration of births and deaths started in 1878. The records are in the custody of the Chief Registrar, General Registry, Douglas, Isle of Man. The office does not undertake genealogical searches but will supply certified copies of extracts, provided sufficient details are given by the inquirer. A fee is charged.

Church Records
Most of these are also in the custody of the Chief Registrar and the same fees apply. Church of England baptismal records date from 1611 and are on file until 1878. Since that year they are in the original churches. Church of England marriages from 1629 to the present date, and dissenters' marriages from 1849 to date, are on

file. Burial records in the office cover the period from 1610 to 1878 (Church of England).

The records held before civil registration are not indexed, and so a number of years may need to be searched if you cannot supply the exact year. Roman Catholic records date from 1817 and are in the Catholic Church, Douglas, Isle of Man. Nonconformist registers from 1800 are in the various local chapels. No central list or index is available.

Census Returns

Censuses have been taken every ten years since 1821 (except in 1941). The first six censuses are open for public search. Those from 1821 to 1871 are in the Manx Museum, Douglas, Isle of Man, and those since then are in the Public Record Office, London.

Directories

Many of these date back to 1808 and are in the Manx Museum and local libraries.

Newspapers

These start from 1793. For the period from then until the present day they are in the Manx Museum.

Societies

There are two useful and helpful societies on the island:

The Manx Society, c/o The Manx Museum, Douglas.

The Family History Society: Mrs. I. J. Lyle, The Old Manse, Kirk Michael.

Wills

The Isle of Man was in the Province of York and the Diocese of Sodor and Man. Until 1884 wills and probate matters were under the jurisdiction of the ecclesiastical courts, which alternated for parts of each year between those of the vicar-general of the bishop and those of the official of the archdeacon.

The records of the two courts were kept together but indexed separately. These courts continued without interruption at the time of the Commonwealth—unlike the situation in England and Wales—although the diocese was vacant from 1644 to 1661. The ecclesiastical officials were replaced by judges and a registrar.

After the abolition of the archdeaconry court in 1874 the bishop's consistory court had sole jurisdiction. From 1885, probate became the business of the High Court of Justice. The pre-1847 wills are now in the Manx Museum, and those since that date are in the General Registry, Douglas. The earliest will on record dates from 1628.

The Consistory Court of Sodor and Man: For the period 1628-1884, wills, administrations, and inventories are indexed. The period 1600-28 is not.

Archdeaconry Court of the Isle of Man: Wills, administrations, and inventories are indexed from 1631 to 1884.

If the deceased lived or owned property outside the island, his will might have been probated in either the prerogative courts of Canterbury or York, or possibly in the consistory courts of Carlisle, Chester, or Richmond.

Other Records

These include manorial records (1610-1922) in the General Registry; books of common pleas in the Manx Museum and the General Registry; mortgages from 1709 to 1846 in the Manx Museum, and after that date in the General Registry; and monumental inscriptions (tombstones) from 1611 to date in the Manx Museum.

More limited in their scope are some of the other records in the Manx Museum. For example, there are a few Bishop's Transcripts covering the period from 1734 to 1799, but only duplicating the entries already available in the parish registers. There are military records of interest if your ancestor served in the Royal Manx Fencibles between 1793 and 1802, as well as volunteer muster rolls from 1864 to 1916. There are records of inquests (called enquests on the island) from 1687 onwards; books of the Court of the Exchequer—civil disputes, company records, licences, etc.—from 1580 to date; and Books of Common Pleas from 1496 (court records).

The Channel Islands

The Channel Islands are located in the English Channel off the coast of France and consist of five main islands and a number of small ones. The main islands are Jersey, Guernsey, Alderney, Sark, and Herm. The Channel Islands have been a possession of the Crown since 1066 and are largely self-governed. They consist of the Bailiwick of Jersey and the Bailiwick of Guernsey (this includes Alderney, Sark, and Herm).

1. Jersey

Family History Society
This society also serves other islands.
(See page 89 for remarks concerning Family History Societies.)

Archives
The Judicial Greffe, States Building, St. Helier.

Civil Registration
This started in 1842. Before that date the only records were kept by the churches. Civil registration records of birth, marriage, and death are kept by the Superintendent Registrar, States Building, St. Helier.

Church Registers
Information about Church of England registers can be obtained by writing to the Dean of Jersey, The Deanery, David Place, St. Helier. Details of Catholic records can be obtained from the Bishop of Portsmouth, Portsmouth, Hampshire, England.

Census Returns
These are exactly the same as in England. Information about microfilm copies can be obtained from the Superintendent Registrar, States Building, St. Helier.

Wills
The Channel Islands were in the Province of Canterbury and the Diocese of Winchester, but have always been administered separately from that diocese. In Jersey, probate was subject to the ecclesiastical court until 1949. Wills, which date from 1660 up to the present, are in the custody of the Greffe, Royal Court, St. Helier, Jersey.

The records of the Ecclesiastical Court of the Dean of Jersey are indexed:

Wills of personalty, 1660-1964
Administrations, 1848-1964
Wills of realty, 1851 to date

2. Guernsey

Family History Society
See under Jersey.

La Société Guernesiaise
Peter Johnson, Courtil à l'Herbe, Route des Bas Courtils, St. Saviour, Guernsey. The society has a thousand members and is mainly concerned with natural sciences and local history. It does not have a genealogical section and does not do research of any kind for overseas inquirers. The Family History Society of Jersey is more likely to be able to put you in touch with local record-searchers.

Civil Registration
The compulsory registration of births, marriages, and deaths started in 1840 and all records are in the custody of the Registrar General's Office, St. Peter Port, Guernsey.

Church Registers
Church of England registers are in the original churches, as are records of marriage before 1919. These parishes are St. Peter Port, St. Sampson's, Vale, Castel, St. Saviour's, St. Peter-in-the-Wood, Torteval, Forest, St. Martin's, and St. Andrew's. Information about Catholic records can be obtained from the Bishop of Portsmouth, Portsmouth, Hampshire, England.

Inquiries about church registers on Alderney should go to the Clerk of the Court, Alderney, and for Sark to Le Greffier of Sark, on Sark.

Census Returns
These are exactly the same as in England and are in the custody of the Registrar General, St. Peter Port, Guernsey.

Wills
Intestacies and wills relating to personal estate only come under the "Court of the Commissary of the Bishop of Winchester in the Bailiwick of Guernsey". This is the only ecclesiastical court in Great Britain with jurisdiction over probate and estate administration. It also has jurisdiction over Alderney, Sark, Jethou, and Herm. The records date from 1660 and remain in the custody of the court. Inquiries should be sent to the Registrar at 12 New Street, St. Peter Port, Guernsey.

Wills referring to real estate in Guernsey only are in the Royal Court of Guernsey, but only date from 1841. There can be no real estate on Herm and Jethou as the land belongs to the States of Guernsey. In Sark all estates and landed property must descend intact to the heir, until the fifth degree of kinship. Failing such relatives, the property reverts to the Seigneur of Sark. The widow has a right to a dower of one-third. There is also a fixed rule of descent for Alderney. All the wills for that island were destroyed during the Second World War.

14
PREPARING A FAMILY HISTORY

Once you have completed your family tree, you should write up the history of the family. This will put flesh on the bare bones—or perhaps I should say leaves on the bare branches! It will bring the whole story of the family together, and it will be much more interesting than just the family tree itself. When you have done it, you can send photocopies to relatives who have helped you in your search. More importantly, you can lodge copies in the local library in the place where your family originated, with the public or county archives there, and with the Genealogical Society. In this way, all your hard work will become of help and interest to the generations which come after you.

A family history sets out in easy-to-read language the family story from your earliest ancestor; it should include extracts from diaries and letters if they exist. I hope at this point in your genealogical research you have developed an interest in social history—so that you are finding out *how* your forebears lived, as well as where they lived.

Perhaps an example will help to show you what I mean. Of course, you must bear in mind that each family is unique. Some of you will have discovered a great amount of information about your ancestors—how much they paid for their land, and letters and legal documents which tell you a great deal about their character; others will have found out very little beyond the dates of birth, marriage, and death. You have seen passing references to my personal research during the course of this book. Perhaps the following family history will give you a better idea of what I was able to discover, and what remains unknown after many years of research.

The Baxters of Swindale and Morecambe

Swindale is a remote dead-end valley located in the Westmorland part of the county of Cumbria, in the English Lake District, about fifteen miles north of Kendal. It has one tiny village (Bampton) and the ruins of several farmhouses, most of which were owned by the Baxter family at one time.

The area was colonized by the Romans in A.D 80, and after their departure it became part of the Kingdom of Strathclyde, centred on Dunbarton, Scotland. In about A.D. 616 the English infiltrated Cumbria from the east, followed by the Danes in 875 and the Angles in 925, although the area was still nominally under Scots sovereignty. After the Norman Conquest of 1066, the new masters occupied the main centres on the road north, and by 1092 King William II (Rufus) had completed the Norman occupation of Cumbria. Most land in Westmorland (separated from Cumberland in 1190 and reunited with it in 1974 under the name of Cumbria) was occupied by tenant farmers who had security of succession. The land was poor and the local economy depended on the rearing of cattle and sheep and the production of wool.

Since the original Saxon inhabitants were not disturbed unduly by the Normans, it seems likely that the Baxters were descended from Saxon ancestors. The name Baxter (or Bacastre, Baecestre, Bakester, Bagster, Bakster, Backster) is Saxon for baker. The first mention of a Baxter in the area was in 1195 when John le Bacastre (John the baker) owned land at Helton Flechan (near Bampton and now known as Helton). In 1303, William le Bakester, "a free tenant", held half a carucate at Castlerigg, some ten miles to the northwest, and paid fourpence per annum for it to the Manor of Derwentwater. This was part of the vast estates of the Radcliffe family (later Earls of Derwentwater). Under the feudal system a carucate was as much land as could be tilled with one plough and eight oxen in a year. On the fells (low hills) above Helton an area on the map is still shown as Baxter Rash. "Rash" was a local dialect work for "a narrow piece of arable land left uncultivated" or "a narrow strip of rocky or overgrown land". (Both explanations are given in *Place Names of Westmorland*.)

In 1362 John Baxter, of Helton Flechan, and his wife, Beatrice, are mentioned in the will of Sir Thomas Lengleys, who left them forty sheep. From this date until the present day the family records are complete. Soon after, in 1366, Thomas Baxter was living at Cliburn, about seven miles northwest of Helton, and with him was

Joan, widow of Walter Baxter. Of course, with an occupational surname there is no certainty that they were connected with the Helton family, but I believe we may safely assume that they were.

In 1469 the family had moved the few miles to Bampton, and by 1496 they had prospered and built Bampton Hall, in the centre of their one hundred and sixty-seven acres of land. They were well-to-do "statesmen" with other neighbouring families such as the Lowthers, the Curwens, and the Gibsons.

At this point I should explain the origin of the term "statesmen" as it applied to yeoman farmers in the Lake District. Originally, in Saxon times, they were freemen owning their own land. After the Conquest, they found themselves tenants of their new Norman lords, but they kept far more of their independence than the unfortunate "villeins" in other counties who became serfs. This was because they held their lands by "border tenure", which meant they retained their land as their own in return for their promise of military service in repelling any Scots invasion. The Normans and their successors, constantly threatened from north of the border, continued this arrangement for many years.

One attempt was made in 1605 to end border tenure and transfer ownership of the land to King James I and the great lords. There was a trial in the Courts and the decision was that the lands were "estates of inheritance", quite apart from the promise of border service, and so the "estatesmen" (statesmen) came into existence. They were their own masters—each farm was a separate, independent estate, and each family raised or made its own food and clothing. The fluctuations of the markets and the national economy did not affect them directly, if at all.

In Swindale, the Baxters lived a particularly idyllic existence. They were economically independent and they were not affected by the plagues of 1208, 1268, and 1319, or by the Black Death of 1348. They were immune from the Scots border raids since the main thrusts of the attacks were to the east and west of the remote valley. The Scots came south to Penrith, and then went by way of Mardale and Windermere, or sometimes through Shap and Kendal—either way they left Swindale and the Baxters quiet and peaceful in the middle.

For this reason the houses were not fortified as were more exposed ones. There is no evidence of any pele towers in the valley, whereas on the main invasion routes they abounded. The Baxter ancestral home, Bampton Hall, is built of local slate, low to the ground, and has two storeys. The house still stands and looks much the same as it did when it was built five centuries ago.

Although the Baxters had no trouble with the Scots, apparently they did have problems with their neighbours to the east, the Gibsons of Bampton Grange. On May 1, 1469, the two families signed a bond in which it was agreed that their disputes should be arbitrated by Sir Thomas Curwen and Thomas Sandford. Part of the document is missing and so the cause of the quarrel is unknown. Probably it was a dispute over boundaries or grazing rights for the sheep or cattle. Each statesman had his own area on the fells for grazing and this was called a "stint". The Herdwick sheep raised in the area were reputed to know their own stints and to observe the boundaries—perhaps, in this case, the Baxters and the Gibsons were too trusting!

The John Baxter who built Bampton Hall married Elizabeth Lowther in 1450. She was the daughter of Sir Hugh Lowther, one of Henry V's knights at the Battle of Agincourt. Her mother was Margaret de Derwentwater. This marriage allied the Baxters with the two most powerful families in Cumbria.

John Baxter's grandson, another John, cemented the alliance still more strongly in 1518 by marrying Mary Lowther, daughter of Sir John Lowther and his wife, Mary Curwen—and so the third most powerful family (the Curwens) were linked by blood to the Baxters.

The next generation—John Baxter (1520-94)—brought "brass" and not "class" into the family. He married Isabel Wilkinson, whose family had a small but prosperous iron-foundry at Pennybridge. The son of this marriage, William (1540-1606), married Janet Holm, daughter of another wealthy local family. Her father was a part-owner of coal-mines near Whitehaven, where William Baxter had financial interests. Quite apart from the enormous fell area over which he had grazing rights, William also owned over twelve hundred acres in Swindale, covering most of Bampton and Swindale commons. This was probably the peak of the Baxters' wealth and power. They were related by blood to the Earls of Derwentwater, the Earls of Lonsdale (the Lowthers), and the Curwens, who had acquired a baronetcy and were active in the political life of the North.

The Baxter-Holm marriage produced five sons and one daughter. The latter married Thomas Curwen, and the five Baxter sons farmed the ancestral land. The eldest, John, lived at Bampton Hall, while the others had the farms at Talbert, Bomby, Swindalefoot, and Swindalehead. History does not record whether the son who farmed the latter was bothered by the Swindale Boggle. This was the ghost of a woman in flowing white robes who haunted the fells in that area. She was supposed to have been a woman who starved to death in a remote fell cottage nearby.

In 1600 the youngest son, James, married Mabel, daughter and heiress of Sir James Preston, of Ackenthwaite, near the border with Lancashire. He farmed a large estate there for the rest of his life, and died in 1677, aged 101—the only centenarian in the Baxter family. He had three sons, Thomas, John, and Miles. Nothing is known of the last two, but Thomas (1619-86) married Janet Long and had three sons and two daughters.

The eldest son, Richard (1646-1720), married Elizabeth, daughter of Thomas Gibson of Bampton Grange, his second cousin. The Baxter-Gibson feud of 1469 had probably ended when Janet Baxter of Bampton Hall married Thomas Gibson of Bampton Grange in 1592.

It was at this point that the fortunes of the younger branch of the family started going downhill. Richard had six sons and one daughter, and obviously the Ackenthwaite lands could not support them all. The family scattered over the years, and the estate was sold after Richard's death. His eldest son, William (1690-1737), farmed first at Priest Hutton and later at Yealand—both in Lancashire—and had five sons and one daughter. Once again the family scattered. However, I have been able to trace many of them up to the present time.

The eldest son in each generation remained in Swindale, where life went on as before. In 1703, Thomas Baxter, then the leading man in the area, gave three hundred acres as an endowment to finance the building of a school. The indenture reads:

> Thomas Baxter, in consideration of his great affection towards the inhabitants of Swindale, and to promote virtue and piety by learning and good discipline, grants a messuage of 260 acres 3 rods 33 perches at Wasdale Foot in his manor of Hardendale, and another 31 acres 2 rods 9 perches in his manor of Crosby Ravensworth, that the trustees may build a school-house on some part of my grounds at Bampton, and make convenient desks and seats, and maintain a well qualified person to teach the English and Latin tongues, etc.

The school was built near the chapel and over the next century and a half the school produced many graduates who went out into the world to become clergymen, lawyers, and architects. It was said at the time, "In Bampton they drive the plough in Latin in these days." Seven years after the school was built Thomas Baxter provided a free library. He was obviously far ahead of his time, for in 1710 a tiny village in a lost valley with a grammar school and a free library was unique. His own son, Thomas, was a parson in the Church of England and had the livings of Mardale, near Swindale, and Greystock, in Cumberland.

In 1777 the Baxters were given laudatory mention in a history book: "This Mr. Baxter and his forefathers for time immemorial have been called Kings of Swindale, living as it were in another world, and having no one near them greater than themselves." However, the dynasty of the "Kings of Swindale" was soon to come to an end. The family remained in Swindale until 1796, when the last member of the older branch of the family sold the estate to the Earl of Lonsdale. The sheep remain on the fells, the Swindale Boggle is still seen from time to time, but the Baxters are scattered across the world. Their only memorial is a short lane beside Bampton Hall still called Baxters' Lane, and the Hall itself— still as solid as on the day it was built five hundred years ago.

15
CONTINUATION

This is usually the place in a book for the Conclusion, but there is really no end to your search for your ancestors—there is no conclusion to the search, no end of the road, no finish to the story. Unless you have been incredibly lucky, there will always be gaps to be filled and questions to be answered. You may have traced a family back for six hundred years—but in one generation you may have a wife's first name but not her surname; in another you may have a date of birth or baptism but not of death or burial. These gaps do not mean your proven descent is incomplete, but you will still worry away at them over the years.

As I mentioned earlier in the book, I am still trying to trace my Caley ancestors back beyond 1778, and I have been trying for forty years! Every few years I take out the file and study all the mass of documents and papers. Every now and then I come up with a new idea and try it out—and every time it doesn't work out, but I still go on. Never be discouraged, never give in, never compromise on the accuracy of your information, and eventually all problems may be solved.

When we were tracing my wife's Pearson ancestors back in 1949, we could find no record of the marriage of a man named Christopher Pearson. We knew it must have taken place between 1700 and 1705. We did not even know the wife's name because in the baptismal entries for the children (three sons and a daughter named Jean), only the name of the father was given. Apparently the minister did not realize it takes a man and a woman to produce a child.

Nearly twenty-five years later I was in Scotland and visited a small library near Glasgow University. It was a casual visit because someone had told me there were some interesting old books there—certainly I had no thought of the missing marriage. I found a record of some vague land transaction in the Dumfries area, and a mention of a Margaret Cunningham selling some property called Gareland, near Sanquhar, in 1739.

I knew that Gareland had been owned by Christopher Pearson

and so off I rushed to Edinburgh and the Record Office to look up the Register of Sasines for Dumfries. (As I mentioned in Chapter 11, this register is a record of land transactions.) In it I found that Margaret Cunningham, widow of Christopher Pearson, and her daughter, Jean, had sold the property to Alexander Telfer. The sale was indexed under the name of Cunningham, and not Pearson, because it often happened in Scotland that greater importance was given to a woman's maiden name than in many other countries.

So, after twenty-five years, we knew the full name of Christopher's wife. We have since learned that the Cunninghams were a prominent family in Dumfries as early as 1350, and that their family mansion in Queensberry Square, with its ornate "painted chamber", was destroyed by fire in 1505. But we still do not know where and when the marriage of Christopher and Margaret took place. We are working on it, however, and perhaps I may have more to report in the next edition of this book!

Apart from the dull parade of dates of "vital events" which make up your family tree, your search will bring you excitement and romance. You will have the thrill of the chase as, step by step, you go further back into history. You will have those magic moments when you open a long-awaited letter from overseas to find you have gone back another generation or found the location of a house or discovered a will. You will find moments of intimacy in old letters and diaries. You may discover touching tributes to some of your ancestors—like one of my wife's Copland forebears who had these words inscribed on his parents' tombstone:

> If all those who well knew and could record his integrity, public spirit, and benevolence, and her amiable manners and worth, had been immortal, this memorial need not have been inscribed by their eldest son, William Copland of Colliston. AD 1808.

As you trace your family back you will want to know much more about the work they did, the clothes they wore, the houses they lived in, the area in which they were born. You can find all this, and more, in local history books, old newspapers, books on sociology, and so on. I found out when the Baxters took their sheep to market in Kendal—every Wednesday; how much they got for their wool—8 shillings for 14 lb. in 1705; when they took the flocks up to the high fells for summer grazing—early in April. These are the details which put vivid foliage on the bare branches of your family tree.

During all these years my wife's Pearson ancestors were living some sixty miles away on the upper reaches of the River Tyne. Their life was very different from the Baxters'. Although they had originally been hill farmers, they developed a nose for business and were soon owning lead-mines and coal-mines and ever-increasing estates—they were lords of the manors of Haltwhistle and Allendale and Hexham—totalling thousands of acres of good farmland, and stone quarries, and lead-workings. They married the daughters of the Earls of Derwentwater and played an active part in the fashionable life of Newcastle and London. They sent one son to manage lead-mines in Scotland (the Christopher Pearson I mentioned above) and another to fight in the lost cause of the Jacobite Rebellion in 1715.

You will discover many such stories about your own ancestors if you dig deep enough. We know Thomas Baxter and Christopher Pearson almost as well as if we had lived in those days. If you are lucky you may well come into possession of family treasures you do not even know about now. In due course you will be making contact with distant relatives in the old country—eventually you will meet them and who knows what heirlooms may be passed on to you?

We discovered a very distant cousin of my wife's on the Copland side of her family tree, and with great generosity she gave us a damask tablecloth and napkin especially made in Ireland for the marriage of Alexander Copland and Ann Gordon in Dumfries in 1735. They had been used ever since for wedding feasts in the Copland family. We have continued the tradition and used them at our daughter Susan's wedding in 1981.

Perhaps you will find, as I once did, the ruins of an old house once lived in by your ancestors. I doubt, however, if any find could be more romantic than mine. Many years ago on a spring morning, just after daybreak, I was poking about in the ruins of an old farmhouse in Swindale called Swindalehead. The silence was total and there was no living creature within ten miles of me—except for a few sheep grazing near by, perhaps the descendants of the tough Herdwicks bred by my ancestors. I found a massive beam which must have been the original support for the bedroom over the living-room. Suddenly I noticed some faint carving in the wood. I rubbed away at the dirt and grime, and picked away at the indentations with an old nail. Finally, I could decipher it—JB ⚭ IB 1539.

I knew who they were! John Baxter and his wife, Isabel Wilkinson, and 1539 was the year of their marriage. I also knew that in that year John was nineteen and his wife was eighteen, and they had been given the farm as a wedding present by John's father. Standing in the ruins in the silence and the stillness of that lonely, lovely valley of my ancestors, I could picture the two youngsters setting up house together—John carving the initials in the heavy beam, and Isabel holding firm the chair on which he stood. In that moment all my ancestors crowded around me and all my searching for my roots was worth while.

BIBLIOGRAPHY

This is not intended to be a complete list of every book ever written about ancestor-hunting in Great Britain and Eire. There is not enough room to give details of all books written on the subject—particularly the ones about specific localities. This list includes some of the books I have found particularly useful over many years in tracing my own ancestors and those of the hundreds of people who have come to me for assistance, or have asked for suggestions at public meetings and on TV and radio programs.

It does not include books written about individual families or small local areas. Once you have found a particular area in which you are interested, you should get in touch with the County Record Office (if one exists), the Family History Society, the nearest public library or museum, or the provincial or national archives, and they will tell you what books of genealogical interest have been published locally.

Note: The books listed as published in Baltimore, Maryland, U.S.A., were reprinted by the Genealogical Publishing Co., 1001 North Calvert Street, Baltimore, Maryland 21202, in the year shown. All were originally published in the United Kingdom, and in most cases had been out of print for years. It is worth while to place your name on the mailing-list of this company.

England and Wales

Barber, Henry. *Family Names*. Baltimore, 1968.
Bardsley, Charles. *English Ancestral Names*. Baltimore, 1968.
Baring-Gould, S. *Family Names*. Baltimore, 1968.
Bridger, Charles. *An Index to Printed Pedigrees*. Baltimore, 1969.

Camp, Anthony. *Tracing Your Ancestors*. London, 1971.

———.*Wills and Their Whereabouts*. London, 1974.

Cox, Jane, and Padfield, Timothy. *Tracing Your Ancestors in the Public Record Office* (PRO Handbook No. 19). London, 1982.

Dalton, C. *English Army Lists 1661-1714*. London, 1960.

Ellis, Henry. *The Domesday Book*. Baltimore, 1968.

Ewen, Cecil. *Surnames of the British Isles*. Baltimore, 1968.

Fairbairn, James. *Crests of the Families of Great Britain*. London, 1905.

Fox-Davies, A. C. *Complete Guide to Heraldry*. London, 1969.

Frith, Sir C., and Davies, G., *The Regimental History of Cromwell's Army*. London, 1940.

Gibson, Jeremy. *Wills and Where to Find Them*. Chichester, 1974.

———.*Guide to Probate Jurisdictions*. Banbury, 1980.

———.*Census Returns, 1841, 1851, 1861, 1871, on Microfilm*. Banbury, 1980.

Guppy, Henry B. *Family Names in Great Britain*. Baltimore, 1968.

Hamilton-Edwards, G. *In Search of Ancestry*. Baltimore, 1974.

———.*In Search of Army Ancestry*. Chichester, 1977.

Harris, R.W. *England in the Eighteenth Century*. London, 1963.

Hector, L. C. *Handrwiting of English Documents*. London, 1966.

Kaminow, Marion. *Genealogical MSS in British Libraries*. Baltimore, 1967.

Kitching, F. and S. *English Surnames in 1601 and 1602*. Baltimore, 1968.

Kitzmiller, John M. *In Search of the Forlorn Hope*. (British Army Records). Salt Lake City, 1987.

Marshall, W. *The Genealogist's Guide*. Baltimore, 1973.

Phillimore, W., and Fry, E. *Changes of Name 1760-1901*. Baltimore, 1965.

Pine, L. G. *The Story of Surnames*, London, 1965.

Reaney, P. H. *British Surnames*. London, 1966.

Richardson, J. *Local Historian's Encyclopedia*. New Barnet, 1974.

Rye, Walter. *Records and Record Searching*. London, 1969.

Sims, R. *Index to the Heralds' Visitations*. Baltimore, 1971.

———.*Pedigrees and Arms*. Baltimore, 1970.

Smith, Frank. *Genealogical Gazetteer (England)*. Baltimore, 1969.

Unett, John. *Making a Pedigree*. Baltimore, 1971.

Wagner, Sir Anthony. *Heraldry in England*. London, 1946.

Whitmore, J. A. *Genealogical Guide*. London, 1953.

Willis, Arthur. *Introducing Genealogy*. London, 1961.

Debrett's Peerage of England, Scotland, and Ireland. London, annual.

Burke's Peerage. London, annual.

National Index of Parish Registers. London.

Scotland

Adam, Frank. *Clans, Septs, and Regiments of the Scottish Highlands*. Edinburgh, 1908.

Black, G. F. *The Surnames of Scotland*. New York, 1965.

Ferguson, Joan. *Scottish Family Histories Held in Scottish Libraries*. Edinburgh, 1960.

————.*Scottish Newspapers in Scottish Libraries*. Edinburgh, 1965.

Graham, H. G. *Social Life of Scotland in the Eighteenth Century*. London, 1937.

Hamilton-Edwards, G. *In Search of Scottish Ancestry*. Baltimore, 1972.

Hewison, J. K. *The Covenanters*. Glasgow, 1908.

Innes, Sir Thomas. *Scots Heraldry*. Baltimore, 1971.

————.*The Tartans of the Clans and Families of Scotland*. Edinburgh, 1964.

Jones, M. *Essays in Scotch-Irish History*.

Perceval-Maxwell, M. *The Scots Migration to Ulster in the Reign of James I*.

Plant, Marjorie. *Domestic Life of Scotland in the Eighteenth Century*. Edinburgh, 1952.

Sandison, A. *Tracing Ancestors in Shetland*. London, 1985.

Scottish Sources. National Index of Parish Registers, Vol. 12. London, 1975.

Smith, Frank. *Genealogical Gazetteer of Scotland*. Logan, 1971.

Statistical Account of Scotland, 1790. (This remarkable set of volumes is of little value genealogically, but once you know the town or village in which your ancestors lived, it will tell you more about how they lived than any other book I know.)

Stuart, Margaret, *Scottish Family History*. Baltimore, 1978.

Whyte, Donald. *Scottish Genealogical Research*. Edinburgh, 1980.

Northern Ireland and Eire

Berry, H. F. *Registers of Wills, Dublin, 1475-1483*. Dublin, 1898.

Bolton, Charles. *Scots-Irish Pioneers in Ulster and America*. Baltimore, 1967.

Breffney, B. *Bibliography of Irish Family History*. Dublin, 1973.

Clare, W. *Irish Wills*. Baltimore, 1972.

Coffey, H., and Morgan, M., *Irish Families in New Zealand and Australia*. Melbourne, 1985.

Crisp, F., and Howard, J. *Visitation of Ireland*. Baltimore, 1973.

Dickson, R. J. *Ulster Emigration to Colonial America 1718-1775*.

Eustace, B. *Irish Quaker Records*. Dublin, 1957.

Falley, Margaret. *Irish and Scots-Irish Ancestral Research*. Evanston, Illinois, 1961.

ffolliott, Rosemary. *Genealogy in Ireland*. Dublin, 1967.

Gardner, Harland, and Smith. *Genealogical Atlas of Ireland*. Salt Lake City, 1964.

Goodbody, O. *Guide to Irish Quaker Records 1654-1860*. Dublin, 1967.

Hackett, D., and Early, C. M. *Passenger Lists from Ireland*. Baltimore, 1972.

Harrison, J. *The Scot in Ulster*. London, 1888.

Heraldic Artists, Ltd. *Handbook on Irish Genealogy*. Dublin, 1978.

Hill, G. *The Plantation of Ulster*. London, 1877.

Jones, H. *The Palatine Families of Ireland*. Studio City, California, 1975.

Lewis, Samuel. *A Topographical Dictionary of Ireland*. London, 1847.

Marshall, W. F. *Ulster Sails West*. Baltimore, 1979.

Matheson, R. *Surnames in Ireland*. Baltimore, 1975.

MacLysaght, E. *Irish Families, Their Names, Arms, and Origins*. New York, 1970.

———*Surnames of Ireland*. Dublin, 1973.

Mitchell, Brian. *Irish Emigration Lists 1833-39*. Baltimore, 1989.

Mitchell, Brian. *Irish Passenger Lists 1847-71*. Baltimore, 1988.

Myers A.C. *Immigration of Irish Settlers into Pennsylvania 1682-1750*. Swarthmore PA, 1902.

O'Hart, John. *Irish Pedigrees*. Baltimore, 1976.

Phillimore, W., and Thrift, G. *Indexes to Irish Wills, 1536-1857*. Baltimore, 1970.

Schliegel, D. *Passengers from Ireland 1811-1817*. Baltimore, 1980.

Vicars, Sir Arthur. *Index to the Prerogative Wills of Ireland 1536-1810*. Baltimore, 1967.

Woulfe, P. *Irish Names and Surnames*. Baltimore, 1969.

The Isle of Man

Feltham and Wright. *Monumental Inscriptions in the Isle of Man*. London, 1948.

The Channel Islands

Balleine, G. R. *A Biographical Dictionary of Jersey*. London, 1948.
Payne, J. B. *An Armorial of Jersey*. London, 1859.

Jewish (England)

Gartner, L. P. *The Jewish Immigrants in England*. Detroit, 1960.
Hyamson, Albert. *The Sephardim of England*. London, 1951.
Roth, Cecil. *Archives of the United Synagogue, London*. London, 1930.
_____.*Anglo-Jewish History*. Baltimore, 1966.
Rottenberg, Dan. *Finding Our Fathers*. New York, 1977.
Rubens, Alfred. *Anglo-Jewish Portraits*. London, 1935.
Bevis Marks Records: *Sephardic Marriage Registers, 1837-1901*. London, 1973.

INDEX